ADVANCE PRAISE

"*Putting Trauma to Sleep* by Drs. Reitav and Thirlwell is a must-read for any psychotherapist dealing with patients suffering from trauma and its repercussions. By demonstrating that sleep problems like insomnia are not just a symptom of PTSD but a core issue, a strong case is made that sleep-inclusive trauma treatment should prioritize restorative sleep as an ultimate resource for our patients to recover successfully from trauma."
　　—**Dieter Riemann, PhD,** professor of clinical psychophysiology, Freiburg University Medical Center, dept. of psychiatry and psychotherapy, Germany

"A rich introduction to sleep neuroscience and the treatment of sleep disturbance. Their hypothesis that shock—at a brainstem level—is the origin of sleep disturbance is supported and astutely observed by the authors' review of the latest neuroscientific research. This elegant hypothesis is nourished by several case studies using a novel therapeutic approach. Through these pages we can see the application of deep brain reorienting in reestablishing the restorative function of sleep."
　　—**Hannah Young, PhD,** coauthor of *Deep Brain Reorienting: Understanding the Neuroscience of Trauma, Attachment Wounding, and DBR Psychotherapy*

"*Putting Trauma to Sleep* is a deeply academic dive into how trauma affects our brains, our bodies, and our sleep. The authors discuss the biological mechanisms of sleep, trauma, and healing, and provide ways to assess clients and help them heal, connect with themselves, and experience better sleep. It contrasts EMDR with DBR (deep brain reorienting) as ways to heal embodied trauma. It opened my eyes to many new things, and I think you should read it."
　　—**Robin Shapiro, LICSW,** psychotherapist, clinical consultant, lecturer, and author of *The Trauma Treatment Handbook* and *EMDR Solutions I and II*

"Fantastically insightful and meticulously researched, this book provides an essential antidote to the shocking disregard for sleep in established trauma treatments. As such, it is an excellent resource for trauma therapists looking to up their game and provide their patients with immensely valuable help.

Putting Trauma to Sleep offers a radical new understanding of how to resolve trauma 24 hours a day—not only with standard daytime behavioral therapies, but with powerful sleep interventions to stabilize the autonomic nervous system. With this holistic approach, trauma sufferers are guided toward the most supportive neurobiological framework for deep healing."
　　—**Clare Johnson, PhD,** www.deeperluciddreaming.com, author of *Elixir of Sleep* and *The Art of Transforming Nightmares*, and past president and CEO of the International Association for the Study of Dreams

**PUTTING
TRAUMA
TO SLEEP**

The Norton Series on Interpersonal Neurobiology
Louis Cozolino, PhD, Series Editor
Allan N. Schore, PhD, Series Editor (2007–2014)
Daniel J. Siegel, MD, Founding Editor

The field of mental health is in a tremendously exciting period of growth and conceptual reorganization. Independent findings from a variety of scientific endeavors are converging in an interdisciplinary view of the mind and mental well-being. An interpersonal neurobiology of human development enables us to understand that the structure and function of the mind and brain are shaped by experiences, especially those involving emotional relationships.

The Norton Series on Interpersonal Neurobiology provides cutting-edge, multidisciplinary views that further our understanding of the complex neurobiology of the human mind. By drawing on a wide range of traditionally independent fields of research—such as neurobiology, genetics, memory, attachment, complex systems, anthropology, and evolutionary psychology—these texts offer mental health professionals a review and synthesis of scientific findings often inaccessible to therapists. The books advance our understanding of human experience by finding the unity of knowledge, or consilience, that emerges with the translation of findings from numerous domains of study into a common language and conceptual framework. The series integrates the best of modern science with the healing art of psychotherapy.

PUTTING TRAUMA TO SLEEP

ATTACHMENT-BASED NEUROMODULATORY INTERVENTIONS FOR STABILIZING THE BRAINSTEM

JAAN REITAV
CELESTE THIRLWELL

Norton Professional Books

An Imprint of W. W. Norton & Company
Independent Publishers Since 1923

Note to Readers: This book is directed to professionals practicing in the field of psychotherapy and mental health who work with people who have undergone trauma, trauma survivors, and people experiencing difficulty sleeping. It is not a substitute for appropriate training or clinical supervision. Standards of clinical practice and protocol vary in different practice settings and change over time. No technique or recommendation is guaranteed to be safe or effective in all circumstances, and neither the publisher nor the authors can guarantee the complete accuracy, efficacy, or appropriateness of any particular recommendation in every respect or in all settings or circumstances.

Except as otherwise indicated, identifying characteristics of all patients discussed in this book have been changed. All emails and transcripts quoted have been reproduced with permission. Certain patients elected to be referred to by their actual first or middle names; all other patient names have been changed. Any URLs displayed in this book link or refer to websites that existed as of press time. The publisher is not responsible for, and should not be deemed to endorse or recommend, any website other than its own or any content that it did not create. The authors, also, are not responsible for any third-party material.

Copyright © 2025 by Jaan Reitav and Celeste Thirlwell

All rights reserved
Printed in the United States of America
First Edition

For information about permission to reproduce selections from this book, write to Permissions, W. W. Norton & Company, Inc., 500 Fifth Avenue, New York, NY 10110

For information about special discounts for bulk purchases, please contact W. W. Norton Special Sales at specialsales@wwnorton.com or 800-233-4830

Manufacturing by Versa Press
Production managers: Gwen Cullen and Ramona Wilkes

ISBN: 978-0-393-71477-7 (pbk)

W. W. Norton & Company, Inc., 500 Fifth Avenue, New York, NY 10110
www.wwnorton.com

W. W. Norton & Company Ltd., 15 Carlisle Street, London W1D 3BS

1 2 3 4 5 6 7 8 9 0

This book is dedicated to the sleep and trauma pioneers, each of whom has made enormous contributions to the foundation that anchors the book you hold in your hands: Sigmund Freud, Carl Jung, Nathaniel Kleitman, Wilder Penfield, Wilhelm Reich, Bessel van der Kolk, Harvey Moldofsky, Rosalind Cartwright, Ernest Hartmann, Charles Morin, Dieter Riemann, Francine Shapiro, Anne Germain, and Frank Corrigan.

Contents

Introduction: Every Trauma Therapist *Is* a Sleep Therapist   ix

Part I: Interpersonal Neurobiology, Neuromodulation, and Sleep Processes in Trauma

1. Restorative Nighttime Sleep: An Essential Target in Trauma Treatment   5
2. The Attachment-Based Approach to Sleep Repair   37
3. The Intersubjective Collaborative Cascade in Trauma Treatment   58
4. Active Attunement and Empathic Communication Builds Therapeutic Alliance   85
5. The Yawning Breath: Teaching Agency   102

Part II: Addressing the Four Enemies of Sleep

6. Identifying and Removing Major Sleep Roadblocks to Trauma Work   123
7. Sleep-Wake Reorganization With Zeitgebers   146
8. Flashbacks, Nightmares, and Intrusive Thoughts   171
9. Targeting Restless REM Sleep: From Nightmares to Dreaming   197
10. Somatic Distress and Self-Regulation   228

11.	The Life-or-Death Crisis and Neurochemical Dissociation	265
12.	Putting Trauma to Sleep	285

Epilogue: Integrating Sleep Repair Into Your Trauma Treatment	317
Acknowledgments	327
References	331
Index	345

Introduction:
Every Trauma Therapist
Is a Sleep Therapist

"A growing body of evidence shows that disturbed sleep is more than a secondary symptom of PTSD—it seems to be a core feature." —Victor Spoormaker and Paul Montgomery (2008, p. 169)

"I was once fond of saying, 'Sleep is the third pillar of good health, alongside diet and exercise.' I have changed my tune. Sleep is more than a pillar; it is the foundation on which the other two health bastions sit." —Matthew Walker (2017, p. 164)

Congratulations! You have started a journey of learning about how sleep can benefit you and your work. Sleep repair has long been ignored in mainstream trauma treatment. You clearly have an open mind and a healthy curiosity, and a desire to truly help your clients and patients. While most in the trauma field have not paid attention to sleep at all, almost everybody who has experienced trauma knows sleep is impossible.

Hence the main title of our book, *Putting Trauma to Sleep*. Our goal is to show that attending to sleep is a very productive part of trauma therapy. That part of the title is easy to understand. The rest of the title, *Attachment-Based Neuromodulation to Stabilize the Brainstem*, may have left you puzzled. What do *attachment* and the *brainstem* have to do with sleep?

To address this question, it's important for us as the authors to provide some insight into our backgrounds. Collectively, we possess over six decades of expertise in assisting individuals grappling with insomnia and sleep apnea, conditions that are overlooked but prevalent, particularly among those who have undergone trauma. Over the course of our careers, we've delved into various treatment methods and techniques for sleep disorders. This has included working overnight shifts in sleep clinics, administering sleep tests, and subsequently aiding patients in deciphering the significance of their results. Building rapport and earning the trust of our patients has been paramount. By incorporating sleep therapy into our psychiatric and psychological practices, we have facilitated constructive changes in their mindsets and behaviors, which have enabled them to experience the profound satisfaction of waking up fully refreshed. It's been immensely rewarding guiding individuals both one-on-one and in group settings, employing strategies such as maintaining sleep diaries, introducing yoga practices, and fostering avenues for self-expression and self awareness. Six decades of collective experience have been dedicated to alleviating the impact of trauma on sleep, and now the effects of poor sleep on trauma recovery.

Through our encounters, it gradually dawned on us that what we initially perceived as the root cause (or central issue) of the sleep problem wasn't actually the true underlying cause. Like numerous professionals in our field, we were initially trained to assist individuals in altering their sleep habits and cognitive perceptions surrounding sleep. While interventions of *Cognitive and Behavioral Therapy for insomnia* (CBTi) proved beneficial for many, resulting in significant improvements in their sleep, regrettably we, and others, have found that two out of every five patients saw minimal enhancement in their sleep patterns (Riemann et al., 2022). Among those who had undergone trauma, nonresponders were in the majority. It became apparent to us that there existed a deeper, underlying issue that needed to be addressed.

The next step in our quest to help patients was to shift deeper into the brain, so to speak. We were trained in trauma therapy. We shifted from a cognitive focus to the *emotional* turmoil orchestrated by *the limbic system*. And for quite a while we found particularly good results, desensitizing patients of their emotional distress. You will soon read the example of Mike, one such patient. While that significantly helped many, we discovered that some of these patients returned with the same problem months or years later. How could that happen? We desensitized the brain's emotional activations. Apparently there was yet another, deeper level to the mystery of broken sleep.

This has been the conundrum of trauma therapy. It is as if a stealth circuit in the brain was holding the pattern of sleep disruption and we could not see it, or change it. Popular wisdom was that relieving the emotional distress would solve the problem. Like many researchers of trauma, we found that trauma treatment does not necessarily resolve the underlying sleep problem.

As we applied ourselves to solving this "who done it" (finding the root cause of sleep problems after trauma), we could not neglect the other equally pressing issues in the patient's day to day life. Namely, helping them with relationships that were unpredictable and unstable, and significant physical and medical problems that were persistent. And, of course, being unexpectedly triggered by something that threw them back into "trauma time."

All clinical trauma treatments are directed at changing the undesirable symptomatic states of the patient. Psychotherapeutic and pharmacological interventions in trauma treatment have, quite rightly, concerned themselves with identifying therapeutic strategies and techniques that reliably attain profound changes in clinical states. These have included:

1. transforming states of emotional dysregulation (e.g. terror) to an internal state of safety;
2. converting physical distress and pain to feelings of embodiment, connection, and vitality;
3. and reorganizing a disconnected sense of self/distrust of others/fragmented identity to an integrated experience of self in relation to others.

What has completely escaped the attention of the field of traumatology is that these important transformations of disrupted clinical states occur within a more foundational rhythm of state changes. Namely, between the state of waking consciousness (being active in the world), with that of unconscious withdrawal from waking consciousness (in order to integrate these self experiences during deep sleep).

THE BRAINSTEM AS THE MASTER HUB OF NEUROMODULATION

Transmission of neural signals in the brain occurs in two distinct ways: (1) synaptic transmission and (2) neuromodulation (Solms, 2021). Synaptic transmission is the direct neuron to neuron communication of a neural signal across a single synapse. It provides a targeted and immediate response in the receiving neuron, and is fastest and most effective way of activating a specific response in post-synaptic neurons.

In contrast, *neuromodulation* refers to the release of neuromodulators that diffuse over a wide area of brain activity. Once the neuromodulator is released, it modifies how large groups of neurons in that area respond to inputs. Neuromodulators influence ion channel conductance, receptor sensitivity, and gene expression. *Neuromodulation brings about changes in brain states, while synaptic signals effect isolated responses.*

Furthermore, most of the neuromodulatory processes are activated by norepinephrine, dopamine, serotonin, acetylcholine, and histamine—all of which are released from the brainstem. We can therefore refer to the brainstem as the master hub of neuromodulation. Its activities will modulate basic biological rhythms like breathing, heart rate, and sleep, and also activities in the limbic system and neocortical areas. All of these are intrinsically critical in *"putting trauma to sleep."*

In authoring this book, we have discovered something important. It is our view that the "villain" at the heart of sleep disturbances is the same one that's at the heart of attachment difficulties, traumatic memories, and significant bodily symptoms. That villain is a *dysregulated autonomic nervous system (ANS)*. And the ANS lives in the brainstem, below our cognitive awareness, and most importantly it responds to danger prior to our emotional response, in order to instinctively intervene to save our life.

Antonio Damasio (1999) suggested that this "proto self" is present at the brainstem level. Bjorn Merker (2013) proposed that the initial integrative hub for sensory (environmental) and somatic signals into a responsive first-person perspective occurs in the superior colliculus (SC). From this brainstem based foundational sense of self, other brainstem structures activate critical brainstem nuclei and their neurotransmitter systems. The most important of these are the locus coeruleus–norepinephrine; dorsal raphe–serotonin; ventral tegmental area–dopamine; pedunculopontine structures (PPN, PPT, LDT)–acetylcholine; and the tuberomammillary nucleus–histamine). These brainstem nuclei modulate arousal when they work together (Solms, 2021), *or* can be dysregulated by trauma. And once dysregulated, the brainstem can maintain dysregulation for life (Corrigan et al., 2024).

Understanding the role of brainstem structures in either creating harmony or failing to create harmony is the key to healing. The four main triggers disrupting harmony in the ANS are: traumatic experiences, attachment difficulties, bodily distress, and sleep disturbances. These four TABS provide the therapist with clear direction about how to go about repairing autonomic dysregulation, to better modulate the brain and return it to harmony. What we are excited to share with you, dear reader, are the practical skills to neuromodulate and change that dysregulated ANS by targeting the brainstem. It has taken us decades to find these answers. While these may not be the whole of what is needed, we are certain that it will remain a core part of the answer. We provide you with the TABS model so you can arrive at more productive results in your trauma therapy work, within months rather than decades.

We trust that these clarifications now help you make sense of *Attachment-Based Neuromodulation to Stabilize the Brainstem*. But as we said, it has taken us the better part of our careers to arrive at this understanding, so don't be dissuaded from reading if this does not yet make sense. That is what reading the rest of the book is for: to provide the clinical evidence and the neurobiological underpinings to what Anne Germain (Germain et al., 2017) described as a "paradigm shift reconceptualizing sleep disturbances as biologically relevant and modifiable predisposing, precipitating, and perpetuating factors of PTSD" (p. 84). This book will give you the tools for "putting trauma to sleep."

An excellent starting point for all trauma treatment is to ask where the normal integrative processes of the brain have broken down. From a functional perspective, for trauma patients these include intense emotional reactivity, poor impulse control, inability to sustain relationships, negative self-image, and dysregulated emotions and behavior. All these dysfunctions have their root in a dysregulated brainstem.

Critical to repairing these dysfunctional patterns is understanding the role of sleep in providing a sustainable foundation for emotional regulation, physical energy, and cognitive capacity. *Without attention to returning the traumatized patient to a stable sleep-wake rhythm, a full recovery and ongoing sustainable integration of cognitive and emotional functions will not be possible.*

Sleep disorders undermine the normal psychophysiological rhythms that support and sustain integration, health, and well-being. However not all sleep disorders are equally disruptive of health and well-being and therefore as important in resolving trauma. We can place sleep disorders on a spectrum from most impactful to least impactful. In decreasing level of impact on your treatment outcomes these conditions include: trauma-associated sleep disorder, sleep apnea, narcolepsy, night terrors, sleepwalking, insomnia, nonrestorative sleep, and nightmares. This spectrum has practical implications for how to integrate sleep interventions into trauma work.

Trauma hijacks the nervous system, not just for 16 daylight hours, but rather for 24 hours a day! Most trauma therapists treat trauma as if it is over when the sun goes down. Nothing happens at night, so why include that in your clinical formulations?

The basic fact is that trauma overwhelms the nervous system day *and* night. This book explores the benefits of considering trauma as a 24/7 phenomenon. Not just affecting daytime activity. Not just affecting daytime difficulties, or managing emotions or relationships, but also dysregulating the very core of the nervous system, at the heart of the brainstem.

In our view, understanding the root of trauma as a persistent brainstem dysregulation helps to understand not only the reported PTSD symptom experiences of the patient, but also provides a pathway toward directing treatment to brainstem dysfunction. This allows neuromodulation, healing, and integration to proceed, and finally to *put trauma to sleep*. An important reason that we decided to write this book was to draw attention to a deficit shared by the five most quoted guidelines for trauma treatment (see Hamblen et al., 2019). Shockingly, our review of these guidelines found that not a single internationally recognized trauma treatment guideline even mentioned sleep! One included a reference to sleep, but *no current trauma treatment guideline considered sleep, nightmares, apnea, or dreaming as an important treatment focus, to guide the trauma patient to recovery.*

In this book, we will provide trauma therapists with a different perspective, a new way of understanding the nervous system. Seen in the 24-hour context, trauma shapes the daytime symptoms but also subverts the healing powers of nighttime sleep. The 24-hour cycling between daytime activity and nighttime sleep provides a neurobiological framework for three complementary brain states (waking, NREM, REM), which, when pendulating, create the necessary conditions for healing and integration to occur.

Alternating periods of activity and rest provide for stabilization of the autonomic, emotional, metabolic, endocrine, and immunological systems. Lack of sleep undermines nightly recharging, reorganization, and reintegration, which instead becomes a period of fragmentation and disconnection. We aim to make the case that these interventions can easily be integrated into the trauma work that all trauma therapists are currently doing.

The purpose of this book is not just to identify sleep as another important symptom that can be added to other established symptom treatment targets, but that sleep is an *essential core target* for trauma treatment. This perspective emerges from two underlying dynamics: (1) sleep actively maintains physical and emotional health, and disrupting sleep disrupts health and wellness, and (2) the brainstem autonomic mechanisms that disturb the sleeping brain are the same mechanisms that activate daytime trauma symptoms that disrupt healing from traumatic events.

This volume is written to expand the clinical efficacy of the psychological treatments provided for traumatized patients. Our goal is to provide the background neuroscience that tells us that the dysregulation that is precipitated by traumatic events dysregulates not only daytime symptoms of the patient, but equally the nighttime sleep and dream experiences of that person. The daytime symptoms and the nighttime disruptions are intertwined because both are generated and coordinated by the brainstem.

OBSERVE YOUR TWO HANDS

Hold your two hands up in front of you. Let's reflect on how we go about understanding a problem. We hope that this exercise will illustrate how the important task of integrating an awareness of sleep problems into trauma treatment has been missed.

Exercise: Examine your hands carefully. Make observations on a sheet of paper. Continue until you have completed observations (you can't think of anything else). Write these down on a sheet of paper until you are satisfied that you have characterized all important features of your hands. Return to reading when you are done.

Now consider this. Your observations should relate to physical characteristics, function, and internal sensations. Did you include all three? When you held your hands up, chances are that you held them with palms facing you. Did you move your fingers? Your wrists? Did you rotate the hands so you observed the backs of your hands? Our point is that if you only made observations with your hands as they were facing you, you have not captured accurately the whole picture of how your hands look: from the front *and* back.

For example, you might conclude that the thumbs are distant from each other and that the skin is smooth and without hairs. If you turned your hands to face away from you, you would see that those observations were correct, but incomplete. There *is* a bigger picture that can only be obtained by observing the hands from all perspectives, front, back, and sides. Each adds to our overall picture and corrects for some observations that apply in only some limited ways.

Your physical observations lead to understanding function of the hands. And function of the hands leads to awareness of the subjective qualities of touch. The point is that each area of observation leads to understanding function in a more integrated way.

Understanding the traumatized person can also *only* be understood in full by observing their mind, their behaviors, and their symptoms across the 24-hour period and in all social contexts. It is only in this more ecologically valid perspective that we can begin to tease out the importance of and interrelationships between symptoms that are evident in the daytime and symptoms that are evident from sleep. In addition, we only begin to appreciate how ignoring the nighttime symptoms actually hampers your patient's recovery once we begin to deal with these important experiences.

This book is meant to guide your work with patients in a way that begins to integrate your observations of the sleep-wake cycle with interventions to correct sleep disturbances in a simple, yet systematic way. Case illustrations are used throughout, as this book aims to teach about trauma sleep therapy in an experience-near way. We learn by observing with our own eyes and ears. So let's start with a case study that illustrates how central to the goal of recovery from trauma the resolution of sleep problems is.

MIKE'S STORY: "I HAVE BARELY SLEPT IN 5 MONTHS"

This edited case study, in Mike's own words, reviews the results of the treatments provided after a high-speed motor vehicle collision.

The accident resulted in whiplash and a concussion. The key symptoms were: severe headaches, insomnia, nausea, and sensitivities to noise and smell.

"Mike" (not his real name) was a 52-year-old male in excellent physical and mental health, with no history of substance abuse. A single parent, he had a successful career and no health or sleep issues. Mike recalls events immediately before the collision, but has no memory of the collision itself or the minutes that followed, including a 10-minute period of unconsciousness.

After a battery of tests, he was discharged from the hospital and advised that he likely had a concussion:

> MIKE: For the first few days following the accident, I had a steady but mild headache and generally just felt extremely tired. I also experienced nausea, which came on quite suddenly, upon which I simply laid down and went to sleep.
>
> After 1 week, I felt I had rested well enough and was ready to try and go back to work. During the first 2 hours of working on my laptop, I became

extremely nauseated and had to stop working. Nausea was something that I had almost never experienced prior in my life. My boss advised me that I likely had a concussion. She thought that I should seek help prior to coming back to work; which I did.

On the advice of my doctor, I waited two weeks and then returned to work on modified duties: 2 hours per day for 4 days. I also used up the rest of my vacation time and made some changes to my diet.

I have never slept so much in my entire life as I did the first 4 weeks following the accident. With all that sleep, I was still exhausted during the daytime. For those first 4 weeks, I continued to have a steady, mild headache and frequent bouts with nausea.

On Figure I.1, the intensity of Mike's headaches is rated as: 0 = none, 2 = mild pain; 4 = moderate throbbing pain; 6 = strong stabbing/throbbing pain, 8 = severe stabbing pain of migraine intensity, 10 = Call 911.

FIGURE I.1 Headache Intensities for the 10-Month Period After the Accident

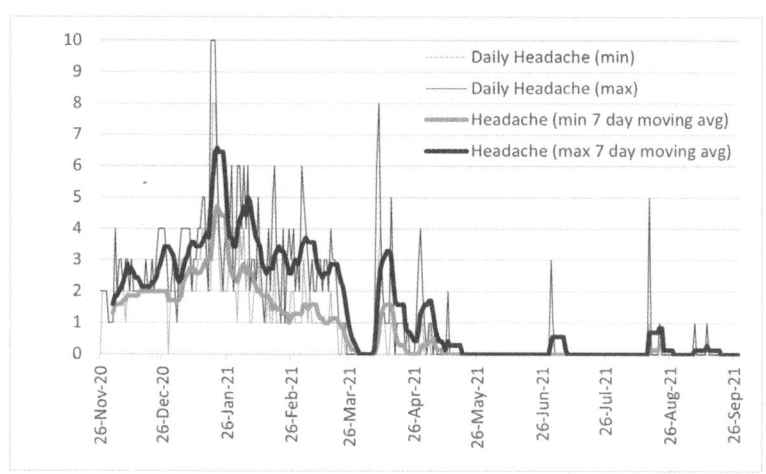

MIKE: I slept an average of 10 to 12 hours per night. However, at the 4-week mark post-accident [see arrow, Figure I.1], the nausea started to disappear. But this was replaced with increasingly stronger headaches, and my sleep rapidly declined to less than 3 hours per night [see Figure I.2].

The headaches continued to intensify, never really going away. By 6 weeks post-accident, mid- to late January, they had become completely debilitating. There was a period of 3 consecutive days and nights in the latter half of January where the pain felt like someone was driving a 3-inch nail into my right temple every second or two. This continued nonstop, day

Introduction: Every Trauma Therapist Is a Sleep Therapist

and night, for 3 days straight. I had always considered myself to be fairly resilient, but this was far more painful than I was capable of handling. By the third day I had simply given up. There was no strength left in me to continue fighting. By the fourth day, I felt like a lifeless and emotionless shell.

My sleep pattern was very inconsistent [see nightly TST on Figure I.2]. One night I would not sleep at all. The next I might get 3 hours. Then none again. Then 6 hours. Because it was so unpredictable it was very frustrating. I never knew what my next day would be like.

FIGURE I.2 Total Sleep Time for the First 4 Months Post-Accident

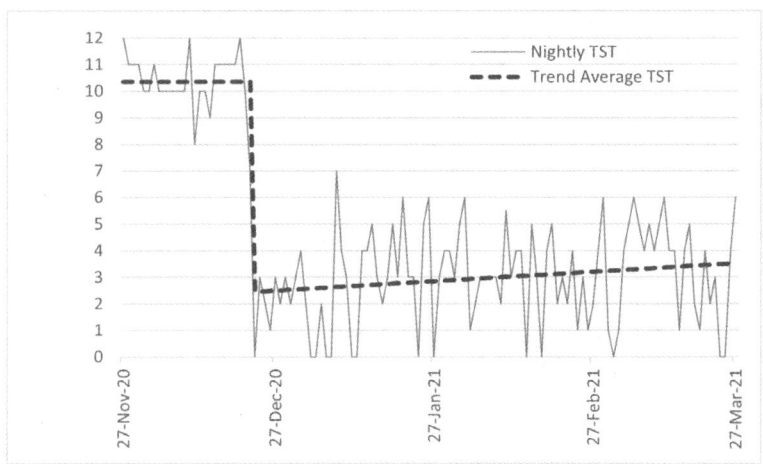

MIKE: I had also become aware that I had developed an unusual sensitivity to noise [see Figure I.3].

On Figure I.3, the sensitivity to noise is rated as: 0 = none, 2 = mild sensitivity; 4 = moderate sensitivity and need to distance self; 6 = strong sensitivity and need to isolate self, 8 = extreme sensitivity causing pain.

MIKE: It wasn't that noises sounded much louder than before. But I heard all noises around me all the time, with little ability to filter anything out. It made it difficult to focus on anything. All sounds flooded in: outside traffic noise, the air conditioner running, etc. Simply walking outside was distracting because of being overwhelmed by traffic noise, people talking as they passed by, sirens, and more.

FIGURE I.3 Post-Accident Sensitivity to Noise

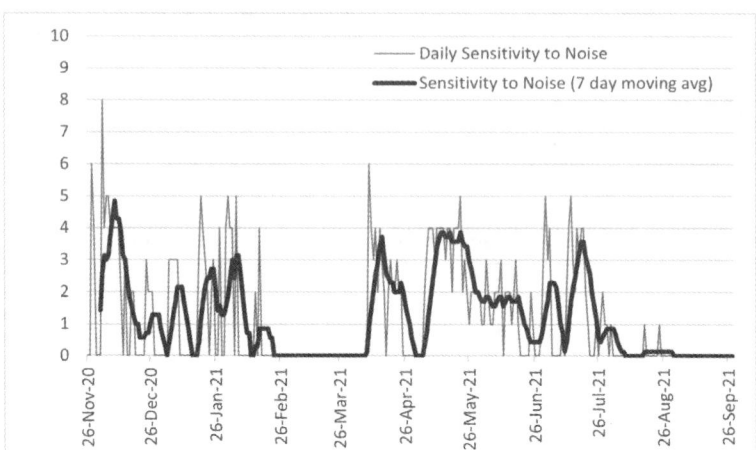

MIKE: During the first 5 months, I averaged one night per week with absolutely zero sleep. I would lie in bed, completely alert. I continued to be exhausted during the daytime and was functioning at a very limited capacity.

In addition, I had also developed a strong sensitivity to smell. My doctor had referred me to a concussion specialist. I was seen by two concussion specialists, who conducted a thorough assessment. On a memory test, I scored 20%! I knew my memory had been worse since the accident, but this bad? Accepting the results was crushing. The specialists described this as a traumatic brain injury but were optimistic, estimating it would take 1 to 2 years to make a full recovery. They prescribed physiotherapy, occupational therapy, and antidepressants to help me sleep.

I felt completely shattered by their prognosis and the prescription for antidepressants. I'd tried so hard to do everything right in managing my concussion and was perhaps naively hoping they would tell me it would only be a few more weeks, but 1 to 2 more years of this? What would this mean for my career? Would I even have a career? How would I be able to support my child, continue to pay my mortgage, and could I even survive that much more of this? It took several discouraging days for me to reluctantly accept my fate.

A few weeks thereafter; finally, some good news. My MRI tests came back negative. I also noticed that I was getting some relief from my headaches as a result of the antidepressants. No difference however to my sleep, still averaging about 3 hours a night.

At about that time I started physiotherapy. Then I switched to chiropractic therapy. I noticed little to no benefit to my key symptoms—particularly sleep. Nonetheless, I stuck with it for 3 months, thinking it would show benefits eventually. Unfortunately, it did not.

Around that time, I spoke with a friend who had experienced similar symptoms. For the first time, I felt that somebody understood what I was going through! He shared what therapy he had received, including from an acupuncturist and a sleep therapist. He believed that he had obtained the greatest benefit from the sleep therapist.

I had gone 4 months with very little sleep, while trying to manage through headaches that were more painful than I had ever imagined possible (see Figures I.1 and I.2). I immediately reached out to both the sleep therapist and the acupuncture therapist.

My Recovery Journey: The Benefits of Trauma Sleep Therapy

MIKE: I obtained benefit from the acupuncture therapist, particularly with minimizing my headaches and reducing the stiffness in my neck muscles. However, the most significant benefits came from my sessions with the sleep therapist. He explained how my autonomic nervous system was stuck in "fight-or-flight" mode, which was why I was having difficulties sleeping. It all made perfect sense.

He assured me that with some exercises he would be able to help. He started with some breathing exercises that I practiced every day. Next, he introduced me to bilateral eye movements. I thought to myself, "If I weren't so desperate, I am not sure I would be open to this treatment." It was different, but I was frantic to get more sleep. So I keenly engaged with the exercises and the EMDR treatment, no matter how unorthodox they seemed. After a couple of sessions, I started to believe that this would help me.

We spent several sessions conducting EMDR with bilateral eye movements. He had me focus on my experience in the moments leading up to the crash. I was almost spooked; I felt like I was actually reliving the accident. Muscles had tensed up in various parts of my body and I could recall visual images of the vehicle that cut in front of me with such clarity. As we continued the treatments, my stress level declined. Only then, for the first time, could I think back to the accident with a certain calmness.

The sleep therapy also taught me additional breathing exercises, one of which (the yawning breath) I found incredibly powerful for helping me fall asleep quickly.

Even with these tools, the amount of sleep I was getting had not improved significantly in the first 6 weeks of treatment [see trend lines in Figure I.4]. The therapist suggested that more than one traumatic event had resulted from the accident. Two more, as it turned out. The first, the severe headaches. The second, hearing the prognosis from my concussion specialists. I should have been happy to know what I was dealing with and yet it felt so incredibly defeating.

FIGURE I.4 Total Sleep Time Before and During EMDR Therapy

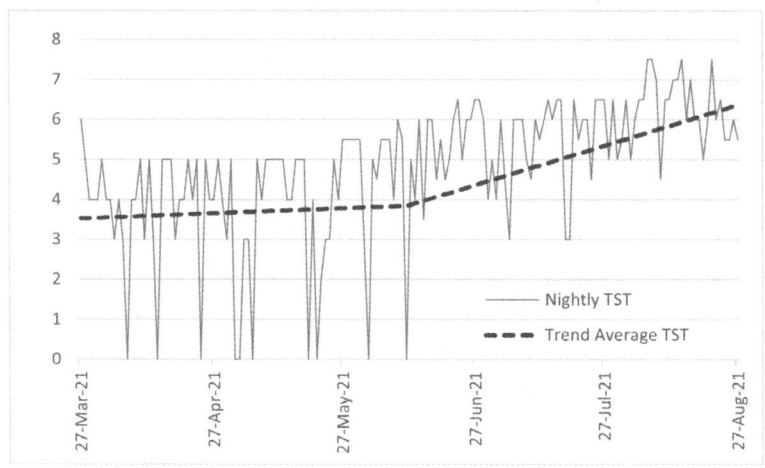

MIKE: We continued with more EMDR sessions focusing on the severe headaches. I had no trouble remembering how intense the physical pain was, but until I revisited them, I had not realized just how emotionally, physically, and mentally beaten I felt by these severe headaches. There was really nothing left of me and I recalled that my body and mind felt like they were shutting down. It felt so eerie: morbid in fact. It was a very difficult session on many levels. But it was mostly difficult to allow myself to sit with and internalize just how bad my situation had become.

This led to some relief: a first true recognition of how fortunate I was to have survived the accident. The EMDR work was helping put the overwhelming pain experiences into the past. It was also not long after the sessions focusing on the headaches that I started to feel more at ease with my recollections of them. And at that time, I also started to see the first real sign of improvement with the average amount of sleep I was getting. This was huge progress [see the steady increase in total sleep time from early June in Figure I.4].

Introduction: Every Trauma Therapist Is a Sleep Therapist   xxi

Finally, we focused on the traumatic event of the specialists communicating my prognosis. By the end of this EMDR session a huge weight had been lifted off my shoulders. I had a newfound level of energy. Upon returning home, I simply felt good, normal, and healthy for the first time since before the accident.

At this point, the EMDR trauma work with me was completed. I was still averaging less than 6 hours of sleep per night (compared to about 7.5 hours per night prior to the accident) and was a little reluctant to close the sessions.

I had been logging my symptoms daily since the accident, mainly to know exactly what was working and what wasn't. When plotting my progress, it was clear that my average sleep was a roller coaster week to week. How could I be sure that I was actually better? We scheduled a follow-up session a month later. While I am writing this, I have not had that session yet. But for about a week now I have been averaging almost 7 hours of sleep a night and climbing. I don't feel even tired anymore in the morning. While I am not yet at 100% of my old self, I am probably at 90% or so. That is pretty amazing given the trajectory I was on in my earlier stages of postconcussion syndrome!

Results

MIKE: Table I.1 lists the five most striking symptoms that I struggled with during the months after my accident. Of these, the insomnia and the headaches were clearly the worst. What was striking to me was that as nausea and dizziness decreased after the first month, insomnia and headaches became far worse. Treatments like the antidepressant medications and acupuncture did help reduce the headaches, but none of these conventional treatments improved the insomnia (see Tables I.1 and I.2).

TABLE I.1 Mike's Summary of Key Symptoms and Treatment Results

Key Symptom	Description	Treatment Results
Insomnia/Sleep Deprivation	5 months of averaging just over 3 hours of sleep per night, before things started to improve 24 nights with zero sleep Completely alert when lying awake in bed at night	Sleep therapy yielded greatest results by far
Headaches	Mild to severe headaches, often debilitating I experienced nonstop headaches for 4 months straight, day and night with a couple of weeks relief before they started up again for another two months straight as I went back to work full time	Amazingly, eating a lot of blueberries seemed to be the first thing that made some difference Antidepressant medication also helped a lot Acupuncture seemed to also help a fair bit
Nausea & Dizziness	Generally triggered by screen time, these were typically short (a couple of hours or less), but could be quite strong Really only an issue in the first month or so after the accident	This naturally went away as my insomnia started and headaches became far more severe
Sensitivity to Noise	Everyday noises would often feel overwhelming, making it very difficult to concentrate/focus More manageable than the other symptoms, as I merely had to ensure I was in a quiet place	Oddly enough, these seemed to dissipate as my sleep was restored I have to credit the sleep therapy here
Sensitivity to Smell	Heightened sensitivity to odors While both good and bad odors were much more prevalent, bad odors would at times turn my stomach—odors that others couldn't even smell	Very much aligned to my sensitivity to noise, also went away as my sleep was restored Again, I have to credit the sleep therapy here

This not only shows how serious my situation was, but also how many conventional techniques and therapy had only minor impact on my post-concussion symptoms (see Table I.2).

TABLE I.2 Mike's Summary of Conventional Treatments and Their Impacts

Treatment	Duration	Impact
Physiotherapy	12 days	No noticeable impact, but perhaps too short to assess
Chiropractic	2 months	No noticeable impact to key symptoms, but some relief to stiff neck/whiplash
Acupuncture	3 1/2 months	Good relief to stiff neck / whiplash Some relief to headaches Minor help to improve sleep
Sleep Therapy	3 months	Every session had a very noticeable impact—both bad (short term) and good (long term) This was the only approach that addressed the root cause of my sleep disorder and I believe was responsible for the overwhelming majority of my improvement Also, the only treatment that benefited my sensitivity to noise and smell

Ultimately, the combination of these *trauma sleep therapy* techniques (diaphragmatic breathing, muscle relaxation, the yawning breath, and directly focusing on traumatic memories activating autonomic dysregulation), were absolutely key in helping make a full recovery. What I experienced was that targeting the traumatic memories in treatment was effective, even though they also increased some of the symptom difficulties initially. For example, my sensitivities to noise were elevated (see Figure I.3) throughout the EMDR treatments (as we revisited these memories). The experiences in the treatment sessions felt like I was reliving the accident all over again. In these initial EMDR sessions, I also noticed that my nausea returned (after a few months of absence).

Trauma Sleep Therapy Helps Resolve Key Postconcussive Symptoms

MIKE: These techniques were the only ones that I came across that addressed the root cause of the symptom problems. I believe it has been the only one that has enabled me to make a full recovery. It has been a trying 9 months, to say the least. But 3 months of sleep-directed therapy have made all the difference. Interestingly enough, as my sleep deprivation subsided, so did my sensitivities to noise and smell.

I was quite surprised by how little direction was available in the health care system to getting effective treatment for my concussion. It was really through pure luck that I stumbled across this sleep therapy. Any therapy that addresses the root cause will always be more effective than one that merely treats symptoms.

Commentary on Trauma Sleep Therapy as a Postconcussive Treatment

Mike's account of his experiences helps us understand how critical disturbed sleep can be in exacerbating and perpetuating a variety of other symptoms difficulties, like increased moodiness and anxiety, poor mental focus, recurrent pain problems, and sensitivity to noise. However, every treatment case is unique. It is difficult to draw definitive conclusions from a single treatment that could apply to all trauma patients, let alone all postconcussive patients. However, there are many noteworthy issues that this treatment raises.

First and foremost, the fact that Mike kept consistent daily records of his symptom experiences for years after his accident provides us all with an unparalleled opportunity to track the ebb and flow of five distinct postconcussive symptoms after a major high-speed car crash. Rarely do we have consistent longitudinal data about pain, dizziness, nausea, insomnia, and noise and smell sensitivity. Looking at these data and seeing patterns of change is helpful to draw hypotheses that can later be evaluated in rigorous studies.

An initial important observation is that these symptoms wax and wane. None of them turn off quickly, once and for all. For example, dizziness and sensitivity to noise had both improved prior to active trauma treatment. Both returned as active EMDR treatment of the traumatic events began.

While Mike's sleep did improve with the trauma sleep therapy he was provided (and will be described in detail throughout this book), there was no visible improvement in sleep patterns for almost 6 weeks into treatment. And it was only after 4 months that it was clear that the insomnia could be successfully resolved. Only after this important clinical change occurred could the relationship between the sleep repair and reduction of his other postconcussive symptoms be clearly seen.

Many studies have shown that treatment of depression, pain, or anxiety does not necessarily improve sleep. Mike's case suggests that resolving sleep problems has broader significance for the underlying state of the autonomic nervous system. Targeting sleep problems may provide ripple effect benefits to many other distressing symptoms.

Still, questions persist. What is the relationship between Mike's dizziness and his prolonged sleep pattern in the first month after the accident? Why did both reverse at the same time? Why did his headaches worsen in parallel with his sleep worsening? And what are the brain mechanisms that are responsible for these changes in clinical status?

As you work through the chapters of this book, you will discover the answers. There are two parts to the book. Part I reviews sleep processes, both normal restorative sleep, as well as the different patterns of dysfunction that trauma might exert to distort sleep. Tools to assess these sleep difficulties are provided, both in the form of suggested clinical interview inquiries, and questionnaires to evaluate the presence and intensity of specific sleep issues. Following that, we review intersubjective collaboration and active attunement as critical skills in applying the interventions documented in the second half of the book. Also reviewed is the importance of educating the patient about the dynamics of the autonomic nervous system and how to use breathing to actively recruit and boost the parasympathetic system to improve sleep patterns.

Part II moves to understanding what we call the *Four Enemies of Sleep* and what can be done to resolve their negative impact on sleep. The four enemies include hypoxia, sleep-wake desynchronization, autonomic dysregulation, and distressing bodily symptoms (like pain, numbness, etc). Each of these are approached from a clinical perspective, with case examples of treatment of the problem, discussion of the interventions used, and, most importantly, a thorough discussion of why the interventions work. Throughout this book we use "patient" as opposed to "client." The reason is that all of these individuals had significant sleep and medical problems, in addition to their trauma.

Parts I and II require delving into the deeper activities of the brainstem, as the master hub of neuromodulation. As it turns out, the roots of sleep disturbance lie buried in the dysregulation of the brainstem centers that activate the brain's major neurotransmitter systems (norepinephrine, serotonin, glutamate, GABA, dopamine, acetylcholine, and histamine). When you resolve the dysregulated roots of sleep disturbance in the brainstem, you are also resolving the root cause for body tension (trauma guarding), dissociative shutdown, sympathetic overdrive, emotional dysregulation, and cognitive hyperactivation (flashbacks, rumination. and intrusive thoughts). Stabilizing the brainstem effectively neuromodulates not only the limbic system, but also other cortical areas and the spinal cord (see Figure 1.5).

While discussion of the neuroscience must be included, the chapters are written so that you can go to the clinical case and start by only reading that. Take a seat in the consulting room and watch the therapeutic process as it unfolds. Direct experience of the work that the patient and the therapist are doing together allows both to track the process of change and link symptom changes to the brainstem structures that are stabilizing. For most therapists the transcripts would be the best place to start reading the book.

Each of the clinical chapters includes an exploration of the neurobiological reasons why these interventions work. These inferences, while speculative, allow a preliminary understanding of the underlying neurobiological processes accounting for the symptoms in the first place. While some of the neurobiology gets dense, it is hoped that these accounts will gradually increase your curiosity and patience for wading through the neurobiology. The authors fully understand that this aspect of the book is difficult. However, it is essential for understanding the nature of the sleep disturbances and the interventions necessary to resolve them.

To provide you with a road map for these discussions, we refer you to Figure I.5, Allan Schore's (2012) outline of the organization of the brain's main circuits. From the bottom up, these are: the autonomic nervous system, the limbic system, right-brain memory circuits (procedural, emotional, and context), and left-brain circuits (language, meaning, and knowledge). The autonomic nervous system (with its brainstem responses) is the building block at the very foundation of our neural system. It is at this level that trauma sleep therapy focuses.

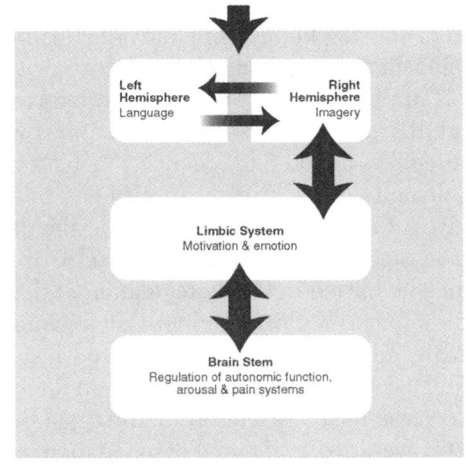

FIGURE I.5 The Integration of Implicit (Right Brain) into Explicit (Left Brain) Memories
Source: "Figure 3.2," from THE SCIENCE OF THE ART OF PSYCHOTHERAPY by Allan N. Schore. Copyright © 2011 by Allan N. Schore. Used by permission of W. W. Norton & Company, Inc.

EVERY TRAUMA THERAPIST IS A SLEEP THERAPIST

All clinical work begins with an evaluation of the strengths and difficulties of the patient. This can consist of information obtained by interview, corroborating accounts from others, results of questionnaires, and other physiological, behavioral, and medical tests. All trauma therapists have their way of doing this. But they may be missing one key ingredient: What happens at night?

We will make suggestions on how therapists can integrate key questions about sleep-wake rhythms into their interviews, support those findings with additional tests of patient sleep problems, and guide you to making good decisions to help patients move forward most effectively in their individualized trauma treatment plan. Sleep treatment is *not* an add-on to your trauma treatment. It is a lens you learn to see through, to identify what is driving your patient's difficulties in order to educate them and gain their cooperation in repairing sleep problems as part of your overall integrated trauma treatment protocol. Table I.3 provides a range of starting points to begin the process of engaging your patient in being curious about their sleep.

TABLE I.3   Reitav-Thirlwell Trauma Sleep Inquiry for Therapists

Domain	Clinical Questions
Onset of Sleep Problems	When did you first start having problems with your sleep? Did you have a hard time sleeping as a baby, getting up for grade school, high school, college/university, or work?
Initial Insomnia	How long does it take to fall asleep? What time do you generally fall asleep?
Maintenance Insomnia	How many times do you wake up at night?
Terminal Insomnia	Do you wake up earlier than expected? What time do you generally wake up?
Non-Restorative Sleep	Do you feel refreshed when you wake up? Do you feel unrefreshed even after sleeping for 8 to 10 hours?
Sleepiness vs. Fatigue	Sleepiness: Do you have the urge to fall asleep during the day? Fatigue: Are you exhausted during the day but cannot fall asleep?
Cognitive Impairment	Do you have problems with memory, concentration, or multitasking? Can you remember details after reading a paragraph or chapter of a book? Can you follow what is happening in a TV show?

Psychological Impairment	Do you have problems with irritability, mood, or anxiety? Are you prone to have accidents at play, work, or when driving?
Chronic Pain and Chronic Illness	How does your quality of sleep affect your pain/illness? How does pain affect your sleep/illness? Do you have any gastrointestinal issues or suffer from irritable bowel syndrome? Have you ever had a concussion or been in a motor vehicle accident?
In Utero	Was your mother under stress during her pregnancy with you? Was she in any accidents or had any illness when she was pregnant with you? Any complications during the delivery?
Early Development and Attachment	How was your relationship with your mother? With your father? Who were you closest to growing up? What was going to school like for you? Any traumatic experiences, physical, mental, or emotional, while growing up?
Environment, Interpersonal, Intergenerational	Is there anyone or anything that causes you to wake up from sleep? Did your parents and/or grandparents suffer any trauma or have any issues sleeping?

We will walk you through the core principles of sleep repair and show you how to apply these with your patients. What background concepts do you need to ask the right questions? What do you do with the information you are told? How do you communicate your understanding of their symptoms to them, so you are both on the same page to consider treatment options? And how do you conduct those interventions? That is what you will learn in reading this book.

Trauma Treatment Begins With Collaborative Assessment

Sleep disorders undermine the normal psychophysiological rhythms that support and sustain health and well-being. But not all sleep disorders are equally disruptive of health and well-being and therefore as important in resolving trauma. *Trauma Sleep Therapy* follows along five critical clinical choice points (CCPs), which are integrated with the overall treatment plan:

Comprehensive Clinical Assessment of Trauma,
Attachment, Medical Conditions, and Sleep
1. The primary clinical objective is for patient and therapist to collaborate on identifying the treatment need(s) and goals for successful trauma treatment. Our approach highlights four core areas of clinical focus in your work with your patients: trauma, attachment, body symptoms, and sleep (TABS). This TABS approach provides you, as a therapist, with maximal flexibility to integrate what you are learning here with your earlier trauma training and existing skills.

Active Exploration of Sleep Problems

Screening for Sleep Problems
2. Clarification of the nature and severity of sleep-wake problems. An initial screen of a variety of possible sleep problems is done, and the presence of sleep disorders is actively considered. Checklists and screening instruments help us think about the most likely underlying conditions. The sleep repair battery of five paper-and-pencil tests can be completed within 15 minutes and provides a good starting point for further discussions about the value of sleep repair to the recovery plan. As part of this ongoing exploration of the nature of sleep, and how it impacts the patient's daytime symptoms, the patient can be asked to complete a Consensus Sleep Diary for 2 weeks (see Carney et al., 2012). The sleep diary provides a picture of the nature, severity, and frequency of important disruptions to the patient's sleep pattern.

Educating Patients About Sleep and
Reasons for Obtaining a Sleep Study
3. Screening tests can outline the presence of a disturbance in the sleeping state but cannot tell you exactly what it is. Determination of the nature and severity of the underlying sleep problems can only be seen from the results of a full polysomnographic study of your patient's full night of sleep. To prepare the patient for this test, there is a necessary initial process of educating the patient about the real impact of sleep disorders. This often involves a discussion of the importance of sleep to their recovery and highlights the impact of one or more undiagnosed underlying sleep problems to the patient's specific symptom picture. Once the links between a possible sleep disorder and their daytime complaints are understood by the patient, the importance of obtaining an overnight sleep study becomes obvious. Any concerns or resistance about going for a polysomnographic study are addressed. This psychoeducational step is necessary and will be critical to successful resolution of all the patient's symptoms.

Interventions Addressing the Four Enemies of Sleep

Hypoxia

4. Once the sleep study has been conducted, the results are reviewed with a particular focus on identifying the presence and seriousness of apnea, autonomic dysfunction, periodic limb movements, and narcolepsy. A sleep intervention plan is developed. Complications and setbacks are managed through education, support, and guidance. CPAP treatment is initiated, the challenges to a regular and predictable sleep pattern identified, and interventions continued until CPAP use is stabilized.

Sleep-Wake Desynchronization, Autonomic Dysregulation, and Physical (Body) Distress

5. The focus shifts from sleep disorders requiring specific sleep treatments (apnea and narcolepsy) to sleep disorders that respond to psychotherapeutic treatment (nightmares, intrusive thoughts, chronic insomnia, chronic pain). Sleep is stabilized using sleep therapy strategies, and the therapist then returns to their overall treatment plan and identifies the next priority for trauma treatment.

These five clinical choice points (CCPs) are intended to provide you with an effective strategic approach to guide you in using this book as a treatment manual for integrating sleep repair into your clinical work. To help adopt this clinical framework, the book provides the background knowledge needed to understand how sleep supports your patient's recovery. Each chapter also provides an outline of the key concepts as well as an application section. These will guide you to practice using the tools and principles.

The clinical cases in Part II provide both the clinical strategies and the steps needed to address the four most common causes of disrupted sleep patterns in trauma. The clinical cases demonstrate what to do and how to do it. Each chapter also provides a grounding in the neurobiology of the disorder to provide insight into why the interventions work. Enjoy reading and learning from the clinical examples elaborated in this book! And feel free to use this treatment manual in the way that best supports your clinical work. Start with whatever chapter interests you the most, or which resonates with the work that you are doing with a current patient.

KEY MESSAGES FOR THERAPISTS

1. Integration of Sleep Treatment in PTSD Protocols: Many have advocated for a paradigm shift to include sleep treatment in PTSD protocols based on persistent relationships between trauma, sleep disturbances, and

PTSD symptoms. Despite these efforts, current PTSD Treatment guidelines still lack adequate integration of sleep treatment in trauma recovery.
2. Neurobiological Roots of Sleep Disturbances: Increasingly, animal and human studies reveal that brainstem neurotransmitters, particularly norepinephrine, serotonin, and dopamine, are crucial for regulating both healthy and disrupted sleep. Dysregulation in brainstem functions underpins sleep disorders and PTSD symptoms, emphasizing the need for targeted sleep interventions. Understanding these neurobiological foundations helps develop effective treatments for trauma patients, addressing the roots of their sleep disturbances and improving overall therapy outcomes.
3. Clinical Necessity of Targeting Sleep Disturbances: The book stresses the importance of addressing sleep disturbances alongside trauma treatment. Therapists must recognize the necessity of targeting sleep issues to collaborate effectively with patients. The text provides practical steps and tools for therapists to ensure a comprehensive approach to trauma therapy, incorporating sleep treatment to enhance therapeutic effectiveness and support patients' recovery.

PUTTING TRAUMA TO SLEEP

PART I

Interpersonal Neurobiology, Neuromodulation, and Sleep Processes in Trauma

"Therapists need to consider that the chronic sleep disruption associated with nightmares may affect the efficacy of first-line PTSD treatments, but targeted sleep treatments may accelerate recovery from PTSD."
—Anne Germain (2013, p. 372)

"Understanding sleep problems and their role in the development and maintenance of PTSD and TBI symptoms may lead to improvement in overall treatment outcomes"
—Karina Gilbert, Sarah Kark, Philip Gehrman, Yelena Bogdanova (2015, p. 195)

1

Restorative Nighttime Sleep: An Essential Target in Trauma Treatment

"It has long been thought that interventions focusing on trauma itself would eventually reduce disturbed sleep. But accumulating evidence shows that sleep disorders play a central role in both the development and maintenance of PTSD and therefore require clinical attention."
—Marike Lancel, Hein van Marie, Maaike Van Veen, Annette van Schagen (2021, p. 1)

"Targeted sleep-focused therapeutic interventions can improve sleep symptoms and mitigate daytime PTSD symptoms."
—Janeese Brownlow, Katherine Miller, Phillip Gehrman (2020, p. 301)

One of the earliest voices calling for the integration of sleep treatment into trauma treatment protocols and guidelines was the prominent PTSD researcher Anne Germain. For two decades she has conducted groundbreaking research into the complex interactions between trauma exposure, sleep disturbances, and the development of PTSD. She contributed an important research tool for investigating sleep disturbances in PTSD (the Pittsburgh Sleep Quality Index Addendum for PTSD [Germain et al., 2005]). The research which followed led to a review article (Germain, 2013) and then proposed a conceptual model for "a paradigm shift" (Germain et al., 2017, p. 84) to acknowledging the decisive role of sleep in the development of PTSD. Her life's work has been a clarion call to integrating sleep treatments into PTSD protocols.

Since Anne Germain (2013) first called for integrating sleep treatment into PTSD treatment guidelines over a decade ago, her conclusion that "there is no consensus or guideline regarding the inclusion of evidence-based sleep treatment strategies in the context of trauma and PTSD management" (p. 379) still prevails. The hard truth is that targeted treatment of the sleep difficulties of trauma patients has not been adequately integrated into treatment guidelines. This book provides the neurobiological rationale, clinical examples, and practical tools for addressing sleep issues during trauma treatment. As the reviews of the literature on sleep disturbances in PTSD cited in the epigraphs above have all concluded, *sleep and trauma* (as well as mTBI [Wickwire et al., 2016]) *are inextricably linked* and there is increasing recognition that to optimize trauma therapy, *sleep issues also require assessment and treatment*. Part of this problem has been the lack of a clear treatment manual that can guide trauma therapists to incorporating sleep into their trauma treatment. Part I of this book provides the background knowledge and the tools to correct this gap.

Animal studies have only recently confirmed that the neurobiological roots of healthy and disrupted sleep lie in the brainstem. The critical issue is how the brainstem-activated neurotransmitters (norepinephrine [Osorio-Ferero et al., 2022], serotonin [Oikonomou et al., 2019]), and dopamine [Hasegawa et al., 2022]) interact, *which then permit normal, restful sleep, or disrupt sleep*. Review of human studies of sleep problems in PTSD patients all point to the same conclusion., namely that sleep disorders and the various hyperarousal, emotional, and avoidance symptoms of PTSD all have their origins in dysregulation of brainstem functions, but that there are multiple resulting patterns of disruption (Germain, 2013; van Wyk et al., 2016). This plasticity of symptom responses to a given traumatic event is best illustrated by the neuroimaging of brain reactions in a husband and wife after a horrendous car accident. His brain was hyperaroused and hers was shut down (Lanius et al., 2003). Each is an independent feature of the overall PTSD clinical picture and targeting just one symptom does not make any others disappear. All elements of the dysregulated brainstem need to be clinically evaluated and targeted with evidence-based interventions.

This section of the book will not review the considerable research evidence that has documented the comorbidity of daytime PTSD symptoms and sleep disturbances. Those can be found in the review articles cited in the epigraphs above. Instead, this book focuses on the next step. Once therapists appreciate the clinical necessity of targeting sleep disturbances, this book will provide a guide to collaborating with your patient in the examination of their sleep problems and then specifically target their sleep disturbances.

While the importance of addressing sleep disturbances can no longer be questioned, what is not entirely settled is what does a comprehensive approach to these disturbances include? Is it sequential or integrated?

A sequential approach refers to treating sleep disturbance as a preparatory step and then beginning the trauma treatment. A recently reported field trial with CBTi provided as a first intervention before introduction of the trauma treatment reported superior results with this way of augmenting standard trauma treatment (Pigeon et al., 2022).

An integrated approach refers to integration of sleep treatment with the trauma treatment you are providing. This book aims to give you an understanding of what is required to treat the many ways that sleep can be dysregulated in trauma. While it is intended specifically for therapists, providing both the knowledge base and the intervention tools to integrate sleep treatments into your trauma practice, it is hoped that both trauma survivors and family members may find the information helpful in their healing journey. Our goal is to provide readers with a clear idea of what sleep problems are found among trauma survivors, what needs to be done about these, why it is important to do something about sleep specifically, and how to go about it for those ready to do it.

Whether you are a trauma therapist or a person who has experienced significant trauma yourself, this chapter will provide you with an overview of what fixing sleep can mean to recovery from trauma. The central thesis of this book is that *sleep is about your relationship with your "self."* Period. Nothing more.

Trauma is like an earthquake in your life. It disrupted everything about who you were: your self. What you were doing, feeling, and knowing prior to that moment was cataclysmically disrupted. As every earthquake has aftershocks, some a few minutes after, some days or weeks after, every trauma has aftershocks in your mind and your body. However, the earth does not have a memory system, so after the earthquake and its aftershocks, that disruption is over and done with.

Your brain, on the other hand, does have multiple memory systems. And your brain's survival systems try to protect you from further quakes by remembering every element of what happened in the trauma. These memories of the trauma are present both in your mind (as memories and flashbacks) and in your body (as tension, emotion, vulnerability, and foreboding). To restore sleep to a normal restorative pattern, the first step is identifying the intrusive aftershocks that trauma has left in the mind and in the body. This book will walk you through how to identify each of these.

This chapter will review the nature of the various sleep disturbances commonly found to be comorbid with PTSD. Whether you are a person who has had trauma, a family member, or a therapist working with trauma, you need a perspective about why sleep is important to normal functioning. It is only after we understand that sleep is one of the body's most precious resources that we can start to make the changes necessary to support optimal restorative sleep.

At times, the goal of enjoying truly restorative sleep for the trauma survivor can feel more impossible than taking a trip to a far-off galaxy. Disrupted sleep has often been present for decades, even dating back to infancy. Yet setting the firm intention and goal of stabilizing sleep right from the outset of trauma treatment is the strategy that is most likely to succeed, by including attention to sleep alongside attention to traumatic events, attachment dynamics, and body reactions.

SLEEP AS A RESOURCE FOR TRAUMA RECOVERY

Sleep-inclusive trauma treatment will prioritize restorative sleep as the ultimate resource you can provide your patient for their trauma recovery and for their life. It includes a number of elements: (1) clearly understanding the critical contribution of sleep as the body's natural healer in recovery from trauma, (2) knowing that there are a variety of different sleep problems that can impair full recovery (not just one), (3) knowing how to investigate the specific features of your patient's sleep pattern, and (4) knowing there are useful clinical interventions that target sleep-related barriers to recovery. Overall, these steps provide a pathway for the sleep-challenged trauma patient to reestablish a strong connection with their body's ability to heal and recover a healthier self.

In this chapter, we first review what the target of *restorative sleep* looks and feels like, so we know where we are going. Only if you know where you need to go with treatment will you be able to start sharing that goal with the person struggling to recover from trauma. Then, we introduce you to the range of common sleep disorders with which your traumatized patients may be struggling. This will help you understand what you are looking for. In the next chapter, we will review the tools you will use to determine the specific sleep disturbances your patient may have.

What I will learn in this chapter to become a better sleep and trauma therapist:
1. I will be able to describe sleep's five major restorative functions, including: reenergizing physical energy, modulating emotion, regulating metabolism and appetite, downregulating inflammation, and reorganizing long-term memory.
2. I will understand that trauma can disrupt sleep in multiple diverse ways, not just as a single trauma-related disruption of sleep.
3. I will know the key features of nightmares, insomnia, sleep apnea, narcolepsy, restless legs, trauma-associated sleep disorder, sleep paralysis, sleepwalking, night terrors, and circadian rhythm disorders.
4. I will be able to describe how sleep is *the most essential resource* to bring to the trauma survivor, to install in their daily repertoire and help with the restoration of their healthy self.

RESTORATIVE SLEEP

Sleep Quality: A Composite of 5 Factors

What is it that happens across the night that provides a good, deep refreshing night of sleep? There are five factors that contribute to sustained deep sleep at night (Ji et al., 2023; Parrino et al., 2016):

1. Timing: having a regular time to go to sleep and wake up
2. Regularity: consistency of those times across two weeks of sleep tracking
3. Duration: nightly sleep duration of 7 hours or more of total sleep time (TST)
4. Rhythmicity: excellent sleep depth (good intensity of slow wave sleep [SWS])
5. Efficiency: stability and continuity of sleep across the 7-hour sleep period (with few awakenings and with swift return to sleep)
6. Daytime alertness: an active daytime agenda including exposure to sunlight, physical activity outdoors, regular meals, and face-to-face time socializing with others.

The sixth factor may have surprised you into thinking, "That is not a part of sleep." True, but it is included because one of the core concepts we want to get across is that you are *not* isolating sleep as a separate entity to improve. We always look at the rhythm of activity and rest, activity and rest. Sleep has no value separate from its value to create the conditions for you functioning at your best across the day. Your daytime activity is still the focus of who you are, what you care about, and what you seek to accomplish. And sleep is your absolute best resource for accomplishing that.

When all these elements are present, your sleep-wake rhythm supports sustained daytime physical, social, emotional, and mental health. So what does the brain do, to get into a restorative sleep? Unlike our conscious awareness, which is "on" or "off," our brain shifts down into sleep in a series of four steps. Think of a car that has to downshift from third gear, to second, to first, and then neutral. The brain works similarly. What this healthy sleep looks like is represented by the *hypnogram*. The hypnogram is a graph of the sequence of the brain's activity across the night. Figure 1.1 is a hypnogram illustrating the cascade of sleep stages across the 7 hours of sleep in a sleep lab.

SLEEP STAGES

Sleep is divided into several stages, each characterized by distinct patterns of brain activity, eye movements, and muscle tone. These stages are typically measured using polysomnography, which includes electroencephalography (EEG) to monitor brain waves, electrooculography (EOG) to monitor eye movements, and electromyography (EMG) to monitor muscle activity. The main stages of sleep are:

Non-Rapid Eye Movement (NREM) Sleep

NREM sleep progresses in three distinct stages:
Stage N1: This is the transition from wakefulness to sleep. It's a light sleep stage during which muscle activity decreases, and people can easily be awakened. Brain waves start to slow down, and there may be occasional muscle twitches.

Stage N2: This is a deeper stage of sleep characterized by further slowing of brain waves, along with occasional bursts of rapid brain activity called sleep spindles. Eye movements stop, and heart rate and body temperature decrease.

Stage N3: Also known as slow-wave sleep (SWS) or deep sleep, this stage is characterized by slow brain waves known as delta waves. It's the deepest stage of sleep, during which it's most difficult to awaken someone. Muscle activity is minimal, and various bodily functions, including hormone regulation and tissue repair, occur.

Rapid Eye Movement (REM) Sleep

REM sleep is characterized by rapid eye movements, hence its name. It's associated with vivid dreams and increased brain activity, similar to wakefulness. Muscles are relaxed, almost paralyzed, to prevent acting out dreams. Heart rate and breathing become irregular, and blood pressure increases.

These stages do not occur in a linear fashion throughout the night. Instead, sleep typically cycles through multiple cycles of NREM and REM sleep, with each cycle lasting roughly 90 to 120 minutes. The proportion of time spent in each stage varies across the night, with more time spent in deep sleep (N3) during the earlier part of the night and more REM sleep occurring in the latter part.

Brain states during sleep can also be classified based on EEG patterns:

Delta activity (slow-wave sleep): Dominant during deep NREM sleep (Stage N3) (indicating a silent Reticular Activating System (RAS) but active thalamocortical rhythms).
Theta activity: Present during lighter NREM sleep (Stage N1 and Stage N2) (indicating activity of the RAS in the absence of sensory inputs).
Alpha activity: Occurs during relaxation and drowsiness, often seen during the transition to sleep (also indicating activity of the RAS in the absence of sensory inputs).
Beta activity: Associated with wakefulness and active thinking, typically absent during sleep (indicating the RAS processing external sensory data).
Gamma activity: Associated with enhanced cognition, peak performance, bliss, and quality of life (fully conscious RAS processing of external signals).

Understanding these stages and brain states helps researchers, doctors, and therapists assess sleep quality, diagnose sleep disorders, and tailor treatments accordingly.

Each of the stages in this hypnogram represents a shift in the underlying brain rhythms that are present in normal sleep (see Figure 1.1). After about 20 minutes of being awake in bed, the sleeper shifts into a brief state of light sleep called non-rapid eye movement stage 1 (NREM1), followed by a brief state of moderately deep sleep (NREM2), to finally arrive in deep sleep, called slow wave sleep (SWS, or NREM3). After about 45 minutes in this deep sleep, brain waves shift back through the lighter sleep stages and then into the first REM sleep for about 10 minutes.

FIGURE 1.1   Hypnogram of Brain Sleep States Across the Night of Sleep

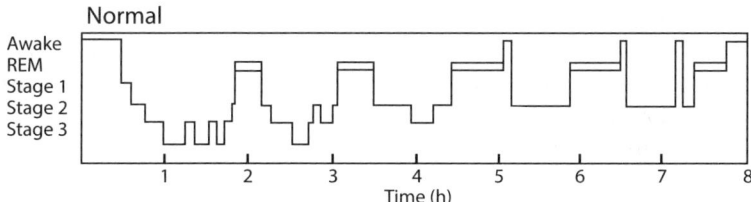

The rhythm of these shifts takes about 90 minutes, and these repeat four to five times across the night. This 90-minute cycle that repeats is called an *ultradian rhythm*, and in a healthy sleeper there is an orderly shifting through the NREM stages and ending in a REM period each time. This 90-minute rhythm continues for another four cycles in a healthy, good sleeper. At the end of these cycles, the sleeper awakens refreshed.

From the flow of these stages, the brain has an orderly sequence of initiating and transitioning from stage to stage. It is apparent that most of the deep, slow wave sleep, occurs in the first 4 hours of sleep, and most of the REM sleep occurs in the last 4 hours of sleep. If any of these factors are compromised or absent, our daytime experiences are marked by having difficulty concentrating, feeling moody, and not having the energy we need to make it through the whole day.

The hypnogram traces out the progression of sleep stages that is a signature of good sleep, but the preparation for that good sleep begins well before you lay your head down to sleep. About 2 hours or so prior to sleep the darkness of sunset triggered the release of melatonin by the brain. Melatonin, the "darkness hormone," travels through the body to let every cell of the body know that sleep is coming. Melatonin does not put you to sleep; it gets all bodily organ systems to synchronize and begin their transition into sleep. It activates these preparatory physiological, restorative processes in all organ systems, and this collective shift in metabolism throughout the body allows a graduated slowing down that ends in going to sleep about 2 hours later. When the sleeper lies down in bed and turns the light off, it still takes about 20 minutes to let go of the lingering mental activity from the day.

All the features of restorative sleep are illustrated in the hypnogram (Figure 1.1). In clinical practice, though, we rarely have hypnograms to review. Instead, we work from the patient's reports of how easy or hard it was to get to sleep, stay asleep, and awaken from sleep. In the next chapter we will describe how to use sleep diaries and screening questionnaires to evaluate these aspects of a person's sleep. First, we describe in more detail the elements of restorative sleep. After the body has begun to slow down, to permit sleep, how does the brain use the opportunity to get into a deeper sleep?

Sleep Quality and Cyclical Alternating Patterns

Restorative sleep does not just happen when we start sleep. It requires a considerable amount of brain wave activity to create an uninterrupted period of sustained deep sleep. That effort to get into deep sleep is seen in sleep recordings from the night. They are called A1 cycles and can be seen clearly as the white bars in Figure 1.2 and note how A1 cycles push sleep into SWS (see hypnogram lower panel).

Examination of the cyclic alternating patterns (CAPs) across sleep reveals that there are underlying cycles of cortical activity that either promote sleep stability (A1 cycles, see white bars in Figure 1.2) or signal the activation of motor centers (A2 cycles, black bars) or autonomic activity (A3 cycles, also black bars). The healthy sleeper in Figure 1.2 demonstrated a total of 214 A1 events during sleep. Notice how many of these A1 cycles happen across the first hour of sleep. These are what shift the sleeper into deeper sleep.

FIGURE 1.2   Frequency and Timing of Cyclic Alternating Pattern (CAP) Subtypes in a Healthy Sleeper   Source: Reprinted with permission: Parrino et al. (2005 p. 2237)

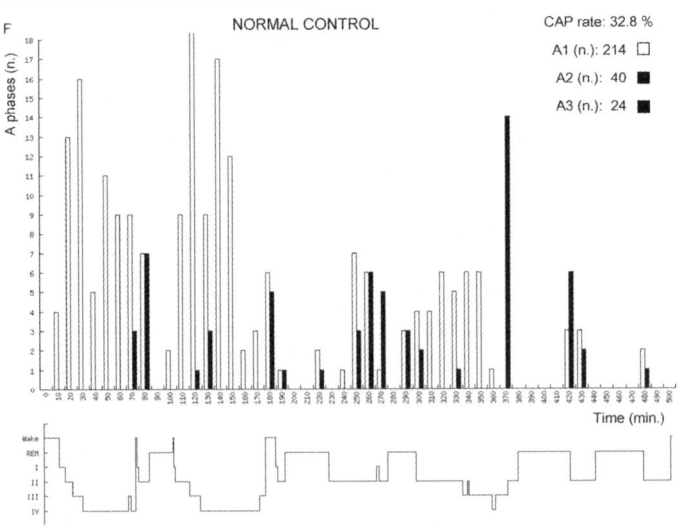

The presence of these microstructure (A1, A2, and A3) events is not random. While the A1 subtypes were more present in the early part of the night, the activating patterns (A2 and A3) ramp up autonomic activation before every REM sleep period. What we see in Figure 1.2 is the brain activating memories of unfinished business from the previous day, so that the creative REM sleep time can first desensitize the emotional load of these memories and then begin to actively reprocess what needs to happen to resolve these challenging problems.

Figure 1.2 demonstrates the role of A1 CAP subtypes in progressively and actively deepening sleep across the first two ultradian rhythms. Each bar on the upper histogram indicates the number of CAP subtypes observed in the past 10 minutes of sleep. Note how the abundance of A1 subtypes (white bars) across the first 3 hours of sleep results in two episodes of lengthy SWS (see hypnogram inserted under the CAPs graph). You can also detect an increase in A1 toward the morning, reflecting the presence of a strong circadian sleep drive.

In the third ultradian cycle, A1 subtypes are relatively absent and A2 and A3 subtypes begin to occur with more frequency. Note also that A2 and A3 subtypes are rarely present when the sleeper is in SWS. However, as the transition into REM sleep begins, there is a reactivation of A2 and A3 subtypes, which participate in generating the REM sleep experience. A3 subtypes reflect activity of the autonomic system, and these are present prior to all five REM periods throughout the night. A2 and A3 subtypes prompt the transition from NREM into REM sleep. For these reasons CAP has been referred to as a master clock that determines the progression of the sleep stages across the night. The hypnogram in Figure 1.2 shows that this sleeper went through five of these 90-minute ultradian rhythms (switching between NREM and REM) across the night.

Core Sleep and Drowsy Sleep

The whole sleep period has two qualitatively different phases of sleep. The first, composed of three 90-minute sleep cycles takes about 4.5 hours. It contains most of the SWS for that night. This first 4.5-hour period of sleep has been called "core sleep" (Parrino et al., 2016). In contrast, the remaining 3 hours of sleep is a light drowsy sleep. Sleep is shifting back and forth between light NREM2 sleep and REM sleep. Many sleepers awaken repeatedly during this later half of sleep, but it is *not* the time to get out of bed. The brain is continuing to do important work in processing negative emotions and reorganizing long-term memories. Calming the body and shifting away from thinking patterns can help to stay in this drowsy sleep.

While drowsy sleep is lighter sleep, it is just as necessary for healthy functioning. The REM sleep that is necessary for restorative sleep has not yet really begun until after the core sleep. Getting out of bed after 4–5 hours of core sleep will mean that your total nightly REM sleep will be less than 10% of your total sleep time—half of what is necessary for both cognitive and emotional stability.

The first three cycles of ultradian sleep (90-minute rhythms) are primarily GABAergic, while the last two are mainly cholinergic states (Parrino et al., 2016). That switch in underlying acetylcholine (Ach) presence boosts the duration of REM sleep. In addition to the prevalence of Ach in the last half of sleep, oxytocin, adrenaline, and cortisol also increase, adding complexities to the active neurotransmitters supporting REM sleep. This more complex soup of neurotransmitters also increases the complexity of recalled dreams. Morning dreams contain more elements from much earlier life experiences, the presence of different people in the dreamer's life, and the introduction of a range of emotional and visceral bodily states into the dream. These dreams just before awakening are integrative of the dreamer's current emotional struggles.

Many hormones increase across the sleep period. For example, testosterone takes at least 3 hours of sleep to reach its heightened level at night. Oxytocin levels peak about 5 hours after the start of sleep, coinciding with the onset of more productive REM sleep. Adrenaline and cortisol are both released in the last 2 hours of sleep. All these hormones can influence sleep and dreams. The relative absence of oxytocin in those with developmental trauma means their dreams will be dominated by increased levels of sympathetic activity and stress hormones, resulting in more nightmares and in terrifying mood states.

In patients with PTSD, many of the normal rhythmic ebbs and flows of hormones have become dysregulated. Intense sympathetic arousal by brainstem mechanisms, dysregulated hormones, and absence of oxytocin all contribute to aggravating and perpetuating the disruption of sleep. For example, patients who have suffered from PTSD for decades will have low testosterone levels and likely suffer from adrenal fatigue. Thus, the normal circadian cortisol and adrenaline surge that happens before awakening in the morning does not occur. This adds to the experience of real fatigue upon awakening. Not only was their sleep short and not restorative, but the lack of testosterone and oxytocin adds to anhedonia and lack of drive to start the day.

Normal State Transitions Awakening (NREM to REM, or REM to NREM)

Awakenings across the night of sleep are common and normal, especially before and after a state change (from NREM to REM or REM to NREM). A normal awakening from NREM sleep would mean a gradual awareness of your sleep room. You would notice where you are and may decide that you need to go to the bathroom. Even a 5-minute trip to the bathroom would be under a state of *sleep inertia*.

In sleep inertia your mind is not fully awake, but you are perceptive enough to navigate to the bathroom and back. Sleep inertia allows you to get back to bed, lie down, and fall asleep within 10 minutes. Sleep inertia means your mind never actually becomes fully awakened during a nighttime awakening.

Just enough of the brain wakes up to get the job done. However, it is important not to cue the brain to wake up. Turning on lights, beginning to think about daytime activities, or going for a nighttime snack all tell the brain that we are finished sleeping and to wake up fully! Those struggling with trauma may have awakened with pain or from a nightmare. These nightly states of activation undermine their ability to easily return to sleep.

To summarize, when the brain and body are allowed to do their normal internal housekeeping duties (by getting 7 to 8 hours of decent-quality sleep) they get the job done. During restorative sleep your nervous system will unconsciously (without your conscious direction) identify memories that were emotionally tagged the previous day (NREM2), replay them to move them to the neocortex (long-term memory; NREM3), and consolidate these fresh memories with old memories (REM). That sequence of brain states across the night functions to desensitize negative emotions and reorganize the sleeper's self-system to include recent experiential learning from the day before.

Role of Visceral Integration for Signaling Normal Morning Awakening

Key to the understanding of the many functions that sleep supports is its role in integrating the visceral information from every organ system. Emotions are a vital component of this visceral information, but not the only element. During waking life, each organ system operates independently, interdependently, and holistically, integrated with the rest of the body through circadian cycles. It regulates its functions based on the load put on it by the organism operating in each environmental context. Most of the time, there is no overload.

However, when distress and trauma dysregulate somatic systems, all these systems require better integration. *These visceral states include visceral sensations of cramping, nausea, pain, and physical discomfort, and these get compartmentalized as bodily symptoms. This sets the stage for holding the trauma in the body rather than it being addressed, integrated, and healed.* According to Pigarev's *Visceral Theory of Sleep* (2014), the drive for sleep at the start of the night in part reflects the body's accumulated drive to neutralize and balance these visceral states during sleep. However, in the fragmented trauma state, this does not occur.

The body is a critical driver of the need to sleep. Pigarev (2014) saw these visceral states as a critical component of what Borbely (1982, 2022) termed the "homeostatic" drive for sleep. Across the day, the component visceral systems of the body accumulate information on the need to sleep. In a safe environment, with no other competing needs or dangers, the transition to sleep at the end of the day can occur easily with the first signs of tiredness.

However, a hyperaroused fear system in PTSD that is terrified of sleep will override these visceral signals, make sleep impossible to start, and quickly and repeatedly interrupt sleep throughout the night. This corresponds to storms of

A2 and A3 CAPs that override the sedating A1 CAPs, overwhelming the sleep urge and awakening the sleeper. As a result, in the absence of persistent restorative sleep patterns, the somatic distress often seen in PTSD is not resolved or integrated. Not sleeping exacerbates the visceral sensations of cramping, nausea, pain, and physical discomfort, and these in turn further undermine sleep.

To summarize this section on the characteristics of restorative sleep, as a therapist you are looking for patients who describe that they have regular sleep times, they can get to sleep easily, and can stay asleep for most of the night. Also asking about somatic bodily symptoms can be predictable clues that sleep is not restorative. Link these troublesome visceral problems with lack of sleep, so the patient can understand that improving sleep can benefit their physical symptoms.

In normal, restorative sleep, if they do wake up, it is for a brief period, and they can stay in bed and get back to sleep. By morning they will have been in bed for no longer than normal, 8 hours, and will have slept for 7 hours or more of that time. Patients can also be encouraged to record their morning dreams and bring these into their treatment sessions.

That pattern of restorative sleep accomplishes many tasks. For the physical body, sleep restores the energy in mitochondria to allow a full day of activity. For the hormonal system, it restores levels of metabolic hormones that limit eating and allow for a sense of satiety. For the immune system, sleep recharges the ability of the immune army to effectively find and fight invaders like cancer cells and viruses. For the emotional system, sleep brings stability and a sense of well-being. And for the cognitive system, sleep reorganizes long-term memories. All these critical functions support wellness. All effective trauma treatment brings the patient to resolution of their sleep disturbances and reactivates these restorative processes to support a healthy self.

THE MANY FACES OF DISTURBED SLEEP IN TRAUMA

> Insomnia and nightmares are viewed as core symptoms of PTSD. Yet, relations between disturbed sleep and PTSD are far more complex: PTSD is linked to a broad range of sleep disorders and disturbed sleep markedly affects PTSD-outcome. (Lancel et al., 2021, p. 1)

Clashes between the survival drive system and sleep circuitry generate various sleep disorders. We will review those that are most common among PTSD patients.

In addition to the three most common sleep disturbances in PTSD, of insomnia, nightmares, and sleep apnea, we can add circadian rhythm disturbances, depression, restless leg syndrome and periodic limb movements disorder (PLMD), nonrestorative sleep, sleep paralysis, alpha-delta sleep, confusional arousals, sleepwalking, narcolepsy, and night terrors. All can be found among PTSD patients. We will review these according to which stage of sleep they tend to disrupt, first the cluster that disrupts NREM sleep, and then the cluster that disrupts REM sleep.

Blatant Disruptions of Sleep: How Danger Impacts Sleep

To respect our overarching need for survival, it is important to understand from the outset that sleep has a master. That master is the circuitry of the autonomic nervous system (ANS), which is exquisitely designed to take incoming sensory information about both external (environmental) and internal (visceral) dangers and act on those immediately. External threats include present conflicts with others as well as recent and past traumatic events. Internal threats include inflammatory responses, pain signals, and visceral sensations like nausea and fatigue. The presence of both types of danger prior to bedtime in PTSD patients will override the usual tendency to relax and allow the body to slow down for sleep.

Many trauma patients have had horrible experiences late at night, some even in the bedroom. When these date back to preverbal childhood (before age 3), overall tightness in the musculoskeletal system of the body can be a clue that the ANS is on high alert. These memories activate the autonomic system, including upregulation of cortisol and adrenaline, as well as the psychological sense of being on guard for threats to safety. In some patients this autonomic activity is more like a storm. The intensity of their distress is physically and emotionally palpable. Some go to great lengths to avoid sleep. This engine of autonomic dysregulation will create multiple problems, both increased daytime symptoms as well as severe interference in initiating and maintaining sleep.

When the arousal systems override the normal homeostatic and circadian rhythms that prepare for sleep, during periods of traumatic distress or depression, the result can be unwanted and debilitating insomnia (Saper et al., 2005, p. 1262), as well as several NREM disorders the sleeper may not recall in the morning on awakening. We will review the sleep symptoms patients report after trauma in the sequence in which these symptoms typically develop. There is considerable evidence that the occurrence of either persistent developmental stressors or intense overwhelming life-threatening events initially result in repetitive nightmares.

Nightmares

The occurrence of nightmares immediately after traumatic events predicts persistent problems with insomnia in the weeks to follow (Kobayashi et al., 2008). Moreover, if the nightmares are replicative of the traumatic event (repeated flashbacks to the events) those individuals will demonstrate higher fear of sleep than others whose nightmares are not replays of the traumatic event (Davis & Wright, 2007; Krakow et al., 1995).

In recent studies of sleep disturbances among PTSD patients, the role of *fear of sleep* has been highlighted as a significant and unique perpetuating factor for trauma-induced insomnia, and distinguishing it from insomnia among those without trauma (Werner et al., 2020). The biggest part of this fear of sleep is the fear of loss of control that surrendering to sleep requires (Pruiksma et al., 2014). Such pronounced fears are likely to activate hyperarousal, and a PTSD study of those with disturbed sleep found that those with hyperarousal (versus without) had higher levels of norepinephrine metabolites (van Wyk et al., 2016). *Finally, studies of combat veterans who completed trauma treatment, among those who no longer met PTSD criteria clinically significant insomnia continued in 48% (Zayfert & DeViva, 2004) and 57% (Pruiksma et al., 2016) of those whose daytime symptoms are remitted.*

In a review of sleep studies conducted to 2016, Anne Germain and her colleagues found that 50–70% of trauma survivors continue to report regular nightmares (Koffel et al., 2016). These occur on a spectrum of intensity. At the most intense end of the spectrum, the nightmare is described as a replicative posttraumatic nightmare, like a flashback in sleep. In between, there are nonreplicative posttraumatic nightmares with enough intense emotions to awaken the dreamer. At the less intense end of the spectrum are nightmares with the same theme of overwhelming danger, but with changes in the setting, participants, and events. At this less intense end, the dreamer is aware of the intense danger but is engaged in the symbolic reworking of the traumatic event into a posttraumatic dream experience.

Screening for Nightmares

To summarize, intense autonomic dysregulation is often first apparent in intense replicative nightmares immediately after trauma. Therapists can explore the impact of individual traumatic events by asking about the occurrence of nightmares immediately following the traumatic event. Asking about the content of the nightmares, their intensity, and how long they were up after awakening from a nightmare can also give a better picture of the impact of the trauma on the nervous system, as well as the likelihood that these disruptive sleep events will continue and require targeted sleep treatments.

A straightforward way to get the current clinical picture of the presence and seriousness of nightmares is by giving the Nightmare Disorder Index (Dietch et al., 2021). This scale was constructed to mirror the *DSM-5* criteria for nightmare disorder. It is composed of five items that provide a measure of how frequently the patient has nightmares, as well as how much nightmares distress and cause difficulties for the patient.

Insomnia

> Growing evidence supports the assumption that insomnia is not limited to a sleeping complaint, but should be considered as a 24-hour disorder. . . . Research showed that the best differential diagnosis of insomnia was made with the use of CAP variables. (Cortoos et al., 2006, p. 263)

Most (70–90%) of those diagnosed with PTSD report insomnia as an associated sleep disorder (Brownlow et al., 2020). Insomnia is defined as difficulties getting to sleep or staying asleep or waking up too early in the morning. In short, insomnia reflects the underlying state in which the sympathetic nervous system is actively fighting the sleep instinct. Psychologically, this is evident in an elevated level of fear of sleep. While there are multiple reasons that someone may develop insomnia, among the population with PTSD it is the fear of sleep itself that is a key element that maintains the disorder (Werner et al., 2021).

How is this tension between the parasympathetic drive toward deeper sleep and the sympathetic drive to remain awake evident in brain wave activity? It is most clearly seen in the activity of cyclical alternating patterns, or CAPs. Comparing Figure 1.3 directly with 1.2 shows some dramatic differences in both the hypnogram of brain activity (bottom of diagram) as well as the cortical CAP sequences driving those changes (top of diagram). The CAP signature includes many clear features. First the CAP rate of insomniacs is twice that of healthy sleepers. Second, healthy sleepers have mainly A1 sleep promoting subtypes

FIGURE 1.3 Frequency and Timing of CAP Subtypes in Primary Insomnia
Source: Reprinted by permission: Terzano et al. (2003, p. 1719)

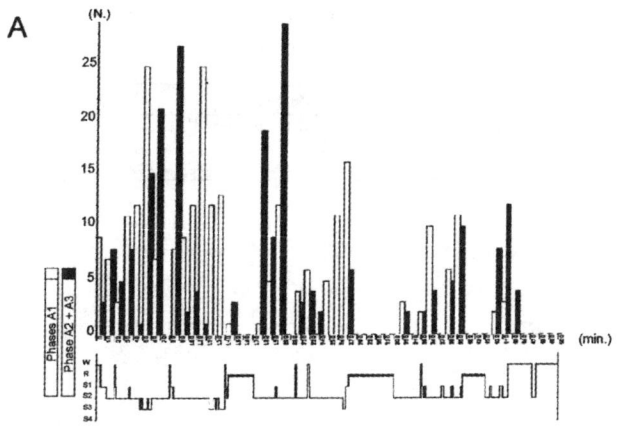

in the first three hours of sleep, whereas insomniacs have mainly A2 and A3 arousal subtypes.

There is intense A2 and A3 CAPs activity right from the start of sleep and persisting throughout sleep. In the first 2 hours of sleep, these activating cycles led to multiple awakenings before the first REM sleep period emerged. There are only very brief moments when A1 predominates over the activating cycles, resulting in very brief SWS. REM periods still did appear after those brief forays into SWS. The overall result is the pattern of activated and fragmented REM sleep we review in Chapter 9.

These differences in the brain wave activity underlying sleep in PTSD have been demonstrated by increased arousal levels (reduced depth of sleep) as indicated by the combination of reduced NREM delta power and increased gamma power in the frontal cortex during REM and NREM sleep (Wang et al., 2020). These physiological differences are also evident in correlations between measures of fear of sleep and reduced total sleep time (Kanady et al., 2018), longer sleep latency, more nighttime awakenings, and reduced sleep efficiency at night (Baglioni et al., 2016).

Claudia Zayfert and her colleagues began to postulate that fear of sleep was a particularly important variable in understanding the persistence of sleep problems among PTSD patients. They devised the Fear of Sleep Inventory (FoSI) and reported on its psychometric properties (Pruiksma et al., 2014). These researchers found that fear of sleep scores contained two factors: fear of loss of control and fear of the darkness.

FIGURE 1.4 Pathways to Development of Chronic Trauma-Induced Insomnia
Source: Reprinted by permission: Werner et al. (2020, p. 2)

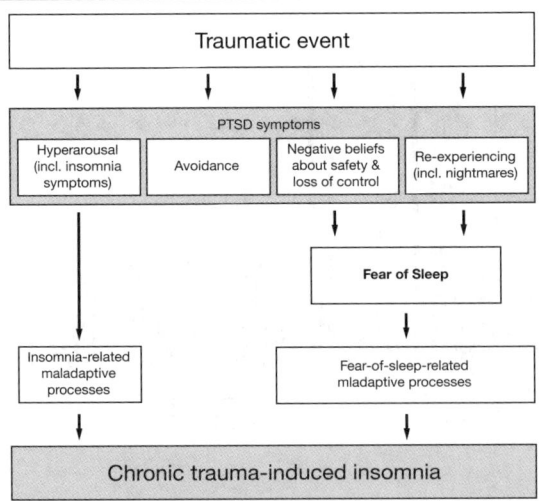

Gabriela Werner and her colleagues (2021) extended this idea by proposing that the fear of sleep construct consisted of three components: (1) the emotional experience of fear of sleep; (2) dysfunctional beliefs about safety during sleep, loss of control, and fear of reexperiencing nightmares; and (3) maladaptive behavior related to these beliefs. The difference between insomnia resulting from poor sleep habits and trauma-related insomnia is illustrated by Figure 1.4.

The conceptual model that these authors propose highlights the clinical importance of distinguishing between insomnia that relates to poor sleep habits and generalized arousal (left column of Figure 1.4) from insomnia that includes specific fears about sleep itself (right side of Figure 1.4), along with the heightened fears of loss of control and the increased pre-sleep somatic symptoms with which these patients often present.

Screening for Insomnia

There are two screening instruments that allow the therapist to evaluate the seriousness and impact of the patient's current insomnia. The Sleep Condition Indicator (SCI) was developed to mirror the *DSM-5* criteria for an insomnia diagnosis. The questions are phrased positively, with higher scores indicating more restful and satisfying sleep. Scores below 16 indicate the likely presence of clinical insomnia.

The second screening instrument asks more specifically for the presence of fear of sleep. The Fear of Sleep Inventory-Short Form (FoSI-SF; Pruiksma et al., 2014) is a 13-item questionnaire that provides a measure of the intensity of fear of sleep demonstrated by the patient. Their study confirmed that PTSD patients endorsed more FoSI items than the undergraduate sample. More importantly, factor analysis revealed a two-factor structure: fear of loss of control and fear of the dark.

Depression: Absence of SWS with REM Storms

Depression is another common symptom complaint in PTSD patients. It may seem odd to include depression as a sleep disturbance. However, Michael Perlis and his colleagues (Perlis et al., 1997) demonstrated that among patients successfully treated for depression, those who went on to relapse into clinical depression first experienced disrupted sleep, then they became depressed.

Not only is insomnia a precursor for the development of clinical depression, but depressed patients have a unique sleep signature (Cartwright, 2010, Chapter 4). The normal transition from stages 1 and 2 into NREM stage 3 (delta or SWS) sleep happens within the first hour of sleep. In depressed individuals, SWS is strikingly absent. It is one of the defining sleep signatures of depression. As a result, their first REM period happens much more quickly, as soon as 45 to 50 minutes. Their REM sleep is abnormal in other ways as well. The first REM period is twice as long as the normal 10 minutes. And the eye movements are either too sparse or too dense (Cartwright, 2010, p. 51). When the eye movements are dense, they can appear as eye-movement storms.

However, if you awaken the depressed sleeper, the dream reports you get are sparse and lacking in both the complexity and emotional variability you find in dreams of healthy dreamers (Cartwright, 2010). Why? One of the critical functions of the NREM period that precedes the REM period is to replay tagged emotional memories from the day before and transfer those memories from short-term memory (replaying them in the hippocampus) to the neocortex, which stores long-term memories. This is accomplished by the resonating neural activity between hippocampus and cortex during SWS. The SWS replays emotional memories prior to the REM episode, not all memories, just those that were tagged with emotional (dopaminergic) signals, stimulated during the previous daytime's activities.

Dopamine (DA) is the neurochemical tag that gets activated and attached to events and experiences that are enjoyable. In depressed patients these signals of enjoyment have been blocked through intervention of the lateral habenula (LHb). The LHb neurons regulate the DA reward system, and when the LHb shuts down DA activation in the VTA and NaC, there is no brain activation of DA responses.

As a result, the LHb has a vital role in managing aversion, and when it blocks DA in depressed patients, it dysregulates goal-directed behavior. Reward processing of all kinds is mediated by the VTA and the NAc. Reactivation of reward circuits becomes a major goal of clinical intervention with depressed patients, and restoration of sleep patterns, paying particular attention to the pre-sleep experience of the patient, is a big part of this. These will be illustrated by clinical cases in Chapters 2 and 3.

Screening for Depression

Most trauma therapists already screen for depression with the Patient Health Questionnaire (PHQ9), the Beck Depression Inventory (BDI), the Center for Epidemiological Studies Depression scale (CES-D), or the Zung, Hamilton, or HADS depression scales. These all have items that ask about sleep, fatigue, and having trouble concentrating. Review of these items should trigger consideration of giving one or more screens for the other sleep disorders.

Circadian Rhythm Disorders

Many patients with PTSD begin to have highly irregular sleep patterns. One night a patient may stay up late or not sleep at all. The next night they may fall asleep after dinner and sleep till the next morning. The absence of a recurring regular pattern for sleep is very disruptive of the brain's restorative functions. A regular bedtime means the sequence of hormonal and immunological rhythms that occur across the sleep state can proceed predictably. For example, growth hormone is released in the first SWS episode, which usually occurs about an hour into the sleep time. If bedtimes are inconsistent, the normal release of this hormone will be disrupted and become blunted.

There are three ways that circadian rhythms become disrupted: sleeping too early, too late, or inconsistently. Adolescents and many trauma patients are night owls, regularly going to sleep at midnight or later. On the other hand, older patients are morning larks and go to sleep early and wake up early. It is the inconsistent sleepers, with erratic sleep times, who are most common among the trauma population. And these inconsistent sleep times play havoc with the underlying hormonal levels required to maintain the brain and body and prepare it for the next day.

Screening for Circadian Rhythm Disorders

When asked about their sleep during the interview, patients with irregular sleep times will not be able to give an unqualified answer to questions about time in bed, time awake, and total sleep time across the night. The extent of their circadian rhythm disturbance will become apparent when they begin keeping a sleep diary (see next chapter for details).

Unobtrusive (Stealth) Sleep Disruptions: How Danger Impacts Sleep

The remaining sleep disorders to be reviewed all share an important characteristic: patients may have no clear sense that these disruptions are occurring during their sleep period. When there is no subjective complaint of a problem it increases the likelihood that the underlying problem is not detected or treated. It often becomes known because of the reports from bed partners of disturbances during the night. Some of these do have objective findings that are evident on polysomnographic sleep studies, but others do not. Episodic problems are hard to identify but are still important to understand as they can seriously impact the overall sleep-wake rhythm.

Restless Legs Syndrome: Periodic Limb Movement Disorder

During NREM sleep many patients will experience periodic flexing of their legs or arms. These occur every 90 seconds or so. These limb movements can be intense enough that they wake the sleeper. Periodic limb movements have been found in about 33% of veterans with PTSD. Most are unaware of the movements, but they are very aware of waking up repeatedly across the night. The cause of the movements has not been identified, but some think that they represent the action sequence of the flight response to trauma, that is, the sleeper is aware of an overwhelming stressor and is making every effort to escape the danger while sleeping.

Alpha-Delta NREM Sleep

Alpha waves are characteristic of an awake mind. Delta waves are characteristic of NREM stage 3, a deeply sleeping mind. Alpha-delta sleep refers to the sudden appearance of an alpha awakening signal in the deepest part of SWS. The paradox of alpha-delta sleep is that the deeply sleeping brain suddenly has the impulse to awaken (Moldofsky & Scarisbrick, 1976). While the alpha wave signal attempts to awaken the sleeper, it does not result in awakening—but the intrusion of the alpha waves disrupts the restorative function of deep sleep. As delta sleep is the only sleep stage in which the reticular activating system is quiescent, this intrusion represents the re-engagement of the autonomic system, disrupting deepest SWS.

In the morning, the sleeper whose deep sleep was visited by repeated intrusions of alpha brain waves will awaken with the feeling that they have not slept at all. This has been called *nonrestorative sleep* (NRS) because the amount of total sleep time is fine, but the quality of the sleep that was obtained was poor because an activated autonomic system is fragmenting both NREM and REM sleep stages throughout the night. This problem does not appear to terminate the deep sleep of the sleeper, but the intrusion of an activated mind into the most restful part of sleep fragments the restorative sleep process. Nonrestorative sleep is typical of fibromyalgia and other clinical conditions in which fatigue, physical tiredness (physical and mental fatigue), pain sensitivities, achiness of body, and listlessness are typical.

When NRS persists, the inflammatory system is activated, causing the release of inflammatory factors, which cause the sensation of aches and pains in the body. As well, chronic NRS adversely affects hormonal systems. Therapists can be alert to the difference between sleepiness and fatigue. Sleepiness is the uncontrollable urge to sleep. Fatigue is different. Patients will tell you, "They are tired." This needs clarification by the therapist. "Are you saying you are feeling depressed? Do you want to avoid speaking about something? Do you feel overwhelmed by anxiety? Or does it feel like you are physically or mentally fatigued? Or are you feeling both sleepy and fatigued?"

Confusional Arousals

The first sleep cycle lasts for about 90–100 minutes. During this time, the sleeper's sleep need is at its maximum and most sleepers are unlikely to wake up. However, there are sleepers who do wake up, but in a very disoriented state. This is usually due to intense activation of the sympathetic system. The sleeper may be disoriented, confused, or unresponsive to efforts to communicate. Their behavior may be strange or unusual, or they may engage in common activities. These can last from seconds to a few minutes. Sometimes they last longer. They can be triggered by periods of sleep loss, irregular sleep-wake schedules, stress, ongoing use of sleeping medications, excessive caffeine, travel, or other undiagnosed sleep problems (e.g., apnea). The following morning the sleeper usually has no memory of the confusional arousal.

Somnambulism (Sleepwalking, Sexsomnia, and Other Driven Behaviors)

Sleepwalking is most common among 11- to 14-year-old children, whose brains are not fully developed. Sleepwalking only occurs in NREM sleep, usually within the first 2 hours of sleep onset. While it is a common developmental phenomenon, it can persist for some sleepers and there are family histories of sleepwalking patterns across generations.

When the sleeper is more active in these confusional awakenings, they may be engaging in more complicated behavior but without their usual sense of self-awareness. These internal states are called somnambulism, as they are not clearly waking or sleeping states. Among the drives that can be initiated during these sleep behavioral states include exploration (sleepwalking), eating, sexual or aggressive actions, and even working at tasks without any awareness of it the next day. Awakening someone in this state can result in confusion and agitation. The sleep environment should be made as safe as possible.

Night Terrors and Night Panic

As the name suggests, the hallmark feature of these experiences is awakening in a state of absolute terror. In these states, the sleeper may jump out of bed and across the room. Often the sleeper is unable to awaken fully for a while. They may moan, gasp, cry, or scream uncontrollably. Night terrors occur in NREM sleep and are most likely to occur in the first 2 hours of sleep. While these are more common in children, they can occur at any age. The cause of the night terror or night panic is a sudden surge of activity in the autonomic system. The terror can last for up to 10 minutes in length and may re-occur the same night. Afterwards it may take a while to get back to sleep, owing to the intense autonomic discharge.

Narcolepsy

Narcolepsy is a rare neurological condition caused by the loss of a considerable number of orexin neurons of the hypocretin-orexin system. The original cause was a childhood viral infection, usually between ages 5 and 15. The result of the damage caused by the virus is a weakened orexin system. As the ventro lateral pre-optic nucleus is the gating mechanism that determines whether the person remains awake or falls asleep, the weakness of the system creates major challenges for the person. At night, narcolepsy prevents them from staying asleep through the night. In the daytime, they get sleepy and experience sleep attacks. Some experience cataplexy, a bout of muscle weakness often triggered by a strong emotion. Overall, problems both day and night make it difficult to manage daily responsibilities. While narcolepsy is never the result of trauma, it can seriously compromise their tolerance of emotions. The resulting sleep attacks during active trauma treatment can delay or undermine their response to treatment.

Sleep Apnea

By far the most important sleep disorder to identify in working with PTSD patients is the presence of underlying sleep apnea. Apnea comes from the Greek words for "without breath." As many as a half of PTSD patients will have moderate or severe apnea (Krakow, 2006; Lydiard & Hamner, 2009). The apneas occur because the upper airway is soft and relaxes during sleep. When it relaxes, it collapses into the passage, creating an obstruction in the upper airway. The obstruction results in lower oxygen levels in the blood, which triggers the autonomic system to awaken the sleeper to breathe. The obstruction can last from 10 seconds to a few minutes. The longer it lasts, the lower the person's oxygen levels will drop. In extreme cases, oxygen saturation drops into the 70% range, or lower (compared with a normal level above 92%).

While apneas do not occur exclusively in the REM period, there is a reason they are more likely to occur in REM, and in sleepers who sleep on their backs. During the REM period all striated muscles in the body are paralyzed. As a result, the remaining working breathing muscle is the smooth muscle of the diaphragm significantly limiting the pulling power of the respiratory muscle. Sleepers sleeping on their backs will have the added element of gravity, which will pull their tongue down into the upper airway space, exacerbating the difficulty of preventing the blockage that obstructs air flow.

Instead of sleeping all night, the apnea patient stops breathing repeatedly, activating the stress system to awaken them. The stress system will always have your back, but the cost to your health is enormous: (1) you do not get into deep sleep (especially REM sleep) increasing the risks of depression and diabetes, (2) your oxygen levels drop repeatedly throughout the night and you may be spending as much as 20% of your sleep time in a dangerously low desaturated state, i.e., below 92% (increasing risks of cell death especially in the brain), (3) you activate your autonomic nervous system repeatedly when your oxygen saturation drops due to partial or complete blockage of your airway, (4) resulting in high levels of stress hormones in the body throughout the night (resulting in shallow sleep and atrial fibrillation), and (5) the repeated activation of the autonomic system also stimulates the activation of the immune system, resulting in systemic inflammation and running down your body's immune reserve to fight viruses and cancer during the daytime.

FIGURE 1.5 Proportion of CAP Subtypes in Untreated Sleep Apnea
Source: Reprinted by permission: Parrino et al. (2005, p. 2234)

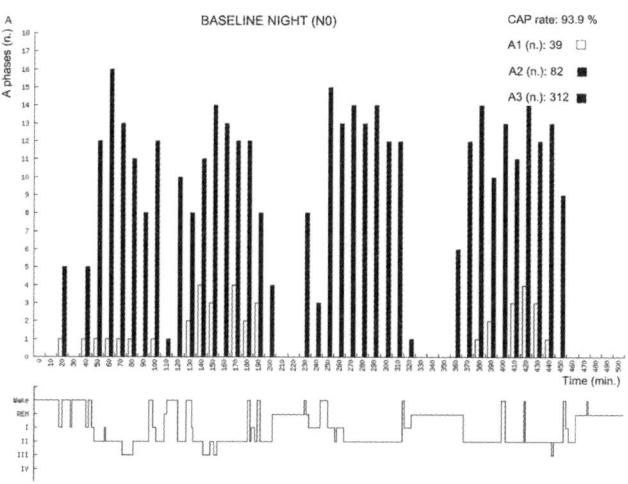

Figure 1.5 illustrates the profile of CAP activity for a typical apnea patient. What stands out is the radical shift in CAP activity, compared with the insomnia patient in Figure 1.3. The insomnia patient is still getting A1 CAP activity, even though it is crowded out by A2 and A3 CAPs earlier in the night. Once the initial hyperarousal of the autonomic system has settled, the sleeper will get some degree of SWS.

The paradox that every therapist needs to be aware of is that most apnea patients will tell you they have no sleep problem. They say that they "sleep like a baby," often adding that they fall asleep "as soon as my head hits the pillow." Figure 1.5 shows why: we see a 10-fold increase in A3 subtypes (compared to normal) in Figure 1.5 and the halving of A1 sleep-promoting subtypes. The trauma patient with apnea is getting almost no SWS and the restricted REM they will get is rarely after SWS sleep.

Why is apnea so devastating to emotional and physical health? The answer is lack of oxygen. Levels of oxygen circulating in the bloodstream are illustrated by the oximeter readings across the night of sleep in Figure 1.6 which shows that this sleeper spent half the night with oxygen levels below 92%.

Healthy sleepers will not experience oxygen levels dropping below 92% at any point across the night. This is considered an important threshold. Readings below 92% indicate hypoxia and put the survival of cells in the body at risk. Cells that do not get oxygen supplied to them for 5 or more minutes are at risk of dying. Apnea leads to a range of downstream physiological dysfunctions that put cognitive processes at risk. These include hypoxia, hypoxemia,

FIGURE 1.6 Blood Saturation Levels of Oxygen Across the Night
Source: Author's data.

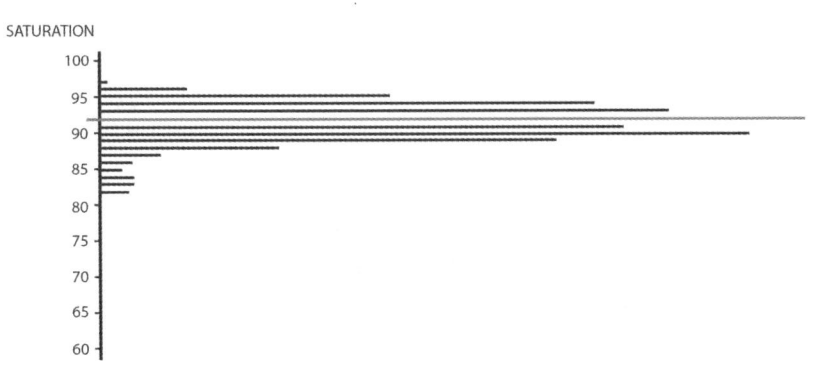

neuroinflammation, endothelial dysfunction, and oxidative stress. Taken together, these processes create major health challenges for the sleeper, including cardiovascular risks from hypertension, atrial fibrillation, and plaque building, as well as four times the risk of a heart attack or stroke.

Many of the cells that are at greatest risk of neuroinflammation (from low oxygen saturation at night) are in the nucleus tractus solitarius (NTS), which plays an essential role in activating the sympathetic and parasympathetic systems (Daulatzai, 2012). Mak Daulatzai concludes that an inflamed and dysfunctional NTS (along with other similarly compromised brainstem structures) may play a pivotal role in triggering memory and cognitive dysfunction in apnea patients. Also, the other functions of the NTS can similarly be compromised, including distorting pain signals and other somatic signals relayed here.

The oximeter readings in Figure 1.7 show the impact of obstructive apneas across the night of sleep. Apneas are more likely to happen in REM because the body's striated muscles are paralyzed from the neck down during REM. That means that the only remaining motor driving inspiration is the diaphragmatic smooth muscle (smooth muscles are not paralyzed during REM). All the collateral muscle groups (pectoral, intercostal, rhomboids and deltoids) are on vacation during REM. As a result, the collapsed upper airway cannot be overcome, and a longer period of apnea persists. During NREM sleep all the collateral muscle groups are still functioning, so apneas in NREM are less likely. In severe apnea there are apneas in both NREM and REM sleep.

Panel A shows the disastrous loss of blood oxygen during a REM episode from 4:35 to 4:50, despite the heroic efforts of the sympathetic system (see the spiking of pulse rates). Two and a half hours later, at 6:55 a.m., during the morning REM time, the autonomic system shifts to a collapsed state (bradycardia evident from dropping pulse rate) to manage the apneic risk. Trauma therapists

FIGURE 1.7 Impact of Apneas During REM
Source: Author's data.

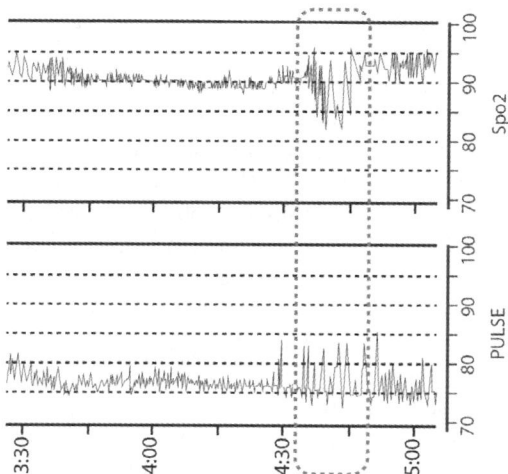

Panel A. Mobilization of dorsolateral PAG response with REM onset at 4:35.

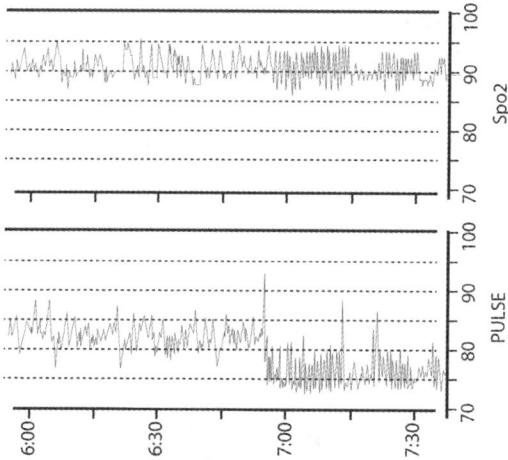

Panel B. Ventrolateral PAG-vagal shut-down at 6:55 to manage hypoxia.

will understand that such a collapse in the autonomic system indicates a system in a desperate situation, which it cannot escape.

Trauma therapists are aware of the impact that life-threatening perpetrators have on their victims. The nervous system tries to survive by fleeing. If fleeing is not possible, we fight. If fighting is hopeless, we collapse. None of us would ever suggest that our traumatized patient should visit the predator, who overwhelmed their ability to manage a hopeless situation. So why do we, as therapists, ignore the nightly suffocating attacks of apnea on our patient's autonomic system? It is the same situation we are putting our patient in when we do not act, especially when there is a solution. Air! Supplied to the lungs all night. When the patient chooses to use the CPAP machine, they are providing their body and nervous system with an escape from life-threatening danger. Providing a steady supply of air every night allows the nervous system to shift back to normal again.

The challenge to using this remedy is that the benefits will take from weeks to months to fully change the patient's internal physiology. For example, Figure 1.8 shows the change in CAPs structure from Figure 1.5. As well as the normalization of CAP rates, notice the normalization of the brain stages in the hypnogram below.

Standard treatment for sleep apnea is with Continuous Positive Airway Pressure (CPAP). This device provides a gentle pressure to air supplied through a nasal or face mask at just enough pressure to prevent the airway from collapsing, thus removing most of the obstructive events occurring during sleep. As the patient continues with treatment, their autonomic system is no longer needed to keep the obstructed airway open. As a result, a shift begins to occur, but it takes months for autonomic activation to dampen.

Liborio Parrino et al. (2005) note that the neural systems governing sleep and wakefulness undergo significant synaptic and postsynaptic change under the persistence of sleep apnea. Recovery of some functions may not be possible, and others may take months to years. In their study they found that REM sleep measures rebounded within the first 30 days, as did the CAP rate, A3 subtypes

FIGURE 1.8 CAP Activity After 30 Days of CPAP Treatment
Source: Reprinted by permission: Parrino et al. (2005), p. 2237

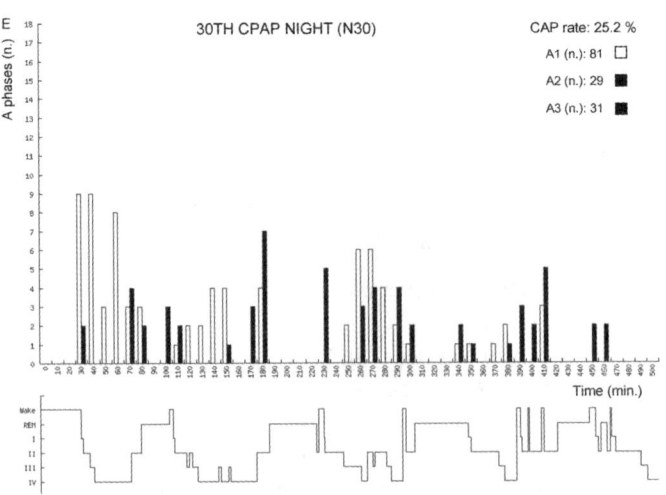

and arousals. However, what did not recover even by day 30 were the sleep-promoting A1 cortical waves. Similarly, we know that measures of executive functioning like concentration, memory, and problem-solving ability take half a year or longer to recover. The good news, however, is that with regular CPAP treatment, recover they do.

A further complication is that as many as two-thirds of apnea patients struggle to use their CPAP machines regularly. Published research with PTSD patients with OSA suggests that the average apnea patient uses their CPAP machines only about half the time in the first 3 months. This is not enough to allow the autonomic system to relax its protective vigil of the body and brain. And as many as a third of patients stop using their machines entirely.

Screening for Obstructive Sleep Apnea

The only way of knowing whether a person stops breathing at night and how much of an impact these stoppages in breathing have on their circulating blood oxygen level is for the patient to complete an overnight sleep study (usually at a sleep clinic). During this test, called a polysomnogram, the patient's body is wired up to measure many biological functions across the night of sleep. The *sleep test* is not really a test of whether they sleep, but a test of what their body and brain do when they have an opportunity to sleep 7 hours.

As there are no paper-and-pencil tests that can approximate what the overnight polysomnogram tells us, the screening tests are compilations of risk factors that are typical in patients who have tested positive for severe sleep apnea in the past. The sleep apnea screening test that is easiest to use is the STOP-BANG test (see Table 2.2). It is a compilation of eight risk factors (four clinical and four demographic). If a person reports three (or more) of these eight screening items triggers a discussion about the value of a sleep test (polysomnogram). As the test has good sensitivity, but low specificity, recent guidance suggests that at least two of the four STOP items should be endorsed. In other words, if the person endorsed three demographic factors (they are an obese male over 50) but does not have any of the clinical risks, that screen is considered negative.

Restless REM Sleep and Amygdala Adaptation

One of the consequences of autonomic dysregulation, either from apnea or chronic insomnia, is what has been termed REM instability (Riemann et al., 2012), or *restless REM sleep* (Van Someren, 2021). This is not an official diagnosis, but it refers to an important clinical phenomenon. Namely, repeated autonomic activation during REM sleep can disrupt the REM state, terminating REM, and awakening the dreamer.

Rick Wassing, Eus Van Someren, and their colleagues in Amsterdam have completed a series of studies that highlight the role of REM sleep in the dynamics of resetting the amygdala's hyperarousal. They induced self-conscious states in normal sleepers and insomniacs and reassessed them after a period of sleep (Wassing, Benjamins, et al., 2019; Wassing, Lakbila-Kamal, et al., 2019).

On retest they found that for healthy sleepers the amount of amygdala reactivity had decreased in proportion to the total amount of consolidated REM sleep in the intervening sleep period. In contrast, insomniacs had higher levels of restless REM sleep. Restless sleep was measured by frequent awakenings from REM, which the authors inferred were due to activity of the locus coeruleus. Experimentally enhancing both the favorable effect of increasing the duration of REM sleep or increasing the unfavorable actions of restlessness of REM sleep further accentuated these effects.

These investigators concluded that the spindle-rich period in transition into REM as well as the duration of the REM period both *contribute to the adaptive process of resetting the amygdala* for the next day (Wassing, Lakbila-Kamal, et al., 2019). They also note that chronically disturbed REM is a feature of PTSD, resulting in chronic insufficiency of overnight adaptive processes in these patients, rendering the adaptive value of REM useless for these patients. The result is sustained daytime hyperarousal and nightly experience of being stuck in replicative traumatic dreams. The finding that insomnia directly compromises the nightly normal adaptive resetting of the amygdala/emotional system cannot be overstated. The earlier observation that half of those treated for trauma, and whose daytime symptoms remitted, still had clinically significant insomnia, thus increasing the risk of relapse. Much like the patient hospitalized for low hemoglobin who is transfused and discharged, but has to return, as the underlying problem has not been resolved.

Sleep Paralysis

Sleep paralysis occurs as one is coming out of a period of REM sleep. During REM sleep the body is paralyzed from the neck down, while the eyes are in REM, the heart is beating faster, and the diaphragm is working to maintain breathing. The paralysis during REM is normal and protects the sleeper from thrashing in the bed if they are dreaming of running away from a lion. However, when the dreamer awakens and the muscular paralysis continues, that is terrifying. Becoming conscious with no ability to move arms or legs can be deeply troubling. As the state lasts for less than a minute or so, most adults easily adjust to the troubling experience. If it repeats, they come to appreciate that it will end quickly on its own.

However, when sleep paralysis happens to a child, the result is often traumatizing. The feeling of being unable to move any limb creates an intense horror that one is vulnerable and helpless to control threats and dangers. When this happens in childhood it can result in PTSD symptoms that are disabling and continue into adult life.

Isolated REM Behavior Disorder

Isolated REM behavior disorder (iRBD) can occur for either neurodegenerative or functional reasons. During normal sleep, every REM period is accompanied by atonia. Atonia means that all the striated muscles in the body from the neck down are paralyzed during REM. When REM ends, the paralysis ends. With aging, neurodegeneration of brainstem centers that regulate REM can deteriorate, resulting in a loss of atonia. This results in dream enactment behaviors, from jabbing to thrashing. Forty-five percent of patients with iRBD go on to develop such neurodegenerative conditions as Parkinson's disease, dementia with Lewy body dementia, and multiple system atrophy. Isolated RBD can appear as an early sign of such neurodegenerative conditions, as early as decades before the full clinical syndrome. However, atonia can also appear as an extreme response to severe trauma. In such patients, there can be a replicative dream of a catastrophic situation that was inescapable.

The dreamer, who is seeing a bomb land beside their bed, will leap across the bed to safety. The danger is that many reactions could occur to their dream, and those reactions can include lashing out to protect from danger, putting the dreamer and their bed partner at risk for injury. Alcohol and drug withdrawal can also aggravate the condition. iRBD has been incorporated as one element of a proposed new parasomnia sleep disorder, trauma associated sleep disorder (TaSD).

Trauma-Associated Sleep Disorder

Traumatized patients can present with any of the sleep disorders reviewed in this chapter. However, none of those diagnoses are specific to trauma. Trauma-associated sleep disorder (TaSD) is a recently proposed diagnosis to add to the sleep disorders already enumerated in the sleep diagnostic manual (Mysliwiec et al., 2018). This proposal comes from work with returning veterans, many of whom had overwhelming life-threatening terror when hopelessly caught in battle. It captures the extreme end of the spectrum of autonomic intensity that starts with constant replicative dreams, and continues through to nightmares, to the bad dreams found among most trauma survivors. These inescapable life-threatening situations result in unrelenting flashbacks that intrude into the dream experience: the dreamer screams, thrashes about, and awakens in panic. As the first effort to identify a syndrome that occurs directly after an overwhelming traumatic event, TaSD highlights the unique elements of sleep disruption that reflect an underlying overwhelming level of autonomic arousal, which can result in the arousal causing a dissociative state that overwhelms REM atonia. This REM sleep without atonia (RWA) is a functional breakdown of normal REM that is unique to TaSD.

As the autonomic disturbance diminishes, these reenactments begin to shift and the inherent ability of the REM state to integrate nontraumatic elements into the dream experience is restored. The reenactments diminish and then disappear. The existence of a continuum of nightmare intensities accords with clinical observations and allows us a way of identifying where in this underlying spectrum the patient's nervous system is currently at in resolving the trauma.

While TaSD has not yet been integrated into our current diagnostic manuals, it introduces an important awareness of the multiplicity of different sleep reactions possible after trauma. Indeed, any sleep disorder reviewed in this section could apply to the trauma patient with whom you are working. So, how would you go about identifying the nature of the problem and decide what to do about it?

That is, fortunately, not too hard to do, even in a busy practice. As with any other task, if you have the right tools, you can do the job easily. Without the tools, it is exceedingly difficult. In the next chapter we will move on to review the ways to evaluate which sleep disorders may be impacting the sleep of your trauma patient.

CONCLUSIONS

You now have an appreciation of all the diverse ways that trauma can disrupt sleep. A bit overwhelming when you think that many of these sleep problems have existed undetected for years in those struggling with the aftermath of trauma. These unrecognized sleep problems are like the volume of the iceberg under the water level. And just like the iceberg under the water level, what you do not see can sometimes cause terrible injury.

Knowledge of these conditions is the first step toward exploring whether any of these disruptive elements to healing are present for a trauma patient. Your understanding of the sleep disorders common in trauma (usually unbeknownst to them) can guide more curiosity about sleep to identify what may be happening under the surface.

It may sound like a lot of work, but it really isn't. Discussing the importance of restorative sleep and the way trauma can undermine it will engage the traumatized patient to work toward their own recovery. It is in the scope of every trauma therapist to understand the risks that disturbed sleep presents to full recovery.

While sleep disturbances can undermine trauma treatment, all are modifiable. As you engage more in using this knowledge, you are likely to see further improvements in mental, emotional, physical, and social well-being. The usual pattern of change with sleep treatment includes the following sequence of steps: (1) a gradual decrease in fragmented sleep, (2) an increase in nightmares (as REM sleep becomes more consistent), (3) replicative nightmares changing to nightmares with various themed content, (4) intermittent intense dreams in the context of short sleep, and finally (5) rich and complicated dreaming in the context of more restorative sleep.

This sequence describes the progression of symptoms when trauma treatment incorporates sleep along with the more usual (daytime) targets of trauma treatment. The rest of this book will elaborate on the TABS model of trauma treatment. TABS includes attention to: Traumatic experiences that need to be processed, Attachment wounds that need to be resolved, Bodily symptoms that require attention, and Sleep disturbances that can be identified and treated. The TABS therapy approach is flexible and modular. TABS therapy allows addressing each of the four domains that a destabilized autonomic system impacts. TABS is a strategy that permits dealing with sleep-wake rhythm disturbances when they become the primary roadblock to recovery.

If you understand the importance of being curious about sleep disorders, then the next chapter will give you the tools you need to find the underlying sleep problems that can threaten to undermine your trauma treatment. We look forward to seeing you there.

APPLICATION

You did not start reading this book for academic reasons. To make effective use of the information you have been reading, we invite you to engage yourself and the patients you work with in a brief opening dialogue about their sleep:

Demonstrate Curiosity: How has your sleep been lately?

Is Your Sleep Restorative: Does your sleep get you through all of what you want to do the next day?

Explore Attitudes: What attitudes about sleep did you learn from your family? Did you know that sleep problems can make all your trauma difficulties worse?

Explore Readiness to Change: Would you be interested in learning about how to make sleep your ally, not your enemy?

Identify a Starting Point: If you could make one important change in your sleep, what would you want to improve in your sleep?

Key Messages for Therapists

1. Sleep is the ultimate resource to stabilize patients and prepare them for trauma work. The orderly, uninterrupted ultradian transitions in nightly brain waves alternating between non-REM sleep and REM sleep restore energy, reorganize memories, and modulate emotions. Laying the groundwork for optimal sleep-wake rhythm supports the best self.
2. Danger always interferes with restorative sleep. If you are in danger, survival is the first imperative. Sleep is potentially dangerous. If you miss seeing the lion because you were asleep, you die. Trauma activates survival instincts that undermine sleep, which is the body's natural resource for health and well-being.

3. Trauma dysregulates sleep in countless ways. In this chapter, we introduced the major disruptions to look for. Of all the sleep disorders to be mindful of, apnea and narcolepsy are two of the most important. Apnea because it actively corrodes both physical, cognitive, and emotional health, and narcolepsy because patients have a limited tolerance of emotional experience before they shut down.
4. Insomnia, nightmares, and sleep apnea are the sleep disorders encountered most often because these interfere with patient functioning in the most noticeable way. All sleep disorders can be effectively treated as part of the trauma treatment plan.

2

The Attachment-Based Approach to Sleep Repair

"Increased earlier-life traumatic event exposure was associated with increased rapid-eye-movement sleep (REMs) fragmentation, and increased REMs fragmentation was associated with increased later-life disruptive nocturnal behaviors."

—Salvatore Insana, David Kolko, and Anne Germain (2012, p. 570)

"From a life-course perspective on health and disease on the basis of the reviewed evidence, we may hypothesize prenatal–early-life stress to be related to the development of insomnia in newborns and later in adult life."

—Laura Palagini, Christopher Drake, and Philip Gehrman, et al. (2015, p. 454)

Secure attachment is a cornerstone for establishing lifelong quality sleep. A systematic review regarding sleep and attachment concluded, "The majority of the studies reviewed suggest a relationship between attachment style and sleep difficulties in all ages. Secure attachment is associated with better sleep quality while insecure attachment styles are linked with poorer sleep" (Adams et al., 2014, p. 505).

Secure attachment plays a significant role not only in the infant's learning of how to regulate their emotions, but also in learning how to self-soothe and regulate their internal physical state to get to sleep and stay asleep. When these self-regulatory skills have not been acquired in childhood, the growing child is more vulnerable to periods of distress resulting in periods of increased nervous system arousal and hypervigilance, thus disrupting sleep.

The operation of these developmental processes is not limited to childhood. Attachment and learning self-regulation are prepotent elements of effective trauma treatment. Specifically, it is attention to the dyadic, intersubjective resonant relationship between patient and therapist that is a necessary element effecting repair of the dysregulated autonomic system. The therapeutic relationship, when combined with a systematic targeted approach to fixing sleep, reactivates that prepotent latent capacity of the brain to reorganize sleep-wake patterns to a more functional level in traumatized patients.

In the following systematic targeted approach to fixing sleep-wake rhythms, we will review a 5-step pyramid of clinical interventions, or clinical choice points (CCP). The underlying principle of this model is that all conditions of the previous step are met in full before movement to the next level of clinical intervention is indicated. Figure 2.1 illustrates the ascending levels of CCPs. Intrinsic to this 5-level approach to intervention is the TABS model of trauma assessment.

The attachment-based approach is anchored in starting with a collaborative assessment of all patient difficulties: trauma, sleep, attachment, and all comorbid medical and psychological conditions. A key part of this assessment is an understanding of early attachment patterns relative to current life relationships, because insecure attachment styles pose challenges to developing effective treatment alliances. As well, as explained above, insecure attachment styles predispose and perpetuate sleep disorders in clients. Examples of frameworks for such attachment assessments can be found in Maureen Kitchur's Strategic Developmental Model (Kitchur, 2005, p. 8) and Dan Siegel's Attachment Interview protocol (Siegel, 2015a, p. 163).

FIGURE 2.1 The Five-Level Pyramid of Clinical Choice Points in the TABS Model

CCCP5: Seamlessly integrate validated sleep interventions into a flexible sequence cycling through: trauma work, increased relational security, body symptoms, restorative sleep

CCCP4: Collaborate in identification of a progressive treatment plan that prioritizes trauma, attachment, body, and sleep (TABS) symptoms in the order that optimizes the patient's full recovery

CCCP3: Initiate psychoeducation to propose restorative sleep as the prepotent resource for trauma treatment, and clarify the benefits of a sleep lab study to identify unseen barriers to achieving the restful sleep needed for full recovery

CCCP2: Actively evaluate multiple possible sleep problems, to identify all barriers to regular, predictable daily rhythms alternating between activity and restful sleep

CCCP1: Establish a safe, collaborative relational context with attending and attunement from which to explore trauma, attachment, body, and sleep symptoms (TABS)

What you will learn in this chapter to become a better sleep and trauma therapist:

1. Understand the 5-step clinical choice point (CCP) approach to integrating sleep evaluation into your collaborative TABS trauma assessment.
2. Refine the nonverbal skills of attuning to the patient's responses to you to establish an increasingly safe, intersubjective, relational field from which to proceed with the TABS trauma assessment and intervention work (CCP1). This is further elaborated in Chapters 3 and 4.
3. Describe the clinical tools and strategies that can be employed to evaluate the range of dysfunctions of sleep-wake patterns of your trauma patient (CCP2), as discussed later in this chapter.
4. Integrate psychoeducation to communicate the resource value of sleep with patients, integrating sleep into their trauma treatment plan from the start.
5. CCP3 is elaborated in Chapter 6 and CCP4 and CCP5 are illustrated by cases in Chapters 7 to 12.

COLLABORATIVE INTERSUBJECTIVE CLINICAL INQUIRY: PART I

The first clinical choice point (CCP1) is recognition of the frailty of the intersubjective relational field in which all clinical work with complex trauma patients unfolds. This part of the inquiry refers to the nonverbal, sensory, visceral, and relational aspects of the therapeutic interaction between patient and therapist. It focuses only on the textural characteristics of the interaction between patient and therapist, not the content of the discourse. Patient and therapist learn to expect to collaborate and to acquire trust in being able to repair misunderstandings and missteps.

The therapist learns to look for cues of hesitation, worry, concern, and fear. The frown on the face, tension in the jaw, quivering lips, looking away from the therapist, and recoiling from a topic are all examples of the patient's underlying distress and perceived lack of safety. The therapist can respond by softening their voice, mirroring back, and providing nonverbal cues to convey compassion and understanding, thus establishing the grounds for collaboration and the development of healthier attachment. All of these establish the intersubjective field of right brain to right brain that provides the sense of resonant safety required to explore the clinical issues that need repair (Schore, 2019).

The moment-to-moment, continuous attention to the quality of the therapeutic partnership is a process that does not end at any point through the therapy. It is the foundation that supports all the inquiry and practice and especially the forays into the most horrible aspects of the traumatic events experienced by the patient. The trauma recovery journey is a partnership from the outset (see elaborations in Chapter 4).

Patients with complex trauma are continuously wary of betrayal and abandonment. Any statements, phrasings, choices of words, or gestures that signal rejection will trigger withdrawal and rupture of the therapeutic alliance. The patient's symptom difficulties bring them in, to begin their therapeutic work, but the patient's attachment difficulties will repeatedly undermine their efforts to continue with that work. It is best to point out to the client that the instinct to recoil from the therapeutic alliance is in fact an expected response of a nervous system that has had to deal with the pain of rejection repeatedly in life. The recoiling is a protective mechanism that the client developed in earlier dangerous situations. And only by the patient learning to recognize this protective pattern can they begin to develop healthier, more adaptive patterns of interaction. Our joint task is to notice when that skittish, untrusting part has been reactivated and encourage the patient to talk openly about that, whenever it occurs.

A few words to clarify what is meant by the *intersubjective two-person field* in which all therapy occurs. This phrase draws attention to the dynamic interaction between the two persons who are engaged in a common task. It is not just what one person says or does. Nor is it just the words in the response of the other. It is the quality of the emotional dance between the two as the work proceeds. That dance includes the smiles, the leaning forward toward each other, deep sighs of profound comfort, or the opposite: tense, darting movements with head and eyes. All of these provide the critical *felt sense of rapport*, working together on something that both value, appreciate, and feel an indispensable part of. It resonates with the Rogerian approach (Rogers, 1951), which highlighted the genuine person-centered approach to therapy with empathy, congruence, and unconditional positive regard. The "intersubjective" is the resulting memory of these moments of accord that becomes the transformational glue that supports the ongoing work together.

A more detailed discussion of the clinical elements to establishing this holding environment is elaborated in the following chapters.

ACTIVE EXPLORATION OF MULTIPLE SLEEP CONCERNS: TABS MODEL

Sleep is defined as the extended nightly period with the chief feature of absence of consciousness. Its role is to ready the sleeper for the next day's activity demands. How well, or how poorly, the patient is accomplishing this *is not* inherently obvious to either the sleeper or the therapist. Only active exploration of the characteristics of both the sleeping and awake state will surface how functional the patient's resting state is. What quickly becomes apparent to therapists exploring these states is that not all sleep is restorative sleep. This can set up a vicious cycle for the patient, with poor sleep affecting daytime functioning, which in turn disrupts the next night of sleep.

The most important clinical pearl regarding sleep disturbances among trauma patients, is that *any* of the sleep disturbances reviewed in the previous chapter can be present. There is about an 85% chance that the traumatized person has insomnia, sleep apnea, and/or nightmares. Many have all three. Add a 20% chance that they may have sleep paralysis on awakening, sleepwalking, night terrors, and/or isolated REM behavior disorder. Again, there is a possibility that more than one can be present. A dysregulated autonomic nervous system is both a hallmark of PTSD, as well as consistent with one or more disturbances in the sleep-wake rhythm.

Sleep problems do not exist in a vacuum all by themselves. They have evolved from earlier difficult experiences, which overwhelmed and/or threatened the person. In these contexts going to sleep may itself have become too dangerous. Sleep was not a restorative refuge; it became a threat triggering the sympathetic overdrive of the fight or flight response. Not all patients welcome the opportunity to withdraw from the world and take care of their body and brain by resting and recharging both.

Many patients are afraid of being alone, fear the darkness of the night, and avoid the loss of control that is necessary to enter sleep. Their attitudes and feelings about sleep reflect feeling unsafe, alone, and vulnerable, not seeing sleep as an opportunity to let their guard down and rest fully. This necessary period of self-care reveals instead a range of difficulties waiting to torment them.

The opposite is also found. Patients retreat into sleep to hide from the world. Many of these patients find the isolation of sleep comforting. But it is not a comfort that prepares them for going out into the world to do more. It is a comfort that is meant to avoid going out into the world altogether. The challenges of that world are too overwhelming to cope with, so sleep becomes the safe house which permits hiding from the dangers of the world.

A skilled therapist can frame explorations of sleep as an investigation of the patient's ability for self-care. Daytime activity requires engagement with the world. Nighttime offers the possibility of withdrawal from the demands of the world, retreat to an oasis that permits healing, energizing, desensitizing the emotional system, and consolidation of learning. Being fully in each state is what supports its opposite. We don't live to sleep: we sleep to live.

Particular importance should be placed on understanding the patient's experience of the transitions: both the transition from wakefulness to sleep and from sleep to awakening. Start treatment with understanding the barriers that prevent them from having restorative sleep. A case illustration of how to address this clinically is presented later in this chapter.

What approach does the patient take to caring for their brain and body? Initial questions may need to be integrated with some psychoeducation about the role of sleep to their ongoing health and well-being. This can also be a transition point to asking about what they learned about the value of sleep in their family environment. What importance was placed on it? What efforts were placed on valuing sleep as an essential part of taking good care of their self?

What are the best clinical strategies for asking about sleep problems among these patients? There must be some prioritizing of evaluation of the overall impact of any underlying sleep disturbance on their daytime functioning and trauma symptoms. Clinical experience suggests screening for sleep apnea first, then establishing the severity of the sleep disturbance and identifying the causes of the autonomic dysregulation.

On identifying the most critical treatment need(s), patient and therapist together decide on the most critical treatment target (sleep, daytime trauma symptom, interpersonal problem, or medical issue). Intervention must begin with what the patient experiences as the most significant challenge to their well-being.

When sleep problems are *not* the primary issue troubling the patient, keep sleep problems in the back of your mind and have a discussion of those when the sleep problems (cannot sleep, nightmares, fatigued or sleepy during the day) come up in the assessment process. When the assessment is completed, sleep problems can be identified as a primary target for treatment or as a background contributing factor to preventing full resolution of the primary goal of treatment.

Trauma therapists are already well acquainted with the evaluation of trauma, attachment disturbances, and medical issues like pain, endocrine, and immune problems. These will not be reviewed in this book. Instead, we will focus on the many ways that sleep issues come up in the assessment of trauma patients. In this chapter we will introduce the main themes that will be elaborated with clinical strategies, tactics, and examples of interactions with patients, to provide readers with an introduction to the range of topics elaborated in the chapters that follow.

Most trauma therapists conduct their initial assessment with a combination of patient interviews and completion of validated screening questionnaires. The remainder of this chapter approaches assessment of sleep issues with an eye to providing readers with detailed descriptions of how to complete both effectively.

The Clinical Assessment of Sleep in the Trauma Patient

A good start to the assessment is asking the patient what brought them in for treatment. Understanding the nature of the problems and symptoms is the first task. Once you have clarified a reasonable picture of the problems facing them, I usually ask what they are expecting therapy to achieve. "If this treatment is completely successful, what will the new improved you look like? What will you be able to do that you can't do now? What symptoms and difficulties will be minimal or gone? How will you and I know that we have completed the treatment?"

As you engage the patient in that dialogue, listening carefully to what is important to the patient, there will be many opportunities to ask about their energy, their sleep, their concentration, and their mood. Table 2.1 provides examples of ways to ask directly about these important themes.

None of these questions are difficult. What is required is curiosity about how the daytime experiences and the nighttime sleep pattern are working together

TABLE 2.1 Questions to Explore Sleep Difficulties

Domain	Clinical Questions
Is Sleep Adequate	Are you currently getting enough sleep to get you through your day without problems?
Sleep Need	How many hours of sleep do you need each night to get through your day?
Sleep-Wake Patterns	Can you describe a usual 24-hour day? When you go to sleep and wake up? What you do across the day?
Sleep Aids	What helps you sleep better? Are there any sleep aids/medicines that you take?
Sleep Challenges	What do you think is disturbing your sleep the most?
Onset of Sleep Problems	When did your sleep problems begin?
Past Sleeping Patterns	Have you ever been a good sleeper? If so, when did this change?
Development of Sleep Problems	If sleep has gotten worse across time, what age(s) did it change most?
Sleep Goals	If this treatment is 100% successful, what will your daily sleep-wake routine be like?

or undermine each other. In addition to clinical interview questions, it can be extremely helpful to give one or more screening questionnaires, to determine the presence and intensity of underlying sleep disturbances. Table 2.2 includes a list of common screening surveys that can be used to evaluate a range of common sleep complaints.

The TABS Sleep Repair Survey

The purpose of clinical questionnaires is to identify key symptom concerns, evaluate their overall severity, and put these together into a bigger clinical picture. The bigger context is determining the priorities for an overall treatment plan. Sleep assessment is part of trauma assessment. Hence the goal of screening for sleep problems is a part of your evaluation of trauma symptoms.

As most of the existing guidelines for assessment and treatment of trauma do not mention sleep at all, there is a need for a standardised survey of the sleep patterns of trauma patients. Table 2.2 lists validated questionnaires that provide

TABLE 2.2 TABS Sleep Repair Screening Questionnaires

Screening Questionnaire	Value of the Questionnaire	Clinical Cutoff Scores
Self-Assessment of Sleep Scale (SASS and SASSY)	To provide a quick snapshot of subjective sleep experience	No cutoff scores: overview of sleep quality and quantity across week
STOP-BANG	Screens for the presence of sleep apnea with 4 clinical (STOP) and 4 demographic (BANG) risk factors	Total score > 3 (Provided at least two of the 4 clinical (STOP) items are endorsed)
Nightmare Disorder Inventory (NDI)	Five questions that evaluate the presence of nightmares as well as their impact on daytime functioning: mirrors the criteria for nightmare disorder in *DSM-5*	Total score ≥ 7 (Provided the three impact items are endorsed "somewhat" or greater)
Sleep Condition Indicator (SCI)	Eight questions that evaluate the presence of disrupted sleep at night as well as its impact on daytime functioning: mirrors *DSM-5* insomnia disorder criteria	Total score ≤ 16
Fear of Sleep Inventory-Short Form (FoSI-SF)	Thirteen questions evaluate the presence of fear of sleep (with two factors: loss of control and fear of the dark)	No validated cutoff Suggested cutoff ≥ 10
Pre-Sleep Arousal Scale: Somatic Experiences (PSAS)	Eight questions evaluating the presence of somatic arousal	Subscale score ≥ 14
Pre-Sleep Arousal Scale: Cognitive Experiences (PSAS)	Eight questions evaluating the presence of cognitive arousal	Subscale score ≥ 20
Pittsburgh Sleep Quality Index (PSQI)	Nineteen items for 7 components combined into a global score	Global score ≥ 5
Pittsburgh Sleep Quality Index PSQI – Addendum for PTSD	Seven sleep disturbance items commonly reported in PTSD	Endorsed items ≥ 4

a good starting point for screening for the presence of the most common sleep problems of trauma patients.

These can be administered prior to the first meeting with the patient, along with other questionnaires that are part of the paperwork completed on opening a file. Alternately, the completion of the survey can be conducted after an initial interview and can be conducted in stages, based on the needs of the patient. If only one questionnaire is given initially, start with the STOP-BANG. It will alert you to the possibility of an underlying sleep problem that the patient themselves *may not* be aware of, which will have the greatest impact on your trauma treatment outcome.

CLINICAL APPLICATION OF RELATIONAL WORK WITH INSOMNIA

For the remainder of this chapter, we will review a clinical case that illustrates the application of the TABS model of trauma assessment presented above. First, we reflect on the clinical exploration of emotional dysregulation and attachment problems and how these can actively undermine sleep and create sleep disruption. We wrap up the chapter with an interaction between a trauma therapist and supervisor, reviewing the potential impact of sleep problems of the treatment of a patient.

The following edited transcript is taken from the evaluation of the sleep-wake transitions in a complex PTSD case. The patient is a mid-30s female I will call Sally (not her real name). She entered treatment for what she described as: chronic insomnia (trouble falling asleep). "I also suffer from C-PTSD, GAD, and ADHD. I believe trauma is a factor in my insomnia." She added that she had been seeing psychotherapists and psychiatrists from a young age:

> I think my sleep patterns are a huge factor in my quality of life, and I definitely need help with the other psychological conditions I mentioned, because I think they affect my ability to fall asleep. My mind is always racing, and it's like I can't relax. I try to go to bed around 12 a.m., but I don't normally doze off until around 2 a.m.

The transcript focuses on the examination of the transitions into and out of sleep. Her description of her experience highlights the role of attachment issues as potent disruptors of the normal pattern of relaxing at the end of the day that allows sleep to begin.

After a brief exploration of her mood, we lead into discussion of her sleep challenges:

> PATIENT: I'm feeling down. I cried a lot about my sister and grieved that whole situation. I am struggling with leaving my sister behind. I'm scared

that things won't change. That they will just end up getting worse. I think the worst time for me is at night, where it feels like anything after 10 o'clock is just not working. That's causing my sleep issues.

Commentary. She sees a connection between her emotions being harder to manage at night, particularly after 10 p.m., and her sleep problems. Her feelings of loneliness are quite overwhelming after 10 p.m., and they interfere with her readiness to go to sleep. She has no internal resources to deal with that. She is also beginning to understand that her family relationships were not responsive and nurturing for her. She must move away from her unresponsive and critical sister, but being alone is terrifying to her.

PATIENT: I'm trying to distract myself with social media, but it keeps me awake at night. The other thing too, is I have all these bottled-up feelings about my sister. How much despair and loss I'm feeling about the whole thing. And I feel I can't reach out to people about it.

Commentary. During the time of day she should be relaxed and winding down, she feels intense sadness and despair about the loss of support from her sister. Second, she feels totally isolated, which makes understanding and coping with her feelings harder. She is left with distracting herself with social media, which interferes with sleep and perpetuates her sleep problem. The amount of despair and loss is overwhelming and this peaks in the evening just before her sleep time. Her attachment relationships are causing heartbreak at night, with no sense of a capacity to self-soothe. Sleep research has highlighted that our emotional system tends to be characterized with the most negative mood occurring between 2 and 4 a.m., and that dip is amplified by sleep deprivation (Benjamin et al., 2024).

This sense of isolation combined with the intensity of the feelings she is trying to handle is paralyzing her just before her sleep time.

THERAPIST: Earlier when I was teaching you how to do the breathing, one of the first things you noticed was as you calmed down, suddenly it created this paradoxical reaction: you were freaking out. What is going on there is that you begin to shift out of your normal. And you're into this new normal that feels freaky. Like something you have not really experienced. And so the brain says, "Whoa, this is crazy," and it wants to shift back into the more familiar chaotic internal experience.

Commentary. Here the therapist is reminding the patient that her breathing practice, which activates parasympathetic calm, resulted in a paradoxical reaction of increased stress. Such paradoxical reactions are common among the patients who have not had a positive affective nurturing experience in their childhood. The physiological experience of calm feels strange and can be very alarming. It activates fear, not comfort.

> THERAPIST: We want to focus on those internal states as you begin to calm down. Just shift into that state of feeling relaxed, and just notice. "What does this feel like?" When, or how, does the brain start to freak out? When does it say, "Wait a minute, I don't like this. This isn't good. It's not comfortable for me." Notice those kinds of reactions. We can look at that as an opportunity for you to pay attention to what is going on. And to learn to tolerate and accept that being in a calm state is a good thing. And it is something that you can become more comfortable with.
>
> And you can begin to shift, the reactiveness that kicks in. That makes you feel, "Oh, this doesn't feel calm at all. This feels unsafe."
>
> PATIENT: I think that might have a lot to do with the bedtime routine. As I am trying to relax and go to sleep. All of a sudden, I'm having these fake arguments. Planning out what I would say. Imagining what arguments I would be in, and how would I best prove myself? Who would be on my side, and who would betray me? Stuff like that.
>
> I will say though that lately and to my own credit, when I have been in relationships with chaotic people, eventually, I find out. I'm overtaken with the chaos with them, and my immune system basically dies. I get infections and colds and horrible things. I eventually pull away. I've always been able to break up with abusive relationships.

Commentary. The patient makes a critical connection between these interpersonal tensions and their spontaneous appearance at night as she is trying to fall asleep. These come as *intrusive thoughts* and she is swept up in a reenactment of her earlier life situation of feeling betrayed. From her description, she has no conscious control of this. Her overwhelming loneliness has been triggered by a fear that her wishes for a close relationship will always be dashed and she is destined to be alone forever. Once it has begun, it dominates her pre-sleep experience, creating a repeated experience of feeling overwhelmed and fighting to find arguments to protect herself.

At this point the therapist underlines that isolation is emotionally overwhelming to the mind. The intensity of these feelings combined with the idea of being completely alone in trying to deal with them is what the treatment must address to create pre-sleep conditions more conducive to sleep.

> THERAPIST: There are two steps that I'd like to explore and see how this can work for you. Because I agree with you. If you can begin to allow a shift, especially at bedtime, of getting calmed down and feeling comfortable in your own skin, and learn that you are safe, that is such an important idea. "I am safe," and also "I am not alone."

When you get that internal sense that you are not isolated it gives you a sense of connection. And that's critical for all of us, to have that sense of being connected. That connectedness is important, but as well, that sense of feeling and allowing yourself to be calm. Allowing that feeling of relaxation, making it the norm without falling apart.

I want to use our time today to begin to figure out, and do a little practice, to see how these feelings can begin to settle in more comfortably for you. It is a process and I think if you and I can find a way for you to notice that, you can allow yourself to calm down. You can do the breathing exercise and notice the physiology. Notice what's going on in your body and not fall apart. Or to get that shock of, "Oh my gosh, what's going on?" That was what was happening before.

PATIENT: It was a completely subconscious process. I found myself doing it and I would recognize it. And it would be its own cycle. I want to definitely learn these steps for sure. And see if I can get to that point.

Commentary. This is a critical moment in the session. The patient recognizes that these internal reactions have not been consciously activated. They are subconscious and automatic. They arise from our early implicit attachment memories. Before she knows it, she is experiencing not being seen, valued, or heard and is reenacting internal arguments to fight off these feelings. The other particularly important development is that as the patient recognizes the challenge, she is becoming more motivated to change these patterns. Awareness creates space for change, when held in a safe therapeutic environment.

PATIENT: I second guess myself a lot. I have a fear of getting too close to people because I'm afraid that I will get hurt. Which has been the running theme for most of my relationships, so it's sort of new for me to have normal relationships. And friendships with people who are normal, in my opinion.

Commentary. Again, the patient is realizing that the same internal dialogue that comes up to interfere with her sleep is also linked to her fear of intimacy. The root of both problems lies in the unresolved conflicts about attachment.

Now that the patient grasps the connection between the unresolved attachment issues and her ongoing sleep problems, the therapist begins to educate the patient about the importance of transitioning effectively from the awakening state to the sleep state, and then back again into rest.

THERAPIST: Let's focus on what happens internally at night. During the daytime as you're busy and active, you're out in the desert, doing stuff. Stuff that we all have to do to take care of ourselves. At the end of the day, you must get out of the desert! You have to get to what I call *the oasis*. An oasis means a place where you can sit down, you can be calm. A place where there is shade, where you get out of the sun that beats down on you during the day. There must be a transition from daytime activity when you push yourself to get things done to a focus on nurturing yourself. Being comfortable in your own skin.

PATIENT: Do you want me to tell you exactly what my process is right now?

THERAPIST: Let's start with that. It is important that we understand what's happening as you're trying to get into that oasis place.

PATIENT: This is what I usually do on weekdays. I will wake up and it will be difficult for me to wake up. There is tension there and I'm usually tired by the time I do get up. I turn the computer on, and I start setting up for the workday.

Then my anxiety level goes really high, and my blood pressure goes up. I have constant anxiety and tension in my shoulders. And while I'm doing my work, there is this weird belief that I'm not doing what I'm supposed to do, or I'm not doing enough. I just feel that type of weight.

Then I become a little bit depressed and apathetic about the work that I'm doing. I'm not happy with it. By the time the afternoon rolls around, or maybe the end of the morning, I start feeling better but not too much better.

Then the day ends, and I'll eat my dinner. I feel guarded because I'm eating dinner with my parents. Sometimes I disassociate at the dinner table and my mind is somewhere else. I'm physically there just eating and having a pretty surface-level conversation.

At that point I am forced to spend time with my own thoughts. I'm not being distracted by work. That is when all the social media stuff and the shows and the phone scrolling comes out. I try to distract myself until I know it's getting late and that I have to get ready for bed and I've failed that again, not getting to bed at the right time.

I get in the shower and then I'm upset about my sister still. I start having feelings of hopelessness. Then I finally get out of the shower, and I go back to scrolling again, because I can't manage those feelings. And eventually I pass out. Then I do it all over again. And I feel like my life is going nowhere.

THERAPIST: That is a good summary of how it feels on the inside and how you've tried to manage your feelings. Let's think of that as a default setting.

If we can begin to make a change at one of those moments, what would you want to change? The evening, or the morning? Where would it be most helpful for you to begin to break the pattern?

PATIENT: I want the evenings. That is supposed to be my time, but I'm using my time to distract myself. And I'm not even doing anything that I love. I'm just a vegetable. I want to take back my evenings and then get to the point where I don't have to have these draining conversations. My bedtime routine is torture. That is what I want to change because I would like to not have insomnia.

THERAPIST: I am going to help you with that. Tell me about the voice in your mental dialogue. There's something that voice is trying to do.

PATIENT: The general sense I have of the voice is that I am feeling small and that I don't have the power to make people believe me. The conversations come from a place of feeling I don't have power, and that no one will believe me. Or care. Then I have to prove myself and I have to make a case. When I'm having these conversations, it is always practicing what exactly I will say.

Like if my sister accuses me of this, and it didn't even happen, how can I say this in a way that is cool and collected and puts her in her place? I have this feeling that my parents don't believe me and that they will side with my sister. Then I suffer. I always feel my guard is up.

THERAPIST: You are sensing that she's going to criticize or attack you?

PATIENT: I am. Not being believed and not being heard.

THERAPIST: Here's the important piece. As we're talking about you getting ready for sleep, and you going to the oasis where you can feel calm, what is happening is the part of you that has felt *not heard* and *not seen* and not valued is being activated at night. You and I must find a much better way of taking care of that part of you. Because that part needs to know that she is valued, that she matters, and that she is important. How far back do you think that goes? That younger part of you that very early on realized that you weren't being heard or seen? What age does that feel like for you?

PATIENT: It's got to be young. In senior kindergarten. I don't know if that's 5 years old. I just feel I can picture myself.

The Clinical Picture Emerging From the Exploration of Sleep and Trauma

To summarize, the purpose of the exploration of sleep issues during the interview is to focus on the two important transition periods, from waking to sleep and from sleeping to wake. The purpose of this review is to identify the factors that interfere with the normal process of relaxing at night to allow the body and mind to release all engagement with daytime activities (being in the desert) and allow the peace and quiet of being fully at the oasis. If the initial trauma began at a young age, the patient might never have had the lived experience of being in an oasis prior to and during sleep. They have no idea what it is to relax, feel safe, and sleep.

In this exploration, the patient provided a clear picture that the transition to calm is undermined for her. Instead of relaxing, she describes an automatic activation of feelings of being unseen, unheard, and unvalued in her family. She becomes engaged in a nightly ritual of defending herself against these emotional reactions. Finally, toward the end of the interview she indicates that these emotional issues go back to about age 5. This window into the issues at age 5 then becomes a springboard for therapy targeting the reaction to traumatic events and resultant ANS dysregulation that occurred at age 5 (and before) for this patient.

In the chapters that follow we review the interventions that can be used to remedy this psychological tension that undermines the possibility of restorative sleep.

It is also important to stress that the character of these attachment problems is not likely to respond to cognitive behavioral therapy for insomnia (CBTi), the traditional first-line insomnia treatment. CBTi focuses on synchronizing daily activity with the light-dark environment (see Chapter 7). Only interventions that address the root cause of her nightly distress: her attachment failures and the subsequent intrusive feelings of hopelessness, injustice, and loneliness (that are dysregulating her autonomic nervous system), will her sleep pattern improve (Chapter 8).

Corroborating Evidence From Screening Surveys

While the interview experience provides specific information on the nature of the underlying conflict that maintains the sleep disturbance, it does not provide a profile of the intensity of these emotional distresses. The battery of sleep questionnaires introduced earlier in this chapter provides a clearer picture of how disruptive these emotional factors are to the patient's pre-sleep experience. Sleep questionnaires also provide a tool for monitoring progress and improvement of sleep throughout the therapeutic process for both the therapist and the patient.

The battery of tests includes three sleep tests, the Sleep Condition Indicator (SCI), the Pre-Sleep Arousal Scale (PSAS), the Fear of Sleep Inventory-SF (FoSI-SF), as well as a trauma questionnaire, the PTSD Checklist for *DSM-5* (PCL-5). Each of these provides a unique perspective: the PCL-5 about the intensity of non-sleep symptoms, and the others about the intensity of the sleep disruption. Let's begin by reviewing the PCL-5. The PCL-5 is an evidence-based evaluation of the symptom experiences typically found in persons who have experienced significant posttraumatic stress. The PCL-5 provides measures of symptoms in each of the four symptom clusters necessary for a PTSD diagnosis:

1. Intrusion symptoms (nightmares and flashbacks).
2. Avoidance symptoms (distancing self, or detaching, from external reminders).
3. Persistent negative emotions (fear, horror, irritability, shame, and guilt).
4. Hypervigilance (disturbed sleep and problems in concentration).

Sally's total score at the start of treatment was 55. The overall intensity of her symptoms is well above the threshold (≥33) for considering PTSD as a diagnosis. The four component symptom clusters are all elevated. The intrusive symptoms score was 14/20; avoidant symptoms were 5/8; persistent negative emotions were 16/20; and hypervigilance was 20/32.

Four of the 20 individual items were rated as "extremely." This usually gives a good idea of what needs to be tackled to gain some symptom relief early in treatment. The four items endorsed at the maximum are: (2) repeated, disturbing, and unwanted memories of the stressful experience, (11) having strong negative feelings such as fear, horror, anger, guilt, or shame, (12) loss of interest in activities you used to enjoy, and (20) trouble falling or staying asleep. These four intense experiences underline that the descriptions obtained in the exploration of her sleep are centrally involved in the traumatic symptoms she is endorsing and must be central to the treatment plan.

The SCI provides an evidence-based evaluation of the patient's experience of the quantity and quality of their sleep, along with their sense of how much their poor sleep affects their daytime functioning. Results are scored positively, with higher scores indicating better sleep. The range of scores is between 0 and 32. Scores below 16 indicate that the patient most likely meets the criteria for a diagnosis of chronic insomnia. Sally's score was 7/32, indicating seriously disturbed sleep with clear negative impact on daytime functioning. On the eight individual items, all were endorsed at the two most intense levels, except for the question asking about problems waking up during the night. Sally does not have a problem with broken sleep. Once she is asleep, she usually sleeps through until the morning.

The PSAS measures the intensity of pre-sleep arousal experiences. Two factors are measured: somatic arousal and cognitive arousal. The threshold values for considering the level of reported distress at or above typical of patients with PTSD are somatic ≥ 14, and cognitive ≥ 20. Sally's scores of pre-sleep arousal were somatic arousal = 20, and cognitive = 37. Both are elevated, and both are well above the levels typical of other PTSD patients.

Six of the eight cognitive items were answered as "extremely," the maximum rating. These include: (10) review or ponder events of the day, (11) depressing or anxious thoughts, (12) worry about problems other than sleep, (14) can't shut off your thoughts, (15) thoughts keep racing through your mind, and (16) being distracted by sounds and noise in the environment. Among the somatic items, she endorsed two at "a lot" (one level below the maximum): (3) shortness of breath or labored breathing, and (4) a tight, tense feeling in your muscles.

Taking the elevated PSAS total scores and the number of individual items that are scored at near maximum into account, it is clear that Sally's pre-sleep experience is intensely disruptive. These results corroborate her stated objective of wanting to reclaim her pre-sleep period for herself as her first priority.

Finally, there is the Fear of Sleep Inventory-Short Form (FoSI-SF). This measure has been shown to be particularly relevant for PTSD. It evaluates fears related to loss of control at night, including problems in relaxing and getting to sleep, as well as problems with awakening from nightmares. There are no published cutoffs, but the validation study found that the total scores of the nonclinical sample ($x = 5 \pm 8$) was lower than that of the PTSD patients ($x = 18 \pm 13$) (Pruiksma et al., 2014). Sally's score of 14 was elevated.

Sally's score is not as bad as many with PTSD as she is not experiencing nightmares or nighttime awakenings. Examination of the individual items indicates that Sally reported no problems with nightmares or other awakenings during the night, fear of the dark, or feeling vulnerable when asleep. However, she endorsed four individual items at the maximal, or next to maximal, values. These included: (3) I was fearful of the loss of control that I experience during sleep, (7) I was afraid to close my eyes, (10) I stayed up late to avoid sleeping, and (11) I tried to stay alert to any strange noises while going to sleep.

She made the following comments on item 3: "Loss of control with respect to traumatic flashbacks, feelings of hopelessness about my future, that I'm a failure, not knowing what to do about it." And with item 7: "When I close my eyes my thoughts attack me, and I often wake up crying."

To summarize, the psychometric measures of Sally's sleep disturbance all indicate that both her traumatic symptoms and her sleep disturbance are severe. They suggest that traumatic symptoms and sleep difficulties are entangled, and both relate to her attachment problems going back to earliest childhood. Intervention in this case needs to deal with reducing pre-sleep hyperarousal by providing her with the opportunity to develop positive internal experiences with relaxation. The chapters that follow this one will outline the variety of interventions that can be incorporated into the treatment plan for Sally and other trauma patients like her.

In the last section of this chapter, we use the context of a supervision session between a trauma therapist curious to incorporate attachment-based sleep interventions into their treatment plans with a new patient they are beginning to treat.

COMPLEX ISSUES IN APPROACHING SLEEP EVALUATION IN TRAUMA

To step back and illustrate how to integrate sleep treatment into the overall treatment plan, let's review some of the clinical dilemmas that come up in collaborating with these patients. We will sit in on a discussion between a trainee and supervisor as they consider the many issues that must be considered in working with a new patient, a pharmacist who was robbed at gunpoint.

> TRAINEE: My patient is a 50-year-old pharmacist. He was robbed at gunpoint one night at work about a month ago. He has flashbacks of the robbery. He is not ready to go back to work because of his anxiety, panic, flashbacks, and nightmares.
>
> He says he has nightmares a few times a week. On those days he can't get out of bed. He's like, "I am barely functioning. How can I cope with forcing myself to wake up for work?"
>
> He is very anxious and has had some panic attacks, and because of that he can't get to sleep easily either. He is afraid to close his eyes at night, for

fear of a flashback or nightmare of the robbery. The other factor that goes into it is that he is worried he's going to make a mistake when he's filling prescriptions. So, he is off work on disability.

SUPERVISOR: What is affecting him more, the nightmares, the flashbacks, or the early morning awakenings?

TRAINEE: The nightmares. He wakes up with his heart pounding. He is now afraid of going to sleep and avoids bed. And once he falls asleep, he awakens within an hour of falling asleep.

SUPERVISOR: Are the nightmares replicative (like reliving a movie of the robbery), or does the content of them change?

TRAINEE: I think they are replicative, but I am not sure.

SUPERVISOR: Another important question is how soon after the robbery did the nightmares start? And the flashbacks?

TRAINEE: I don't know.

SUPERVISOR: Does he have signs of other sleep problems, like apnea or narcolepsy?

TRAINEE: How would I know that? He hasn't mentioned anything.

SUPERVISOR: Apnea, periodic limb movements, and narcolepsy can only be noticed in a sleep test, called a polysomnogram. While there aren't any questions that tell you he definitely has apnea (or narcolepsy), there are questions that will tell you he is at risk for having it. You can give him the STOP-BANG screen and ask him about other symptoms like awakening with headaches, dry mouth, back pains, and frequent nightly trips to the bathroom. All of these are often present with apnea. You can have a discussion with him about what sleep apnea is and how it will delay his recovery should he have it.

Having a full discussion of the way apnea can undermine mental, emotional, and physical health is important in the early stage of treatment. It will give him the knowledge he needs to make good decisions for himself. It arms him with information about what to be on the lookout.

If he has multiple risk factors, have a discussion with him about having a sleep study. Keep the possibility of more serious sleep disturbances in the back of your mind. Because those problems seriously undermine the outcome of your trauma work, and because they lurk in the background, invisible to you and the patient, you must always consider their presence.

The issues related to surfacing major sleep roadblocks to recovery is a critical issue for successful treatment of trauma. These considerations are discussed in detail in Chapter 6.

TRAINEE: What he does say is that his sleep is terrible. Some days he only sleeps a few hours, has a nightmare, and can't go back to sleep again.

SUPERVISOR: How many days does he have poor sleep?

TRAINEE: The problem is that it is variable. He says some weeks he wakes up with nightmares three times. Other weeks, he sleeps right through.

SUPERVISOR: You can mention the topic of getting a more detailed picture of his sleep by asking him, "Since the robbery, how many days have you had nightmares? When did they start? Are the nightmares a replay of the robbery? Can you get back to sleep after you awaken? How many hours of sleep are you getting in an average night? How many hours of sleep do you need to function normally?" You first want to get the big picture, before you start talking about solutions.

As he provides answers to those questions, you can introduce the importance of having him complete the Sleep Repair screening survey: a battery of sleep tests that will tell you about his apnea risk, the intensity of the nightmares, how disturbed his sleep is, and how out of control he feels about these problems. Only an overview of all these sleep problems will give you the information you need to make clinical decisions on the severity of his sleep problems. Those tests will also provide a basis to have a discussion with him about sleep and its importance for his recovery.

Once we have the pattern of how his sleep has been since the robbery, you can ask him what is bothering him most about his sleep. The nightmares or the lack of sleep? How does he want to set up an acceptable regular wake-up time, even if there might be exceptions to it?

You must involve the patient in this first step. When you read the textbooks, they all say "This is how to do it. But in the real world, there is no patient who doesn't have their own feelings about waking up too early or going to bed too late. Those are very emotional issues for people with sleep problems. So, before I recommend anything, I ask the patient, "What would you want improved in your sleep?"

TRAINEE: What if they don't know?

SUPERVISOR: Then I'd ask, "What have you been doing? How do you go about setting your sleep times? What is working and what isn't working?"

Once you get that picture, then you can think about making one change. Frame it as, "If we can tweak one thing to make your sleep a little better, what do you think would be most helpful to you?"

The issues related to helping the patient change their sleep-wake pattern are discussed in detail in Chapter 7.

Setting that collaboration is important, because any intervention that's going to work is going to take some practice using and that's usually painful for at least a few days, even a few weeks. Quite often their sleep pattern is worse before it gets any better. That will be the challenge: sticking with the changes. You want to make sure that you're getting the patient's motivation on board to try making the first change. Also letting them know that it can get worse before it improves.

TRAINEE: What if he thinks of something that for you, as a sleep person, sounds like a bad idea? Suppose he says, "Well, I'm going to wake up at three in the morning and read for a few hours and then go back to sleep."

SUPERVISOR: What I would say is that might work in the short term, but I think it's not going to work to give you a full night of restorative sleep. I would give my reasons that it might not work in the longer term, and then listen to how he feels about it. If he thinks he wants to try that, because he has read somewhere it is a good solution, I will say, "Let's try it out. We have to work together, and this will give you a chance to begin noticing what happens when you do X or Y. For us to know if your idea works, or does not work, we need to track it. Using the daily sleep diary is the only way you can track what happens. You can now know for sure what happens with sleep and daytime activity."

With traumatized patients, sleep treatment must be a very collaborative process. Getting that sleep pattern back into line usually requires a couple of weeks of painful, poor sleep. You both must go into those weeks with a clear felt sense that you are working together on each change you are making.

You will entertain any ideas that they want to try. Sometimes there are quick solutions, but most often these don't work. In that case we move on to other more difficult solutions: for example, of waking up every morning at 6 o'clock.

The issues related to collaboration are discussed in Chapters 3 and 4.

APPLICATION

To make effective use of the concepts described in this chapter, apply them by engaging patients with these important steps in exploring their sleep:

Sleep Can Change: An important starting point is a brief discussion asking the patient about their ideas about the role that sleep plays in their emotional and physical life. This is not a clinical evaluation, but a first engagement about the patient's ideas and biases about what sleep means to them. This discussion can conclude with a direct statement about what aspect of sleep can be most helpful for this particular patient in their recovery journey. Just one specific benefit that your patient may value.

Describe Screening Options: When a patient is interested or describes a problem with their sleep pattern, be ready to engage the patient in completing some screening tests that will provide them information about how they can become a better sleeper.

Reflect on Results: Review screening results to determine a sleep change priority. This should be an open dialogue that provides more information about the value of sleep as well as the options that the patient may find helpful. Often the patient will need time to digest the options after providing feedback.

Decide on TABS Treatment Priority: Consider how the sleep problem relates to the patient's trauma experiences, their attachment wounds, and the most important of their physical symptoms. This is not always easy to see. It can be helpful to highlight the two most pressing issues and ask the patient about which would be more helpful to tackle first. Integration of the sleep issue with other TABS therapeutic targets will occur organically as treatment proceeds.

Key Messages for Therapists

1. Every trauma therapist is a sleep therapist. A sequential 5-step clinical choice point model is provided to seamlessly allow integration of sleep interventions with existing trauma therapy approaches to assessment and treatment of your trauma patients.
2. The strategic importance of monitoring relational aspects of the evolving therapeutic alliance is outlined as the focus of ongoing clinical interventions with trauma patients across the entire course of trauma, attachment, body, and sleep (TABS) treatment.
3. An active approach to inquiry into sleep problems (see Tables I.3 and 2.1); how they may be disrupted; and linking the sleep problems with other (see Table I.3, Trauma Sleep Inquiry, and Table 2.1, Exploring Sleep Difficulties) trauma, attachment, and physical symptom difficulties is reviewed. This includes both interview inquiry and the use of the TABS sleep repair screening questionnaires (Table 2.2) to characterize the nature and intensity of sleep disorders. Additional resources and suggestions for inquiry and assessment can be found at www.puttingtraumatosleep.com.
4. The use of the Sleep Repair questionnaires (see Table 2.2) provides a basis for active discussions with the trauma patient about the value of sleep, as well as how sleep problems may be undermining their recovery. Many trauma patients do not know what it feels like to have a safe, relaxed sleep. It has either been many years since they experienced this state, or if the trauma occurred at an early age, or in utero, they may never have experienced restorative sleep.

3

The Intersubjective Collaborative Cascade in Trauma Treatment

"Emotional attunement, reflective dialogue, co-construction of narrative, memory talk, and the interactive repair of disruptions in connection are all fundamental elements of secure attachment and of effective growth enhancing interpersonal relationships."
—Daniel Siegel (2015a, p. 377)

"[Intersubjectivity] . . . describes the continuous and reciprocal interactions and exchanges typical of human beings from their first days of life, in a process in which 'humans come to know each other's mind' . . . The interaction between the Self and the Other is crucial"
—Massimo Ammaniti and Vittorio Gallese (2014, pp. xv–xvi)

The explosion of sleep research launched by the discovery of REM sleep in 1951 has led to a 70-year renaissance of scientific interest in sleep. The advances that have been made in both basic sciences understanding of the state of sleep as well as the application of that understanding to the treatment of sleep disorders have been explosive. What has driven that expansion has been the ability to quantify sleep. The discovery that sleep was composed of discrete stages or REM and NREM sleep, which could be scored off of brain waves recorded by the Electroencephalogram (EEG), created the perfect storm for decades of discovery.

The modern polysomnographic (PSG) sleep study in a sleep medicine clinic includes EEG, eye movements (electrooculogram, EOG), heart rate, arousals, limb movements, oxygen saturation, body position, and central and obstructive sleep apnea events. Finally, with PSG we had a reliable way of measuring what the brain and body are doing across the night! Objective measurement of sleep stages with the EEG and EOG became the gold standard by which to measure restorative, healthy sleep. Moreover, these normative values created a baseline from which to identify disturbed sleep.

The result was the identification of scores of sleep disorders that had not been visible to those observing sleep. The most recent publication of the American Academy of Sleep Medicine's (AASM) International Classification of Sleep Disorders (ICSD 3rd ed.) contains over 80 different sleep disorders in 7 broad categories (Sateia, 2014).

The Americal Association of Sleep Medicine (Kushida et al., 2005) have not recommended polysomnographic study for diagnosis of insomnia, while the Europeans have suggested a role for polysomnography in managing more complex cases (Riemann et al., 2022). Traditional scoring involves looking at 30-second epochs of data on polysomnogram recordings and scoring each epoch for the sleep characteristic for most of that 30-second epoch (see Chapter 1 for details). A meta-analysis of PSG studies of insomnia (Baglioni et al., 2014) found that compared to good sleeper controls, the sleep of insomniacs was shorter, subject to more awakenings (6 on average), and marked by less SWS and REM sleep.

Using high-density quantitative EEG recordings, Eus Van Someren (2021) and his group scored 3-second epochs within the standard 30-second epoch, to evaluate the presence of mixed states of vigilance in deeper sleep. They found that insomnia disorder (ID) patients demonstrate twice as much concurrent light sleep during their deep sleep epochs. They concluded that in insomnia disorder hyperarousal continues into deepest sleep and that the presence of this biomarker of ID could help in identifying which brain centers participate in creating this disruptive experience, even in deepest sleep. Their conclusion was that conventional EEG scoring is not detailed enough to capture the interplay of brainstem regions with cortical structures.

There are now multiple ways in which the sleep and the awake states can be measured. Physical activity can be measured by use of actigraphy. This device looks like a wristwatch. It straps onto the wrist and measures the movement of the wrist across the night. The data can be plotted to show periods of rest, which stand out in sharp contrast to periods of activity. Periods of activity appear as dark lines on the plot. When the actigraph device is worn for a week or longer, the result is a forest of dark lines across the daytime, and white space at night when the wearer is asleep. Restless sleep would result in the sleeper tossing and turning. Their data plot would show dark forests of activity interspersed across the white expanse of sleep.

As a global measure of activity, the actigraph can be helpful to determine relative periods of quiet from relative periods of activity. Healthy sleepers show a sharp contrast between the awake state and the sleep state. However, poor sleepers show a predictable scramble of dark and white alternating across both the nighttime and the daytime (owing to their fatigue and exhaustion). What the actigraphy plot can't tell us is what the autonomic system is doing during these periods of inactivity, and what triggered the arousals and awakenings.

SLEEP AS BEHAVIOR VERSUS SLEEP AS EXPERIENCE

The brain wave activity of traumatized individuals can vary enormously from one traumatized patient to the next. In a classic study, Ruth Lanius and her colleagues (2004) contrasted the brain waves of two persons who had been in the same horrendous multivehicle carcrash. Both experienced the same external event. One was the driver, and the other was the passenger. Their fMRI results demonstrated that the two exhibited two very distinct patterns of subjective response, autonomic activity, and behavioral response. The driver exhibited classic signs of the hyperaroused fight-or-flight response. His wife, the passenger, exhibited subjective signs of numbness and feeling frozen, characteristic of a dissociative response to the trauma. The authors summarized that their results were consistent with an emerging literature that traumatic experiences can lead to a range of different physiological, emotional, and behavioral consequences based on differences in posttraumatic pathophysiology.

The implication of these findings for sleep disturbances is clear. As individuals subject to trauma respond with different pathophysiological reactions, they also report different subjective experiences and symptoms of the trauma. It follows that these distinct types of subjectively reexperienced states will also result in different sleep problems, based on the underlying neural circuits that have been recruited. The example of Sally, from Chapter 2, illustrates that the pathophysiology of her unresolved developmental relational trauma impacted her pre-sleep mood, but did not result in nightmares.

What I will learn in this chapter to become a better sleep and trauma therapist:
1. Define what is meant by the intersubjective two-person therapeutic field.
2. Understand how verbal and nonverbal interactions between patient and therapist activate the intersubjective experiences for both.
3. Understand that the nonverbal elements of eye contact, prosody, pausing, nodding, encouraging, and smiling are effective as reinforcements of the developing intersubjective field.
4. Become particularly attentive to the topics that trigger withdrawal in the patient.
5. Understand that in all cases of relational trauma, one critical outcome is that the patient will have a range of defenses against allowing *the other* too close.
6. Understand that a large part of the therapeutic work with trauma

involves resolving these defenses in their spontaneous interactions with the therapist.
7. Interact with patients around their experience of breathing patterns to provide opportunities to awaken healthy curiosity about their physical sensations and foster an evolving intersubjective cascade.

THE CHALLENGE OF COMPLEX TRAUMA

The *White Paper on Complex Trauma* by the National Child Traumatic Stress Network of the United States (Cook et al., 2003) outlined the domains impaired by developmental attachment trauma. These seven domains included continuing problems in attachment with others, biology (physiological dysregulation), affective and cognitive difficulties, dissociative reactions, problems with behavioral control, and negative self-concept.

The impact of all these dysfunctional patterns is severe limitation in the child's ability to trust. In short, the trauma from the unavailability, unreliability, and inadequacy of their primary relationships results in the child's nervous system learning to be constantly vigilant, to distance, and to distrust relationships. The problem this poses for any therapy is clear: working toward resolution of the impaired domains requires working together, so the therapist must persistently be attentive to the difficulty the patient's nervous system may have in joining the therapeutic work.

The *White Paper* identified four central goals in providing treatment to these patients: (1) safety in the environment (includes all present life domains: the therapy, school, work, and personal life), (2) develop skills in emotional regulation and interpersonal functioning, (3) meaning-making about past traumas to create newer more positive adaptive views of themselves and (4) enhancing resiliency and integration into their social networks (Cook et al., 2005).

There are many implications for trauma treatments. We will highlight recommendations they made to strengthen the *attachment* between the child and their caretakers: (1) create a structured and predictable environment through establishment of rituals and routines, (2) enhance the adult's ability to tune in to the child's affective state, (3) model the effective management of intense emotions, and (4) use all opportunities to reinforce positive behaviors (Blaustein et al., 2003). While these recommendations were made for working with children with complex trauma, they are just as relevant in working with adults who come to us for treatment. In most cases, they have not been able to resolve these problems (or they wouldn't be seeking treatment).

All these principles, of highlighting the vital role of the relationship, are integrated into the TABS model for trauma assessment and sleep repair, with the therapist actively incorporating an early clinical focus on the patient's sleep pattern, through routine tracking of sleep, *combined with* attentiveness to the patient's affective states. In this chapter we will elaborate on the interactive non-verbal communication between patient and therapist that supports this goal.

COLLABORATIVE INTERSUBJECTIVE CLINICAL INQUIRY: PART II

Dan Hughes (2017) highlights the importance of developing an interactive style with the patient that is reciprocal. These back-and-forth communications are expressive. He stresses that these communications are not just about behaviors, but about what the patient is curious about, what they intend, and what behaviors mean.

Hughes (2017) proposes that these communications have the goal of becoming "in sync." His dyadic developmental psychotherapy treatment derives from the application of attachment theory, elaborating on the significance of improving parent-child interactions. The impact of these begins in the first months of life, well before the child has even a single word. They are present in the expressive sound babbling between baby and mother. The prosody of the voices carries critical information about the internal experience of each. These coordinated in sync affective, nonverbal communicative dances are what constitute what we mean by sharing an *intersubjective experience.*

Hughes notes that our sense of self develops from these early intersubjective experiences. The cooing, laughter, and glee in the voice of the parent communicates that the parent is in love with the baby. These sensory signals are internalized by the infant as a feeling of joy and delight within. When the parent expresses that the baby is delightful, the baby feels delightful. When the parent expresses that the baby is lovable, the baby feels lovable. These gradually internalized working models become the foundation of a basically good sense of self.

When such mirroring responses are absent, the infant has a correspondingly limited internal sense of a good self. Instead, there are plenty of feelings of stress, frustration, and anger that come and go, and due to the unresponsiveness of the caregiver these feelings are usually impossible for the infant to control. Children begin to protect themselves by becoming defensive of the environment and adopting a controlling, vigilant approach. They are constantly on guard for potential bad experiences that will retrigger these affective storms.

Unresponsive parents leave a different quality of intersubjective experience. It is a sense of feeling disheartened and betrayed. These internalized working models of inadequate and unresponsive authority figures will form the prominent mindset of the patient's expectations about the trustworthiness of everyone, including their therapist.

Maintaining a Goal of Synchronizing With the Patient's Affective State

A foundational part of our work with every traumatized client is to find opportunities to resonate with the patient's affective experience—something they feel strongly. Schore (2019) called this right brain psychotherapy. As we notice the feeling and resonate with it, it provides the patient the opportunity to feel felt, to notice the response, and take it in. If they are able to respond again, it allows for the cascade of affective responsive communications back and forth between the two. These moments of reciprocal relational engagement create shared experiences that are the basis of a revised narrative about self and other. The therapist actively holding safe space and reflecting the affective state of the client is a vital step in the client becoming more aware of their affective state. This awareness opens the door for change. However, if there is no reflection on what just happened, the internal working models of attachment will likely remain unchanged, even though plenty of excellent work has been done.

In the TABS model for sleep repair, there are at least four different ways that these principles can be incorporated into the treatment. Introducing an interactive assessment of the patient's breathing pattern allows plenty of opportunities to observe the openness and responsiveness of the patient to interventions. Second, the second CCP (Figure 2.1) includes introducing use of the Consensus Sleep Diary developed by Colleen Carney and colleagues (2012) provides a lens through which to examine sleep patterns together and be curious. What happens at night? What can change? Third, direct inquiry into attachment relationships throughout the treatment permits reflective opportunities. And finally, during the reprocessing of traumatic experiences, multiple moments to resonate with the deeper feeling states of the patients emerge. These create moments of triumph for feeling shared pride in achieved success.

When working with traumatized patients, every behavioral achievement during the sleep fixing can be accompanied by the celebration of the achievement in a way that engages the patient in the reciprocal cascade and positive reframing. The greater the extent and pervasiveness of the trauma, the more important these synchronized intersubjective experiences are to a successful outcome for the therapy.

Sleep research has generated a number of effective strategies, tools, and interventions to change sleep patterns. They work very well when they are applied consistently, with results tracked progressively as the treatment continues. Tracking sleep patterns is the glue that holds this process together. In clinical practice, the tracking is accomplished by use of the Consensus Sleep Diary (Carney et al., 2012).

The sleep diary reveals behavioral patterns that have resulted from a variety of poor choices such as going to sleep late, bringing the phone into bed, and using it through the night, etc. The sleep interventions are also behavioral. In addition, it provides an insight to how autonomic activation is repeatedly preventing and disturbing the transition into sleep. The whole pattern of sleep is looked at, a specific target for change identified, and the corrective behavioral suggestion made.

With nontraumatized patients, often the only clarification needed is to explain the reasons for these suggested changes. Some patients may also ask questions, and then the changes are adopted across a 2-to-3-week period.

However, traumatized patients may have multiple comorbidities, complicating life situations, and ambivalence about the value of the treatment itself. All of these will prove to be barriers to successful adoption of the behavioral change.

Behavioral Observation of Sleep-Wake Patterns

With traumatized patients, sleep is *not* simply a behavioral misalignment. The patient has multiple fears, wishes, avoidance patterns, and complicating clinical issues. A patient who is agitated about going to sleep because of recurrent nightmares is at increased risk of using substances and alcohol to suppress the agitation. Although alcohol initially works as a depressant, it will cause rebound insomnia later in the night. Substances will disturb sleep-wake patterns and have other negative psychosocial effects. Once a treatment plan has been established and sleep is being tracked, the Consensus Sleep Diary will be used to follow changes in sleep patterns (discussed in detail in Chapter 7).

As a general principle, initiation of sleep interventions with traumatized patients requires much attention to: (1) doubts patients have about treatment working, (2) long-standing conflicts about trusting health providers, (3) inconsistency with making the agreed-to changes, (4) complications from other stressful challenges in their daily life, and (5) complications from comorbid conditions that affect sleep.

In the two case studies that follow we will illustrate how therapeutic relationship challenges are managed: (a) when patients come into the assessment with a distrust of health care providers and doubts about whether treatment can ever be effective for them, and (b) when patients come to treatment with a readiness to explore traumatic events.

DEALING WITH THE RESISTANT PATIENT

All trauma patients have sleep problems: many with nightmares, insomnia, and sleep apnea. As they have been struggling with these sleep problems, most will have started taking some sleep medicines or self-medicated with alcohol, marijuana, or other substances.

Usually there have been multiple sleep aid failures. Asking about what sleep aids worked, and which ones have not, is a good place to start. This allows the therapist to understand what has been most frustrating for the patient and to empathize with the frustrations and acknowledge how emotionally painful this has been for the patient.

As sleep problems are reviewed, there will be many opportunities to reframe sleep problems as problems with autonomic nervous system (ANS) instability. Hyperactivation of the sympathetic nervous system (SNS) is at the heart of disturbed sleep. While medicines may put the patient to sleep, they will not change what the underlying SNS is doing. The patient coming to understand that sleep requires the boosting of parasympathetic nervous system (PNS) activity is necessary for reliable change to happen.

SNS overload may be evident in other body symptoms as well, like digestive issues, avoidance behaviors, infertility, pain, and anxiety problems. The presence of any of these difficulties allows the therapist to link the sleep problems with the other mental and physical health problems.

After taking the time to explain how the ANS works, the most important thing for the therapist to do is to pay attention to how the patient responds to this information. Did the patient listen and understand? With what part of the explanation did they resonate? Did they ask any questions? Tuning in to what the patient takes away from this explanation will guide you in how you conduct the rest of the assessment.

It is important to normalize what has happened and provide a pathway to change. Clarify that change is possible, but it comes through participating actively, not passively through drugs or sleep aids. This puts the patient into a place of agency. They will be required to act in their own interests, to retrain their own nervous system. The therapist will coach, but the patient actively participates in treatment. Here is how that can be communicated.

> THERAPIST: Here is how I think I can help you. We have to retrain your nervous system. Not with drugs. They won't help with retraining the nervous system. There are many things that I am going to teach you. Each of them helps, but there is no one thing that is going to do it all. That is an important idea. There is no magic pill or single answer.
>
> We are going to activate the brakes, to make the brakes function better. As you get more practice using the brakes, getting that braking system to be more effective for you, it will start to reset your gas pedal. The gas pedal will be less stuck in the "on" position. It is not going to happen in a week. Not even in a month. But it will begin to shift. We will give the brakes much more support. Does that make sense to you?

Engaging the patient in boosting the PNS braking system is the first priority in the treatment. The therapist underlines that tracking progress will be the only way they will know for sure that treatment is working. This places tracking sleep with the sleep diary at the heart of determining what is, or is not, working in the treatment.

> THERAPIST: The most effective way that I can teach you to use the braking system in a better way is by teaching you therapeutic breathing. Breathing is taught in many different places. You may even have done yoga somewhere.

While the above illustrates how to manage the distrust of a patient with complex trauma, by putting them into the driver's seat in this joint project, vigilance to withdrawal and doubt will continue across the entire treatment of these patients. It is a fundamental part of how this patient's nervous system has been organized: you can't trust anyone in an authority position. When these moments come up, as they will repeatedly, the therapist will always invite their questions and ask if they have doubts about whether the treatment will work or whether the therapist can be trusted.

CLINICAL APPLICATION: THE INTERSUBJECTIVE CASCADE

At one end of the spectrum of trust, the therapist's main task is developing a conscious therapeutic alliance, even if unconsciously the patient is not able to trust. We now turn to the other end of the spectrum, namely to an example of what it looks and feels like when patient and therapist are in sync, tuning in to each other's verbal and nonverbal communications.

To illustrate this process, we will review the clinical session with Mary (not her real name), a woman who was primary caregiver for her husband, John (also a pseudonym). John had been diagnosed with cancer over a decade previously. Over those years, she helped him with activities of daily living. She continued to assist him without ever complaining. They had a wonderful relationship and she described him as gentle, caring, and having a good sense of humor.

John was able to manage for most of the period of decline from his condition. But the last month of his life was in her words "a nightmare," filled with pain and anguish. He opted for the Medical Assistance In Dying (MAID; available in some states) protocol before he lost his faculties and would not be able to make that decision. A date was set, but his physical condition, according to Mary "fell off a cliff." He experienced severe intractable pain for lengthy periods. He would scream and swear at these times. This last month was torture for Mary, too.

The following edited transcript is taken from the trauma work done with Mary. Mary is a woman in her mid-60s. She had no previous traumas and had never experienced any psychiatric difficulties. Her husband had passed away the previous year, just after his birthday.

In the last month, his condition deteriorated markedly, he experienced horrible pain. Mary said that her memories were dominated by these scenes of pain and suffering. She felt robbed of all the wonderful memories they shared across a 3-decade-long marriage. She could not get back to her old self and felt incredibly sad and lonely.

What caused her to call me for treatment was a medical crisis she had. She had organized a Celebration of Life in her husband's memory a year after his death. She invited the friends and family who had been there for her and her husband across the years. The night before the event she considered whether to give a tribute to John herself. She said it made her feel edgy and emotional. She decided she would not be up to it and went to sleep.

She said she had been a good sleeper her whole life. However, that night, she awoke at 5 a.m. with extreme chest pain and unstable blood pressure. After waiting a half hour or so for these symptoms to abate, she called an ambulance and was taken to the hospital. The paramedical team were extremely concerned for her. Her blood pressure was spiking erratically. The ER was swamped that morning. She waited almost 4 hours to see a doctor. She began to feel an urgency to leave. She said she was determined and was able to calm herself. Her erratic heart rate calmed down and the doctors agreed to discharge her from the hospital. She was able to attend the Celebration of Life without further difficulties.

Now we will focus on Mary's experience of the nightmare of dealing with John's anguish when it was at its worst. Mary agreed to begin EMDR for her symptoms. Here is our exploration of the memories she felt "stuck with" after his death:

PATIENT: The big change came the week before his birthday. He was in a real crisis. January 15 was the date planned for his "medical assistance in dying" day by the MAID team. Once you pick a date, they are very reluctant to change that date. Across the last month he constantly asked to have it advanced, but they don't do that. It was a terrible month.

THERAPIST: Can you focus on what part of it stands out as the most difficult for you?

PATIENT: The periods where he was in so much pain and distress that he was screaming. Those were the times that were the hardest to tolerate. Because the rest of the time we were very close, very much together. We still laughed. We still did all the things we'd always done. But he would have these periods in the day, every day, at the end, when he just couldn't tolerate what was going on.

THERAPIST: Let's do reprocessing around that. If you remember what stands out when you were really struck by his pain and anguish, what are you remembering?

PATIENT: It was his birthday. And he was in bed at a time of day that he was normally not in bed. And he was screaming and swearing.

THERAPIST: What does that evoke in you? How do you think about yourself in that moment? Is that a sense of feeling powerless? Or hopeless?

PATIENT: Oh, for sure. The inability to do anything to help. The powerlessness. The horror at watching that. Knowing that he had to suffer that. He'd done relatively well up to that point. And that was such a change, such a turn.

THERAPIST: That's what I'm going to have you notice. The way you felt that sense of powerlessness. And the horror of it. That's the internal moment I want you to notice. What that feels like. And on that scale that we use from zero to 10, gauge how disturbing it feels right now. How would you rate that?

PATIENT: Probably an eight at least.
THERAPIST: We'll do the reprocessing work around that.

Commentary. There are several things to note in the opening 10 minutes of this session. She had done virtual trauma work previously. She did not require any introduction to the procedure. In this session she identified the worst moment quickly and the activation of those memories was apparent in her voice and facial gestures. In this online session, the bilateral stimulation is done by the patient moving her right hand back and forth across the table she is sitting at, tracking the movement of her fingers with her eyes. From her previous sessions, we were using 45-second sets of bilateral stimulation.

THERAPIST: When you're ready, you're going to start by bringing back the memory. Once you've connected with it, then you can begin with the first set. There we go. What are you noticing now?
PATIENT: That feeling of cold and numbness.
THERAPIST: Notice exactly what's coming up. I know this is really hard.

Commentary. The patient is breathing irregularly, gasping for air as the therapist feels the intensity of her distress and provides reassurance through his voice. The therapist has her begin eye movements while he monitors her difficulty breathing. Her labored breathing means that the internal experience of terror around the experience is overwhelming. The therapist maintains voice presence throughout the sets of eye movements. As well, the therapist's acknowledgment of the painful experience is important for Mary to know these feelings are difficult, but a normal part of grieving.

THERAPIST: Take a deep breath in and let that go. What's coming to your awareness now?
PATIENT: All the physical sensations, the numbness.
THERAPIST: The numbness is all through your body?
PATIENT: Feet and chest.

Commentary. In these first sets of bilateral stimulation, her descriptions of her coldness and numbness relate to the state of shutting down and the release of kappa opioids. When the emotional pain of an experience is overwhelming and inescapable, the ventrolateral periaqueductal gray (vlPAG) shuts down the overwhelming internal experiences. The therapist directs her to notice these internal states and continue with the eye movements.

THERAPIST: Notice the way in which the sensations are coming back to your awareness.

Commentary. The therapist continues to monitor all nonverbal cues by taking in her facial expressions, the intensity of the breaths, and the emergence of her sad feelings in her sobs. The therapist notes that she was keeping all of this inside when it was happening.

> THERAPIST: Take a deep breath in. And let that go.
> PATIENT: It's still very physical. Not much imagery. Lots of tingling in the head, in the chest, in the hands, and the feet.
> THERAPIST: Those physical sensations are exactly what we'd expect: all of that stuff you bottled up. You were doing your best to be there for him.

Commentary. Across the past minute or so, the therapist has sensed that Mary needs time to ground in the present moment before resuming the reprocessing. He has given her space to comment on her experience. Also important is her sensation of tingling. This can be a sign that blood flow is beginning to be restored to the areas in which she feels the tingling. If so, we will soon see additional signs that the vlPAG opioid shutdown is starting to release, and the activation of the dorsolateral PAG (dlPAG) and its emotional responses are restored.

> PATIENT: A lot of cold sensation. Cold breath in the abdomen.
> THERAPIST: Notice exactly where you feel that is present. Once you're ready, let's begin with the next set.

Commentary. The therapist has taught Mary how to use breathing therapeutically to manage her distress, and she is intentionally taking long, deep breaths. (Breathing therapeutically will be elaborated in Chapters 4 and 5.) She is using this skill to manage her own level of distress as she continues with the reprocessing. As difficult as the memories are, she is actively managing her level of distress.

> PATIENT: The tingling is settling down a bit.
> THERAPIST: There is still quite a bit of it?
> PATIENT: There's still a buildup.
> THERAPIST: Notice that residual tingling, wherever it is. And it may have shifted where you feel it most in your body.
> PATIENT: It's head and feet.
> THERAPIST: Notice it. We are going to the next set when you're ready. Tapping once more. You are doing really well.

Commentary. Even though Mary is modulating her own distress with breathing, there will be associations or images that emerge across the reprocessing work that surprise or startle her. Particularly at the point when the vlPAG shutdown is released, there is often blood flow restored to other brain regions.

Images of what she saw or heard can now come rushing back. When there is a signal of distress, the therapist again makes his presence known by a short verbal affirmation.

> THERAPIST: Take a deep breath. What's coming back for you?
> PATIENT: A tingling in my mouth.
> THERAPIST: Take a moment to breathe. If it's helpful, you can open your eyes. Notice that you're in a place where you feel safe.

Commentary. The therapist urges Mary to breathe to help manage her internal state. Her emotional level, punctuated by sobs, is markedly higher than when we began. This is quite normal. Titrating the amount of exposure, the length of the sets, the amount of grounding between sets, and the option of stopping entirely if the patient requires that are all options the patient needs to be aware of. The patient gets to decide if they want to continue the session or stop if it is overwhelming.

> PATIENT: Feelings are pretty intense. Pretty overwhelming.
> THERAPIST: A lot of these feelings you were holding onto because you were being strong for him, right?
> PATIENT: For his sake I try not to show emotion.

Commentary. The therapist is in sync with her feelings and her intent that she wants to protect John. The patient is immersed in the memory. Her statement is in the present, even though he passed away a year earlier. Another sign that these overwhelming feelings are activated and intense. The therapist continues to monitor all nonverbal cues by taking in her facial expressions, the intensity of the breaths, and the emergence of her sad feelings. The therapist notes that she was keeping all of this inside when it was happening. The emergence of the sadness indicates that the state of hypoarousal from dorsal vagal shutdown has released and the activation of the dlPAG is now central to the reprocessing work.

> THERAPIST: I know. [The therapist is in sync with her feelings and her intent that she wants to protect John.]
> PATIENT: It's so much harder on him if he thinks you're suffering, and so you keep trying to be strong. It's very hard to lose somebody you love that much.

Commentary. At this point, 10 minutes into the reprocessing, Mary is fully in touch with her sadness and also realizing that she was avoiding it when it happened in order to protect John from the added challenge of her distress. Being able to experience her feelings and to put words to what this experience means to her is critical for recovery. She also has a felt sense of the therapist's intersubjective presence. This marks the shift from hypoarousal (numbness and cold) to hyperarousal (intense distress and heartfelt sorrow).

> THERAPIST: You're so right. You see those feelings, everything you were pushing down to be strong for him. All of that is coming back. This is the way healing happens. We have to, at some point, look at how we feel, what the sensations are.

Commentary. Mary takes two deep sighing breaths, regulating her breath with intentional long, slow breaths. The spontaneous occurrence of the deep breaths is particularly important. It means the tension in her chest and body is easing as she is able to feel and talk about her feelings. It is important for the therapist to note these preverbal expressions of emerging emotional states. They provide the foundation for the ongoing intersubjective exchange between Mary and the therapist. This is a signal to continue with the reprocessing work.

> THERAPIST: Take a deep breath, and I want you to go back to that experience, that starting point. You said his birthday when he was in bed, right? That memory?
> PATIENT: That was so bad. And he was so funny because every day, starting with his birthday, we had people coming to see him to celebrate. And, although they didn't know it, to say goodbye. But we knew it.
> And it was such a bad day. I said maybe we should ask people not to come. And he said, "No, no, no. I'll be okay. I'll pull myself together. I always do." And he did.

Commentary. Mary makes another spontaneous association with how painful it was for her. This association heightens her sense of loss around these memories. The return of specific memories related to these events is a further sign that hyperarousal has begun to ease, and she is able to experience her feelings and begin to put words to these. This marks a transition from hyperarousal to affective modulation.

> PATIENT: When I look back on those photos, he looks so terrible. He almost doesn't look like himself.

Commentary. Mary continues to make important additional associations related to how she is experiencing her deep sense of loss. The therapist tracks her distress, the breaking voice and the sobs, and stays with her to maintain the intersubjective flow in the experiences she is elaborating. Providing her the space to feel her feelings and allow her mind to reflect on her experience without interruption beyond a word or two like "Right" and "Okay" maintains the intersubjective field.

PATIENT: You never quite know if you're doing the right thing. Is that a good distraction, the chance to see the people he cared most about in life?
THERAPIST: But you let him make his own decision.
PATIENT: I think it helped him to get through those days to have a focal point. But his life is so different. How he's getting through every day is so different, how he looks, how he's coping. He just fell off a cliff, right then and there.

Commentary. Mary is now able to remember how he looked and how much worse he was, after he "fell off a cliff." The spontaneous return of the visual images of his state at the end is an important shift from the earlier purely physical sensations of cold and numbness. Each of these images brings another wave of intense affect related to that overwhelming image. As she is now experiencing her feelings, she is putting words to her feelings and the thoughts and memories attached to these experiences. This marks an important transition from intense right brain emotional hyperarousal to affective modulation by integration of the left brain's ability to register places, times, and meanings into a new awareness of the meaning of these experiences. This process usually continues across many sessions.

PATIENT: If we could have timed it differently, I would have spared him that last month. Because it wasn't a great time. There were great moments but there was a lot of pain and suffering, him wanting to be out of it. It was hard to deal with. Every day he asked to have it moved up, to be relieved of it. And that was tough. Very tough.
THERAPIST: But I see the same resolute effort in you, as you were seeing in him.
    That you really did your absolute best. But right now, we're giving your feelings, everything that you've pushed down, the chance for you to deal with and to appreciate what was going on and what you felt.

Commentary. The determination in Mary's voice is a good sign, also the appearance of deep breaths. The therapist draws the focus from the husband back to Mary. How strong she was in pushing her feelings down when she needed to, but that she no longer needs to do that. These communications are important to give Mary a real sense that her pain is being seen, as is her strength in being able to tolerate her feelings. He senses that it is a suitable time to return her to the trauma work.

THERAPIST: We're going to continue with the next set. When you bring that image of him back on his birthday, in his bed, on that zero to 10 scale. How does that feel for you right now?
PATIENT: Pretty terrible. I wish it was a memory I could erase. I had so many wonderful memories. And this one dominates. This is what you're left with. And I don't want it!

Commentary. Despite openly crying and struggling with her breath, Mary states how much these horrible memories have haunted her, as well as her determination to overcome these with the reprocessing. The fact that this intrusive memory has dominated her experience across the past year tells the therapist that there will be more sessions of working on these images and memories, to allow all the buried feelings to be felt and acknowledged.

> THERAPIST: There is a path that we know well, to let it go. And it's noticing all the emotions, everything that's flooding and coming up for you right now. Again, just be aware of what that feels like. And then we're going to continue with the next set.
> PATIENT: That's it.
> THERAPIST: Take a deep breath in. And let it go, rest your eyes. What are you noticing?
> PATIENT: Some of that sensation is leaving and some of it is still there. It's gone from my stomach and my chest. It's still there in my head, my feet. It's sort of abating.
> THERAPIST: It's beginning to move and shift. I know this is really tough, but it's the only way to heal, to let go of this.
> PATIENT: I keep telling myself it'll be worth it.

Commentary. Mary laughs as she keeps reminding herself that this will help her. Clearly, not all of her may believe it, but she is resolute. The laughter is important. It indicates that she is not completely absorbed by the heavy grief. She is able to wonder about herself and whether this trauma reprocessing will work.

> THERAPIST: It'll be worth it.
> You've been through this grind before. And you're a real soldier, you're tough. The shortest way through is to go right through it.

Commentary. The therapist reminds Mary of her successful resolution of a previous trauma a few years ago. He again takes a moment to acknowledge Mary's strength.

> PATIENT: I'm beginning to laugh a little.
> THERAPIST: Laughter is the best medicine.

Commentary. As the therapist joins Mary in her laughter, there is another moment of intersubjective resonance where both can take a moment's break in this very heavy session.

> PATIENT: Funny enough, I didn't think John's Celebration of Life would have influence, but it has. I think that was helpful and therapeutic.

I don't think it's quite the answer. But I think it was more important than I expected it to be. I thought, it's what you do for other people, because they need it.

Commentary. In this moment Mary is able to let go of her caretaking role and notice how important and meaningful that experience was for her. She had spent the best part of the last number of years thinking about others. She was now beginning to be able to think of what this has meant for her.

PATIENT: But it was actually quite a moment for me. Quite a day. And crazy that it was preceded by this silly health thing.

Commentary. Mary calls her medical crisis on the night leading up to the Celebration of Life "a silly health thing," minimizing the importance of the event.

PATIENT: I believe that I willed myself out of the hospital. Because I couldn't see any other way to get out of that hospital. But it was quite helpful. It gives you some sort of line to cross.
THERAPIST: When you reflect on the intensity of the feelings that are bubbling up for you right now, I suspect some of the intensity of all this stuff (which is what you had pushed down) was what was coming up and causing the extreme chest pain that took you to the hospital.
PATIENT: Subconsciously, obviously. Because, out of the dead of sleep. Everybody around me thought it had to do with that day. And I thought not, because I was sound asleep, right? Maybe, in retrospect.

Commentary. Mary rightly appreciates her own strength in making the decision to get out of the hospital to attend the planned celebration. However, as she does not understand the emotional engine to her cardiac symptoms, the therapist elaborates on this. Mary acknowledges that she never connected the two, even though others had told her they saw the connection. Mary did not believe it, as she had awoken out of "the dead of sleep."

THERAPIST: Your brain has been holding onto a lot of very intense emotion and painful feelings. And then that was starting to bubble up in the middle of the night.
 The work you're doing now is heroic. This is hard, but it will make a big difference, because it's allowing the right side of your brain to let go of what caused your cardiac symptoms.
PATIENT: I hope this is the last time. I'm going to have to have a chat with my brain about this. Enough! Enough!

Commentary. The therapist underlines how these memories automatically get locked into our memory networks by our brains. Mary is able to be playful about this. She seems to understand the link between the medical crisis and what she calls her underlying, "subconscious" feelings that are coming up now. She is also spontaneously able to imagine having a chat with her brain and laughs at the thought of that.

> THERAPIST: You have to tell it, "It's okay to be forgetful. You don't need to remember so much."

Commentary. The therapist spontaneously joins in with Mary's imaginary chat. Both laugh heartily for a while, continuing to reinforce the intersubjective experience that even such horrible and painful experiences can be approached and can be interspersed with moments of laughter. This completes the stepping back from the intensity of the grief and loss. We are now about 30 minutes into the treatment and the therapist suggests getting back to more trauma work.

> THERAPIST: We'll continue with the work because I think this is really, really important. And you're doing such an excellent job. You said some of the sensations are leaving, but you're noticing they've shifted from the stomach upward? Where do you feel them now? When you bring that image of John on his birthday, when you bring that back to your awareness, what do you notice?
> PATIENT: I still have tingling in my feet. And I get a funny sensation in my mouth and in my head, sort of tingling. Almost like my whole throat is affected. Something that affects my ability to swallow. A funny sensation in the back of my throat and my head.

Commentary. There continue to be residual physical sensations to be addressed. Many aspects of the memories around traumatic events are stored as body sensations. Mary is now more aware of the physical sensation of choking back and being unable to swallow. This becomes the focus of the next set.

> THERAPIST: Go with that. You don't have to do anything about it. Just notice how you're feeling it.

Commentary. Mary takes intentional long deep breaths, a sign that she is fully engaged in the memories and is attending to her experience.

> THERAPIST: Take a deep breath in. Let that one go. And what are you noticing now?
> PATIENT: Calmer. It feels weird to do the eyes and the hands in the same direction. It's the opposite of how you walk. Quite strange. It feels almost spastic to me. Because my natural inclination is to do opposite.

Commentary. Mary continues to be able to reflect on the puzzling physical aspects of these experiences. She laughs spontaneously and is curious about the process.

> THERAPIST: True, that's going counter to what we're doing.
> PATIENT: Going counter to what we're doing. It feels quite awkward for me to get my eyes to go to the same side that I'm tapping. Feels completely backwards.
> THERAPIST: You have to will your eyes to do something.
> PATIENT: I think, "Am I doing it the right way?" And it's quite a strange sensation.
> THERAPIST: You're definitely doing it the right way. Because as the fingers move, the eyes are moving.
> PATIENT: It feels very counterintuitive to me.
> THERAPIST: In part, your brain is saying, "What are you doing? You shouldn't be thinking about all this awful stuff. Why are you doing this?" It's partly because the brain is trying to minimize pain.

Commentary. Mary and the therapist take a brief time to reflect, both laughing, on the resistance she feels around doing the eye movements. The intersubjective experience of enjoying the strange aspects of the experience is noted, and the therapist suggests that the awkwardness may be arising from the brain's difficulty in allowing the painful feelings. Again, what is important is the openness that Mary has to noticing her actual experience and communicate it openly with the therapist.

> THERAPIST: The reason it's so painful is in large part because you loved him so much. Because you cared deeply, and you shared so many wonderful times and memories and experiences, that just intensifies it. And then at the very end when he is in so much pain, and he's begging you to move up the date, you feel that pain. Even though all the illness is in his body, because you care so much, your empathy brings all of that awful physical sensation into your experience as well.
> PATIENT: We lived that nightmare for a whole month.

Commentary. The therapist makes the comment that John's pain was not only his experience, but because of the empathy she had for him, she experienced his pain as well. When she responded with, "We lived that nightmare" she is confirming that it was, and is, part of her experience.

> THERAPIST: That's why it's important for us to revisit and to let it go because you don't need this after losing him. And you're going to have your memories of him. In fact, once we let go of the painful feelings and sensations,

then what begin to emerge are all the pleasant memories, all the positive things.

PATIENT: I looked through a bunch of photographs recently and I thought back to all the trips and all the travel around the world and all the great occasions and all the great fun we had. But my head is somehow dominated by that last month.

Commentary. With this last comment, Mary recognizes that the trauma work is not done. The nonverbal cue of her voice tensing with her acknowledgment indicates that the memory has been activated again.

THERAPIST: It's the pain. Your brain is saying, we're going to remember everything that happened, because we don't ever want to go through this again. But in the end, it's the wrong strategy. This is completely curable. This is why we're doing this. It will make an enormous difference for you.

I'm going to have you go back to that memory, that starting point of his birthday in bed, and the screaming. Again, bringing back that experience, whatever way it's there. As you reflect on it, on that zero to 10 scale, how does that feel for you right now?

PATIENT: Diminished, but not gone. But it feels less than it did when we started this session. I can still feel it, but I can see it more than I can feel it now. All these funny sensations that I experienced keep changing. So now I've got a twitching in my eyes. And my feet are still tingling, but my head is clear. I am a very funny person, funny in how I experience this stuff.

THERAPIST: This is the way in which the brain has packaged it and tucked it away in your memory. All of these experiences are part of what you actually went through, or part of the internal experience. As it lets it go, you bring your attention to it and it begins to shift and change. Whatever part of it is still bothering you, or as you say, you can see it more than feel it. Whatever way the feelings and the image are present. Put your full attention on it.

Take a deep breath in and let that go. What are you noticing now?

PATIENT: Just calmer, a little bit calmer again. When I first started, I had this feeling of rapid heart rate and innervation in my body. And that's starting to calm down.

THERAPIST: That's the sympathetic fight-or-flight reaction.

PATIENT: I am hoping that's what's contributing to my blood pressure, and it's going to calm down. Because my whole life I had low blood pressure. And now I have high blood pressure.

Commentary. The patient is fully engaged in the process and noticing significant changes in her physical distress. She notes the decrease in her heart rate and the intense "innervation" in her body. She wonders whether these feelings of emotional distress may be the cause of her recent problems with hypertension.

> THERAPIST: We'll know in about two or three more sessions. When you first approach these really painful experiences, it's like all of the intensity of the emotion just floods in. It's beginning to feel a little bit more doable, right? You say it's calmer?
>
> PATIENT: In the beginning, I didn't so much see him as feel it. Now I can see the visual more than experience everything physically. The physical response tones down, it starts to leave in various areas. And then I see the image more clearly.

Commentary. The in sync relationship between Mary and the therapist is now solidly in place. The processing has shifted from hypoarousal (the physical responses) to hyperarousal (visual images bringing intense emotional experiences with them). The solid intersubjective experience in which these feelings emerge provides the necessary resource to continue to allow these eruptions of distress to be noticed, experienced, and put into words. The spontaneous increase in dialogue by the patient confirms the transition from overwhelming feelings (right hemisphere), to modulated affect in which there are words (left hemisphere) to begin to describe internal experiences that are no longer overwhelming.

> THERAPIST: It's like peeling an onion. There are layers. There is some crying, and then there's another layer. But as you go, it settles down. It begins to feel easier.
>
> PATIENT: Can you promise?
>
> THERAPIST: I promise you. No, I absolutely, cross my heart. Promise.

Commentary. The therapist goes along with her laughing request, and both therapist and Mary laugh. The session continues within this evolving intersubjective field in which Mary's experiences and comments are responded to resonantly by the therapist; and then his responses are taken in by Mary and reflected on. We have underlined the essential elements of how the intersubjective field emerges from the spontaneous comments, experiences, and responsiveness of both participants, co-creating an intangible yet reliable intersubjective field. The therapist is able to give a powerful assurance of success based on Mary's response in this session.

SUMMARY OF CLINICAL ISSUES EMERGING FROM THE INTERSUBJECTIVE CASCADE

This edited transcript from an early session with Mary illustrates the ways that nonverbal responses come to be woven together with reflection and putting words to these experiences. When both participants are listening and responding to the other, they create an interpersonal cascade that provides a sense of mutuality. As this intersubjective experience is felt by both participants, it supports the patient's courage in being curious about these new internal states.

Allowing the full experience of these internal states in turn provides a deeper experience of Mary's inner self, as well as understanding herself better. The therapist watches for moments that need to be responded to spontaneously to maintain connection with the affective state of the patient. Trauma work is resumed as the opportunities present themselves.

The therapist's task of maintaining an intersubjective dialogue and presence across the reprocessing of the traumatic memory is essential to titrate Mary's emotional level. By using breaks from the trauma work, providing time to talk about what is being experienced, praising the patient for her strength, responding to her seeing a funny side to how her brain works, and other moments to remain in connection, the therapist enables the patient's felt sense of confidence in the treatment to grow.

Also significant in what the patient and therapist have accomplished is an important working through of the initial experience of emotional shutdown (vlPAG). Mary describes very clearly an important shift that has occurred in her internal experience of witnessing John's anguish. The first sets of bilateral eye movements brought back the physical sensations of feeling cold in her abdomen, feet, and head. As the sets progressed, other physical sensations linked with the initial shock reaction (especially constricted breathing with waves of intense tension) came and went. Gradually, Mary began to be able to visualize the elements of the experience. These other sensory elements were unavailable in the first 10 minutes of the reprocessing and their appearance signaled a shift from hypoarousal (vlPAG) to hyperarousal (dlPAG).

The intensity of these affective storms would be impossible for Mary to face entirely on her own. The context of safety provided by the intersubjective field that exudes a feeling of being held emotionally is what allows her to go inside to allow these overwhelming feeling states. The experience of these overwhelming feelings (hyperarousal) within the context of the in sync relationship provides the opportunity for affective modulation to occur.

Moreover, it is not just the accessing of that inner state that heals the emotional pain. Bilateral eye movements desensitize the pain. The same neural mechanisms of REM sleep that accomplish desensitization of moderately intense negative affects at night work with overwhelmingly intense negative affects in the safety provided by the presence of the therapist. After many such desensitizing sets, Mary spontaneously drew the connection to her medical crisis. During that crisis, a month before the start of treatment, her sleeping mind began to activate the same memory circuits.

The night before, she was thinking about the Celebration of Life organized for the next day. A good friend had flown in for the event and was staying with Mary.

They were up talking about the event during the evening. She felt edgy about the celebration and decided that she was not going to deliver her own tribute because she was still so emotional. All of these pre-sleep affective experiences funneled into the normal nightly processing of affective experiences, which proved too raw and intense. These feelings overwhelmed her sleep, and she awoke with the intense chest pain and somatic distress that sent her to the hospital.

In the therapy session, the safety of the responsive intersubjective two-person field, combined with the eye movements that her REM sleep would have provided her, allowed the traumatic memory to be fully experienced. As the patient senses these affective storms abating, she feels differently, both within herself and in her confidence in the therapy. While the mechanisms that permit this transformation to occur are still not fully explicated, recent work by Marco Pagani of the National Research Council of Rome and his research group have highlighted the role of the eye movements used in EMDR. These researchers confirmed that eye movements induced slow wave patterns in cerebellar functioning that spread to neocortex, hippocampus, thalamus, and brainstem (Born et al., 2006; Carletto & Borsato, 2017; Carletto et al., 2017).

Mary's level of conscious and unconscious trust in the therapist increases. Across time this becomes the therapeutic alliance with the patient. The conscious part can express gratitude for the help she receives, and the unconscious therapeutic alliance allows memories of increasingly distressing intensity to come to the surface, providing ever-richer material to work with. These processes are elaborated in the next chapter.

Aside from illustrating the theme of how the intersubjective field begins to evolve into a therapeutic alliance, there are a few additional points that need elaboration in the material presented. We will expand on two key issues: (1) implications for our understanding of how we define trauma and PTSD and (2) the relation of trauma symptoms with sleep.

The *DSM-5* removed PTSD from the anxiety disorders and created a new trauma- and stressor-related disorders cluster. This reflected the fact that PTSD often involves multiple physical systems such as hormonal dysregulation and autoimmune reactions. These complex somatic components are often more intense, complicated, and chronic than the physical symptoms reported with anxiety alone.

Another critical point that should be emphasized is the nature of the life-threatening event that Mary experienced. Throughout the month of that "nightmare," Mary herself was never in any personal danger. The trauma she experienced was born entirely from her empathy as caretaker for her life partner John. Witnessing her husband's torturous experiences, which persisted for hours every day, day after day for a month was the trigger for her state of emotional overwhelm, resulting in traumatic hyperarousal and the medical symptoms of cardiac distress.

The fact that intense traumatic experiences can be activated by witnessing horrible events is important. None of us have to be in direct danger for us to experience incapacitating traumatic symptoms, either emotional or somatic. This point is especially important for trauma therapists, who can be exposed daily to such painful experiences. As long as our nightly REM period is functioning well, we continue to resolve these feelings. But when this internal safety valve is lost, symptoms will follow. So how does this internal safety valve work, or break down?

THE 24-HOUR MIND

In Mary's case, the nightly REM period was not functioning well. The waking negative emotion was overwhelming. It is important to note that these symptoms did not arise from her daytime activities, but when her brain was in deep sleep. Why would these symptoms arise in the middle of the night, and not in response to some daytime activity or circumstance?

The answer to this comes from the work of sleep researcher Rosalind Cartwright, author of *The Twenty-Four-Hour Mind* (2010). She reviewed evidence from studies of sleep and dreaming and integrated them into an innovative model of the activity of the mind across the 24-hour day-night cycle. The mind *is* active across the entire 24-hour period, but its activity changes as consciousness is lost in the transition into sleep:

> When sampled in sequence across the night, dreams display the progressive down-regulation of disturbing emotion. This process is responsible for instituting adjustments in the organizing schemas [your self], so that these become more useful in promoting waking adaptation to changed circumstances. This function is most effective when waking negative emotion is within a moderate range, neither too little when no major change is needed, nor too overwhelming. (p. 165)

During the first 90-minute episode of NREM sleep, some of the emotionally relevant experiences that were tagged as important during the day are reactivated, and unimportant information is erased (Cartwright, 2010, p. 175). As well, in SWS there is the added stimulus from one or more biological drives which can intensify the physical sensations and emotional experiences that the daytime experiences activated.

During this first SWS period, the transfer of short-term memories (from hippocampus) to long-term memories held in the neocortex has begun. As the SWS ends, REM sleep begins. In the higher activation of the REM sleep state, Cartwright underlined that there is "an abrupt shift from loosely connected thoughts to a new format, with sensory images expressing one or more of the same emotion-related issues, *now energized as urgent concerns* [emphasis added]" (2010, p. 176).

The eye movements of REM serve to connect thoughts (left hemisphere activity) with the emotional experiences (right hemisphere). Also in this first REM period, there is a matching of new emotional material with older emotional memories. After 10 minutes or so, REM sleep gives way to NREM again and the preconscious NREM mental activity picks up and elaborates on the memories that were augmented by the sensory-rich hyper-associative REM state.

These shifts from NREM to REM continue in 90-minute cycles, back and forth, across the night. According to Cartwright, "The mind keeps working throughout the cycles of changes in brain activity, with only a hint of some 'time off' in the deepest of SWS" (2010, p. 178).

In Mary's case, going to sleep thinking about the Celebration of Life event began activating preconscious memories from the year before when they lived the nightmare of the unrelenting anguish and pain. These reflections made her aware that she was too emotional to deliver a tribute herself. As these emotional memories were only sensed and not fully expressed (or dealt with), their intensity (evident from the first few sets of this treatment session) activated increasing distress and autonomic arousal. This activation would be further accelerated across each 90-minute period of NREM and REM across the night.

By 5 a.m. this cascade had fully activated those unresolved feelings of anguish and loss. The intensity of Mary's unresolved emotional experiences overwhelmed her and resulted in somatic symptoms of intense chest pain, accelerated heart rate, and dysregulated blood pressure. What this treatment session illustrates is that the engine to her medical crisis was the internal intensity of the emotional experiences that emerged in the first 10 minutes of trauma work. That *emotional* pressure cooker created the intense *somatic* chest pains and dysregulated cardiac activity that awoke her. The intensity of these feelings overwhelmed the self's ability to process these feelings in REM, resulting in the abrupt awakening out of the depths of sleep.

APPLICATION

To make effective use of the information from this chapter, we invite you to apply the concepts by engaging patients with these important steps in exploring their sleep:

Empathically Explore the Sleep Problems of a Resistant Patient: Engage the patient in an exploration of their sleep pattern along with the efforts they have made to overcome it. Reflect the patient's internal state during this exploration.

Reframe Sleep Disturbance as Autonomic Dysregulation: Describe the autonomic system components of sympathetic (gas pedal) and parasympathetic (brake) and highlight the importance of boosting the braking system to prepare for sleep. Discuss this perspective until the patient fully grasps that the braking system can be modified by a variety of exercises and strategies.

Introduce Therapeutic Breathing to Stabilize the Autonomic System: Let the patient know that the amount of effort they put into doing the breathing exercises will directly impact how well they can stabilize their dysregulated autonomic nervous system. They are not trapped in this state but have agency in regulating their internal state. In particular, patients who are chest breathers will gain the most from practicing these exercises.

Increasing Awareness of, and Fostering of, the Intersubjective Cascade: Notice and respond attentively to the patient's internal experiences of distress. Intervene to augment collaboration. Whenever possible engage the patient's curiosity and sense of competence in managing moments of distress. Creating an atmosphere of playfulness, respect, and acceptance is critical for ongoing trauma work.

Key Messages for Therapists

1. Complex trauma patients are often resistant at the start of treatment owing to long-standing relational trust issues (with health providers and other authority figures). The therapist responds by normalizing these defensive postures and relating the brain's protective stance back to the traumatic relational experience in which such responses were necessary. The therapist continues to encourage communication of these moments of distrust and doubt whenever they come up.
2. The mind is active across the 24-hour day-night cycle. In the transition from wakefulness into sleep emotionally tagged memories are preferentially elaborated across sleep. These continuous mental contents make sleep both a subjective experience as well as a behavioral state. Standard EEG sleep scoring of 30-second epochs does not capture the internal experience of sleep. Intense emotional states, typical in trauma, have the power to disrupt sleep entirely, awakening the sleeper out of sleep, in distress, pain, or with other significant physical symptoms.
3. Framing sleep problems as problems in dysregulation of the autonomic nervous system provides both: (1) a context for teaching necessary skills for improving sleep and also (2) a bridge to moving back and forth between the TABS targets of Trauma treatment, elaborating on Attachment issues, resolving long-standing Body (somatic) symptoms, and integrating Sleep interventions.
4. The therapist takes every opportunity to underline the necessity of (1) the patient being an active participant in their sleep and trauma treatment, as well as (2) the therapist and patient working together to retrain and reorganize the autonomic nervous system to boost parasympathetic nervous system activity.

5. The interventional tools of behavioral sleep treatments (using sleep diaries) as well as interactive mind-body interventions (teaching diaphragmatic breathing) provide opportunities for tuning in to patient internal states and building necessary shared intersubjective experiences through attuned responses that support a cascade of attuned interactions.
6. Repair of sleep problems in trauma requires ongoing attention to the intersubjective relationship, in which the therapist and patient together concentrate on internal emotional experiences that have been too overwhelming for the patient to manage on their own. The developing intersubjective field provides that support.

4

Active Attunement and Empathic Communication Builds Therapeutic Alliance

"It is ultimately the attuned relationship that is reparative, and it is only in the context of that relationship that a therapeutic agenda or strategy can be safe and effective."
—Maureen Kitchur (2005, p. 10)

"This patient tells me that what has helped her in our work together is that she 'feels felt' by me. . . . This attunement of states forms the nonverbal basis of collaborative, contingent communication."
—Daniel Siegel (2015b, p. 94)

At the first meeting in a psychotherapeutic journey, both participants are ready to engage in building a sense of trust and comfort with the other. Both will intuitively know that such a strong foundation is necessary to weather the storms of emotional distress that trauma treatment will visit on them. While the appreciation of the critical importance of the connection is understood, what is likely not as well understood is that both participants come to this journey with a previous map of what relationships are and how they can be safe or dangerous. It is this map, encoded in intrinsic memories of past experiences, which will dictate how the relationship unfolds and how effectively it can address the emotional challenges that trauma treatment must overcome.

The study of how to best go about building that therapeutic alliance runs through all forms of experiential psychotherapy. Freud noted that the attitude of the therapist should aim toward an "evenly hovering attention" to the patient: "suspend judgement . . . and give impartial attention to everything there is to observe" (1909, p. 23).

Since the time of Freud, countless others have elaborated on the attitude, technique, and skills that the therapist must bring to the session. Among the most important of these is the more recent highlighting of *safety* as an essential backdrop for all therapeutic activity. For example, Ogden and her colleagues (2006) highlighted that trauma can significantly alter the safe boundaries of the person's personal space. She emphasized the importance of tracking the nervous system by careful monitoring of the patient's body signals. She will collaborate with the patient regarding the seating arrangements for the session, with the goal of empowering for the patient to find the relational space that permits them to feel completely safe in their bodies so therapy can proceed.

In fact, Ogden's paradigm (2006) of early therapeutic attention to bodily reactions in session, including the sense of safety, has now become widely accepted in the trauma field. It is also broadly accepted that trauma lives in the body: trauma memories are body memories (van der Kolk, 2015). Dan Siegel's (2015b) interpersonal neurobiology approach integrates tracking, alignment, and resonance into the interactive process that constitutes the active engagement of the patient's internal experience by the therapist, called attunement. As so many of the internal experiences that disrupt nighttime sleep emanate from the body, attention to the memories that the body has locked into its inner experiences is critical to sleep repair.

What I will learn in this chapter to become a better sleep and trauma therapist:

1. Know what is meant by active attunement and know how to approach the trauma patient by skillfully applying active attunement in each session.
2. Understand that paying attention to the nonverbal cues of physical symptoms is the gateway to activating buried emotional distress.
3. The most powerful therapeutic intervention to deepen attunement is exploring breathing dynamics with a behavioral assessment of breathing.
4. Demonstrating proper technique in breathing exercises is the first necessary step in activating the parasympathetic braking system.
5. The systematic activation of the parasympathetic braking system provides a critical tool facilitating the transition from wakefulness into sleep.

ACTIVE ATTUNEMENT AS CATALYST TO INTERNAL PSYCHIC CHANGE

In *The Developing Mind* (2015b) Dan Siegel drew attention to the power of relationships to transform who we are. He provided a detailed review of how our interpersonal worlds activate and enrich our neural networks to create new internal experiences. Experiences that are either negative and aversive can be changed to positive, enjoyable, and creative experiences. At the center of how interpersonal experience can fuel transformation of the internal world is the active, dynamic process of affective attunement. What were the essential elements of this transformative process? Here are Dan Siegel's conclusions:

> A transforming attuned relationship would involve the following fundamental elements: contingent, collaborative communication; psychobiological state attunement; mutually shared interactions that involve the amplification of positive affective states and the reduction of negative ones; reflection on mental states; and the ensuing development of mental models of security that enable emotional modulation and positive expectancies for future interactions. (2015b, p. 143)

In the above we have a road map for transformation and change. The road map includes the openness to engage in this reciprocal dialogue, which was discussed in the last chapter. It also includes an exquisite attentiveness to both psychobiological states (one's own and the other's). Attunement to these internal states is not the entire story. It is the beginning. And from this beginning, what we are heading toward is coregulations of the negative states, so that positive experiences can emerge. And after these positive experiences have emerged, that is not the end either. These form a basis for Siegel's "development of mental models of security" (2015b, p. 143), which become the internal resources that can be accessed to provide a reliable foundation for emotional modulation and the ability to maintain positive expectancies for the future.

What Daniel Stern (1985), Allan Schore (1994), and others call attunement can be understood as being composed of three processes that Siegel (2015b) called "tracking, alignment, and resonance" (p. 313). Tracking is focusing our whole attention, moment to moment on the other person's internal states. The purpose is to stay present with these internal states. Tracking provides the foundation for alignment.

Alignment is the intentional alternation by one or both members of the therapeutic dyad to bring their internal state into a state approximating that of the other. Bringing one's internal state into alignment with the other allows the other to feel felt. This internal synchrony between the two provides a powerful sense of being understood at a deep level. This creates a powerful unconscious therapeutic alliance.

Siegel (2015b) notes that the overall process of attunement leads to the possibility of each member of the dyad being able to mutually influence the other. He describes this new possibility as "resonance" (2015b, p. 313). This resonance can continue after alignment has stopped. The mutual influence of the earlier alignment of states actively persists within the minds of each of them after the aligning experience has long been over.

Siegel (2015b) adds that all our human relationships are prone to rupture, and these moments of rupture require active repair of the misunderstanding. In his words, "Repair is an interactive process in which the rupture is recognized, reconnection is established, and attunement and resonance are experienced as a soothing process that enables the relationship to continue on a supportive path" (p. 314).

Relevance of Attunement for Sleep Treatment

All the elements of the road map for transformation through attunement apply to sleep treatment. Sleep is a psychobiological state of exceeding importance to everyone's physical and mental health. The disrupted sleep of the traumatized patient is healed by the processes of tracking internal states of hyperarousal, attending to the impairment of parasympathetic activity necessary for sleep, and realigning these states by boosting parasympathetic activity. This creates the opportunity to recognize the emotional distress from traumatic experiences and then use therapeutic breathing to desensitize these feelings, which are blocking emotional modulation in the pre-sleep period. As breathing patterns mirror the underlying balance between sympathetic and parasympathetic activity, attuning to the trauma patient's breathing patterns is a critical tool in preparing for its transformation.

ATTUNEMENT TO BREATHING PATTERNS

The psychotherapeutic process involves developing a meaningful and honest connection between the therapist and the patient. This connection includes both connection with the patient's story as well as connection to their internal state. Probably the most important aspect of an individual's present state is their internal level of distress, as determined by the autonomic nervous system. Moment to moment, the balance between our sympathetic and parasympathetic systems creates an internal state that is somewhere on a continuum from extremely relaxed and content through to a hyperactivated system that is hypervigilant for danger and cannot relax enough to permit sleep.

The balance between these two systems is directly apparent in our breathing patterns. When the sympathetic system is highly activated, our musculature is tensed and ready for fight or flight. The tensing of the musculature in turn restricts the normal rhythmic breathing patterns, causing short staccato inbreaths. The restriction in the size of each inbreath means taking many more breaths to supply the necessary amount of oxygen to the body.

On the other hand, when the parasympathetic rest and digest system is in charge, the body is in a state that promotes restoration and healing. To activate this state, there cannot be any clear and present danger. Activation of the parasympathetic state of relaxation is necessary for the mind to shift into restorative sleep. Children learn to relax their autonomic systems with the presence of a caregiver who maintains a consistent, protective interpersonal experience at bedtime. Only when this protective presence is available can the nervous

TABLE 4.1 Behavioral Assessment of Breathing Pattern
Source: Copyright © Jaan Reitav (2016, p. 35). Used by permission.

Step	Direction for Each Step	Observations Check the Appropriate Box		
		Column 1	Column 2	Column 3
1	Number of breaths taken in one minute: (One inhale and exhale counts as one breath.)	[ ] Over 15 # Breaths	12 to 15	[ ] Under 12 # Breaths
2	On INHALE which hand MOVES FIRST?	[ ] Chest	Both	[ ] Belly
3	On INHALE which hand MOVES MOST?	[ ] Chest	Same	[ ] Belly
4	ON INHALE does your right (belly) hand move IN or OUT?	[ ] IN	Neither	[ ] OUT
5	IF your hand moves OUT, how much does it move?	[ ] Moves IN (or not at all)	Moves OUT slightly	[ ] Moves OUT noticeably
6	Make two fists, push into the soft tissue between hips and ribs. Breathe in. Do your fists MOVE OUT?	[ ] No (or they move inward or upward)	A Little	[ ] Yes noticeably
7	In the past month, have you noticed that you sigh, yawn, or take a gulp of breath on a regular basis?	[ ] Yes	Occasionally	[ ] No
8	Take 10 full breaths in and out quickly. After 10 QUICK breaths: Do you feel DIZZY now?	[ ] Yes	A little	[ ] No
TOTAL (Add up the check marks in each column)				

system let go of the prepotent activation of the sympathetic system. Survival always trumps sleep.

A relatively easy way to engage the patient in a reflection on their current state of balance or imbalance in the autonomic system is to walk them through some observations of their breathing pattern. The breathing assessment consists of eight behavioral observations on how the person's body accomplishes breathing. What muscles are recruited to breathe in and out? These results will tell us whether the patient is a shallow "chest" breather, or a deeper, diaphragmatic "belly" breather. Sympathetic hyperarousal shifts breathing to the "chest" breathing pattern. Chest breathing is labored, and each breath is short. Most of the breathing muscles activating breath are the striated muscles of the chest and shoulder area. The large diaphragmatic smooth muscle is largely absent from breathing.

Table 4.1 provides an overview of the eight observations that evaluate whether the person is mainly a chest breather or a diaphragmatic breather. Observations that cluster in Column 1 on the form indicate a shallow, chest breathing pattern. Observations that cluster in Column 3 on the form indicate more of diaphragmatic breathing pattern. Patients whose observations are somewhere in between those two poles indicate a mixed picture of both patterns contributing to the overall breathing mechanics.

Understanding the balance between the sympathetic and parasympathetic systems is critical for the patient to understand early in the treatment. It provides the person with a snapshot of how their body's internal autonomic state is balanced. As well, tools that transform these patterns can be introduced to systematically create a more relaxing, parasympathetically dominant pattern. Patients can be taught to use diaphragmatic breathing to enable the shift from the awake state into sleep.

Assessment of the Current Breathing Pattern

The following edited transcript, an assessment of a patient we'll call Kelly, provides the rationale and the interactive attuned manner in which these breathing observations are conducted.

> THERAPIST: We are going to count how many breaths you take in 1 minute. This means you're letting your body breathe whatever way it needs to breathe. You're watching the breath happen. A count of one breath is both the exhale and inhale. So those two together make one complete breath. I'll tell you when to start counting and then when I say stop, you're going to tell me what number you got to. Any questions?
>
> Start counting. And stop.
>
> PATIENT: 21.
>
> THERAPIST: Next, I'm going to have us both stand up. You can watch what I'm doing. We're going to use our hands as a way of telling us where the breath is going. Your left hand is going to go up here on the chest. The sternum. That is the bony part up here. And your right hand is going on the belly. My belly button is here. Just above the belly button. Your legs are going to be bent at your knees a little bit. You're feeling solid on your feet. Now you'll take a couple of deep breaths. As you take breaths into and out of your lungs, I want you to see what movement you feel in

your left and right hands. Take a couple of breaths in and out and notice whether you can detect any movement in your hands.

Now if the hand that's on your chest moves, it will tend to move in a vertical direction: up and down. The hand that's on your belly, if it moves, will tend to move horizontally: in and out.

Commentary. Notice if the patient is comfortable or not. Engage them in discussing how they feel, if necessary. You may need to talk about the importance of tracking their breathing for their specific treatment goals. If the patient appears uncomfortable, ask what you can do to help them feel more comfortable.

THERAPIST: Take a couple of breaths, and tune into and notice where you feel the movement in either hand. When you begin to breathe in, you start your inbreath. Which hand is moving first?
PATIENT: My left.
THERAPIST: And secondly, when you take a full breath in, from beginning to end, which hand is moving most? Left, right, or both about the same?
PATIENT: Both are about the same.

Commentary. As the assessment continues, the therapist is observing the engagement of the patient. Is Kelly curious about her breathing? Does she follow the directions easily? When there are signs of confusion or lack of interest, we will pause and address her questions. If the patient is too stressed about doing the assessment, they will disengage from the process entirely. In some cases, it is helpful to pause the assessment and ask the patient how they are feeling. Does this remind them of anything that was difficult or aversive to them before?

THERAPIST: The next thing is to focus on the hand that's on your belly. When I start to breathe in, this hand could move in one of two directions. It can move inward toward the spine. Or it could move outward away from the spine. As you begin to breathe in, which direction does that hand start to move in?
PATIENT: It's barely moving in. Toward the spine. I'm feeling it slightly outwards. If I concentrate, I can feel it moving out.

Commentary. Providing time for the patient to sense what is happening in her body is very important. She is attending to the sensations carefully. In the beginning she felt the hand move inward. As she focused on the sensations, it began to shift outward. Attending to these shifts in experience is important. The patient's shallow chest breathing pattern released to a deeper belly breathing pattern as she made that observation.

THERAPIST: Moving out. Does it move out a little bit? Or noticeably?

PATIENT: All the breathing is not very noticeable to me. It's extremely shallow.
THERAPIST: The next thing is you're going to make two fists. And you're going to push the fists into your middle section here. Just below your lowest rib. There's a soft spot in there. I'm tucking the fists in there. As you breathe in and fill the lungs, I want you to tell me if you notice any movement in the fists themselves. They could move up, move inward, move out, or move downward.
PATIENT: Upward, the top I can feel it going up and down.
THERAPIST: When you breathe in, does the fist move up on the inbreath?
PATIENT: Yes. I can feel this better than the other way.

Commentary. The assessment focusses on multiple ways of tuning in to the physical sensations related to how her body is breathing. The fact that Kelly can notice that one way of feeling where her breath goes is better than another way also provides a sense that she is able to notice each of the signals and keep her observations in mind, to compare how each feels different for her. In this case, this observation suggests a chest breathing pattern, consistent with Kelly's first observation on the previous test. Inconsistencies and changes in breathing patterns do happen across the eight tests. Breathing is a dynamic process that can shift, with elements of both chest breathing and diaphragmatic breathing appearing.

THERAPIST: We are going to sit down again. There are a couple more questions. Across your day: morning, afternoon, and evening, do you find that you regularly take in an extra gulp of air? Some people call it a sighing breath or a yawning breath.
PATIENT: No, what I noticed sometimes is not breathing at all! Once in a while I catch myself when I've realized, "I'm holding my breath." I don't even know that I am.

Commentary. This spontaneous observation is quite important. Half or more of the chronic insomniacs I have assessed demonstrate this pattern of shallow breathing. Holding the breath is a normal part of the sympathetic system's alert response. It is the first vigilant response when facing an uncertain situation that could signal danger.

THERAPIST: And then the last thing. We'll do it together. We're going to fill and empty our lungs, 10 times, very quickly. Fill the lungs and empty them. It'll be like if you've run for the bus, and now you're trying to catch your breath. It's like panting to catch your breath.

I'm going to demonstrate it and then then we can do it together. So, it's going to look like this.

Ready and go.

Now here's the question: Do you feel lightheaded or dizzy?

PATIENT: I usually always feel dizzy and lightheaded. Lately. Even my daughter would say I feel so dizzy. It's been lately we've been seeing that. So, we're thinking, "Is it some kind of flu that's been ongoing for these past several months"?

Commentary. The sensation of dizziness in these 10 quick breaths comes from clearing out the carbon dioxide in the blood stream. Carbon dioxide travels in the blood as carbonic acid. When it is removed with quick breaths, the carbonic acid is eliminated from the blood, making the blood more basic. That shift in the pH balance of the blood is detected by the brain and the dizzy feeling starts.

Dizziness is a benign symptom. When patients report that the breathing exercises make them feel dizzy, I compliment them. "You were doing the exercises so well. The dizziness is your gold star for doing so well. Please know that it is a benign symptom. It is a signal that your body recognizes that your breathing has changed and is more efficient now. When you get the dizzy feelings, just stop that practice session. It will go away quickly. As you continue doing active breathing, this symptom will gradually disappear on its own."

There are many other reasons that Kelly might have felt dizzy for the past month. If this continues past the first week without change, you can suggest that she contact her physician to investigate it further.

Relaying the Results of the Assessment

THERAPIST: As we've been doing these eight observations, I've been keeping track of your answers. Each of these observations is in one of three columns: one, two, or three. The total tells us the type of breather you are. Column 1 is observations that show us you're mainly a chest breather. This is a pattern of shallow breathing. Column 3, the last column, means that you're breathing down into your belly. That is called being a belly breather. Kelly, four of your eight observations were in chest breathing column. Three were in the middle column, somewhere between chest and belly breathing. Only one observation indicated that you are mainly a belly breather.

You are probably wondering what this means. Briefly, when you're mainly a chest breather, that happens because you've been using the sympathetic system, the gas pedal, over and over. When the nervous system is constantly shifting into fight-or-flight mode, when you are stomping on the gas pedal, your breathing changes to the shallow, chest breathing pattern. That is how the brainstem prepares you for action. You also said that you notice that you stop breathing. That is actually the signature of an overactive sympathetic system.

The most important thing that I want to stress to you is that this is not "in your head." This is a change in your nervous system. It has shifted to a very, very hyperalert state. And I think the migraines have been another big consequence of that. Because migraines are triggered by chronic stress and that pain pushes the gas pedal even more. Once that gas pedal gets stuck in what we call hyperarousal, it's next to impossible to fall asleep. You can't lie there in bed and tell yourself to sleep when the gas pedal is pushed to the floor.

The good news is that you will benefit so much from the breathing exercises I am going to teach you. I will show you how to boost the parasympathetic system. We must get the brakes to start working again.

Commentary. The most important point in this review of her results is to relate the results of her breathing assessment to what these tell us about how her nervous system is functioning now. The therapist stresses that chest breathing is a normal part of hyperarousal. The second and more important message is that this pattern can be changed with a few weeks of practice.

The results of the assessment are also an invitation for the patient to start tuning into their breathing patterns and start paying attention to their body. As she changes her breathing pattern, she will boost parasympathetic activity and reduce sympathetic activity. The message that this can change within a few weeks is an invitation for the patient to become active in her own treatment. In summary, agency, attunement, and the promise of change are all key messages to deliver on reviewing the results of the breathing assessment.

Introduction to the Breathing Practice

THERAPIST: The muscle we will retrain is the diaphragmatic muscle. When you've been using the gas pedal it creates the state of hyperarousal. I see this over and over again with sleep patients. Often people have big problems with sleep because they've become stressed and tense, and this shows as the chest breather pattern. The good news is that with consistent practice it can change in 2 to 4 weeks.

Your nervous system has shifted your breathing into very shallow breaths. For that reason, you have to take lots of them. You took 21 breaths in a minute. Somebody who is really relaxed maybe takes half as many, 10 or 11 breaths in a minute.

Commentary. At this early point, you want the patient to understand that the breathing practice is a *retraining* of the muscles of active exhalation. The three muscle groups that work together on diaphragmatic breathing are the diaphragm, the intercostal muscles (between the ribs), and the abdominal core muscles (front of the belly). For the breathing pattern to change from shallow chest breathing to slow and deep belly breathing will require a few weeks of regular training practice.

THERAPIST: We want you to breathe better. To use more of the lungs, not just the little shallow breaths. When you do that, you fill your lungs with each breath. That boosts the parasympathetic system, boosting the braking system. And that will begin to bring the overactive gas pedal down, down, down.

This is going to take a few weeks. It's not like what I show you today, you do it, and then tomorrow you're going to say, "Wow, I am sleeping again." What we're doing is we're retraining the nervous system by using breathing as an effective tool. Some people call this kind of belly breathing diaphragmatic breathing.

THERAPIST: The diaphragmatic muscle is a huge muscle, one of the bigger muscles in the body. It goes all the way across the middle of your body. It's shaped like a parachute or an upside-down salad bowl. It's anchored to the lowest rib on both sides. And it is also anchored onto the spinal column. When the muscle contracts (and all muscles work by contracting) it flattens out.

That's the muscle that we want to work at getting the air into your lungs. Your assessment shows us that you can make a big improvement in how much you use that muscle. The lungs themselves are sitting right above that muscle, on top of it. Getting that muscle to pull the air into your lungs is what's going to make the most improvement in your breathing.

But the problem is that muscles are grouped into two kinds: striated and smooth. Striated muscles are ones you can consciously control, like deciding to raise your arm. The main difference between striated and smooth is that smooth muscles do not take orders from your thinking brain. Examples of smooth muscles are your heart, the diaphragm, and your arteries. Your thinking brain can't tell your heart, "Go faster." It's a smooth muscle.

Smooth muscles take orders from your autonomic nervous system and the brainstem, not from your thinking brain. The brainstem is at the base of the brain. This is what controls your heart rate, the blood pressure in your arteries, and it controls your breathing with the diaphragmatic muscle.

I'm going to teach you how to retrain your breathing. But we can't directly tell that diaphragmatic muscle to work harder. What we can do is focus more on the exhale, on blowing the air out. How do we do that? What are the muscle groups that push the air out of the lungs? Those are your *abdominal core muscles*. The abdominal core muscles consist of five sets of muscles located here on the front of your body. Between your ribs and down to the hips. When those muscles contract, you are exhaling. As you blow the air out, you are pushing the diaphragmatic muscle up to get it ready to pull the air in on the next inhale. When I'm doing a good job of exhaling, these abdominal muscles are tightening and getting the diaphragm ready to do a better job on the next inhale.

To activate these core muscles, purse your lips and blow out through that small opening. Some people call this "straw breathing." If I had a drinking straw in my mouth and I was pushing the air through that straw, I would make a whistling sound as I blow that air out.

PATIENT: So as I blow out, they're contracting.

THERAPIST: Do you hear that? That sound you're making. What makes that sound for you are these abdominal muscles that are pushing the air out.

These belly muscles are all contracting. And when they contract, they are pushing that diaphragmatic muscle up so it will be ready to breathe in. Focus on controlling the exhale, doing a really good job of the exhale, so we can get the diaphragmatic muscle ready to do a better job of the next inhale.

PATIENT: So, it's important to exhale properly. If I exhale properly and I contract that muscle, it's going to force the diaphragmatic muscle to expand upwards.

Commentary. After the therapist demonstrates where to put the hands and how to make the breaths, and shows a video, Kelly now appreciates the mechanics of proper breathing. She practices the exhale as I explain it. There is an attunement between therapist and patient. The therapist makes a playful comment aimed at highlighting that good things can happen in the treatment. Kelly does not respond directly to this, but she realizes she is learning more than she anticipated. In an important moment in this session, Kelly asks for exercises to practice on her own.

THERAPIST: Now I know why you didn't want to come for treatment in the beginning. It's because you've done probably everything you've read about. And nothing has worked. The breathing is not the whole answer, but it is an important part of the answer. And you will start doing that more effectively.

Commentary. The therapist brings up Kelly's reluctance to attend the session in the beginning. This is meant to provide an opportunity to assess any residual resistance to treatment and to allow Kelly to talk about any concerns she may still have about treatment.

PATIENT: I see I have not been breathing right. I haven't been breathing at all. I'm so shocked.

THERAPIST: Because you noticed that you often stop breathing. You've never activated that diaphragmatic pump: that lung space to use it effectively. It's like you've been driving around in a car with a gas pedal and no brakes.

Commentary. The review of the assessment and its implication for starting a process of change has engaged the patient. At this point she is enthusiastic about what she is learning and is excited about the prospect of continuing with treatment. Kelly's full attention and her improved motivation are both essential to getting through the details of breathing practice. The therapist then walks Kelly through how to do the breathing exercises on her own that week.

The Mechanics of Therapeutic Breathing

To get the diaphragmatic muscle engaged and functioning at a higher level, because it's a smooth muscle and we can't directly make it work, we need to exhale.

Most of us breathe in and out through our nose. The mouth is closed. And we're breathing through the nose and that's comfortable. That is the way we are designed to breathe. But if we do that, we can't really use that exhale. We want to get that exhale to be better. To do that, we have to exhale through pursed lips. When you make that small opening, like pushing the air through a drinking straw, two things happen. The first thing is that making the opening small, you're going to make the exhale longer, right? The second is that you make a noticeable sound, which gives you feedback about whether you are doing the exhale correctly.

The breathing in is through the nose, then there's a pause, then exhaling through pursed lips, and then at the end of it, another pause.

The other thing that we want to do is we don't want to have the breath up here in the chest as much and we want to get the abdominal and diaphragmatic muscles working together and doing more of the work. What we can do for that is isolate the belly muscles, so we don't cheat and use those chest muscles. *It is best to do the breathing exercises lying down on the floor.* The therapist demonstrates by lying down on the floor. The patient needs to see exactly how it is done. Most patients will also lie down and practice along with the therapist. That is the best way to see and mirror the patient's practice.

You can lie down on a couch as an alternative. It's important to have your knees up, because when your legs and feet are flat on the ground, it puts tension on the lower abdomen. You can feel tightness there. So your abdomen isn't working 100% on the breath. When you put the knees up, you're relaxing all these abdominal core muscles, because these are the ones that you want to use for the exhale. They are going to be pushing the air out better.

Breathe in through the nose, pause, and then out through the mouth. Now because we don't want the shoulders and the chest to be as involved in the breathing. What we're going to do is put our arms above our head. When the chest is already fully extended, all the breathing must come from the belly. Demonstration of the proper posture is essential to proper technique. Knees should be up to relax the abdomen and arms should be above the head, to isolate the abdominal and diaphragmatic muscles. Both therapist and patient can be lying down. The therapist can take the posture that the patient is demonstrating. This can help in understanding blockages to feeling into the breathing practice. Experiencing what the patient is experiencing is most important in teaching this psychomotor skill to patients.

Many patients require more time to get comfortable with the posture and steps in the breathing practice. If there are no questions, the therapist can take 2 minutes to do the breathing practice together with the patient, mirroring the pace of the breathing. The sense of comfort in relaxing, doing the exercises, and in reaching a point of feeling enjoyment with the practice by the end are also very important.

When the whistling sound of the exhalation comes out evenly all the way through, the abdominal core muscles are engaged.

Completion of the demonstration is arrived at when the patient understands the rhythm of the cycle. Ask them to demonstrate in their own breathing that their abdominal core is fully engaged in the exhale, and that the inhale is actively moving the belly up, with little or no movement of the chest and shoulders. The experience of doing the breathing together, mirroring the patient's breathing posture and pattern, provides an initial experience of attuning to the autonomic reactivity of the patient.

Limit the practice to 5–10 breaths only. All chest breathers must start slowly. There are many potential problems if they try to do too much. They may strain some muscles and get aches and pains. They may get very uncomfortable with the new relaxed feeling and have a *paradoxical reaction*. A paradoxical reaction means that the new state of relaxation is experienced as too novel and disturbing. Their nervous systems activate the flight-or-fight response, and they begin to think that the breathing is not working for them. In the first week of practice, you want the patient to do a steady amount of practice, so they can begin to get comfortable with the practice, but not experience any setbacks. In the next follow-up appointment, the therapist can adjust the amount of practice, but only after the patient has been given a chance to do their best in a comfortable way.

It will probably take a week or two before the patient notices the benefit on their sleep in making it a little easier to fall asleep.

Doing the practice six or seven times across the day will give better results than once a day. The more retraining, the quicker the nervous system shifts and flips back and gets that braking system operating. The therapist closes the session with a clear statement of the practice goals. This is also a place where you can ask the patient how many times a day, they think they can do the practice. Once they offer a number that they think is possible, you can ask them how confident they are that they will be able to do that every day.

Summary of Clinical Issues Emerging From Active Attunement to Breathing

From the preceding transcript, there are several important messages for therapists. Attending to the patient's breathing pattern early in treatment provides a rich opportunity for (1) the therapist to attune to the patient's autonomic nervous system, (2) the patient to begin to link their physical sensations of tension (chest breathing) with the hyperaroused state, (3) the patient to start feeling the release of that tension with breathing practice, and (4) the patient to understand that they have the power to make that transition happen (agency).

Dan Siegel (2015b) has provided an important way to understand the attunement process in therapy. Earlier we identified the three stages he highlighted in the attunement to patient's affective challenges: tracking, alignment, and resonance. Identifying distress early in a session is an important way to set the stage for the emergence of feelings:

> Emotional resonance . . . involves more than the alignment of states; it also includes the ways in which the interaction affects the individuals in other aspects of their minds. . . . The mutual influence of the alignment of states persists within the mind of each member after direct interaction no longer occurs. (pp. 313–314)

The importance of this experience of hope is what Dan Siegel highlighted as the emotional resonance of patient and therapist. This is what builds the therapeutic alliance for the next stages of the therapy.

What Role Does Active Attunement Play in Managing Sleep Disturbances?

Without active attunement by the therapist to a patient's distressed state, emotional resonance does not occur. Each time such resonance is achieved, there is a partial resolution of the previously aversive memories that have fueled the hyperarousal related to those memories. Bringing these overwhelming experiences to focus, in the context of safety and alignment, provides the opportunities to experience emotional resonance in the shared relationship. This gradually affords increasing trust in the other and a more secure internal sense of security. As this grows, the improved emotional modulation and positive self-assurance of the patient can be used directly in preparing for sleep. Being alone does not feel anywhere as dangerous for the patient.

At the end of the day, when we turn out the lights, we must have the emotional capacity to feel comfortable in our own skins. No fears or worries. No sense of abandonment or betrayal. If we can achieve a state of comfort and accomplishment, looking back at the day just ending, and find the moments of growth and personal significance, and sit with those positive experiences, we can activate that rest-and-digest system. That inner confidence allows us to welcome sleep when it decides to arrive.

APPLICATION

To make effective use of the information you have been reading, we invite you to apply the concepts described in this chapter by engaging patients with these important steps to learning skills that will help in retraining their sleep patterns:

Conduct a Few Behavioral Assessments of Breathing: The first step in using the breathing assessment is to start with yourself. Conduct all eight steps of the assessment. Then complete the process with a friend or family member. That should give you a good sense of what you are doing in completing the assessment. Most people complete the assessment in 15 minutes or less.

To engage a patient in an assessment, start with someone with high anxiety or panic. They are usually happy to hear there is something not involving medications they can do to manage their anxiety.

Review the Results of the Assessments: Describe how belly breathing is different from chest breathing. Be able to describe chest breathing as a normal consequence of distress. You could show the patient a video on how the diaphragmatic muscle works. That muscle is what the exercises are meant to activate and strengthen.

Demonstrate Therapeutic Breathing: Practice the breathing exercises first yourself. When you are confident in doing the exercises, try teaching a friend or family member. Describe the mechanics of inhaling and exhaling to transform chest breathing to belly breathing. Demonstrate how to do the breathing lying down or leaning over a desk.

Key Messages for Therapists

1. Active attunement is a reciprocal, affect-focused stance in the therapeutic interaction that permits a deeper sense of understanding each other's internal experiences. The patient feels felt, which provides a feeling of safety that allows previously overwhelming feelings to emerge.
2. A brief interactive breathing assessment engages the patient in looking inward to notice how they are breathing. Results of the assessment help the therapist and patient both to feel and understand their current autonomic balance point. Sympathetic hyperarousal shifts breathing to the shallow "chest" breathing pattern, characterized by quick, short breaths that perpetuate the SNS hyperarousal.
3. Chest breathers can be taught to use breathing practice to boost the parasympathetic brake. Chest breathers who practice the retraining breathing exercises regularly will notice a shift to diaphragmatic breathing within 2–3 weeks (depending on frequency of practice and the level of imbalance). With greater awareness of the breath and practice, shallow chest

breathers transform to deeper diaphragmatic breathers, allowing for the balancing of the SNS and PNS systems.
4. When active attunement is used to connect with patient's internal states it leads to alignment of therapist and patient and permits a deeper exploration of emotional states. These boost the conscious and unconscious therapeutic alliance between patient and therapist.
5. In facing these previously overwhelming feeling states directly, the patient begins to have the internal experience of these aversive feelings changing: negative internal states can begin to calm down, more positive feelings can emerge unexpectedly, and more positive experiences of self (enduring mental models of security) can be restored or emerge de novo.
6. The TABS model of trauma assessment and sleep repair treatment approach considers both active attunement and diaphragmatic breathing as essential components of working with trauma patients. Restorative sleep cannot be achieved without boosting the parasympathetic system prior to sleep. The combination of using diaphragmatic breathing and resolution of pre-sleep aversive states through trauma work are both necessary.

5

The Yawning Breath: Teaching Agency

"Breathing is exquisitely sensitive to the condition of safety and threat, and it is neurophysiologically linked to the behavioral response modes [of safety and threat] . . . An effortful breath therefore, is a diagnostic indicator of the emotions and sensations that have been suppressed by current and past situations of threat, as well as emotions that may be suppressed in the moment, but not yet part of embodied self awareness."

—Alan Fogel (2013, pp. 234–235)

"Yawning is powerful and pleasurable action, the experience of which can reach deep into our bodies and activate an emergent awareness of how we feel . . . yawning stimulates the afferent pathways of the parasympathetic nervous system."

—Alan Fogel (2013, p. 227)

When the therapist mindfully observes the patient's breath patterns, this provides invaluable therapeutic insight into the physical, emotional, and mental state of the traumatized client. Throughout the therapeutic session, breathing patterns can vary significantly: from the terrified freeze response of holding one's breath, to the short, shallow breaths of a fight or flight state, and finally to the slow rhythmic breaths that come after the release of traumatic material. After deep emotional release clients will often feel sleepy and yawn, denoting an activation of the parasympathetic nervous system. "Yawning activates many muscles, stimulates breathing, enhances the flow of hormones such as oxytocin and neurotransmitters like serotonin, which increase feelings of well-being and pleasure" (Fogel, 2009, p. 227).

Breathing pattern as a barometer of how safe or how threatened we feel is a direct expression of the contributions of the two arms of our autonomic nervous system. The activity of the sympathetic nervous system (SNS, or the *fight-flight-freeze* reaction) is evident in the activity of the *phrenic nerve,* and the activity of the parasympathetic (PNS, or *rest and digest* response) is evident in the activity of the *vagus nerve.* The activation of the vagus nerve allows for the dampening of phrenic nerve activity, thus acting like a *vagal brake* to the autonomic system (ANS). In addition to being clearly visible in the way the body is breathing as you conduct your session, it is also reflected in the respiratory sinus arrhythmia (RSA), not seen, but powerfully important in reflecting the overall state of health and well-being.

RSA is a normal alteration in cardiac rhythm generated from the stimulation of the vagus nerve and changes in cardiac-filling pressures during respiration. A healthy heart rate is not constant. It increases when you breathe in and decreases when you breathe out. Slowing your breath, and extending the out-breath, increases the time between heartbeats and increases your RSA.

BREATHING WHEN SAFE

The following is a clinical example of a patient who has reached a state of safety in the therapeutic process. In this example, I am sitting down to do a follow-up session with a patient who resolved his family conflicts in sessions that ended more than a year ago. As he opens his video link, I am greeted by a warm smile and a hearty welcome. He is sitting in his den, the familiar setting from which he joined me for his sessions. Nothing has changed in the room and space around him. However, much has changed in what I am seeing in him. He smiles broadly. He is leaning toward me and appears eager to tell me what he has been doing.

His breaths are slow, deep, and measured. His chest is relaxed. A feeling of calm is palpable from his relaxed features. As he begins to tell me more, there is a feeling of being fully engaged. There is nothing rushed about how he begins. He comments on how quickly the time has flown and is smiling broadly at the prospect of spending the next hour reflecting on his life. His body is relaxed but engaged. His face has color, and the facial features shift and change as he relates different experiences.

What is supporting this clinical presentation in the example? In a word, safety. When we are safe, there is a steady and enduring balance between the SNS and PNS contributions to breath. The phrenic nerve activates the muscles of respiration as required. The impulse to inhale begins with the strong contraction of the diaphragm (the large muscle at the base of the lungs), which brings air into the deepest part of the lower lung space. From that foundation, the muscular cascade moves up the torso, recruiting the dorsal intercostal muscles (located between each of the ribs that encircle the lungs). This ripple effect continues ascending the torso, now recruiting the accessory muscles (around the neck, shoulders, and chest), which complete the inbreath into the top of the lungs. Each breath in is relaxed and each exhale is slow, steady, and complete.

Also when we are safe, the breath is not hurried, and the heartbeat is slowed and steady. There is ample time to pause after both inhalation and exhalation. You can gauge the depth of each breath from the slow, steady rhythm of the breath. The parasympathetic contribution of the vagal nerve is actively modulating the hurried insistence of the phrenic nerve to rush to the next inhalation.

When vagal and phrenic activity are balanced, our RSA is increased, and our subjective internal state is pleasant, warm, flexible, and playful. In this state we are more open to connection with others, resulting in release of oxytocin and the very gratifying experience of surrendering to the experience of being immobilized, but without fear or apprehension.

Breathing and heart rate work in concert to support these internal states. The heart's sinoatrial (SA) node maintains a regular rhythm of heartbeats through its intrinsic pacemaker activity. Under conditions of safety, the vagal nerve releases acetylcholine, which binds to muscarinic receptors on the SA node, slowing down the heart rate. Under conditions of danger, sympathetic activation releases noradrenaline, which overrides the PNS and accelerates the pumping of the heart.

BREATHING WHEN IN DANGER

An example of the opposite of feeling safe is the following clinical example. I am sitting down for a consultation session with someone who has sought treatment for sleep problems that began many years ago and have gotten so bad in the past 2 years that she has trouble functioning now on most days. She is sitting in her living room. Her body is tensed and barely moving. Her voice is squeaky and tight. I invite her to begin, and she bites her lip and pauses. It appears that she has stopped breathing. I can't detect any movement in her chest and shoulders. Then they engage and there is a visible awkward movement of her upper torso.

This pattern of short staccato breaths punctuated by complete cessations of breath is a hallmark of the chronic insomniac. How does this pattern of chronically tense breathing begin? And how does it progress to this state of rigid inflexibility in the breathing muscles?

Breathing responds instantly to a neuroceptive shift from safety to danger. The appearance of a social or physical threat is first perceived in the brainstem at the level of the superior colliculi, which integrates the incoming sensory information. These signals of danger are relayed to the periaqueductal gray (PAG) and the locus coeruleus (LC), which activate and coordinate a cascade of biobehavioral responses to ensure survival. These orchestrated responses include the options of fight-flight-freeze as immediate responses to the danger.

A central part of the biobehavioral danger response is to accelerate breathing in order to provide the necessary aerobic energy boost required to escape danger. This is accomplished by the dual action of increased SNS firing and withdrawal of the PNS firing. The surge in SNS activity through the sympathetic-adrenal medulla axis provides neural activation that is reinforced by the dumping of adrenaline into the bloodstream. This accelerates heart rate and breathing. The withdrawal of the PNS vagal brake on the heart results in an instant increase of heart rate from about 70 beats per minute (bpm) to 105 bpm.

Other physiological mechanisms also support this instant heightened defensive response, allowing for a continuation of the defensive capability to escape from danger (for more detail, see Fogel, 2013). The combined impact of these more persistent states is chronic muscle tension, which is always associated with chronic thoracic-diaphragmatic muscle tension. Muscle tension in these muscles means patterns of chest breathing during the daytime, as well as hyperarousal across the nightly sleep time.

In parallel with changes in respiration are changes in heart rate. The SA node on the heart (the natural pacemaker of the heart) responds instantly to the sympathetic surge. Sympathetic activity enhances its depolarization rate, which speeds up the pumping of the heart. In parallel with this, the increased sympathetic activity also accelerates the conduction of electrical signals through the AV node, which decreases the delay between contractions of the atrium and the ventricle. This increases the heart rate, and sympathetic activation also improves the strength of the contractions of the heart. All of these changes accelerate the speed, strength, and endurance of the pumping action of the heart. Together, the action of the sympathetic system on the SA and AV nodes reduces the time between heartbeats, which shrinks the RSA.

When the stresses activating these stress responses continue week after week, month after month, and year after year, the musculature of the entire body ratchets up in preparation for the next shoe to drop. Surveillance is continuous and the breathing patterns get stuck. This shift from occasional to chronic preparedness for danger happens with little or no conscious awareness. Very few patients who consult me have any awareness of how much their breathing has veered off course due to a stress-related contracted diaphragm, resulting in shallow breathing. The result is that the body's reliable resource that would help to dissolve daily stresses has been hijacked to become an inflexible rapid taskmaster that locks bodies in perpetual distress and contracted musculature.

REVERSING EMBODIED CHRONIC STRESS

Reversing these chronically stressed breathing patterns is indeed possible, usually within a few weeks. The key to reversing this chronic stress is understanding that the stress is not just being held in the muscles of respiration, but indeed is held in all the muscles of the body. The stress response activates the whole body for response to danger, so all muscle groups are tonically tensed.

Reversal of these patterns of chronic stress in both the thoracic-diaphragmatic muscle as well as the many coordinated muscle groups that together orchestrate inhalation happens in stages. The first step is accurately identifying the problem of shallow chest breathing for the patient. The second step is introduction of breathing exercises that begins to overcome the chest breathing by actively recruiting the diaphragm and resynchronizing the orchestra of breathing muscles from the shallow stressed breathing pattern to the deep diaphragmatic pattern (these steps are reviewed in Chapter 4).

The third step is practicing the longer, deeper breaths for longer periods. The fourth step is slowing the breaths down to five breaths a minute. The fifth step is activating whole body breathing. One way that whole body breathing can be implemented clinically is to begin using what is called the *yawning breath*. This chapter will guide the therapist to reliably direct patients to achieve these reversals in danger-based (fight-flight-freeze) breathing patterns.

How can these changes be introduced in a way that helps the patient unlock these physically locked muscles? The key is attention to the exhalation. Exhalation activates relaxation. However, it is usually a passive process that follows from the relaxation of the muscles involved in inhalation. Muscles that can be directly recruited to mobilize exhalation include the expiratory abdominal core muscles and the lateral intercostal muscles. Activating these muscle groups transforms passive expiration to an actively relaxing process. As we continue to activate exhalation, we boost the activity of the PNS, resulting in a shift in the overall balance between the SNS and the PNS.

Respiratory sinus arrhythmia (RSA) begins to increase. As it increases, bodily sensations of relaxation and calm are triggered. For most people, these internal states of calm are relaxing and help to ground them in a sense of contentment. However, these internal states of calm may themselves be triggers for anticipated states of abandonment or abuse. These paradoxical reactions to relaxation take a little longer to resolve, but they are predictable, and most patients learn to overcome them when guided to understanding what their bodies are doing.

Clinically, the introduction of a grounding strategy must be addressed carefully. Observing the individual reactions of the patient to these states is critically important to the continuing benefit of the intersubjective field between you and your patient.

This chapter focuses on the interventions that help the therapist guide the trauma patient to activate the vagal brake and improve their access to states of relaxation and calm. These interventions are designed to allow the patient to access an embodied sense of calm, which is an entirely new awareness of self. It is a deeply satisfying moment-to-moment physical experience, without any intrusion of cognition that evaluates, criticizes, or questions.

What I will learn in this chapter to become a better sleep and trauma therapist:
1. All persistent psychological and physical threats lead to chronic muscle tension that includes increased tension in the diaphragmatic muscle. This increased tension serves the purpose of responding to danger. It is

The Yawning Breath: Teaching Agency 107

     easier for the diaphragm to contract on inhale, which provides support for sympathetic activation under threat, but locks the breather into a state of hyperarousal.
2. To know the cycle of respiratory inhalation and exhalation and use this knowledge to direct patients to use voluntary control of breathing to effectively boost PNS activity, reduce hyperarousal, restore ANS balance, and facilitate the restorative functions of sleep and digestion.
3. To be able to describe the rationale for the yawning breath and guide your patient through a 10-minute experiential exercise demonstrating how to do the yawning breath.
4. To troubleshoot the problems that patients have in adopting the yawning breath into their pre-sleep routines and in using the yawning breath to return to sleep if awakened in the middle of the night.
5. To understand the importance of integrating body relaxation strategies into your work with your patients. These can include teaching: yoga, progressive muscle relaxation, or autogenic training. Regular practice will promote whole body breathing. Integrating these into a wind-down routine prior to bedtime is particularly effective.

CLINICAL APPLICATION OF THE YAWNING BREATH

In Chapter 4 we introduced how to conduct a breathing assessment and demonstrated diaphragmatic breathing as a way of attuning to your patient's internal experiences. As your patient learns to breathe with the diaphragm down into the belly, it provides them with a means of regulating their own nervous system. In this chapter we start that process and build on that foundation. We begin by reviewing how to manage the inevitable difficulties of finding time to practice breathing.

Experiential Review of Diaphragmatic Breathing Exercises

All requests made of patients to find time to do exercises across the week, between therapy sessions, are likely to have marginal success at first. As these new behaviors are not already in the patient's habit repertoire, they need to have a clear and self-evident higher value than the comfort of continuing to do what they have always done. In fact, it is probably good clinical practice to assume that the patient has done little or no practice between sessions.

    The solution to this difficulty in adhering to the treatment plan is engaging the patient in a *tracking, tuning in, shifting, repeating* protocol. The first step is tracking: that is, becoming aware of the times that they are shallow breathing. The second is tuning in to the experience of the breath moment to moment. Third, shifting their breath into the belly. Fourth, this sequence is then repeated to retrain and synchronize the breathing muscles.

When patients do report any effort to include the new behaviors it is important to probe into how they engaged in the exercises, when they did them, and what they felt on completion of the practice. The review of breathing exercises should be experiential, not descriptive. Just asking what the patient did will not uncover the difficulties that are emerging for the patient while doing the exercises. The review of what they are doing must include demonstrations of how they are breathing, not just what they are doing. These principles are illustrated in the following case.

> THERAPIST: Let's start with an update. At our last session we introduced diaphragmatic breathing. What have you been able to do?
> PATIENT: I have consistently used the technique every day. It still is not an instinctive thing for me to remember. It does help when I do it. I'm not starting that quick enough, but it's gotten better the last 2 nights.
>
> It's becoming more normal for me to do it. But I'd like to introduce it throughout the course of the day. Maybe even having a stretch break. That's what I'm planning to put into my schedule. For now it has to be more deliberate. I am trying to do the breathing around 2 p.m. I need to see if I could integrate that more often.

Commentary. His description of his practice includes many conflicting messages. On the one hand he says that it helps when he does it. On the other hand he says he is not starting quickly enough, that it is not instinctive yet, and he has only been able to do the breathing once a day. This frequency of practice is not enough to retrain the breathing muscles. Most of this session will focus on introducing more information and suggestions to help the patient follow through with their stated objective of being more deliberate about the practice.

> PATIENT: I've also had a couple of nights of severe insomnia.
> THERAPIST: From your sleep diary, there is one night you were up for almost 2 ½ hours.
> PATIENT: That's the norm. I have to put a deliberate, conscientious effort into altering that pattern. It is going to take some time, I know.
> THERAPIST: We'll figure out how to intervene deliberately. As you start to notice what is going on, you can start to change it. We'll introduce some specific things you can begin to do for yourself to derail that pattern. Because you're right, it's an automatic pattern that your nervous system has learned. And it has a long history of many decades. But derailing it is possible, and I do not think it will take a lot of time. It does mean doing something deliberately. In a different way. In a healthier way. Diaphragmatic breathing is a very important part of how to derail it.
>
> So let's get into how to deliberately derail that internalization and severe insomnia pattern. Let's go a little bit deeper into the diaphragmatic

The Yawning Breath: Teaching Agency

breathing. You said it has become more normal. When you do the breathing, can you walk me through exactly what you are doing? And across the day, is this something you do once or twice? What's happening?

Commentary. The therapist asks the patient to demonstrate how he is doing the breathing. This is critical. This is an experiential, not descriptive, review.

PATIENT: No, I'm going to have to actually schedule breaks for that. Because it's not happening. Every day I say, "I'll take a few minutes to do that." But I haven't. So I've only done it at night before I go to sleep.

During that process I lie back on the bed and stretch my arms out. And inhaling and exhaling for 5 to 7 minutes or so. To see how I'm feeling. And it has helped. It has helped enormously to get that stress realigned. It feels like a cleansing process.

What I'm aiming for is good sleep hygiene. Where I look to my sleep diary and have some confidence that I am taking the steps that get me better sleep. Of just releasing myself to sleep. That is very new. It's different for me.

So, as I said, I have to continue with that. That's really what my goal is. Am I going to stick with it? I'm building the commitment to that. So doing that every day. I hope that will become a habit for me, right? Something more natural.

THERAPIST: I think the key phrase in what you just said is "building the commitment." When you're doing the exercise, what you're doing is training those muscle groups to work together. To work in a different way. They have to learn that.

From your breathing assessment you are a chest or shallow breather. So the chest muscles are kicking in too early. That is not allowing the deeper, diaphragmatic breath to happen.

The reason we want you to lie down, and especially putting your arms above your head, is that you remove the chest and shoulder muscles from the inhale. Because you have lifted up the shoulders and the ribs you can't cheat and use these muscles to breathe in. You prevent the use of the chest breathing, which opens the door for the diaphragmatic muscle. The diaphragm has not been working for you, but now you are giving those muscles the opportunity to bring air into the lower part of the lungs.

The therapist underlines retraining the breathing musculature and links the patient's assessment result to why this is necessary. The therapist takes every opportunity to engage the patient in observing their breathing pattern. The therapist walks through each element of the breathing practice, underlining how it is important to pay attention to each facet in a conscious way. The therapist repeatedly draws the patient's awareness to his physical sensations. When the therapist slows down the process and describes each component of the inbreath and outbreath, the patient can begin to notice what his body is doing.

> PATIENT: I don't cough generally. But I find when I do these exercises, I am coughing.

The patient begins to understand that repetition is needed to retrain muscles. And he adds an important observation, namely that he had a coughing response as he had been practicing this week. The coughing activated intense health anxieties, which likely significantly reduced his willingness to practice.

The therapist needs to be vigilant for other signs of procrastination or avoidance behaviors. He moves on to engaging the patient in actually planning for success by scheduling regular practice.

The therapist has the patient think carefully about how he might realistically include the breathing exercises into his day. He also notes the plan so his success or difficulties with making that happen can be reviewed next session.

Boosting Motivation to Do Diaphragmatic Breathing

The key to boosting motivation is to teach the patient moment to moment that they have the power to change their breath. Here is the sequence:

**The Power to Change Your Breath → Rebalances your ANS →
Creates a New Internal State of Rest and Restore →
Arriving at Deeper Better Quality Sleep**

It was only by having engaged the patient in an experiential review of his breathing practice did the problems that would have undermined his progress actually became known. Asking him to demonstrate his practice is what allowed a better understanding of a number of difficulties. Firstly, he was minimizing his difficulties in starting to do the practice. Next, he divulged the unexpected problem with coughing (which had not been mentioned earlier). Then bringing his awareness to breathing as retraining helped him see the practice in a new way. Finally, engaging him in setting up a regular schedule for the retraining empowered him to change.

Once the patient is motivated to continue with the regular use of diaphragmatic breathing exercises, it is helpful to provide a clear explanation of how such regular practice can change their sleep and stress problems. So how does the mechanical action of breathing actually calm your nervous system? What follows are the main points you want to make to the patient.

When you fill your lungs, two things are brought into the lungs: air and blood. At the end of the inhale, you have about 900 milliliters of blood in the lung space. Now, the key to calming your nerves is exhaling slowly. Making the

The Yawning Breath: Teaching Agency

"whwhwhwhwhwh" sound right to the end of the exhale engages all your core muscles. Exhaling this way results in only about 200 milliliters of blood left in the lung. So from 900 milliliters at the start of the inhale to 200 at the end of the exhale, you have pushed about 700 milliliters of blood out from the lung. In contrast, chest breathing only pushes out half that amount.

That exhaled larger volume of blood goes out into the artery. While most arteries in the body do not sense expanding or contracting with these surges of blood. The exception is the carotid arteries, up in your neck, which have stretch receptors embedded in the smooth muscle of the artery. Those stretch receptors measure whether the artery is expanding or contracting. The stretch receptors in the carotid arteries tell the brain how much oxygen and glucose are arriving.

Exhaling more completely pushes more blood, and more nutrients, up to the brain. When the brain feels nourished, it activates the parasympathetic brake, to slow the heart. The message to slow the heart is sent by the vagus nerve, the tenth cranial nerve. It goes to the SA and AV nodes on the heart, as well as to the coronary arteries. The parasympathetic signal to the SA node slows down your heart rate. The signal to the AV node increases the pause between the atrial and ventricular contractions. And the signal to the coronary arteries allows them to dilate and provide more blood to the heart. The result is a slower, more relaxed heartbeat and a deeper feeling of calm.

So when you're doing the breathing, visualize that you are engaging your brakes (the PNS). Every breath you take is getting the heart to slow down. But it only happens with the exhalation. The nickname for the parasympathetic is the *rest and digest* system. And the *rest* means you need that parasympathetic brake working in order for you to get to sleep at night.

Up to now you have not been activating the PNS. It is the gas pedal, the sympathetic that remains turned on. It is keeping you thinking and keeping your brain going a mile a minute. The result is that you stay up for 2½ hours, waiting for sleep.

Transitioning From Diaphragmatic Breathing to the Yawning Breath

It is only after the patient has been able to shift their shallow, chest breathing pattern to a diaphragmatic breathing pattern, that you can introduce the yawning breath. For most chest breathers that takes about 2 weeks. It depends entirely on the amount of practice the patient can put in. Practicing four to six times a day will speed up the transition. However, some patients have paradoxical reactions, and these have to be worked through before introducing the yawning breath.

In this next vignette, we demonstrate the usual procedure of identifying an opportune moment when the patient is asking for help with their poor sleep.

Once the focus of the session is on difficulties with falling asleep or staying asleep, the therapist introduces the yawning breath as an intervention to improve sleep.

> THERAPIST: When you say you are tired all the time, when did that start? Did it get worse gradually or suddenly?
>
> PATIENT: It has been a gradual process over the last year or more. It has been a very stressful year. It beat me up quite a bit.
>
> THERAPIST: So your sleep declined gradually and has not snapped back. You are still tired.

Introducing the Rationale of the Yawning Breath

> Our physiology has a built-in mechanism to bring us back to ourselves. So, the next time you yawn, notice not only how it feels good and stimulating, but also that it draws your attention to become more fully present in your body. (Fogel, 2013, p. 227)

The rationale for yawning breath builds on earlier discussion with the patient about diaphragmatic breathing. If this discussion has not already been had, the therapist can begin with that review (see Chapter 4). Once the patient has completed the Breathing Assessment and been guided to using those breathing exercises to access PNS responses, the following discussion will be possible.

> THERAPIST: There's a way of using breathing that can help you get back to sleep. This way of breathing will start you yawning. It creates an automatic reflex of yawning. I call it "the yawning breath." It is especially helpful if you are waking up repeatedly through the night. Many patients I work with are pretty wired, so they can wake up every hour.
>
> When we go to sleep at night, we have to shift from the daytime gas pedal to the brakes. The gas pedal (SNS) gives us energy to do things during the day. But at night we have to take our foot off the gas pedal and put on the brakes. That means activating the PNS, or the rest and digest system.
>
> Engaging that PNS means slowing the body down. Slowing metabolism down. And starting the digestive process. All of us naturally yawn toward the end of the day. That is a signal that the PNS is being activated. It is like your body is pushing the brake pedal in order to slow you down. So that you can lie down in bed and nod off to sleep.
>
> Learning how to engage the yawning breath will help you get to sleep. Not just at the end of the day, but also when you wake up at four, five, or six in the morning. You know you're not fully rested then, so you can do the yawning breath for 2 or 3 minutes. It doesn't take a lot of time.

The Yawning Breath: Teaching Agency

But you do have to do enough to activate the three signals of parasympathetic activation—yawning, salivation, tearing—that that tells you that your PNS is working. Then all you need to do is find a comfortable position, to get back to sleep. Notice that your body is calm. Then be curious about your body sensations, *not* whether you are going to fall asleep or not. You do not have to fall asleep. There is no rush to fall asleep. Just create a good internal state. One that is going to make falling asleep easier.

You are not trying to force yourself to sleep. You are just applying the braking system until you get those three signals. Then you relax and see what happens.

Even as a therapist, I use the yawning breath myself. I wake up in the middle of the night too. Half the time, when I do the yawning breath myself, I am asleep within 10 minutes. The other half of the time I will be awake for longer: 20 minutes, sometimes for an hour or so. I have learned to use the yawning breath so that my *thinking brain* does not kick back in. If your thinking mind does kick back in, you will not get back to sleep.

Describing the Mechanics of the Yawning Breath

THERAPIST: The yawning breath builds on the diaphragmatic breathing we have already done. We learned to breathe in through the nose. We're bringing the air down to the belly. We are filling the lung, and then pausing. The pause is very important. When you are trying to sleep you are slowing everything down.

Because it's nighttime, you don't need a lot of air. Your metabolism is slower. Your in- and out-breaths can be slower and longer. Both are very gradual. Pauses are longer.

And the exhale starts exactly the way I taught you. Make that small opening by pursing your lips and then exhaling. Blow the air out slowly. And you are making that exhalation sound all the way through. The sound is telling you that you're engaging your abdominal core muscles.

The one thing that the yawning breath adds to that exhale is tensing up your lower body. As you are blowing the air out through your pursed lips, you are also tensing up your lower body. From your belly button down to your toes. Tense up all of those lower body muscles. That includes your glutes, your hamstrings, your quads, your calves, and your feet. Hold all of that tight during your slow exhale.

Now we're going to start the exhale. Blowing the air out while tensing the lower half of your body. Just holding tension there. As you get to the end of the exhale, you might start to notice an urge to yawn. Initially, you can yawn voluntarily. It is not really a reflex yet, but by yawning intentionally you are filling your lungs completely.

When your lungs are full, hold that breath for about 10 seconds.

Enjoy the sensation of the lungs filled with air. See if you can relax your whole body. Once you have held your breath for 10 seconds, we start with the next exhale.

Begin to exhale and gradually tense the lower half of the body. Toward the end of the out-breath, notice if you yet have that urge to yawn. Then fill the lungs and hold that breath. This is important. You are going to hold your breath for about 10 seconds. Try to relax your whole body and be comfortable as you are holding your breath. Just see if you can notice any deep relaxation through your body.

Continue with these cycles until you have noticed all three PNS signals: (1) you are yawning, (2) your mouth is salivating, and (3) your eyes are tearing.

[5 minutes later] Let's pause here. What did you notice?

PATIENT 1: It worked. I did have the yawning reflex. The tensing of the lower body was a key trigger to that somehow. I did notice my eyes getting a little bit wet. Salivation not so much. But I found 10 seconds is a long time. That was not a comfortable thing for me.

THERAPIST: If your stress system has been in overdrive, that is partly what's driving the hunger for air. You have to take more breaths because they have been shallower. You don't have to keep to the 10 seconds as some kind of moral commitment. The idea is to fill the lungs and just hold your breath for a comfortable duration. As you continue, and as the yawning kicks in, the yawning will get more intense. You will be able to hold your breath for longer.

Reflecting on Patients' Experiences With the Yawning Breath

Here are some other questions that can come up, about the yawning breath.

PATIENT 2: When you breathe in, do you do that with a conscious effort to yawn?

THERAPIST: The yawn is a reflex to fill your lungs. It quickly gets air all the way down to the bottom of the lungs. The way in which the lungs are configured is that the biggest part of the lung is at the bottom. It's like a pear shape. It's round at the bottom, and it's narrower at the top.

Yawning gets the air right down to the bottom where the lung is larger. Right at the bottom, just above the diaphragmatic muscle, is where there are loads of parasympathetic sensors. When these sensors are activated by the full yawning breath, they boost the parasympathetic response.

Shallow breathers do not get air to the bottom of the lungs. Your usual breathing is not activating the parasympathetic response. So you are not getting that boost. As you start to do this exercise, you can try taking a voluntary yawn (a larger gulp of air). Do that until you start to feel the reflexive yawn kick in.

PATIENT 3: I noticed that I was continuing to keep my lower body tense. Even when I had already breathed in. So I had to be conscious and tell myself, "I've got to relax now."

THERAPIST: The tensing is only to activate the yawning. Once you have completed the inbreath, relax all your muscles. If they do not automatically relax, yes, tell yourself to relax and just lie calmly without any tension. Try to stay with that relaxation for 10 seconds and pay attention to your salivation and tearing.

The yawning breath is a psychomotor skill, just like riding a bike. So you may find that you get very little salivation; some people can't get salivation at all, but they notice a bit of tearing.

Did you notice any salivation or any tearing at all?

PATIENT 4: A little bit. But I felt tired.

THERAPIST: Feeling tired at the start is likely because you have been sleep deprived for a while. If you are doing the yawning breath in bed, you can stop if you think you are about to fall asleep. If you do not fall asleep, resume the yawning breath again. Continue until you get all three signals: (1) you start to yawn, (2) you get some salivation, and (3) you have tearing. Those are the signs of an activated parasympathetic system. The rest and digest system has now been activated.

Once you get the three PNS signals, you do not have to keep doing the breathing. Find a comfortable position and just relax in bed. Half of the time you will fall asleep. The rest of the time you will be resting in a dozy state. It is important that your thinking brain does not kick in. Just practice lying in bed, being relaxed. No worries about, "Am I going to fall asleep?" If you have engaged your parasympathetic system, you are relaxed, and your brain will start sleeping whenever it needs to. You can't push it into sleep. Instead, notice how satisfying it is to rest.

PATIENT 5: I had trouble with it. I was getting to the salivating part and the tearing but not so much of the yawning. Because I have trouble tensing up and then relaxing my whole body. Because I think I'm still tense.

THERAPIST: You may be stuck in that tense mode in which all the body muscles are still holding the tension. That's more than likely because you've had a lot of tension for quite a long time. That is chronic stress, where the muscles themselves are holding on to the tension.

Commentary. Since individual patients may have specific struggles with aspects of doing the diaphragmatic breathing, it is important to ferret out these early barriers and address each of them directly. As patient get more confident with the yawning breath, they will start to feel the benefits of doing the breathing and use it to get to sleep.

Patients who were identified as either "mixed" or "diaphragmatic" breathers on the breathing assessment can be started on 5 minutes of slow abdominal breaths. As they get more comfortable with the breathing, they can be moved directly into the yawning breath without the 2 or more weeks of retraining from chest to belly breathing.

Once all patients are capable of slowing their breaths to 5 breaths a minute and completing 15 minutes of that, they are fully able to use breathing practice whenever they need to use their breath to relax their nervous systems. The following treatment vignette illustrates a patient combining their practice of their diaphragmatic breathing with the yawning breath.

Personalizing the Practice of the Yawning Breath

BACK TO PATIENT 1: I wonder if I need to do almost two kinds of breathing. Because I often get bloated. I kind of clench my gut all day long. Nothing moves through my gut until I can lie down and do some breathing. As soon as I do some breathing, then, all of a sudden, I can hear my gut starting to work overtime.

I'm clenching my lower half most of the day. I need to do one type of breathing first, just to relax my stomach. So I can take a deep breath and open up the diaphragm. And then a second stage where I do the clenching again and trigger the yawning.

THERAPIST: That makes sense. It also tells me that you are tuning into your body.

I agree that is an indication of your stress level. You are picking up that SNS activation. The stress of the last year has created a set point of high stress in your gut.

So start using those two types of breathing: the diaphragmatic breathing to release your gut, and then follow up with the yawning breath to help you sleep. See if you can get that level of tension to reset. Then the gut may not be as clenched through the day. Experiment with it.

Use the breathing whenever you can: morning, afternoon, evening. You have been good with practicing the breathing. So this is just adding another level of activating the PNS. And because it is the rest and digest system, it makes sense to me that it would start to unclench the gut.

Commentary. The patient is becoming more aware of their background level of body tension. This body tension carries the memories of past traumas. The accumulated tension is present in the body armor that he is now beginning to notice. An important part of that body armor is the clenched diaphragmatic and intercostal muscles.

Assigning the Practice of the Yawning Breath

THERAPIST: If you can get into the routine of doing the breathing periodically, just lie down wherever it is most comfortable. Do it periodically throughout the day. See if you get that reset. Less clenching in the gut, maybe less bloating gradually.

It gets easier to activate the yawning as you practice more. You may have to do 20 breaths at the start, to get the three signals. Maybe you just have to do 15. And then it may kick in after 10. It won't be too long after you start doing the yawning breath that you start noticing that yawning reflex, the salivation, and the tearing.

My guess is that your lack of salivation also has to do with that clenching stomach. Your whole digestive system has shut down because of the high level of stress this past year.

The metaphor I use is that breathing is like a garden gate. If you have ever had an unused iron gate, it gets rusty. And a rusty iron garden gate does not move very much. That is like your digestive system. And if you practice the yawning breath, you are moving that gate open and shut. You are oiling it a little bit. You gradually create better movement and more response. These physiological processes take weeks, or even months, to shift back from the hyperaroused, high-stress setting down to a more neutral or calm state.

PATIENT: The diaphragmatic breathing for me has been pretty important. I do use it in bed to relax. And it really does make a difference getting my digestive system cranking again.

Whole Body Breathing

Once the patient is comfortable with diaphragmatic breathing and can do up to 15 minutes of slow rhythmic breathing (5 breaths per minute), it is time to address the chronic tension that has been built up throughout the musculature of the body. Signals of chronic tension provide proprioceptive information that is integrated in the insula. Visceral information is relayed by the vagus nerve to the nucleus tractus solitarius, where it is integrated.

Chronic somatic distress is relayed to the hypothalamus, parabrachial nucleus, dorsal motor nucleus of the vagus nerve, thalamus, amygdala, and the insular cortex. Whether the person is aware of the distress or not, it contributes to an underlying physiological distress that can interrupt sleep. These issues are discussed more fully in Chapter 10.

Interventions that address tension in the neck, shoulders, and jaw are particularly important as these specific signals of muscular tension enter the spinal column right next to the ascending reticular activating system (ARAS). The ARAS is the main "on" switch in the body. The continuous sensory signaling of tension in the neck, shoulders, and jaw muscles activates the ARAS and awakens the sleeper.

Interventions that work very well for this purpose include yoga, progressive muscle relaxation (PMR) exercises, and autogenic training. Adding these exercises into a pre-sleep routine is essential for many disrupted sleepers.

APPLICATION

To make effective use of the information you have been reading, we invite you to apply the concepts described in this chapter by engaging patients with these important steps to learning skills that will help in retraining their sleep patterns:

Complete a 10-Minute Yawning Breath: The first step in using the yawning breath is to start with yourself. Create an audio recording of the directions guiding you to the yawning breath. Listen to the recording and see if you experience the three signals of PNS activation. Continue to use the yawning breath yourself for 2 weeks. Every time you wake up, experiment, and see when and how it works for you.

Review Your Results With Using the Yawning Breath: How often did you use the yawning breath? How often did it work, getting you back to sleep? When it did not get you to sleep, were you able to stay in a dozy sleep state, or did you become completely alert? If it took you some time for the strategy to work, how long was it before you felt completely comfortable with the intervention?

Demonstrate Yawning Breath With Your Patients: After you have practiced the yawning breath yourself and are confident in doing the exercises, start teaching a friend or family member. Describe how the mechanics of the yawning breath activate the PNS. Then start teaching your patients.

Teach Patients Whole Body Breathing: After the yawning breath has become familiar, teach patients to use body relaxation techniques. It can take a few weeks before your patient notices the change in body tension. Ask patients to begin a pre-sleep wind-down routine that incorporates both body relaxation and breathing strategies. These will actively recruit parasympathetic responses prior to sleep.

Begin a Pre-Sleep Wind-Down Routine: The transition into sleep is not automatic. It requires the autonomic nervous system (ANS) to make a major shift from SNS to PNS control. Chronic insomniacs need to set a 30-to-60 minute window to actively recruit PNS activation prior to going to bed (this is elaborated in Chapter 7).

Key Messages for Therapists

1. How safe, or threatened, we feel is measured by the contributions of the SNS and PNS. SNS activity is evident from the phrenic nerve, and PNS activity from the vagal nerve. Diaphragmatic breathing activates the vagus nerve, which dampens phrenic nerve activity, thus acting like a vagal brake to the ANS. This effect is clearly visible in the body and also reflected in an increase in RSA.
2. The key to bringing an internal sense of safety is to teach the patient how to engage their diaphragmatic breath. Here is the sequence:

Diaphragmatic Breath → Boosts PNS → Rebalances ANS → New Internal States of Rest and Restore → Deeper Better Quality Sleep

3. Guiding the patient to modulate their nervous system is accomplished by a Track, Tune in, Shift, Repeat protocol. Tracking means turning awareness to their shallow breathing. Tuning in is deepening into the experience of the breath, moment to moment. Shifting refers to moving their breath into the belly. This sequence is then Repeated to retrain and synchronize the breathing muscles.
4. Reversal of patterns of chronic muscular stress happens in stages:

   - Accurately identifying the problem of shallow chest breathing for the patient.
   - Introduction of breathing exercises that shift from chest breathing by actively recruiting the diaphragm and resynchronizing breathing muscles.
   - Practicing the longer, deeper breaths for periods of up to 15 minutes.
   - Slowing the breaths down to five breaths a minute.
   - Activating whole body breathing. One way that whole body breathing can be implemented clinically is to begin using the yawning breath.

5. The yawning breath is a variation of diaphragmatic breathing in which the patient is guided to slow down their breathing as well as actively facilitate the yawning reflex. This is accomplished by adding lower body muscle tensing to the pursed-lip slow exhale. That triggers a full inhale, which is held for an extended count as the body relaxes. These yawning breaths are continued until the three signals of PNS activation—yawning, salivation, and tearing—are present.

PART II

Addressing the Four Enemies of Sleep

"Overall, literature strongly suggests that consolidated, restorative sleep is an important pathway in sustaining and restoring psychological health in trauma-exposed individuals."
—Anne Germain, Ashlee McKeon, and Rebecca Campbell (2017, p. 84)

"Targeted treatment of sleep disorders in the context of PTSD offers a unique and underutilized opportunity to advance clinical care and research."
—Peter Colvonen, Laura Straus, Carl Stepnowsky, et al. (2018, p. 1)

6

Identifying and Removing Major Sleep Roadblocks to Trauma Work

"Screening of all PTSD afflicted Veterans for OSA symptoms and treating them with CPAP as appropriate will improve the overall quality of life of these patients." —Sadeka Tamanna, Jefferson Parker, Judith Lyons, Mohammad Ullah (2014, p. 631)

"CPAP can significantly improve nightmare and overall PTSD symptoms in these patients." —Ye Zhang, Rong Ren, Linghui Yang, Junging Shou, et al. (2019, p. 172)

Once you have begun to attune to the patient and have had the chance to approach the range of problems they present with, you will have results of screening tests guiding you to consider a variety of sleep problems. Among the sleep problems that are common among trauma patients, the three most common are nightmares, insomnia, and sleep apnea. We can think of these as the real enemies of sleep. Altogether, sleep research has identified four clusters of factors, each of which will undermine sleep.

The four factors that will always wake you out of sleep include: (1) dropping levels of oxygen in the blood (hypoxia), (2) other signals of distress being sent by your body (angina, low back pain, hunger, or cold), (3) sympathetic activation (physical tension, anxiety, emotional distress, night terrors, sleepwalking, ruminating thoughts), and (4) dysregulated sleep circuitry (circadian disorders, narcolepsy, REM sleep disorder, sleep paralysis). Most sleep difficulties will fall into one of these four categories.

The screening inventories in the TABS sleep survey reviewed in Chapter 2 provide a starting point to considering how sleep problems that the patient may be aware of can challenge your therapeutic work. The inventories allow evaluation of nightmares and insomnia, but not apnea. Importantly, the one sleep problem that will have the most negative impact on the outcome of your trauma treatment, is the stealth sleep problem of sleep apnea.

We can consider apnea a stealth sleep problem because most patients are completely unaware of the underlying problem. It happens at night when the patient is unconscious. Sleep apnea is cessation in breathing at night, causing oxygen desaturation, resulting in hypoxia and a cascade of negative physiological and psychological disturbances. This problem can only be detected if you, the trauma therapist, initiate a discussion with your patient. This chapter will focus on the critical importance of how apnea impacts your patient's nervous system, why it is important to consider a sleep study, and how to help them understand the results of their sleep study. This chapter will provide the information you need to be effective in this task of helping patients understand apnea.

What I will learn in this chapter to become a better sleep and trauma therapist:

1. Know the four enemies of sleep: (1) hypoxia, (2) dysregulated sleep circuitry (circadian disorders, narcolepsy, sleep paralysis), (3) body distress (tension, pain, hunger, cold/heat), and (4) sympathetic hyperarousal (shock, emotional distress, rumination).
2. Understand that of the four enemies, *hypoxia is sleep enemy #1*. Repeatedly starving the body of oxygen triggers immediate sympathetic storms that increases physical distress (high blood pressure, inflammation, fatigue, and daytime metabolic hypoarousal), cognitive impairments (poor concentration, memory problems, and problem-solving difficulties), and emotional symptoms (distress, panic, moodiness), collectively called comorbidities. As well, apnea increases the risk of earlier death (mortality) from suicide attempts or disease burden. Learn to communicate these risks effectively to your patients in a simple and direct way, so patients can understand and make informed decisions about reducing these risks.
3. Conduct a brief screen for the likelihood of apnea being a problem and learn how to describe the purpose of a sleep study to determine if they have apnea. This includes answering patient questions to support them in making their decision to arrange for a sleep test.
4. Review the most notable features of the sleep test results, highlighting the importance of sleep fragmentation and oxygen desaturation, taking action to reduce the underlying morbidity and mortality from apnea, and referring the patient back to the sleep medicine professional for more detailed discussions.
5. Anticipate compliance problems with Continuous Positive Airway Pressure (CPAP) treatment and help patients experiment with ways of adopting these treatment devices. Engage the patient in tracking their

adherence to treatment and provide necessary support as they strive to overcome this critical roadblock to trauma work.

CLINICAL INVESTIGATION OF SLEEP APNEA

Identifying the Sleep Disorder With the Greatest Health Risk (Sleep Enemy #1)

Of the 83 sleep disorders listed in the *International Classification of Sleep Disorders, Third Edition* (Sateia, 2014), all impact the quality of daytime experiences and ability to function at your best, but only a few can substantially increase risks of getting other illnesses (morbidity) or even shortening your life (mortality). The most lethal of all the sleep disorders are the sleep-related breathing disorders. These share the feature of reducing the level of oxygen circulating in the blood stream. As oxygen is essential for cells to continue alive, any prolonged periods of reduced oxygen circulating to cells represents a strangulation of their lifeline. Apnea, like cancer, rusts out healthy tissue, slowly killing your body's ability to maintain its health.

"Apnea" comes from the Greek words "a," meaning without, and "pnea," meaning breath. Sleep Apnea (SA) means being without breath during sleep. SA is measured by the Apnea-Hypopnea Index (AHI). An apnea is when you stop breathing altogether for 10 seconds or longer. A "hypopnea" is when your breathing is inefficient (as the airway is partially blocked), and your oxygen level goes down (desaturates) by 3% or more. It means that you are trying to breathe in, but the breathing muscles are struggling to do that, and oxygen levels are falling. The muscles may be deconditioned. They may be getting mixed signals to breathe and to freeze. They swish the air around, but don't move air into the lungs efficiently. You can think of it as inefficient breathing.

The number of apneas and hypopneas are added up into an Apnea Hypopnea Index and reported as an average for each hour you slept. A normal sleeper can have up to five of these events per hour. Our body can cope with that reasonably well. "Mild" apnea is defined as 5 to 14 such events each hour; "moderate" apnea is 15 to 29, and "severe" apnea is 30 or more.

The apnea can be caused by the brain forgetting to try to breathe. This is called central sleep apnea, or CSA. Apnea can also be caused by a blockage to breathing. This happens just above the throat where the air passageway is surrounded by soft, fleshy tissue. When this tissue relaxes, it collapses. Now the passageway is blocked and does not allow air through. This is called obstructive sleep apnea, or OSA. A combination of both CSA and OSA is called complex (or mixed) apnea (CA). The frequencies of these three types of apneas are OSA 84%, CSA 1%, and CA 15% of patients (Morgenthaler et al., 2006). The balance of this chapter will focus on management of OSA, as it is the most common presenting apnea in trauma.

Conveying Increased Risks to Patients

When breathing is blocked (or insufficient) oxygen desaturation occurs and there are decreased levels of circulating oxygen in the bloodstream. The persistently lower oxygen levels activate a nightly crisis response in the brain. The repeated stimulation of sympathetic arousal causes many difficulties: increased blood pressure, nightly trips to the bathroom, systemic inflammation magnifying any bodily pains, unexpected surges in heart rate (atrial fibrillation) and increased risk of stroke, poor concentration and memory, metabolic disorder and weight gain, moodiness, and even severe depression with suicidal thoughts.

In a recent prospective study with over 7,000 adults, Che-Sheng Chu and his colleagues (2023) found that adults with sleep apnea had 4.5 times the risk of carrying out a suicide attempt compared with those who did not have apnea. When adults with mental disorders were excluded, patients with sleep apnea had 4.2 times the risk of carrying out a suicide attempt compared with those who did not have sleep apnea. During the follow-up period, those with apnea also had 3.86 times the risk of repeated suicide attempts compared with those who did not.

Most importantly, apnea can entirely stall our trauma treatment. Here is the message to give patients: When our stress system keeps working at night, dumping stress hormones into our blood all night, we wake up feeling anxious and agitated. We worry more. We may have a panic attack during the day. We can get seriously depressed. The apneas at night are making our trauma symptoms worse and we will have no idea why we are being triggered in this way. We don't even think about sleep as the problem.

A study with male veteran twins who served in the Vietnam War explored the nature of the relationship between having a PTSD diagnosis and the risk for having OSA (Shah et al., 2024). Those with a current PTSD diagnosis had AHIs that were 10.5 events/hour higher than those without PTSD. The effect size of the increased risk of having sleep apnea from the presence of PTSD symptoms was of the same magnitude as that from obesity (a known high risk factor). Every 15 point increase in PCL5 rated PTSD symptoms was associated with a 4.6 increase in AHI. Symptoms of depression were not associated with such an increased risk of OSA. The authors concluded that the dysregulated functional neurobiological and stress pathways of PTSD (but not depression) are hazards for respiratory regulation and airway collapse.

Evidence from recent studies show that starting apnea treatment can reduce many trauma symptoms that we come to treatment to relieve. Not only will we feel more in control, but our body and brain will be healthier as well. On top of that there are risks that we don't see but accrue over time. These include brain cell death, increased risk for diabetes, heart attacks, and strokes, etc. There are many medical, emotional, and cognitive consequences that happen as a result of untreated apnea. However, the most important reason to go for the sleep test is that all of these serious risks can be fixed.

Conducting a Brief Screen for Apnea

Apneas happen when we are asleep (unconscious), so we cannot have any direct experience of them being a problem. If we have a bed partner we might hear from them that we are snoring or stopped breathing at night. If that is not available to us we have to rely on the presence of signs and symptoms that apnea patients typically show. These are best determined from two screening instruments that evaluate these consequences.

Because patients are blind to the problem, trauma therapists must use their awareness of the danger to investigate this potentially lethal problem. Two simple screening tests that take 5 minutes to complete will determine whether the patient has any signs of sleep apnea. These screening tests are the STOP-BANG (Chung et al., 2008) and the Epworth Sleepiness Scale (ESS) (Johns, 1991) which are in widespread use and readily available.

These are not tests for apnea, per se. Only a sleep test at a sleep clinic can determine the presence of apnea and its severity. The therapist's role is to determine whether the patient shows some of the warning signs usually related to repeated apneas at night. From numerous studies of patients with PTSD, we know that about 50% of males with PTSD have apnea. An estimate of the percentage of women with PTSD who might also have apnea has not been determined.

Among veterans, as PTSD symptoms increase in severity, the risk of apnea increases by 40%, particularly when there is comorbid depression (Mysliwiec, et al., 2015). Therefore, all patients scoring high or severe levels of PTSD symptoms on standard validated tests (CAPS-5 and PCL-5) should also be routinely given these apnea-screening instruments.

Conveying the Purpose of the Sleep Test (Polysomnogram)

If your patient is concerned about multiple trips to the bathroom at night inform them that apnea increases: nocturnal awakenings, loud snoring, pauses in breathing, increased urine production, restless sleep, night sweats, dry mouth, and sore throat. In addition there are many daytime symptoms from untreated OSA, which include: morning headaches, excessive daytime sleepiness, difficulty with memory and concentration, increased inflammation with musculoskeletal aches and pain, increased irritability and mood swings, hypertension, and weight gain. On a neurophysiological level untreated OSA triggers a fight or flight sympathetic response due to decreasing oxygen levels. This can result in triggering nocturnal panic attacks, sleepwalking, and other parasomnias due to a hyperaroused state. Overall, all of these affect the person's quality of life and sleep-wake health.

When a therapist recommends a sleep test and explains that it is the only authoritative method of determining what is happening during sleep. Encouraging the patient to go for a sleep test will help screen the patient for these issues, as well as providing objective data on the severity of the autonomic dysfunction and sleep fragmentation being experienced at night by the traumatized patient. The therapist describes the test in detail to reassure the patient that it is important and noninvasive.

Dealing With Resistance to Going for a Sleep Test

If your patient is not willing to go for a sleep test, you will have to skip to the interventions described in the next chapter. Introduce consistent sleep start and stop times, to reinforce a regular sleep period. After those are achieved, add a morning wake-up routine and a 30–40 minute evening wind-down routine. If sleep patterns do not improve with the above, return to discussion of the need to get a better idea of what is wrong with their sleep. Again review the value of having a polysomnographic study.

Review of the Main Findings of the Sleep Test (Polysomnogram)

In the following passage the therapist demonstrates the importance of engaging the patient, Tim (not his real name). Tim went for a sleep test six months ago but was put off by the feeling that the doctor was trying to sell him a machine. That emotional reaction tells the therapist that Tim did not really grasp the way that untreated apnea can undermine both physical and mental health. Sadly, this happens far too often, so the therapist is going to go over some key concepts with Tim.

> THERAPIST: Sleep reports can be difficult to understand. We will look at the main findings and describe how these are important for you.
>   When you got the report, what did you make of it? I'm very curious because medical doctors think they're communicating very clearly. But often, they're trained in all of this language that doesn't make a lot of sense to the nonmedical person. When you read the report, how did you understand it?
> PATIENT: The doctor talked to me about it. The only thing that I got from him is that I should get a CPAP. And he said that from the report, I stopped breathing 33 times in an hour. Those are the only two things that I got from him. Looking at the report, I really didn't understand anything. To be honest, it gives me anxiety. Because I wasn't expecting that I would have this problem. Or is this a problem? This is the first time I've heard of sleep apnea. I don't know anything about it. When I heard that I need a CPAP, I got more anxious . . . like, "Oh, my God, what else . . ."
> THERAPIST: I see what you're saying. Many people, when they go for a sleep test, don't know what to expect. That was the case for you as well. And then when you get the result and they're now telling you, "*You have*

a problem, and you need to use a CPAP," that causes a lot of anxiety and distress.

By definition, when we go to sleep, we lose consciousness. We lose our ability to notice anything or to feel anything. The sleep report brings your attention to problems that you have not seen but are there under the surface.

The way I would urge you to think about it is that you are getting a peek into something that may have existed for years. Your report gives you important information about what, if anything, has been interfering with your ability to get to sleep and stay asleep.

The main aspects of sleep that the sleep test can bring to attention are:

1. An objective measure of sleep efficiency
2. Sleep architecture (a picture of how brain waves shift across the night)
3. Arousals from sleep (how fragmented sleep is)

The sleep report then concludes by pulling these elements together to show the underlying causes for these disturbances. Importantly, there can be more than one sleep problem under the surface.

Sleep Efficiency. Sleep efficiency means how much time in bed was spent in sleep. One hundred percent would mean that the patient fell asleep from the moment they got into bed and didn't awaken until the morning alarm. In that example, 100% of their time in bed was spent sleeping. But nobody sleeps 100%; 85% or better is considered a healthy sleep pattern.

Tim slept 73% of the time that night. That means for every three hours he slept, he was awake for an hour. This measure tells us that Tim's sleep can definitely improve.

Sleep Architecture. The brain is continually active at night. In sleep the conscious mind stops, but the brain doesn't stop. Every bodily function that keeps a person alive continues. While the brain sleeps it is still very actively engaged in maintenance work. Sleep architecture refers to the organized structure of four distinct phases of brain activity that it cycles through at night. These are rapid eye movement (REM) sleep, and three phases of non-REM (N1, N2, N3). In NREM sleep our previous day's experiences are reactivated in the hippocampus and moved to long term memory in the prefrontal cortes. During REM these new cortical memories are integrated with your previous memories into long term memory.

Light sleep is a transitional stage between wakefulness and sleep and is called NREM stage 1, or N1. The brain has to let go of new information coming in before it can do its reorganizational housekeeping. N1 is very light sleep. Many light sleepers are still somewhat aware of their environment during N1.

NREM2, or N2, is a medium level of sleep. In N2 the thalamus stops attending to incoming sensory information and instead actively communicates with cortical areas to prepare for it updating your long-term memory circuits. These are evident from K-complex waves and sleep spindles. The brain has shifted away from daytime activities. And it's beginning to replay the activities from the day that were tagged as important. Those things that happened in the daytime that were noteworthy got tagged with emotion (either a positive emotion like happiness or negative emotion like fear). Those begin to get activated during sleep. All of those memories are kept in short-term memory, in the hippocampus. Memories from the previous day that were kept in the hippocampus get reactivated in that N2, middle level of sleep.

Then the brain begins to generate slow wave sleep (SWS), in N3. In SWS the midbrain structures holding memories begin to synchronize with the cortex, so memories can be moved into long-term memory circuits. The memories from daytime are being replayed in the hippocampus and projected up to the cortex to the long-term memory system.

Tim's N3 was 18.6%, which is much higher than the patient's age norms. Males his age usually only have 2.7% of N3. That's good. It means that the brain is connecting and sending information up to long-term storage. In contrast, the patient had less REM sleep. Only 10.7% of the night's sleep was in REM. Most people Tim's age get about 23%. Something is interfering with Tim's REM sleep.

Arousals from Sleep. The third important measure that a sleep test provides is the number of times the brain was trying to wake up and exit sleep. These would be evident in 10 seconds or longer of arousal rhythms, to awaken, or shift him into lighter sleep. In a normal teen there are about 15 of these arousals and in a normal adult about 25.

There are other waveforms called Cyclical Alternating Patterns, or CAPs, which indicate the brain's activation of the drive to move (subtype 2) or to arouse the nervous system (subtype A3). However, these wave forms are not routinely captured in standard sleep reports.

A sleep report also provides a breakdown of what brain and body activities preceded each time the patient had an arousal from sleep. The usual causes are (1) muscle movements in the legs or arms, (2) apneas, or (3) spontaneous awakenings from sleep.

Let's look at the number and causes for Tim's arousals from sleep.

Periodic Leg Movements

Some people's legs jerk or twitch periodically. Those movements are sometimes enough to wake them up. Tim had very few limb movements. Two an hour is considered normal. Up to five an hour is considered fine. Our brain can deal with it. Tim has no problem with limb movements.

Narcolepsy

In narcolepsy the brain circuit that maintains consciousness (the orexin-hypocretin system) has been compromised from viral damage. As a result, both sleep and wake states are more unstable. It is hard to stay awake in daytime, and it is hard to stay asleep at night. The narcoleptic person will often go directly into REM sleep. That is called sleep onset REM, or SOREMs. The other feature of the narcoleptic's sleep is that they can't stay asleep. They have multiple arousals and awakenings across the night.

Tim did not have any indication of a SOREM. His first REM period happened after 110 minutes, not far off the expected time of 90 minutes.

Spontaneous Awakenings (Autonomic Dysregulation)

The autonomic system never stops its activity. When a person goes to sleep, the body's level of stress hormones (adrenaline and cortisol) should be at the lowest level of the day. For many trauma patients, nighttime is a difficult time, because they have to give up control and surrender to sleep. That is extremely hard when bad things have often happened to them or around them at night. Increased levels of stress hormones keep the autonomic system activated, even when it should be quiet. This makes transitioning into sleep exceedingly difficult. The activated autonomic system will continuously be fighting sleep, either through bodily distress, waves of emotion, or an active mind. Once asleep those SNS prompts to awaken continue and are visible on the sleep test as "spontaneous" awakenings.

Spontaneous awakenings are quite common in trauma patients. These measure how readied the nervous system is for action. Tim's spontaneous awakenings were as frequent as the awakenings due to apnea. These awakenings will be reduced as the trauma therapy successfully revisits traumatic experiences and the patient reprocesses the emotional and somatic memories of those traumas.

Sleep Apnea

The breathing problem. If Tim has apnea, it is important for him to know that, because what apnea does (and has been doing for years) is blocking oxygen from getting to his lungs. When oxygen can't get to the lungs, the blood level of oxygen (oxygen saturation [SaO2]) drops. It is no different than if someone came to your bedroom every night, put their hands around your throat, and started choking you every minute or two while you tried to sleep. SaO2 should stay above 92% all night. Below that and your body is being choked and your organs are starving for oxygen, all of which trigger a psychological and physiological cascade of fight or flight responses.

Your brain's breathing fix. When oxygen drops by a few percent, the brain's alarm turns on the sympathetic system, so you start breathing. It will do that to stop oxygen levels from falling any lower. However, this breathing fix creates many more problems. For one thing, when the stress system is turned on, it dumps stress hormones (adrenaline and cortisol) into the blood. That helps you wake up to breathe, but ends your deep restorative sleep or REM sleep. It also activates your immune system to look for the invader (virus or bacteria). However, there is no intruder to find, so you are just running down your body's defenses against illness and creating an internal state of systemic inflammation. Systemic means that the whole body and brain became inflamed. That aggravates any pains you may have in your body and aggravates anxiety.

The other problems this "fix" creates. The autonomic (stress) system is your emergency system, dumping adrenaline and cortisol in the blood stream so you can deal with danger (real or perceived). With apnea (and the resultant hypoxia) this stress response is triggered over and over throughout the night. The dumping of adrenaline and cortisol will start to make it hard to go back to sleep. It will also get your kidneys working, so you have to go to the bathroom at night. You started with a blocked airway, and you end up with no restorative sleep, a depleted immune system, bouts of accelerated heart rate (leading toward high blood pressure and atrial fibrillation) and across time leading to diabetes, heart disease, and stroke. In the daytime, you will have less adrenaline and cortisol to get you through the day (resulting in tiredness and fatigue all day).

How bad is Tim's problem?
>THERAPIST: The seriousness of the problem is measured in two ways: how many times do you stop breathing in an hour, and how low does the oxygen saturation go at night?
>
>The number of times you stop breathing is the apnea hypopnea index (AHI). It indicates how many times an hour your sleep is fragmented. It measures how compromised the restorative function of your sleep is right now. Tim, your AHI is 33: below 15 is mild, up to 30 is moderate, and above 30 is severe.
>
>The second more important question is how much do apneas compromise your SaO2 level? Oxygen levels below 90% create physiological distress to cells. We measure this in two ways: (1) how low the SaO2 goes at night, and (2) how much of the night are you below 90%.
>
>Tim, your SaO2 (min) is 85%, and your level was under 90% for 10 minutes.
>
>Your report tells us that you have a problem with many sleep disruptions, 33 every hour. That's once every 2 minutes. Think about that. Every 2 minutes of your sleep, your body is threatened with lower oxygen levels. And air is essential for cell health, day and night. Without air, we die. So

your brain will not let you die. It awakens you. You think you are sleeping, while your brain is fighting for its life.

Tim, your report tells us that 33 times every hour you stop breathing, or are struggling to get enough air. The report also tells you about whether you are sleeping on your back or on your sides. You did not spend much time sleeping on your back. That is good, because the numbers would be worse if you did.

Your oxygen level dropped down below 90%, to a low of 85%. That is definitely a problem zone. Dropping below 92% for sure activates more intense survival responses. For 10 minutes at night, your body is not resting in sleep, but is struggling to stay alive. That means dumping adrenaline and cortisol into the bloodstream. And if you are dumping stress hormones into the bloodstream every night, your sleep will become short and fragmented. You will wake up repeatedly, and because of the stress hormones, you won't get back to sleep easily. You can be up for hours in the middle of the night, or wake up by 5 a.m. Deep sleep can only happen when stress hormones are absent or at low levels through the night. Your apnea is preventing any possibility of restorative sleep.

The good news, Tim, is that this is easily fixable. You do not need another drug, or surgery. Just air—pushed with a gentle pressure. That pressure will hold the fleshy tissues around your airway open, the ones that right now are collapsing into the air passage 33 times every hour. Only when you can breathe easily *all night*, can you turn off that survival system. Does that make sense?

PATIENT: I am not sure what to say. I have read the report, but the numbers didn't mean anything to me. Nobody explained how apnea can hurt my body.

THERAPIST: That is why we are taking the time now. I want to make sure you understand how your body is not only struggling to get air, but that that compromises your sleep and your health.

Now let's go on to see how your sleep is compromised. The report shows us that your sleep is not normal. When we are in REM sleep, our body's striated muscles are paralyzed. So your ribs, shoulders, and chest muscles can't help you breathe when you go into REM. In REM you only have your smooth muscle, the diaphragmatic muscle, to do all of the work of trying to pull the air past the blockage in the upper airway. Tim, your report shows us that apnea has reduced your REM from 23% to 10%. For you, REM has become too dangerous. Too many apneas. So your nervous system is keeping you out of REM. That means you lose all of the benefits of REM: managing your emotions better, reorganizing your memories, losing your ability to think and solve problems.

And because the apneas activate your stress system to keep you breathing, it's waking you up repeatedly. And the combination of a nervous system that is fighting for its life, and the soup of stress hormones, makes it impossible to get back to sleep. Your 73% sleep efficiency tells me you are going to continue to be up for an hour or two every night.

Your *thinking mind thinks* you are getting a good night of sleep because you lie down and fall asleep within 5 minutes. But your *body mind* knows it is fighting for its life. Every 2 minutes or so, you stopped breathing, and your survival brain was activated, over and over again.

The solution is a Continuous Positive Airway Pressure (CPAP) machine that makes sure that the passage stays open all night. CPAP is a machine that delivers pressurized room air through a hose attached to a mask that goes on the face, so as to keep the airway open. This keeps oxygen saturation above 92% and the AHI below 5. That allows the brain to begin to move back into its old healthy sleep patterns. The most important message in all of this is that the test found something that, if it hadn't been found, would have created much more serious health problems for you. *If you start using the CPAP, you will be turning off that survival system.* All night. And when you turn that off at night, across the next months, the sleep pattern begins to return to normal. And across the next year, your mental functions improve back to your age levels. Your nervous system will be less on edge.

PATIENT: Do I need to use it for the rest of my life? Or do I need to use it for a few months and then get assessed again? And then they'll say yeah, you don't need it anymore.

THERAPIST: It depends on what the cause of those tissues collapsing into the throat is. There are many reasons they collapse. For example, if your upper airway is very narrow, that's something genetic. You are going to have to use the CPAP for the rest of your life.

Another cause is that you've put on some weight. The higher level of fat in the fat cells could be what's blocking that passage. So, if you exercise more and lose some weight, it is possible that the blockage itself is reduced. In that case you won't need the CPAP machine after you've lost enough weight. It's certainly not a bad idea to try and be as active as you can be and see if you can lose some weight.

The third thing that seems to be involved in whether you keep having apneas or not is the nervous system itself. We know that people who have had trauma, many of them, end up having apnea. Even if their throat is fine, with no blockage, and even if there isn't a problem with weight, the dysregulation of the ANS itself can cause stoppages in breathing. For example, trauma causes your nervous system to freeze, and you stop breathing. This is not a conscious breathing pattern. It's what your nervous system itself is doing, in an automatic way.

But I can give you one reason it doesn't matter as much as it would matter with other treatments. Every medicine that you take may also activate some other, more negative effects. Side effects. Some of these can be serious.

Now if we compare that with a CPAP, all the treatment is doing is it's providing air. It's pushing air into your body. It's not introducing anything that wouldn't be there naturally. It's just guaranteeing that the air that should be in your lungs is going to be in your lungs.

The side effects with CPAP are limited to how uncomfortable using the mask may feel. To have something sitting on your nose and mouth may make you feel claustrophobic. So that is something that can be a problem. The number of people who adjust to the CPAP really easily is matched by a similar number who struggle to get comfortable with using it every night.

Some of the problems that can come up include the air blowing up into their eyelids; or they struggle with tolerating the machine. Most of these side effects have to do with getting used to having something that you use every night, right? But it's a particularly useful machine. It does what it's supposed to do, to protect your sleep and your health.

ADAPTING TO THE CPAP TREATMENT

Decreases of hypoxia in sleep by CPAP treatment are accompanied by reversals of OSA-induced brain changes including a reduction of activation and . . . improvement in neurocognitive function. The amygdala, a significant mediator of the effects of fear memory on arousal and sleep, is also [negatively] affected by chronic OSA. (Zhang et al., 2019, p. 179)

There are multiple ways in which CPAP can improve the symptoms of PTSD. Ye Zhang and his colleagues (2019) conducted a systematic review of PTSD and OSA. They proposed a model that highlighted how reducing hypoxia and arousals from REM would stabilize the autonomic system and promote REM sleep related adaptive processing to improve neurocognitive functions, reduce PTSD symptoms, and achieve better outcomes. From their perspective, anything that can be done to increase adherence to use of the CPAP would result in better outcomes for patients. This next section discusses these strategies and interventions.

Adherence to CPAP Therapy

Adherence to CPAP therapy is a problem for many apnea patients but is even more so for trauma patients. This is because the hyperarousal of the dysregulated autonomic nervous systems makes the discomfort more disagreeable. As a result, PTSD patients do not use CPAP therapy as consistently as OSA patients without PTSD (Collen et al., 2012). Some of the reasons include discomfort with the mask, recurring nightmares, and claustrophobic feelings wearing the mask. Nightmares in particular are associated with higher resistance to CPAP therapy. Finally, individuals with PTSD use CPAP therapy for less that 4 hours a night and on fewer nights. None of them are getting a full night of restorative sleep.

Once a sleep test has confirmed SA, the process of adaptation to the CPAP device begins. It proceeds through selection of masks and machine, titration of CPAP levels, and the patient accommodating to their CPAP machine. For most patients, this process takes up to 90 days. While PAP machines are not the only treatment alternative, they are the most effective for the majority of SA patients, and the most usual first-line treatment.

Failure to comply with treatment means the patient does not want to use the equipment at all. Failure to adhere to treatment is defined as the patient not being able to use the equipment for the minimum duration that would allow correction of the airway problem. Successful adherence is typically defined as using the CPAP machine for 5 nights (70% of the week), for 4 hours or more a night. This is also termed "Medicare criteria" as Medicare only pays for CPAP equipment if its use meets this criterion.

Very few studies of long term adherence to CPAP have been reported. One recent study (Pascua et al., 2021) conducted three years after diagnosis, that 41% of 156 patients diagnosed with OSA refused CPAP at the outset (no compliance). Of those who began treatment, another 27% (more men than women) had dropped out by 3 years (no adherence). At 39 months only 43% of the study cohort of patients were using their CPAP, with a respectable average usage of 6.4 hours a night. These disappointing results, typical of many other studies, of adherence to a life-saving therapy, have led to many studies on how to improve these inadequate adherence rates.

Lewis and colleagues (2004) followed 80 consecutive patients diagnosed with OSA, tracking anxiety, depression, problems encountered at the very start of treatment (at the CPAP titration session, at which the optimal pressure level is determined for the patient), and whether patients lived alone. The anxiety and depression scores did not predict adherence problems, but the occurrence of problems at the outset of treatment, living alone, and having had a recent life event did.

Interestingly, those living alone were less likely to adopt the treatment, as were those who had had a recent life event. Lewis and colleagues (2004) noted that patients having life events were likely still coping with those stressors. However, the most powerful predictor of poor adherence was asking one simple question right at the outset: Did you encounter any problems on your first night of using the CPAP?

Richards and colleagues (2007) wondered whether providing newly diagnosed OSA patients with a structured informational session at the start of treatment would help with adherence. The authors enrolled 100 consecutive patients diagnosed with OSA into a trial of an educational session (ES) compared with treatment as usual (TAU). At 28 days into the treatment, the ES group was using the CPAP for 5.4 hours, while the TAU group was using the machine for less than half that time, or 2.5 hours each night. In total, 88% of the ES group met the 4-hour treatment target, compared to only 39% of the TAU group.

Stepnowsky and Dimesdale (2002) followed 528 CPAP users for 5 months: 63% could not meet the 4-hour criteria for nightly usage; 21% used CPAP from 4 to 6 hours; and only 16% used it for 6 hours or longer. How much is enough? Most professionals in the field would agree the answer is "All night, every night."

Of all the sleep disorders, SA is the simplest diagnosis to confirm, but for many patients, it is the hardest treatment to adhere to. Some patients have trouble finding a mask they are comfortable wearing. Others are mouth breathers at night and cannot get the mask to work for them without very unpleasant "blow-bys" of air. Still others awaken in the night with panic attacks triggered by the terrifying feeling that they are suffocating. These reactions are even more pronounced among those with PTSD, as they are even more acutely aware of cues for potential danger. These problems can usually be very effectively addressed through two to six treatment sessions targeting desensitization of these hyperarousal responses.

There will still be patients who just cannot adapt to the CPAP. In these cases, there are other alternatives that could be very helpful, including dental appliances and oral surgeries. Refer the patient back to the board-certified assessor who evaluated the patient for a discussion of these alternative treatment choices. The balance of this chapter will provide an outline of the eight key issues in helping patients adapt to treatment for SA.

STEPS IN THE INTERVENTION PROCESS

Education and Resistance to Change

Regular use of a CPAP is a major lifestyle change for most patients. As with all major lifestyle changes, the first phase of intervention is evaluation of the patient's motivation to actually use the mask. Many find the equipment bulky and awkward. Some equate it with another sign of deteriorating health or think it unattractive to their mates. Their initial reaction is that they would rather die than use the machine. The therapist's task is to educate the patient that the CPAP is a critical part of disease prevention and health promotion.

The patient can be given homework in the first meeting to do an online search for sleep apnea and come back with a page of information on risks and benefits. The result of this effort is always instructive about the patient's readiness to participate in a serious dialogue about the need for the CPAP. Patients who struggle with looking into risks and benefits are unlikely to take further steps to overcome their resistance to using the CPAP.

Another excellent resource for working with SA patients is an article entitled *Clinical management of poor adherence to CPAP: motivational enhancement* (Aloia et al., 2004). The article provides a clear outline of interventions given across two 45-minute sessions to motivate patients to understand the importance of overcoming barriers to use of CPAP.

Mobilizing Supports

Asking the patient to talk to spouse, family, and friends about the CPAP helps to bring potential problems to the surface quickly by identifying unsupportive, uninformed, or critical support persons. Addressing these potential barriers to adoption is critical to long-term success. This exercise also helps to identify sources of support and encouragement.

Identifying Daytime Burdens of Apnea

Patients should track their sleep with a sleep log for a baseline period. In particular, it is important to assess energy level across each day, number of naps, sleepiness during meetings, etc. A patient who is asked to observe when they get tired, whether they have to pass on certain activities, etc., is becoming more aware of the actual burden of SA on their daily activities. This is most helpful in preparing the ambivalent patient for action.

In the first weeks of treatment, many patients may not be able to keep the mask on for more than an hour or two on most nights. Be encouraging and focus on achievements, but also remind patients that SA kills cells and can make them sick. Their best efforts are critical for both their physical health as well as their emotional well-being. Many patients will also benefit from mask habituation and mask desensitization interventions. Mask habituation refers to a gradual introduction of the mask across many days. Each day the patient is encouraged to use the mask for as long as comfortable while watching TV. The next day, they are encouraged to do a little more. Gradually they feel more comfortable with keeping the mask on. Mask desensitization refers to clinical intervention, where the patient is encouraged to re-experience their distress about wearing the mask and an emotional desensitization strategy (like EMDR) is introduced to resolve these emotional reactions.

When they start to have 1 or 2 nights a week of successful adherence (4–6 hours use), ask the patient to pay attention to their energy levels that day. While not all of the associated symptoms of SA change quickly, at least one or two will, and it is critical to hone in on the positive signs as they appear. Other symptoms will change later, and some not at all. Often, one early sign of change is that patients do not have to wake up to go to the bathroom at night. Once the patient begins to experience at least one real difference in their previous difficulties, the process becomes easier.

Identifying Mechanical Challenges

Progress can be compromised by other clinical problems. Comfort with the mask, mouth breathing, and anxiety reactions all become serious challenges to adoption if not dealt with quickly. The therapist should take the initiative to ask about problems with use of the machine, comfort with the masks, and problems with mouth breathing.

With regard to mask fit, the patient needs to know that there is an optimal degree of tightening of the headgear straps; more is not better as overtightening will impair the seal and will cause the mask to leak. Similarly, use of the nasal pillows can cause rhinitis (runny nose). Without proper guidance, all this can become very discouraging to the patient. At this stage, the best referral is to a large-volume supplier who often has more options and experience with fitting masks for difficult patient situations. The patient should be encouraged to be actively involved in making these decisions.

Panic Attacks and Fear of Suffocation

It is common for some patients to wake up in the middle of the night and feel they are suffocating. Upon awakening, the patient may think "This CPAP machine is choking me." This experience can happen because of claustrophobic feelings but can also be triggered by actual objective mask problems causing a feeling of suffocation.

Specifically, with a nasal mask, opening the mouth will lead to oral air escape which can give a sense of suffocation. In patients with normal nasal function, this will lead to the patient closing their mouth, thus correcting the abnormal air escape. However, in patients with nasal problems or habitual mouth breathing, this may not happen. Taping the mouth shut with surgical tape will often resolve this problem.

Mouth breathers can benefit from changing to a full face mask. Alternatively, because of the larger size of these full face masks (which are more obtrusive and have greater facial coverage), some patients will feel more claustrophobic with a full face mask. In such patients, a trial of nasal irrigation with a mild saline solution prior to bed (like Netipot), or use of a nasal aspirator (like HydraSense), corrects this problem for many patients. If it does not, corrective nasal or sinus surgery can be helpful. Patients have to understand that such surgery does *not* correct their OSA; it will just enable them to use a less obtrusive nasal mask.

Additionally, because of various anatomical factors, some patients will need quite high CPAP pressures, causing tolerance problems. In such cases, certain pharyngeal operations, such as uvulopalatopharyngoplasty (UPPP), may not be curative but will allow the use of a lower CPAP pressure. Similarly, many patients require higher CPAP pressures while sleeping supine. Thus, if the pressures needed are too high, another strategy is to combine an appropriate lower pressure (as determined by the CPAP titration) together with position management to keep the patient off their back.

Panic reactions can be very intense and disturbing to the patient. Ignoring these feelings or focusing on anything else will usually not be credible to the patient. These can often be effectively managed by doing trauma work around the panic triggered by putting on the mask. A patient I treated with EMDR started with her memory of panic triggered by the mask. After a number of sets of bilateral stimulation, she recalled the terrifying experience from decades ago when her then boyfriend tried to strangle her and she ran away. This memory had completely disappeared from her awareness, but the sensation of breathing through the mask retriggered her panic. After this one session, she was able to use her CPAP machine.

Finally, in addition to the comorbid presence of anxiety disorders, there can also be the comorbid presence of insomnia together with sleep apnea. In a recent review of studies that evaluated the presence of insomnia symptoms within their cohort of OSA patients, Luyster and colleagues (2010) found that prevalence of insomnia ranged from 39% to 55% depending on criteria used for defining insomnia. The authors highlight that the existence of an unidentified comorbid insomnia will likely complicate acceptance of the CPAP treatment and that attention to the potential impact of the insomnia on acceptance of the CPAP therapy is important for long-term management of these patients. Interventions in the next chapters can be added after the CPAP use has stabilized.

Relaxation Training

Understanding the dynamics of the panic attacks is not enough to stop the panicky reactions. These are automatic and visceral and can keep occurring for months. To help the patient overcome these anxiety reactions, deep breathing and progressive muscle relaxation can be very useful. Individually tailored exercise prescriptions (e.g., walking 5 days a week) can also be helpful in managing anxiety.

Most patients take 4–6 weeks to get a reliable sense that they can modulate their anxiety. When that happens, they start having confidence in their ability to manage their anxiety and usually begin to report the first nights of using the machine for 6 hours or more.

The alternative to training the patient to relax is to get a machine with a ramp up feature that gradually increases the air pressure across a 30-minute window or to have the patient take a sleeping pill for a 2-week adjustment period. The sleeping pill will help many patients sleep through the panicky feelings initially. After 2 weeks, the underlying anxiety reaction about suffocation is usually deconditioned if the patient has been using the machine across the entire night. If they have not, it can continue to be a problem, and a longer period with the hypnotic may be needed.

Cognitive Challenges

Another complication that can arise is complaints of cognitive impairment by the patient. This can be secondary to the long-term effects of untreated OSA. Or it can be the onset of dementia that could be related to family risk, smoking, or other risk factors that are only being exacerbated by the OSA. In any case, it is often important to evaluate cognitive competence. The Montreal Cognitive Assessment (MoCA; Nasreddine et al., 2005) is one of the more sensitive tests to detect early slippage.

Patients who are in decline should be counseled to be active, get as much bright light as possible during the day, and continue to use the CPAP and other sleep hygiene strategies to optimize their sleep pattern. Recent research has also emphasized the importance of maintaining predictable daily patterns of activity to improve functionality.

Tracking "Good Days"

Once all forgoing clinical tasks have been completed, review of energy levels on "good sleep" days becomes much more meaningful. The patients are more interested in their results and start to experience more regular success. Bringing their attention to the positive days is very important. While setbacks continue to be typical, the patient can now see the good along with the bad. This creates more incentive to put more effort into accentuating the positive gains (see Reitav [2012] for clinical examples).

As the CPAP begins to heal sleep, the patient will be able to experience dreams and nightmares that were previously inaccessible. These events are illustrated in the following clinical example. Working clinically with these nightmares will be elaborated in Chapter 9.

Case Example of Patient's Transition to Adhering to CPAP Treatment

THERAPIST: It sounds like adjusting to the CPAP has been up and down. Are you having any difficulties keeping the mask on?

PATIENT: Sometimes it comes off. I'll wake up and it's on my forehead. My wife told me a couple of times she has put it back on. I don't even wake up. But I have an app on my phone, and it tells me how long I had it on for. Last night my score was 87 out of 100. I had it on for almost 6 hours. I was in bed for a little over 7 hours, so it must have come off at some point. I had 1.2 events per hour, so when it is on, I don't have apnea. It also says my mask came off three times. I might have gotten up to go to the bathroom one of those times.

The night before I had it on for 8 hours and 30 minutes. I had a long sleep. And then I've got a few nights where it was on for 8 hours. It's got all kinds of information on it. Tutorials on videos, you can increase the moisture in it.

Something else I noticed. On nights that I have a couple of glasses of wine, my score is lower. Like I must move around more. Because the mask comes off way more when I've had some wine. I wasn't going to have any wine last night, but my neighbor comes over. He brings his father's homemade wine. I had a couple glasses of wine with him on the porch, and then my sleep was crappier.

The first three nights with this new CPAP, I had nothing to drink. And I slept for 8 hours and 25 minutes; 8 hours and 6 minutes; 7 hours and 45 minutes. And then I had some drinks the next night and I was only sleeping 2 hours and 46 minutes. I think the mask must have come off a whole bunch of times.

THERAPIST: A couple of things are going on. One is that you are moving around more. A second is that wine (or any alcohol) goes back to where it came from. So how do you produce alcohol? You get sugar and you ferment the sugar. Sugar becomes an alcohol. When you drink the alcohol and it goes into the stomach, the alcohol switches back into sugar. And of course, sugar is like gasoline to the body. It is energy.

The alcohol increases your body temperature, like revving up an engine. That is going to make you move around more. You'll also be a little warmer or sweaty, which means that your sleep will not be as deep.

And the final thing that the alcohol does is it relaxes muscles. Which is part of the reason we drink it. We feel calmer. We feel more relaxed, which is all good, except part of the muscle groups that it relaxes are the throat muscles. These soft tissues sink into the throat, closing the airpipe, which causes the apnea. When you drink, they close more frequently. This causes more arousals from sleep and your nervous system has to kick in and wake you up more.

Each of those three reasons contribute. They all play a role in making your sleep worse. What your machine is telling you is that alcohol is not a friend of sleep. It is not going to improve your sleep pattern.

I don't think you should stop drinking altogether. I mean, enjoying a glass of wine with dinner or having a drink with your friends. That is part of quality of life. I wouldn't change that, but what it is telling you is don't go having a couple of drinks one after the other. The more you drink, the more it will affect your sleep.

You are now in the driver's seat. Because the machine lets you know right away how much your drinking is making your sleep worse. The app gives you direct feedback.

PATIENT: The first three nights that I had it, I had long sleeps with it. It worked. When I put it on. When I pulled it off, just a little bit off my nose,

Identifying and Removing Major Sleep Roadblocks to Trauma Work

you really feel how much air it is pushing through. When the seal is poor, then I can feel it. But when the seal is good, you can't really notice it. It's like meditating. Putting the mask on and concentrating on the feeling of the air going in. It helps me fall asleep.

I'm not sure if I told you about this recurring dream I've had numerous times. I always forget it. This morning I remembered it. It's not really a nightmare. I'm in school, whatever university or college or whatever it is. And I realized that I that I'm behind on all my assignments. I get in a panic thinking I'm so far behind I can't catch up. And it's quite a stressful feeling.

I went to school a couple of years ago, for two years. I took a resource drilling course at my college. I never got behind on stuff. I always kept up on it. That was one of my things, "never fall behind." I'm dreaming that I did fall behind.

THERAPIST: We can do some reprocessing work around the emotion. That dream, especially if it's a recurring dream, it means there is a deep sense of fear. This is a deeper fear that has been around for a while.

PATIENT: It creates a fair amount of stress. I didn't have it last night, but I had it the night before. I remembered it and I kept it in my head, so I wouldn't forget it. It's not an end of the world kind of thing, or involving people getting hurt, or anything, but there's still real fear.

THERAPIST: Going back to the dream and that sense of being way behind and feeling that it's hopeless, catching up is going to be impossible.

PATIENT: It's always been in a dream that I felt panicky.

THERAPIST: When do you think you first had the dream that you were behind?

PATIENT: I've had it for months. And I never clued in that it was causing me to wake up. Which it did.

THERAPIST: Could it be that happened on those days that you wake up in a sweat?

PATIENT: It's nothing compared to other stuff. But for whatever reason, it creates a panic and a stressful situation. Like to the point where it actually felt totally real. I wake up and I realize, wait, I'm not in school anymore.

The session continues on by focusing on the anxiety dream, to use this trigger to reset the autonomic system. A detailed example of how this work proceeds can be found in Chapters 8 and 9. What this vignette illustrates is that the sleep challenges are intimately interlaced with other clinical issues, like alcohol use and the emergence of recurrent nightmares. In this instance, the therapist goes on to deal with the emergent anxiety issues. All of this corroborates the TABS model, which underlines that progression across the treatment will inherently involve attending to all four clinical areas: significant traumas, attachment issues, physical problems, and sleep disturbances.

APPLICATION

To make effective use of the information you have been reading, we invite you to apply the concepts described in this chapter by engaging patients with these important steps in exploring their sleep:

Develop an Index of Suspicion and Empathically Explore for Signs of Apnea: Engage the patient in a brief exchange, asking about whether they snore at night, wake up with a headache or dry mouth, feel tired or sleepy during the day, and feel rested enough to get through their whole day without taking a nap.

Develop Confidence in Giving Your Patient the STOP-BANG and ESS Tests: Begin by completing the tests yourself. See how long it takes you. Compare your answers to the scoring criteria. Read the articles that provide validation of the results. Write out the main points you would want to communicate to your patient about the impact of undiagnosed apnea on their symptoms and difficulties.

Develop Confidence in Answering Questions About Sleep Test and Outlining Their Benefits: Describe the process of going for a sleep test to a friend or family member. Get feedback on whether describing the process was helpful to your friend. Then try communicating the same information to a patient who may be at risk for apnea.

Review a Sleep Test, Identify Key Findings Indicating Apnea, and Describe the Importance of These: Obtain a sleep report (yours, or a patient or family member) and look for the sleep efficiency, sleep architecture, and sleep arousal results. Describe the importance of these. Then look at the conclusions made in the report about the causes of those findings. Look for the AHI and SaO2 levels. Compare how serious you think they are with how the report is concluded. Describe the importance of these to your friend. When you are comfortable with this, repeat these steps with your patients.

Answer All Questions Your Friend May Have and Learn to Deal With Their Concerns: Once you are comfortable with the serious impacts of apnea on your patients, see how comfortable you are in dealing with the many resistances of trauma patients to starting or continuing with a CPAP. Learn to become comfortable with the interventions to manage adherence problems as described in this chapter.

Key Messages for Therapists

1. Sleep apnea is the most important sleep disturbance to detect. Of all sleep disturbances, apnea carries the most toxic impact on both trauma treatment outcomes as well as increased vulnerability to numerous serious

health outcomes (like diabetes, chronic pain, suicidality, cancer, heart disease, and stroke).
2. Trauma patients themselves have no idea that they may have apnea and certainly don't understand the health consequences of undetected apnea. Therefore, the responsibility for detecting the telltale signs of apnea rests with the trauma therapist. Developing a healthy index of suspicion for apnea means regularly asking about the typical signs of apnea. Be prepared to follow this initial inquiry by administering the STOP-BANG and ESS screening tests and discussing the meaning of the results with your trauma patient.
3. Develop confidence in discussing these important topics with your patients, friends, and family. This will come slowly with more experiences in having these talks regularly. Reach out to sleep clinics in your community to discuss some of the challenges you face with your patients in going for sleep tests.
4. Anticipate that all PTSD patients will have occasional or persistent problems with adhering to CPAP treatment. Normalize these adjustment problems and discuss multiple ways of tackling them. Become familiar with the strategies described in this chapter and return to them as often as needed.
5. As the patient achieves increasing success with CPAP usage, celebrate these achievements with them. Encourage patients to start tracking the number of good days they have each week. The goal is to achieve four good days each week. Transition the ownership for their efforts at improving their sleep to the patient. This is something tangible they can do to accelerate their resolution of their trauma symptoms.

7

Sleep-Wake Reorganization With Zeitgebers

"Behavioral Sleep Medicine (BSM) refers to a branch of clinical sleep medicine and health psychology that (1) focuses on the identification of the psychological (e.g. cognitive and/or behavioral) factors that contribute to the development and/or maintenance of sleep disorders, and (2) specializes in developing and providing empirically validated nonpharmacological interventions for the entire spectrum of sleep disorders."

—Edward Stepanski and Michael Perlis (2003, p. 3)

"Behavioral rhythms well-tuned to circadian rhythms are necessary for health. Without the deepest sleep [i.e. slow wave sleep (SWS)] . . . coupled with REM sleep, psychological difficulties will ensue."
—Donald Pfaff (2019, p. 100)

Late one December evening in 1951, Eugene Aserinsky observed his 8-year-old son, Armond, as he slept in a sleep lab. Sometime after falling asleep his son's eyes began darting from side to side. At first, Eugene thought that Armond had awakened, but he was astounded to find that the boy was still asleep. Why would his eyes move when he was deep asleep? Eugene was intrigued and kept close vigil that night. This observation marked the discovery of a hidden mystery and an essential element of restorative sleep. The discovery of REM sleep launched the renaissance of scientific investigation of sleep that continues to this day (Aserinsky & Kleitman, 1953).

Investigations into treating sleep disorders accelerated in the 1970s and '80s. By the 1990s five interventions had coalesced to form the core of cognitive behavioral therapy for insomnia, or CBTi. These components included stimulus control, sleep restriction, relaxation training, sleep hygiene, and cognitive restructuring. Randomized controlled trials (RCTs) across the next 30 years have confirmed the power of these interventions, with the result that CBTi has now been endorsed as the frontline treatment for insomnia by the American Family Physicians Association as well as by many other international authorities. These studies of the efficacy of CBTi show large effect sizes for those with insomnia. While the means for the whole group improve, there remains a subgroup of about 20% of insomnia participants who do not improve with CBTi alone. This subgroup is made up of those whose sleep disturbance is the result of trauma, head injury, or other medical conditions like chronic pain.

While CBTi alone is not enough to repair the sleep of trauma patients, it still remains a core part of the necessary interventions to repair sleep in this more complex patient group. This chapter will summarize the ways in which these interventions are integral to the trauma work with these patients. They are an important cornerstone of guiding those with trauma toward healthier sleep, but they are not the entire answer. They do, however, provide a foundation on which the other interventions can rest.

Many factors can disrupt sleep, and many factors have to come together to support sleep. Across the years I have been practicing, almost every patient coming in to see me will tell me, "I've tried that" with whatever I suggest. The solution to fixing the 10 things wrong with sleep is not to fix only one and conclude that treatment doesn't work. It is to fix all 10 at the same time.

Among the most important ideas in this book is the simple suggestion to start by making the simple changes. The simple changes all relate to honoring the basic circadian rhythm that all of us have to live by on this planet. Living in harmony with daily light-dark cycles of the planet we live on is easier and more productive than flying in the face of our biology, our nervous system, and our hormones.

In Chapter 1 we introduced the five factors contributing to sustainable restorative sleep. These included:

1. Consistent times to start and end sleep.
2. Nightly sleep duration of 7 hours or more of total sleep time (TST).
3. Excellent quality intensity (good delta power) in slow wave sleep (SWS).
4. Stability and continuity of sleep across the 7-hour sleep period (with few awakenings and swift return to sleep).
5. An active daytime agenda including exposure to sunlight, physical activity outdoors, regular meals, and face-to-face time socializing with others.

Of these five, only the first and fifth factors are directly under our conscious control. The remainder require sleep-wake circuits that are able to push us into the deeper stages of sleep unimpeded. When there is no interference from the body or from the innate alarm system, brain waves that signal integration of the thalamus and cortex appear spontaneously during sleep and activate stable and continuous sleep rhythms that support healthy functioning.

When the body sends signals of distress (pain, cold, hunger), sleep rhythms are sabotaged. We can't make ourselves sleep 7 hours, nor can we stop our body or nervous system from repeatedly awakening us. How well our nervous system pushes us into deep sleep is determined by the communication between brain centers.

Duration of sleep, depth of SWS, and continuity of sleep are all determined by the underlying stability of the autonomic nervous system (ANS). In this chapter we will elaborate on the ways of assessing how well a person is doing in controlling the behavioral factors over which they have some control. The larger issue of stabilizing the ANS will be elaborated in the remaining chapters in the book.

What I will learn in this chapter to become a better sleep and trauma therapist:

1. Understand that sleep changes from night to night. Many physical, emotional, and cognitive events impact it. One of the best ways to change sleep patterns is to track them across 2 weeks or more with a Consensus Sleep Diary.
2. Be able to guide patients to using the Consensus Sleep Diary.
3. Review the Consensus Sleep Diary with the patient, discussing the indicators of distressed sleep (sleep quality and daytime impact), as well as the measures of sleep that can be changed: (1) regularity of sleep and wake times, (2) sleep fragmentation, and (3) total sleep time. Consideration of these measures leads to review of problems in transitioning into and out of sleep.
4. Formulate the likely causes of the sleep disturbance. How are each of the four enemies of sleep contributing to the sleeplessness of your patient? In order of priority, these are: (1) hypoxia (apnea), (2) dysregulated sleep circuitry (circadian disorders, narcolepsy, sleep paralysis), (3) body distress (tension, pain, hunger, cold/heat), and (4) sympathetic hyperarousal (shock, emotional distress, rumination).
5. Understand that once hypoxia has been addressed, dysregulated sleep rhythms are the next priority. Be able to communicate the importance of keeping to regular sleep-wake rhythms to enhance the body's ability to use the sleep time to refresh, reorganize, and recharge for the next day's activity.
6. Manage common problems in starting to use the Consensus Sleep Diary.
7. Manage complex sleep challenges of trauma patients. Engage the patient in setting a first priority for changing their sleep pattern. Track their adherence to treatment suggestions and provide necessary support as they work to improve sleep and prepare for trauma work.

SLEEP DIARY 101
Normal Sleep Cycles

Our sleep across the night is not uniform. What the brain is doing as we sleep is cycling through SWS and REM every 90 minutes. The last 2 hours of sleep are spent mostly in REM sleep or dreaming sleep (see Chapter 1 for detailed discussion).

REM sleep is particularly important for managing moods. One of the best accounts of what the mind does across the 24-hour day, was provided by Rosalind Cartwright (2010). She highlighted the importance of the repeated shifts from NREM (deep slow wave sleep) to REM, back to NREM and REM. This sequence is repeated four to five times across the night, and each cycle helps the mind reorganize itself for the next day. When that dance between NREM and REM is broken, the mind's ability to desensitize difficult feelings and reorganize your long-term memory system is also broken.

What Cartwright (2010) found is that at the beginning of the night, most people were focused on their negative moods or whatever had upset them. Perhaps it would be a sense of feeling alone. During SWS, these emotional experiences are activated in the hippocampus and transferred to the cortex. In the subsequent REM period the amygdala adapts to the content by desensitizing the emotional reactions. Across the night repeated NREM-REM cycling results in the negative mood changing. In parallel with the emotional desensitization, during REM additional associations from long term memory are triggered by the current problem. The last dreams of the morning became more interesting and more complex. By morning, these repeated NREM-REM cycles transformed the negative evening moods into a positive outlook to start the new day. Importantly, this desensitization did not occur for the depressed participants, as their NREM sleep did not mobilize the emotional memories for processing.

That is how the sleeping brain actively helps us adjust to whatever challenges we might have day to day. It does that for us every single night. But of course, it can only do that if we are getting into SWS and REM repeatedly. If our sleep pattern is interrupted with repeated awakenings, that fragments the healing functions of our sleep. We may not be getting into much REM sleep, or if we are getting into REM sleep, we may not be getting that shift from those negative feelings toward a sense of feeling more confident, or capable of managing the challenges that we face.

That restorative function of the cycling between SWS and REM does not depend on remembering dreams. All of that is happening, even if we do not remember a dream. However, remembering dreams brings that integrative cycling function to our conscious awareness.

If we do remember our dream, we might have noticed that our dreams will vary in how much intense emotion we experience in the dream. The most intense are replicative nightmares that replay an actual traumatic experience over and over. In this instance the emotions are so intense that the desensitization function of REM sleep is overwhelmed, and transformation can't begin. Other nightmares also carry intense feelings, and the transformative processes can begin but are then overwhelmed; the emotions terminate the REM episode, and we wake up in a sweat or a panic.

If affective load is not overwhelming, the dreaming process continues and we wake up with a dream that is more focused on the emotional issue that we are struggling to solve. When dreams are pleasant we are probably going to wake up feeling more refreshed and more positive. In some cases, we may actually have an important insight into a problem with which we have been struggling.

An achievable goal for trauma patients is to improve the consistency and depth of sleep across the night. As depth of sleep improves, they will begin to notice: "I had fewer nightmares"; "I had fewer awakenings"; "I slept through the night"; and "I remember dreaming about something." Even if they cannot remember what they were dreaming, the fact that they are getting into deeper sleep is what is allowing those dreams to happen. And that is good sign, whether they remember the dream or not.

Sleep restores immune functioning and reduces inflammation. A good night's sleep helps the immune system protect the body from viruses and bacteria. Studies have been done looking at what happens when you go for a vaccination. The vaccination presents your immune system with features of the virus you want to fight. When presented with the virus features, the immune system then produces antigens that look for those features of the virus. The antigens become your early warning fighting force. What has been shown is that when you have slept poorly in the period before the vaccination, you produce less fighting force (Prather & Leung, 2016; Spiegel et al., 2002). Those who slept well produced many more antigens than the poor sleepers.

Sleep helps your trauma patients. Not only in feeling in a better mood, having more energy, and more attention to use the therapy session more productively, it also helps them in stabilizing the continuous surges of sympathetic arousal that activate a range of bodily symptoms. Sleep has advantages for both psychological and physical functions. Following are detailed instructions to patients for tracking sleep.

Detailed Instructions to Patients for Tracking Sleep

Tracking your sleep across a two week period is one of the easiest ways to see what is good and bad in your current sleep pattern. This information is necessary for us to understand what we need to do to improve your sleep. Tracking sleep takes 3 minutes at night and another 3 minutes in the morning. You will be tracking your sleep using a form that captures the important aspects of your sleep, the Consensus Sleep Diary (Figure 7.1). You will answer the first five questions every night before you turn off your light. And you will answer the last eight questions (6 through 13) as you are getting out of bed in the morning. During the night, your only task is to do your best to sleep. No watching the clock and no writing.

During the night, please do not try to look at the clock every time you wake up. The sleep diary is about how you remember your sleep in the morning, when you wake up. It is not a minute-by-minute tabulation of the times you were up.

In fact, for the entirety of your treatment, please turn your bedroom clocks to face away from you or move them to a room outside your bedroom. You do not need to know what time it is during the night. Your only job is to relax in bed and be curious about whether you can get to sleep.

Shifting Focus: From Individual Nights to the Overall Pattern of Sleep

One of the most important ideas to appreciate is that no single night of sleep is significant by itself. What we're looking for is the overall integrity of the underlying rhythm of your sleep and waking periods. Are you getting into a restful sleep that is fairly predictable and is long enough to get you through the entire day of activity? We are looking at the stability of the recurring sleep-wake pattern and what prevents it from being more consistent.

This bigger picture will come into focus in the next week or two. Across a 2-week period, you are going to see some good nights and some bad nights. That broader lens will give you a better feel of your sleep rhythm. Continuing to track your sleep will allow you to see the changes happen. At this point, it is normal for your sleep to get better and worse and for it to bounce around. You will begin to see how many good nights you have, and how many bad nights. There are no expectations. You can't get it wrong. We will just be curious about what we find.

REVIEWING THE SIX KEY FEATURES OF SLEEP FROM SLEEP DIARY RESULTS

1. Sleep Quality

The first thing to look at is how each night of sleep feels to you the sleeper. This is the sleep quality rating on the chart (Figure 7.1, row 13). The range is between "very poor" and "very good." When you look across the seven nights that you tracked, there's a range of qualities of sleep possible (from seven "very poor" sleeps, all the way to seven "very good" sleeps). That range is very instructive and gives an initial measure of how distressed you are with your sleep pattern. If all the ratings are very poor, the sleep problem is chronic and will require persistence in making many changes. If there are even 1 or 2 nights that are better

FIGURE 7.1 Consensus Sleep Diary Source: Adapted from Carney et al. (2012)

Today's Date _____	Measures	Example	Day 1	Day 2
1. How long and when did you nap or doze today?	Naps	45 minutes 2:30 p.m.		
2. How much did poor sleep affect you today?	Daytime Impact	0 = none to 5 = severe		
3. Name and dose of any sleep medication you take tonight	Medications	Ambien 5 mg		
4. What time did you physically get into bed?	Time in Bed	10:30 p.m.		
5. When did you start trying to go to sleep or turn off the light?	Lights Out	11:30 PM		
6. How long did it take you to fall asleep?	Latency	60 min		
7. How many times did you wake then go back to sleep?	Number of Awakenings	3		
8. In total, how long did These (#7) awakenings last?	Wake After Sleep Onset	70 min		
9. When did you wake up and not fall back to sleep?	Morning Awakening	6:30 a.m.		
10. What time did you get out of bed for the day?	Time Out of Bed	7:00 a.m.		
11. Time alarm was set or time you intended to awaken? N/A if neither.	Anchor Time	8:00 a.m.		
12. From time to bed (#4) until up for the day (#10), how many minutes were you out of bed?	Time Out of Bed at Night	40 minutes		
13. How would you rate the quality of your sleep?	Sleep Quality	_ Very poor _ Poor _ Fair _ Good _ Very good	_ Very poor _ Poor _ Fair _ Good _ Very good	_ Very poor _ Poor _ Fair _ Good _ Very good

(maybe "fair") then you can begin to reflect on the difference between better and not so good nights.

2. Daytime Impact of Sleep

While the sleep quality tells you how good or bad your sleep felt in the morning, your rating of how much your sleep affected you in your daytime activities shows the seriousness of the impact of sleep on your life. This is a measure of the functional impairment that you feel. Do you have enough energy to finish all the tasks you were intending to, or not? Are you able to concentrate, remember, and problem solve? How is your mood throughout the day?

The Sleep Quality ratings are considered together with the Daytime Impact measures. Across a week or two, there will be both good days as well as bad days for each rating. As we compare the features of sleep that were bad on the bad days and were better on the good days, we will isolate what needs to be targeted for change. Importantly, however, there will be days that the sleep quality was poor, and the daytime impact was not as bad. These instances highlight the disconnect between subjective sleeplessness, which you feel acutely, and the depth of sleep, which you cannot feel. The next four sleep measures are the features that need to be considered to accomplish changes in sleep-wake rhythms.

3. Consistent Sleep Times

For your brain and body to use your sleep time effectively, they must be able to anticipate sleep. If you go to sleep at midnight one night and at 9:30 pm the next night, your brain will not be able to organize all the maintenance and clean-up activities it needs to accomplish. For that reason, the starting point is the consistency of your *sleep window.* A sleep window is the time you are in bed. It gives your body this window of opportunity to sleep. What time do you turn the lights out to go to sleep? Is it the same time every night? When do you wake up? Is that consistent?

Your wake-up time is the most important measure tracked by the sleep diary. A consistent wake-up time anchors your nervous system to the 24-hour cycle of light and dark. Keeping your wake-up time anchored at one particular time is what allows the nervous system to integrate all the activities of your organs and tissues. Every cell in your body has an internal clock, a pacemaker that tells it what it needs to do and when. Waking up at the same time every day is what keeps this internal environment coordinated.

Reviewing the diary. When you review a sleep diary of someone who is not sleeping well, you can expect that there is no consistency with lights out and anchor times. Ask about the activities, obligations, and events that have bumped your patient from keeping regular sleep and wake times. This will provide you with a list of the issues that need to be resolved before a restorative sleep pattern can be established.

4. Total Sleep Time

The guideline for adults is that adults 18 to 65 should get 7 hours or more of sleep each night. That means a 7-to-8-hour sleep window and sleeping for most of it. From the sleep diary, how long were you in bed? How long did you sleep? Did your total sleep time get to the 7-hour target? How many nights?

Commentary. All those complaining of disturbed sleep will not be getting enough total sleep time (TST). Paying particular attention to how often they get a night of 7 hours of sleep is a starting point. Severely disturbed sleepers will have a TST of only 4 to 5 hours. Moderately disturbed sleepers have a TST of 5 to 6 hours. Mildly disturbed sleepers get 6 to 7 hours of TST. The TST of the person you are working with gives you a broad indication of the severity of the sleep difficulty. However, the moderating effect of age is also important to consider (with younger adults tending to sleep more and older adults sleeping less), as is the individual's need for sleep.

On nights that the sleeper did not get 7 hours of sleep, what interfered with their sleep? Is the interference due to the same problem, or are there a variety of disruptors? Creating a list of these factors at the first review of a sleep diary is extremely helpful. This leads to a better formulation of treatment targets.

5. Fragmented Sleep

Waking up repeatedly throughout the night fragments your sleep, breaking it into little pieces of sleep. The more fragmented your sleep is, the less likely you are to feel rested in the morning. Lines 7 and 8 (Figure 7.1) give the information about how many wakes after sleep onset (WASO) and the total time of WASO you had during your time in bed. It is normal to have brief awakenings from sleep across the night. You may awaken to a sound outside, or to go to the bathroom, or from a dream. In these instances, you will usually settle back and fall asleep within 10 to 20 minutes.

Commentary. Multiple nightly awakenings every night, or awakenings that keep the sleeper up 30 to 60 minutes or more, are very corrosive to restorative sleep. On reviewing the sleep diary, inquire into each awakening. Was it a nightmare? Was it pain? Was it a panic attack? There are many reasons why a patient's sleep can be disrupted. You will want to understand what each of these are.

6. Compensations for Poor Sleep

When sleep problems have become chronic, you begin to make compensations to try to fix the problem. These compensatory patterns include drinking coffee or energy drinks during the day or taking naps in the afternoon or evening just to get through the day. Out of desperation, some go to bed earlier, stay in bed longer, or get out of bed in the middle of the night. Many patients come to treatment having started over-the-counter or prescribed sleep medications. You can track all of these compensatory behaviors on the sleep diary on lines 1, 3, and 12.

Commentary. All of these compensations are important. They underline the chronicity of the problem as well as the efforts made to try and fix the problem. As well as getting a list of these, find out how long these patterns have been present. Spending more time in bed, drinking caffeinated beverages, taking naps, and using sleep medications are all measures of how patients try to compensate for poor sleep. On how many of these desperate measures do they rely? Which of these is the patient motivated to change?

IDENTIFYING THE CAUSES OF DISTURBED SLEEP

Let us take the example of a very poor night of sleep, where you woke up more times than any other night throughout the 2-week tracking period. The total time that you were awake for say four awakenings combined was only about 20 minutes. While it's not like you're up for many hours staring at the ceiling, but even so, those four awakenings would really affect your sleep quality. It would also have daytime impact. Restlessness through the night translates into magnified distress through the day.

Commentary. There are two different ways of intervening for disruptions of sleep in trauma, and both are necessary. The first line of intervention is behavioral. Are the sleeper's sleep habits actually helping the nervous system use the sleep time to get restorative sleep? These behavioral anchors of sleep have to be established first. Once you have made every effort to reorganize the patient's sleep around regular sleep times, you will get a clearer sense of the disturbing impact of autonomic dysregulation. The second line of interventions will target the autonomic dysregulation, which are reviewed in subsequent chapters.

Behavioral Anchors of Restorative Sleep

Taking stock of the regular habits that have been developed around sleep is the first step. Many sleep problems are quickly resolved with these adjustments. Once you have made the effort to put them in place, if they do not work, we can begin to identify *why* they do not work. In trauma the typical impediment is dysregulation of the autonomic system.

Commentary. The first step in behavioral intervention is to get the patient to start tracking their sleep. Many patients will struggle with this. It can take weeks for patients to track their sleep regularly. During this time, your role is to educate about the value of getting a clear picture of what is going on with their sleep. This is illustrated by the case example to be reviewed shortly.

Once the patient has started to track their sleep, focus on setting a regular anchor time. The anchor time is what synchronizes all physiological, mental, and emotional activities. Start with negotiating a reasonable time to wake up every day. For example, if the sleeper wants to wake up at 8:30 a.m., that is the first, and only, change to make in the sleep pattern.

Only when the anchor wake-up time has been maintained for at least 5 days a week, should you then add a second focus of intervention. For example, beginning to set the time to go to bed. In this case, midnight would be the start of the sleep window. It is okay for the sleeper to retire to bed sometimes a little earlier and sometimes a little later. If the sleeper aims to be in bed around midnight, and turn the lights out by 12:30 a.m., their sleep window would be from 12:30 a.m. to 8:30 a.m., or 8 hours long.

Once these behavioral anchors have been set, the discussion of which intervention should follow is answered from what the patient is able to accomplish in keeping to these sleep anchors. Most trauma patients will have multiple problems in keeping to these instructions and treatment targets. As the patient brings in more sleep diaries, you can assess the underlying distress that is making it difficult to keep to the plan.

The Autonomic Nervous System Drives Sleep-Wake Rhythms

Sleep is ultimately about calming your nervous system so that you feel relaxed and calm inside across the entire sleep period. Trauma patients will not be able to achieve this with any reliability. But having set this goal focuses attention on the main disruptors as they emerge. At this point, our discussion of sleep problems turns from setting the boundaries of your sleep to the underlying distress that interferes with you keeping those boundaries.

The autonomic nervous system has two branches. The first is the sympathetic (SNS) branch, or your gas pedal. The other branch is called the parasympathetic nervous system (PNS), or the brakes. Its nickname is the rest and digest system. Rest and digest functions both happen primarily at night.

The Parasympathetic Must Rule at Night

Think of when you turn the lights out, and you close your eyes. As movement has ceased and sensory information from the environment fades, sympathetic activity is muted, darkness triggers release of melatonin, and the parasympathetic system slows metabolism and brain activity. This causes systemic changes throughout your body, including heaviness in your eyes, yawning respiration, and heaviness in your limbs. You start to feel your thoughts drift. It is harder to focus your attention, and you fall asleep.

When that braking system is working well, you not only get to sleep easily, but also get into a deep sleep. Your metabolism slows down. Your body temperature drops. Your brain and body are recharging and reorganizing themselves for the next day.

Sympathetic Bursts of Activity Fragment Sleep

What interferes with sleep is when the gas pedal, that sympathetic fight-or-flight system, is overstimulated. It can be from whatever happened the previous day, what will happen in the next day(s), or from what has been triggered by recent events. Something bothered you. It upsets you. And it sits in the back of your mind. Even though you may fall asleep, it acts like an activated memory circuit that continues in operation. It becomes a light switch that keeps flicking on in the middle of your off period of sleep. When memories are survival memories, they will wake you up, and wake you up, and wake you up. Sleep becomes a battleground between two essential neurobiological drives: survival fear and restorative needs.

These constant awakenings through the night from the activated memory circuits of the emotional centers in the brainstem do not allow the braking system to take full control. The more intense the distress, the more awakenings and the longer the awakenings. The result is little or no deep sleep. When you awaken, you don't feel rested and refreshed.

Identifying Sympathetic Triggers

The next task is identifying triggers that have activated your sympathetic system. For example, if you experienced night sweats that were pretty bad that happen a lot with menopause and your whole underlying nervous system is activated, then your sleep will likely be disrupted. In the case that follows, we focus on the initial introduction of the sleep diary into the therapeutic process. We will review edited transcripts of two consecutive sessions to illustrate the way that sleep diaries can be introduced in trauma treatment, and how the tracking of sleep brings to focus the underlying distress issues that must be tackled in the treatment.

COMMON PROBLEMS OF ADAPTING TO THE USE OF A SLEEP DIARY

Many trauma patients have trouble with starting to track their sleep. At the start of treatment they may only have completed 2 or 3 days of sleep tracking. It can be difficult for many different reasons. There may be physical pains, problems with work or family, nightmares, or worries about decisions. Trauma patients have many more disruptions of their sleep, and this can interfere with them really wanting to track their poor sleep. If the therapist begins with an understanding that the sleep-wake rhythm will generally be chaotic, or nonexistent, our first job is to begin to see it accurately.

The therapist should always ask for the completed diaries and take at least a few minutes to review them. Whatever the patient completed should be praised and reinforced. Whatever problems prevented completion should be appreciated and explored, and some solution should be found for the problems.

Once there are regular sleep diaries, the first task is to consolidate nighttime sleep. This means reducing daytime napping (which may be extensive) and reducing nighttime periods out of bed. In some cases, patients get out of bed and begin to do internet searches in the middle of the night. The section after this has many suggestions for how to manage these issues. In early sessions, the best strategy is to engage the patient in a comparison of their best night of sleep that week with the worst night of sleep that week. What was different for them when they think about those two experiences? Could they see a way that they can do more of what happened on the good night of sleep? Encouraging the patient to experiment with better coping patterns to see what happens is key in the initial stages.

As the patient engages in these experiments, some will succeed, and many will fail. Each time things do not work out as expected provides another insight into something of which the patient had not been aware or whose importance the patient had not understood. How they failed to do what they were planning to do is more important than the fact that they failed. These cycles continue for quite a while in the middle part of the therapy.

For example, one of the most common reasons that they fail to keep to a regular sleep pattern is that they experience fear, worry, panic, or a nightmare. All of these happen because their autonomic nervous system is hyperactivated. When these interferences pop up in the treatment process, the therapist can shift to doing trauma work to resolve the causes of the hyperarousal (these are reviewed in Chapters 8 and 9).

During the mid-phase of the treatment, the goal is for the patient to see that they can have 2 or 3 good (or very good) nights of sleep in the week. Highlighting that their nervous systems know how to settle down to get a good night two or more times each week is an important milestone. Many patients are genuinely surprised that this can happen. Others are too focused on the poor (or very poor) nights to even notice the good sleeps. Highlighting what is getting better is critical to break the sense of lack of control over sleep.

One of the paradoxical things that happens as sleep patterns improve is that the patient begins to have nightmares and more dreaming. This should be heralded as an accomplishment. It is only when sleep is deeper that the sleeping brain can even get into REM sleep. While nightmares are never pleasant, it is a sign that the nervous system has been able to begin to process some of these distressing experiences. See Chapters 8 and 9 for more information on how to work with the nightmares.

An important point in the movement toward better sleep is when the patient is able to allow themselves to feel tired and to surrender to sleep. This may require pre-sleep rituals to ensure that they will be safe in their bedroom: for some patients, a lock on their bedroom door; for others, a transitional object with which they can hug and snuggle. The therapist watches for these watershed moments when sleep does not feel as frustrating or as difficult to face for the patient.

In the last phase of the transition to a stable sleep pattern, the patient is able to keep to regular sleep and wake times, achieves a way of calming their nervous system prior to bed, and can collaborate with the therapist around the distressing memories that interfere with their ability to remain in that calm place during the night.

Along with paying attention to these nighttime changes, the therapist is also keeping the other eye on the patient's daytime experiences. Do they have more energy? Are they able to focus their thoughts better? Do they want to participate with others more often? All gradual changes in nighttime patterns will be reflected in better daytime functioning. The patient will not necessarily notice how what they have done at night helps them get through their days. The therapist must draw these to their attention.

The resolution of the background sleep pattern is achieved when sleep improves to four or more good (or very good) nights of sleep a week. At this point, the background sleep pattern is supporting the patient's engagement in the ongoing trauma work. As different traumatic events are worked through in treatment, there will be setbacks in the sleep pattern. However, these usually pass as the issues are resolved. Getting the patient to see that they can get four or more good nights of sleep most weeks is the point at which the sleep focus can be put on the back burner and the focus can switch to trauma and attachment issues.

DISCUSSION OF THE ISSUES EMERGING FROM SLEEP DIARIES

In this final section of this chapter, we will review, integrate, and expand on the clinical themes already introduced. The best way to step back and consider these themes is to take stock of the dynamic forces that are responsible for maintaining insomnia as a major sleep disturbance.

A Classic Insomnia Pattern

Insomnia means that we're not getting enough hours of sleep and that the quantity of our sleep is low compared to what we would hope for or like it to be. The Institute of Medicine in the United States came out with the recommendation that adults between the ages of 16 and 75 should be sleeping 7 hours or more a night. There are some people who can get by with a bit less sleep, but that is rare. Most of us do need 7 hours of sleep most nights.

The key point for treatment of insomnia is that the sympathetic system is in hyperarousal. The gas pedal part of the nervous system is overactive. If our car's gas pedal was pushed to the floor, we would be traveling at 100 miles an hour. And we can't go from 100 miles an hour to zero in 2 minutes. Just as it takes a long time for a car to slow down, it will take us a long time to slow down and transition into sleep.

In treatment we strive to rebalance the activity of the gas pedal and the brake pedal. If the brake is not working well, then the gas pedal easily takes over, and keeps the patient from getting into a deep sleep. Or, if we do manage to get to sleep because we are so exhausted, an overactive gas pedal can wake us up repeatedly and keep us awake for a long time. That is the system that we need to slow down. Teaching the strategies and techniques that slow down the nervous system is particularly important.

Four Enemies of Sleep: Hypoxia, Desynchronization, Hyperarousal, and Physical Distress

What are the experiences that can activate the sympathetic system? There are at least four common factors to consider. In order of the potency of their impact on sleep, these include hypoxia, autonomic hyperarousal, physical distress, and desynchronized sleep rhythms. Of the four enemies of sleep, suffocating from the lack of oxygen is the most dangerous. How to assess it and treat it was reviewed in the last chapter.

Of the remaining factors anything that causes physical distress to the body will disrupt sleep. Pain, especially chronic pain, is important to identify early and to ameliorate. Beyond pain, being hot or too cold at night, hunger, and tension in the muscles, especially the muscles of the shoulders, neck, and jaw area are all potent disruptors of sleep.

All emotions are shortcuts to taking some action: fear triggers moving away from danger, anger mobilizes energies to battle for survival, etc. All of these action impulses override sleep. And thinking itself is the sympathetic activation of the brain, which overrides the braking system. Each of these will be addressed more specifically in the clinical chapters that follow.

For now, we will focus our discussion on the critical role of *synchronizing effective sleep-wake rhythms,* by focusing on improving transitions into and out of sleep.

TRANSITION ROUTINE INTO SLEEP: BOOSTING THE PARASYMPATHETIC WIND-DOWN

Here is what we tell our patients. In order to descend into sleep, your metabolism must slow down. Everything you do to shift toward braking at night will slow metabolism. If your body temperature does not go down, you don't sleep. Prior to falling asleep your body temperature will fall by about a half a degree. Your heart rate goes down and your blood pressure drops. That is called the *dipping* phenomenon.

Dipping of metabolic activity is normal. That is what we are looking to support and enhance. It is optimal for the blood pressure to go down about 15 to 20% and heart rate to go down 15 to 20% and of course, insulin and blood sugars should drop well before sleep, as these upregulate cell energy. Eating too close to bedtime, or doing exercise that raises your body temperature, will undermine transition into sleep.

Sometimes the enemy of sleep is apnea. As we discussed in the previous chapter, when you stop breathing your nervous system has to kick in to keep you breathing throughout the night. And every time that sympathetic system kicks in you get adrenaline dumped into the bloodstream. That increases blood sugars and body temperature. If your blood sugar is going up at night that is something you need to know, as that is an activation sign of the gas pedal being pushed at night for some reason. We do not know why, but it is not a part of normal sleep patterns. If there are elevations in either blood sugar or body temperature you should go for a sleep test.

Certain skills can be helpful in slowing down the nervous system and to help boost that parasympathetic brake. It is really important to practice using these techniques over and over again so that you begin to get that shift happening.

Set Up a Wind-Down Routine to Support the Transition Into Sleep

It is important for you to have a routine and that you keep to that routine most nights. Babies are taught a nightly routine of feeding, bathing, playing, and sleeping. Our nervous system never outgrows the importance of that regular routine for sleep health. Having a regular, consistent time to go to bed and engaging in your best calming strategies in those 30–60 minutes before lights out is very important. For some, doing meditation is helpful. That can slow thinking down. Diaphragmatic breathing could also be helpful. Certain yoga techniques can be helpful. In yoga, there is the yin and the yang. Both Yin Yoga and Yoga Nidra are the more calming yoga practices.

If you are waking up repeatedly through the night or having trouble getting to sleep, you will need a wind-down period of at least 30 minutes. During that time you will actively do what boosts the parasympathetic braking system. Practicing your calming techniques like taking diaphragmatic breaths, listening to music, practicing meditation, or doing yoga will take time, but is essential for a deep transition into sleep.

As we get older, most of us do tend to wake up at least once during the night. But that should not be for about 4 1/2 hours or so. If you're waking up before 4 1/2 hours the gas pedal is too active and it's kicking in and waking you up out of sleep prematurely. Diaphragmatic breathing, muscle relaxation, and meditation can be extremely helpful. We will next review 7 Sleep Practices that can be incorporated into your pre-sleep wind-down routine.

Identifying and Removing Pre-Sleep Triggers

What are some of the things you could do if you're having one of those nights? One is going out for a walk. Moving around can be helpful in burning off some of the stress hormones that build up during the day. But isn't it interesting that as soon as your normal routine is broken, then something else that you substitute may actually aggravate the restlessness?

Sleep Practice 1. Identifying the buttons that disturb your sleep. In the example from the previous chapter, drinking alcohol in the evening caused more awakenings through the night. Other examples include taking phone calls before sleep that distress you, watching exciting shows prior to sleep, starting an interesting book, etc. Tracking your sleep will allow you to notice the activities that disrupted your sleep. Use your sleep diary to identify at least three pre-sleep activities that are *disruptive to* your sleep.

Finding Braking Activities to Befriend Sleep

Some of you may find that reading will usually help you fall asleep. But if you have one of those nights where reading isn't working, I suggest listening to music rather than watching TV. The problem with TV is that nobody makes a TV show meant to put people to sleep. Every TV show is meant to capture your interest and get you thinking about something and that, of course, is all sympathetic activity. Instead of watching TV, listen to music that puts a smile on your face. Choose something that you enjoy. The melody and rhythm in music help the brain calm down. Everyone should work toward having at least 3 late night activities that are calming.

Sleep Practice 2. Use your sleep diary to identify at least three pre-sleep activities that are *calming* for you.

Whole Body Breathing

Whole body breathing means releasing as much of the chronic body tension as possible before breathing practice. This can only happen with regular targeted relaxation of all major muscle groups. Doing 25 minutes of Progressive Muscle Relaxation (PMR) during the wind-down for the next 2 months will accomplish that release.

Sleep Practice 3. Practice PMR and diaphragmatic breathing in the wind-down period before sleep for 2 months. Do 30 minutes of PMR to tune into your body's state. Are you still feeling tension? Do you feel relaxed? Where do you experience those sensations? Can you sit with the relaxation and breathe into it?

Relaxation Means Letting Go of Thoughts and Refocusing on Your Body

Transitioning from the sympathetic to the parasympathetic also means transitioning from thinking and planning to sitting with your body's sensations. Focusing on body sensations allows you to identify areas in which you feel tension. Practicing yoga can be extremely helpful. If you remember some of the yoga poses that you did at the end of a yoga session, they can help you calm down and relax. There are many choices, and just finding things that work easily for you would be a good thing.

Sleep Practice 4. After completing a few minutes of diaphragmatic breathing, take a few minutes to tune into your body sense. As you get more comfortable with pausing and connecting with your body, stay with the relaxed feeling until you fall asleep.

Acceptance of Relaxation Means Giving Up Control and Surrendering to Sleep

The difficult part of sleeping is that none of us can make ourselves sleep. Thoughts like, "I'm not falling asleep, so tomorrow is going to be terrible. How am I going to get through it?" make it even harder to fall asleep.

Grumbling and ruminating about how bad the next day might be activates and charges up the sympathetic system and pushes the moment that you fall asleep even farther away.

Sleep Practice 5. Everyone should find 3 different positions they are comfortable with, to wait patiently for sleep. Long, difficult nights require the option of shifting between these three body sleep positions, all of which are relaxing for you. If you only have one sleep position, these nights will drive you crazy.

Creating Your Oasis: Options for Activating the Braking System

Creating an oasis means building on the previous 5 Sleep Practices. After doing diaphragmatic breathing exercises, some simple muscle relaxation, and focusing on feeling calm and relaxed, consider adding imagery. For example, imagine being on the beach on a nice summer day, and feeling the warmth of the sun. Focus on things that are calming for you. When you do that, you are giving your brain the best chance of getting to sleep.

Sleep Practice 6. Develop imagery of your oasis and practice that each night.

Review Your Day and Search for Moments of Gratitude

When you have learned to be calm and relaxed, you are shifting your internal state. Another important way of doing this is to review your day's activities and find two moments that were enjoyable or memorable. Write those in a gratitude journal in as much detail as possible. Then take 5 minutes to go back into those moments and bring back the internal experience of calm and peacefulness. Take that time to savor the experience of that event. Stay with it until you can feel the calm, the contentment, or the joy.

Sleep Practice 7. Get into the habit of keeping a gratitude journal. After documenting the events, take the time to reexperience how that felt for you. When you have completed that, see if you can learn some self-compassion skills and integrate those into your pre-sleep routines.

TRANSITION ROUTINE OUT OF SLEEP: ACTIVATING THE SYMPATHETIC SYSTEM

Setting a Consistent Wake-Up Time

Even if you are far from a morning lark (getting up between 5 and 6 a.m. daily), you can learn to be consistent with a wake-up time that works for you (say 8:30). Once you have done it for 7–14 days, your brain will keep that schedule. What we do want to communicate to the brain is the regular, consistent period of time that we are going to be resting to take full advantage of getting to a deeper sleep.

Sleep Practice 8. Set a consistent wake-up time for your lifestyle. Keep this the same for weekdays and weekends. Weekly exception: you can sleep in for up to 2 hours on one day each week.

Bright Light Therapy

Once you are up, the next important thing to do is to get exposure to the sun. Right after waking up, get into a room that has the brightest view of the sun. This could be an eastward facing or southward facing room. That's ideal, because the light receptors in the back of the eye get the brain going.

You have five different neurotransmitter systems in the brain and every one of them relies on the light signal to get going in the morning. It's a kickstart. We've got lots of evidence now that getting consistent exposure to light in the morning for 30 minutes is going to help your thinking, problem solving, and concentration. That's important. Your physical energy helps to move you around and do things during the day. After exposure to morning light, your mood is going to be better, too. Those three things are all benefits from light: more mental focus, better mood, and more physical energy. It's the only free lunch that we have on the planet.

***Sleep Practice* 9.** Consider purchasing a light box for the winter. Sit in front of it for 20 to 30 minutes as soon as you wake up. The light should be no more than 2 feet away from your eyes. You do not have to stare into the light, but it should be in your field of vision, so the light gets to the back of your retina.

Regular Meals Across 10 Hours of Wake Time

The other important Zeitgeber that can help is having meals within a 10-hour band. For example, having breakfast at 8 a.m., lunch at noon, and dinner at 6 p.m. Keeping to regular times will help in predictive boosts in insulin levels. Your last meal of the day should be at least 4 hours before bedtime.

***Sleep Practice* 10.** Set alarms for the times you will be starting to prepare your meals and for the times you will be eating your meals. Keep to these times for 2 weeks.

CONSOLIDATING FRAGMENTATION OF SLEEP: SETTLING THE SYMPATHETIC SYSTEM

Tracking Your Sleep Is Descriptive (Not Evaluative)

There is one important issue to be mindful of when tracking your sleep with the sleep diary. In the middle of the night, you will be estimating times, *not* staring at the clock. *Do not* look at your digital clock throughout the night! Seeing that it's 2:31, and then seeing it again at 2:42 will not help you sleep. It is going to drive you crazy!

If you do have a digital clock beside your bed, it's helpful to turn the face of it away from you. You don't need to see the numbers because they are meaningless at night. Whether you're up at 2:30 or 5:30, your task is always the same: to rest! Just keep your morning alarm on. Your only job is to still your mind and body and rest.

Sleep Practice 11. Once you have settled in to sleep, just breathe, notice the sensations in your body, and find the most comfortable sleep position you can. For the really bad nights of sleep, it is important to have at least three different sleep positions to rotate through across a difficult night of sleeplessness.

Even Though I Am Awake, I Am Glad That I Can Care For Myself

If we are trying to follow the guideline of boosting our parasympathetic system and doing things that are calming and relaxing then just practice lying in bed feeling comfortable breathing. Focus on images that are calming and relaxing. That's how you can get yourself back to sleep the quickest. On some days it still might take an hour or more. But if you're calm and relaxed, at least your body is getting much of the restorative value of sleep. And your mind is as well because it's much calmer than if you begin to ruminate about some negative things. For example, you could repeat to yourself, "I'm awake. It is okay. Now is a time to take some deep breaths and practice relaxing." Allow your focus to shift from thinking to focusing on your breath and allowing your body to relax.

Sleep Practice 12. Find a teddy bear to snuggle with. Feeling love towards a cherished object activates your oxytocin system. The oxytocin system is the hormonal response system to love and attachment. You can nurture your teddy bear and care for it. Now send that same feeling of nurturing and care to yourself (practicing self compassion). Learn to use some positive affirmations as you relax in bed. Self-compassion skills of Tenderness, Acceptance, Loving Kindness (TALK) toward yourself can be integrated into your middle-of-the-night routines.

Tension and Pain in the Jaw, Neck, and Shoulders

Any kind of tension or aching in the mouth, the jaw, the neck, or the shoulder will disrupt your sleep. If there is tightness, tension, or pain in those structures, they send those signals of distress up to the brain via your spinal column. Where these signals enter the spinal column is right beside the main activating center that awakens you out of sleep. When these signals of tension or pain come into the spinal cord, these innervations spill over and also activate the ascending reticular activation system (ARAS). The ARAS wakes you up. If you grind your teeth at night, or have any dental pain, these send signals to the brain throughout the night. That usually means you will wake up repeatedly all night. Once these areas quiet down, you do not get that constant waking up over and over again. Anything that you can do to take care of tooth, jaw, neck, or shoulder issues is going to help your sleep. But it can take weeks for that to settle down.

Sleep Practice 13. Learn to do shoulder and neck rolls to relax the shoulders and neck. Taking magnesium glycinate or having an Epsom salt bath 1–2 hours prior to bedtime can be very helpful in releasing this muscle tension.

Medications and Sleep

All medications will affect your sleep in some way. Some will increase the amount of REM sleep; others will decrease it. Beta blockers (a class of medicines that end with "lol" like bisoprolol and atenolol) will typically fragment your sleep. If you do take beta blockers, one of the things that may help to reduce the negative impact on your sleep is melatonin. Studies done with those who were prescribed beta blockers have demonstrated that adding melatonin as well, helps to consolidate the sleep (Scheer et al., 2004 and 2012). While it is not a sleeping pill, it can help to glue your sleep together so it does not fragment as much. Consult your doctor before adding to your beta blocker regimen.

Melatonin would usually be taken about two hours before going to bed (or the same time as your nighttime medicines). Melatonin comes as three, five, or ten milligram tablets. Three or five is fine for most sleepers. Try taking melatonin for a trial period of four weeks. Tracking your sleep will allow you to see whether there is any shift in your sleep pattern.

If you are having problems falling asleep, get sublingual melatonin. Putting them under your tongue gets the melatonin working right away and helps you get to sleep faster. On the other hand, a slow-release melatonin tablet will release across the night, which will be more helpful for someone who is waking up repeatedly throughout the night. Melatonin is not a "sleeping pill"; melatonin is a messenger. Basically, it tells all the systems in the body to slow down.

Sleep Practice 14. Consider taking melatonin as a sleep aide.

Napping and Sleep

If you are napping for 2 hours, that counts toward your total sleep hours for that day. For example, if you had 6 hours and 20 minutes of sleep at night and a 2-hour nap, that adds up to sleeping for 8 hours and 20 minutes for that day. Naps boost the total sleep time (TST) you get. If you need to take a nap, go ahead and nap. On days that you may need a nap, any time after lunch is great, but do try and get the nap done before 3 o'clock.

The other issue is how long to nap. Research tells us that the best benefit for energy and alertness from a 20- to 40- minute nap (Brooks & Lack, 2006). A longer 60-minute nap will result in grogginess on awakening, but can improve memory and cognitive functioning (Stepan et al., 2021). However, if you nap for 90 minutes or longer, you have a bigger problem. You complete a full NREM-REM cycle and now your brain starts thinking, "Oh, we are starting our real sleep time." That makes it hard to wake up out of the nap. Your whole metabolism is slowing down much more than it would from a half-hour nap.

Sleep Practice 15. Nap if you need to, but keep to the two rules for naps: (1) nap before 3 p.m. and (2) keep your restorative nap to 20–40 minutes. For example, you can set an alarm for 45 minutes. If it takes you 5 minutes to fall asleep, you'll get a good 40-minute nap in, and the alarm will wake you up. Naps longer than 40 minutes will interfere with your nightly sleep.

Wearable Sleep Information

Wearables (like Fitbits, Garmins, and Apple watches) provide feedback on physiological measures of your nightly sleep. However, they all capture those physiological signals from your wrist. Your wrist does not sleep like your head sleeps. For example, there are no brainwaves in the wrist, so the wearable starts with a smaller array of neurobiological measures than you would get in a sleep study. Sleep studies capture information from your eyes, nose, neck, as well as brainwaves. Wearables track the movement of your wrist and your heart rate, and then guess what the brain is doing from that limited segment of psychophysiological data. They cannot be 100% accurate because they do not measure your brain wave activity. They do provide you with a reasonable guess about your sleep stages, but they will overestimate your awake times.

Sleep Practice 16. Most wearables (Fitbit, Apple Watch, Garmin, Muse) distill the physiological information down to an (arbitrary) rating out of 100%. Anything better than 80% is a good result.

SUMMARY FOR THERAPISTS

In this chapter you learned the importance of tracking sleep with the sleep diary, how to describe the importance of this tracking to your patient, and then how to guide your patient to using any of the 16 Sleep Practices to improve transitions into sleep and out of sleep. Tracking sleep is the foundation for integrating sleep work into your trauma work with your patients. It is especially important to see what happens as changes are introduced. As sleep patterns improve, there are opportunities to reorient treatment back to any of the four TABS targets (traumatic events, attachment wounds, physical symptoms, or continued sleep work). These will be elaborated in the remaining chapters of this book.

APPLICATION

To make effective use of the information you have been reading, we invite you to apply the concepts described in this chapter by engaging patients with these important steps in exploring their sleep:

Develop a Curiosity About Sleep-Wake Rhythms: Ask the patient if they get enough sleep. If they don't, what is preventing them from getting good sleep? Have they had good sleep in the past? Are they interested in exploring what they can do to improve their sleep?

Become Familiar With the Consensus Sleep Diary: Begin by tracking your own sleep for 2 weeks. How easy or hard is it? Use the discussion of reviewing the sleep diary in this chapter to find the strengths and weaknesses of your own sleep pattern. Is there anything you would want to change? If so, make one adjustment in your sleep pattern this week.

Develop Confidence in Using the Consensus Sleep Diary: Describe how to use the sleep diary to a friend or family member. Get feedback on whether that was helpful. Develop a 2-minute talk about how sleep helps your physical and mental health. Listen to the patient's response. If they are interested, show them how to keep a sleep diary.

Review Your Own Sleep Diary to Identify Key Areas of Difficulty: From your diary look at the pattern of Sleep Quality and Daytime Impact ratings. Is there a problem? Describe the importance of these to your friend. When you are comfortable with this, repeat these steps with your patients.

Know the Key Behavioral Interventions for Transition Into Sleep, Out of Sleep, and Consolidating Fragmented Sleep: Once you have identified which of the three problems is your patient's primary target for change, introduce one behavioral intervention and stay with it until the patient has mastered it.

Key Messages for Therapists

1. Understand that sleep changes from night to night. Many physical, emotional, and cognitive events impact it. The only way to change sleep patterns is to track them across 2 weeks or more with a sleep diary.
2. Be able to guide patients to using the Consensus Sleep Diary.
3. Review the sleep diary with the patient, discussing the indicators of distressed sleep (sleep quality and daytime impact), as well as the measures of sleep that can be changed: (1) regularity of sleep and wake times, (2) sleep fragmentation, and (3) total sleep time. Consideration of these measures leads to review of problems in transitioning into and out of sleep.
4. Formulate the likely causes of the sleep disturbance. How are each of the four enemies of sleep contributing to the sleeplessness of your patient? In

order of priority, these are: (1) hypoxia due to central, mixed, or obstructive sleep apnea, (2) dysregulated sleep circuitry (circadian disorders, narcolepsy, sleep paralysis), (3) body distress (tension, pain, hunger, cold/heat), and (4) sympathetic hyperarousal (shock, emotional distress, rumination).
5. Understand that once hypoxia has been addressed, dysregulated sleep rhythms are the next priority. Be able to communicate the importance of keeping to regular sleep-wake rhythms to enhance the body's ability to use the sleep time to refresh, reorganize, and recharge for the next day's activity.
6. Managing common problems in starting to use a Sleep Diary.
7. Managing complex sleep challenges of trauma patients. Engage the patient in setting a first priority for changing their sleep pattern. Track their adherence to treatment suggestions and provide necessary support as they work to improve sleep and prepare for trauma work.

8

Flashbacks, Nightmares, and Intrusive Thoughts

"Dreaming makes connections guided by the dominant emotion. . . . What happens following a trauma as it resolves is that gradually more and more 'usual' dream material is introduced along with the direct or metaphorical representations of the trauma."

—Ernest Hartmann (2000, p. 18, 27)

"Adding one or two sessions specific to nightmares and sleep—symptoms known to be treatment resistant—could prove to be an important addition without taking away from the essential components of established [PTSD] treatments."

—Joanne Davis (2008, p. 206)

Mental clarity, emotional balance, and sustained energy are what we all look for to start the day. These internal states depend on the appropriate amount of neurobiological maintenance work being accomplished across sleep at night. The normal rhythm of cycling through NREM and REM periods of sleep provides the physiological support for brain and body repair necessary to support daytime well-being.

A traumatic event is characterized by intense sympathetic activation in the nervous system, an explosion of hormonal activation (adrenaline and cortisol), and excessive pro-inflammatory responses in the immune system (release of endorphins and kappa opioids). These intertwined physiological responses allow intense activation of fight-or-flight energy.

While this cascade of responses provides an adaptive advantage *to act* in the moment of traumatic challenge to survive, it also creates an internal memory experience (saturated by sensory and emotional overflow) that literally develops a life of its own and can be reexperienced, over and over. These memories are so intense the person says it feels like they are back in the traumatic experience. When these intrude into waking life they result in an intrusive thought, a panic attack, a flashback, or dissociation. When they intrude into sleep they result in insomnia, a nightmare, somnambulism, or night terror.

The intensity of these surges in autonomic activity not only disturbs the normal transitions from waking to sleep and the recurring 90-minute cycling between NREM and REM that continues throughout sleep, but also continues into waking life to disrupt daytime functions. As these nighttime symptoms can be managed relatively easily, this chapter will review the nature of the autonomic hyperaroused states disrupting sleep and how to work with nightmares productively in trauma treatment.

IMPACT OF TRAUMA ON SLEEP

The impacts of trauma on sleep include: night terrors, somnambulism, bruxism, restless legs syndrome (activation of the fight or flight muscles at night), restless REM, insomnia or nonrestorative sleep (NRS), and nightmares. Night terrors are intense surges of autonomic arousal occurring as the person is transitioning into NREM sleep. They occur most often in the first 2 hours of sleep, are raw surges of amorphous emotion, and have no narrative. They can result in the person jumping out of bed and across the room. Somnambulism includes a range of activities that occur in NREM sleep, also most commonly in the first 2 hours of sleep. Such activities can last from 10 minutes to hours and include sleepwalking and nighttime binging as well as sexual and aggressive behaviors.

Nightmares are among the most common symptoms of trauma. The American Academy of Sleep Medicine (AASM; 2014) describes nightmares as *"recurrent episodes of awakening from sleep with recall of intensely disturbing dream mentation, usually involving fear or anxiety, but also anger, sadness, disgust, and other dysphoric emotions."*

The specific *DSM-5* (American Psychiatric Association, 2013) criteria for nightmare disorder are as follows:

1. Recurrent episodes of extended, extremely dysphoric, and well-remembered dreams that usually involve efforts to avoid threats to survival or security or physical integrity. The nightmares generally occur in the second half of a major sleep episode.
2. On waking from the nightmare, the individual rapidly becomes oriented and alert.
3. The episodes cause significant distress or impairment in social, occupational, or other areas of functioning.
4. The symptoms cannot be explained by the effects of a drug of abuse or medication.

5. The nightmares cannot be attributed to another mental disorder (i.e., posttraumatic stress disorder, delirium) or medical condition.

Importantly, nightmares are not only a nocturnal event. The distressed nervous system that generates a nightmare continues into daytime to impair daytime functioning. Also of interest in the *DSM-5* definition is the exclusion (5) that indicates that nightmares are considered an integral part of a PTSD diagnosis. They are expected and do not have to be diagnosed separately. However, the fact that an individual diagnosis is also possible is significant in itself. It means that there are many people who do not suffer from a full PTSD syndrome, but their underlying ANS is still hyperactivated (persistent SNS activity) and this results in reporting repeated nightmares.

Not All Nightmares Are Alike

There are other important considerations beyond that as well. For example, the Boston psychiatrist Ernest Hartmann (2000) compared nightmares of combat veterans who had had lifelong nightmares with those traumatized in active combat (often losing a close friend), and a control group of veterans who had not been in active combat. Those who were traumatized in active combat had nightmares in the first half of sleep while those with lifelong nightmares had theirs in the last half of sleep. The content of dreams was different as well. The traumatized soldiers' dreams replicated what had actually happened on the battlefield and these video clip-like replicative nightmares repeated over and over. In contrast, the lifelong nightmares were terrifying, but the imagery content of the nightmares continuously changed.

Hartmann (1996) concluded that the PTSD nightmares are "a different phenomenon, a kind of memory intrusion—not truly a nightmare at all" (p. 113). It is a flashback memory experience that occurs during REM sleep. He also noted that these replicative dreams share some similarities with night terrors. Specifically, both occur in the first half of sleep, both include an overwhelming sense of terror, and both entail muscular activity and partial arousal. Night terrors do not have the visual imagery or movie narrative that PTSD nightmares have, as they are not REM state experiences.

Hartmann also noted that such replicative nightmares are not as typical in women who have had significant trauma. He ascribed this difference to the fact that women are not as likely as men to avoid emotion or to avoid emotional contact with others. The traumatized veterans did both, which he thought supported the view that these replicative nightmare experiences occur because the veterans were in his terms "encapsulating" the overwhelming emotional aspect of their wartime trauma experiences (Hartmann, 1996, p. 113).

We will elaborate on the specific neural activation patterns that are characteristic of nightmares and how to manage these clinically.

What we have already learned from previous chapters about management of the sleep and trauma patient:

1. Use the TABS overview of patient needs to determine an appropriate focus for each phase of trauma treatment. If traumatic memories are predominant, use trauma treatment interventions, like eye movement desensitization and reprocessing (EMDR), prolonged exposure, or cognitive processing therapy (CPT) to reduce distress from these experiences.
2. Stabilize sleep as much as possible and continue with stabilization skills alongside trauma treatment (Chapters 6 and 7). Initial sleep screening identifies risks requiring a sleep test. Further sleep repair includes CBTi interventions to stabilize sleep patterns (e.g., the use of the sleep diary) to anchor regular sleep times, wake-up routines, daytime activities, and wind-down routines.

What I will learn in this chapter to become a better sleep and trauma therapist:

1. If sleep issues like nightmares and insomnia are predominant, these should be targeted directly. Nightmares can easily be addressed by teaching imagery rehearsal therapy (IRT) interventions to reduce the sensory and emotional arousal states that cause awakenings from sleep throughout the night. Insomnia will be discussed in Chapters 9 and 12.
2. The intense arousal reactions locked into the trauma victim's implicit memory system will disrupt sleep as well as daytime symptoms. Beginning by addressing the nightmares can provide quick relief of these disturbing symptoms, which can empower the patient and motivate them to continue with their trauma treatment.

Neurobiological Maturation of Brain Systems

The developmental perspective of brain maturation is critical to understanding the trauma patient's PTSD symptoms. Allan Schore (2011) has provided a synthesis of our understanding of the sequence of normal early neurobiological development (see Figure I.5). He highlights that memory consolidation proceeds by integrating information from four different areas of brain activity: brainstem, limbic system, right hemisphere (imagery focused) and left hemisphere (language focused). The sequence by which information is integrated into memory proceeds from the autonomic arousal systems in the brainstem, to the emotion processing in the limbic system, to the development of implicit (right hemisphere) memory circuits, and finally to the verbally based, consciously explicit left hemisphere memory circuits.

Importantly, the newborn arriving in the world has fully operational brainstem and limbic circuits and begins in earnest to create a felt sense of the body (within) and the world (outside). These right brain implicit memories are initially to identify specific objects as permanent things around the child (object

FIGURE 9.1   Awakenings from REM Instability in Insomnia vs. Healthy Sleepers
Source: Reprinted by permission: Eus Van Someren (2021, p. 1000) and Dieter Riemann et al. (2012)

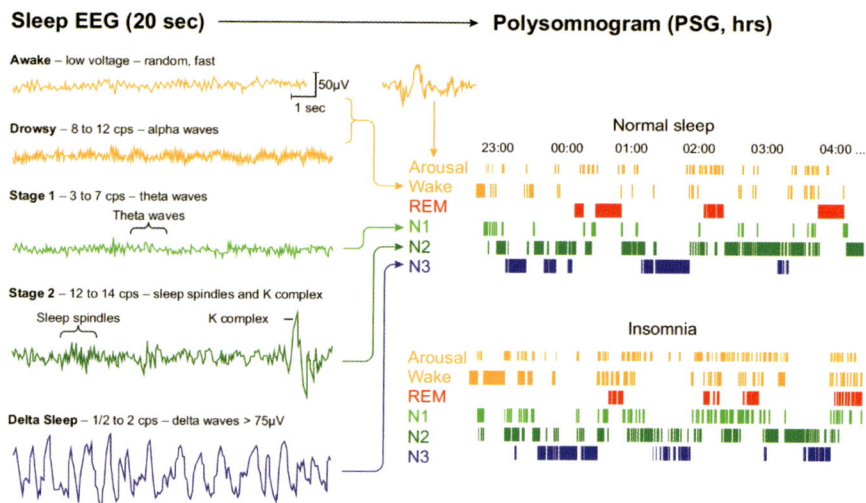

FIGURE 9.2   Normal REM Sleep With Amygdala Adaption vs. Restless REM Sleep
Source: Permission of Eus Van Someren (2021, p. 995) and Rick Wassing et al. (2019)

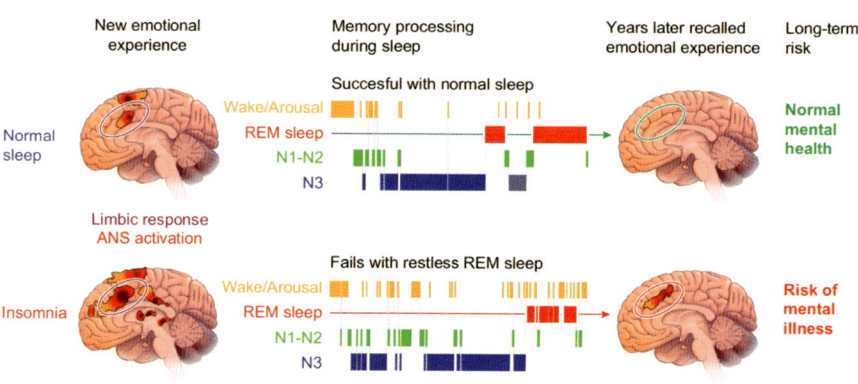

FIGURE 10.1   Impact of Secure (top) vs. Insecure (bottom) Attachment on Somatic Sensory Integration   Source: Reprinted by permission: Kearney & Lanius (2022, p. 11)

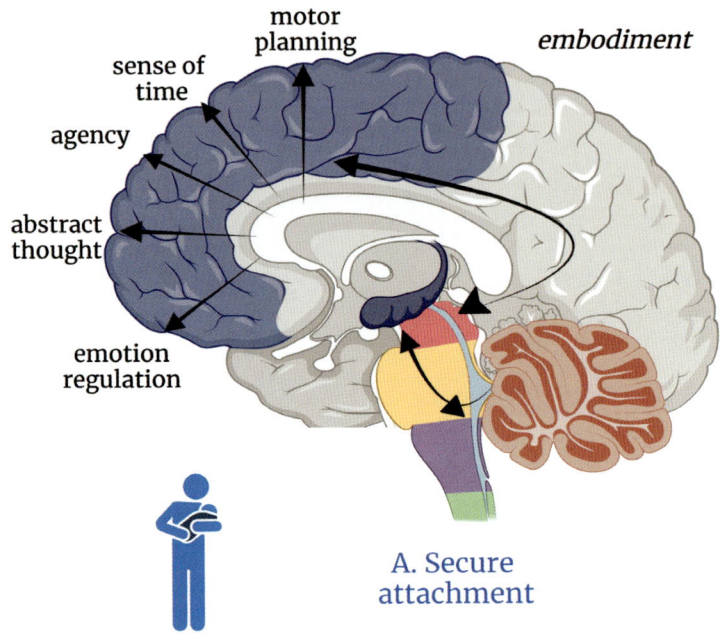

A. Secure attachment

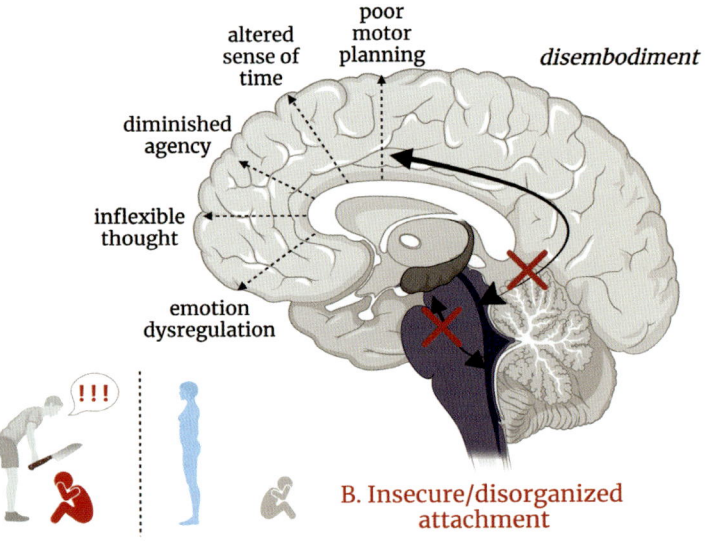

B. Insecure/disorganized attachment

permanency). Then the child begins to recognize that a specific caretaker shows up, or does not show up, to respond to their physical needs (hunger, pain, discomfort). From age 18 to 36 months the child's main mental activity is compiling thousands of experiences to create an internalized map of what living in the world feels like (how much distress there is, whether it is responded to, how safe it feels). These experiences lead to the development of reliable right brain implicit schemas of self and other, as well as strategies to best interact with others to protect the self while getting one's needs met. The composite of how the right brain has integrated these schemas is activated every night and can be seen in the dreams of the adult patient.

The left hemisphere's encoding of explicit memories must await the myelinization of the hippocampus. This occurs around age 36 months. Important attachment experiences as well as early experiences of feeling safe and protected in the world have already been encoded into years of implicit expectations about what attachments and safety in the world feel like. These are all rooted in right hemisphere implicit memories, which are stored as internal body sensations as well as visual images providing context for those sensations and feelings.

Only in the last step does a memory of being at a specific place at a specific time come into being. These episodic memories form the basis for the development of autobiographical memory, which are personal memories of specific events and experiences across our lifetime. When taken together, these create a narrative of the person's life story. This forms their sense of identity and sense of self.

The most critical function for an organism is survival. Survival is assured by the prompt response of the salience system. The salience system is responsible for being vigilant for threats to safety and then to immediately respond to that danger. This critical process happens in the brain at the first level at which incoming sensory signals (visual and auditory) are integrated, which is the superior colliculus (SC).

The SC mobilizes an *orienting tension* (OT) that recruits the involvement of three nearby brainstem structures (LC, PAG, and cerebellum), as well as the limbic system (amygdala and hippocampus). Once the SC has directed attention to the threat, the other brainstem nuclei act in a coordinated way to mount a *survival response* to the danger. Initiation of the fight-or-flight stress response is a coordinated response of all these brainstem and limbic structures. Importantly, the prefrontal cortex (PFC) (the seat of our conscious experience) is not aware of, nor involved in, these initial survival responses.

The Alarm Reaction of the Locus Coeruleus Releasing Norepinephrine

With the incoming danger signal from the SC, the LC activates the *innate alarm response* by releasing norepinephrine (NE) into widespread brain structures including the cerebellum, PAG, limbic system, and the thalamus. This surge of NE shifts all attention onto the sensory signals that are tracking the danger. These images, sounds, and somatic sensations are etched into the memory circuits providing the persistent grist for flashbacks and nightmares.

In life-or-death situations, the hyperactivated LC is continuously activating the norepinephrine circuits of the whole brain. This recruits the entire brain into a hyperaroused state. Intensified mental alertness, physiological arousal, and mobilized bodily sensations become recurring states that will now enter conscious awareness. These intense experiences of what the mind captured of the sensory and emotional right brain experiences of the traumatic event can recur spontaneously as flashbacks.

The intensity of these hyperaroused survival reactions overwhelms the usual shift into sleep at the end of the day and predisposes the individual to developing anxiety, insomnia, depression, and PTSD. A recent study with mice confirmed that acute psychosocial stress disrupted sleep (Antila et al., 2022). Specifically, stressful conditions activated the stress-regulatory LC-NE neurons during sleep. This undermined restorative NREM sleep (by increasing microarousals [MA] and reducing sleep spindles), and also reduced REM.

When stresses are amplified or continuous, such sleep disruption can persist for weeks, months, or years. This results in persistently disturbed sleep from continued elevations of LC-NE activity. Moreover, because these automatic reactions occur at the brainstem level, they occur below conscious awareness. The traumatized person will only be aware of their mental and somatic distress, and their urge to avoid whatever sensory signal triggered the danger signal.

The brainstem nuclei (SC, LC, and PAG), relay these states to the limbic structures (amygdala and hypothalamus), which interact with the thalamic nuclei to relay auditory and visual threat [via the medial and lateral geniculate nuclei (MGN and LGN)] to cortical structures [anterior cingulate cortex (ACC) and the insula] as well as the centers in which visual [inferior temporal gyrus (ITG)], auditory [superior temporal gyrus and sulcus (STG and STS)], and somatosensory temporo-parietal junction (TPJ) memories are integrated and stored.

Motor responses to *danger!* are learned and revised by signaling between the cortex [ACC, insula, ventrolateral prefrontal cortex (vlPFC), and dorsolateral prefrontal cortex (dlPFC)], the extended amygdala [central amygdala (CeA), bed nucleus of the stria terminalis (BNST), basolateral nucleus (Bn), amygdalohippocampal transition area (AHI), and nucleus accumbens (NAc)], brainstem tegmentum (red nucleus), and cerebellum.

In summary, a traumatic *danger!* experience floods the nervous system at the brainstem level with intense responses (at the very base of this sequence). The autonomic system (ANS) is overwhelmed by an intense response, equivalent to the intensity of the *danger!* in that moment. When that *danger!* is life or death, the nervous system responds with every noradrenergic fiber in the locus coeruleus (LC), every sympathetic nerve fiber of the SNS, and every drop on adrenaline available to it at the adrenal medulla. This in turn activates the most intense feeling of terror, horror, and helplessness at the limbic level.

More importantly, these internal life-or-death experiences are critical to prevent future danger, and so these memories of what the body experienced and the global context in which this reaction was triggered are locked into the right orbitofrontal cortex, as well as the brainstem salience system, especially the extended amygdala. This physiological storm of autonomic activity, when reactivated in the daytime, results in panic attacks, and when reactivated at night, creates the intense arousal leading to night terrors and nightmares.

Trauma Undermines Normal Sleep and Results in Nightmares and Restless REM Sleep

Until these experiences are downregulated, they cannot be integrated with contextual information stored in the hippocampus and then transferred to the left hemisphere of the cortex. The normal process of transforming affectively tagged memories (which routinely happens in REM sleep) is undermined by the intensity of the sensory and emotional charge of these memories. Moreover, this is not an accident. Intense raw and amorphous emotions have an intensity that overwhelms and discontiues the REM state. The nervous system has intentionally designed a system that does not erase memories with potentially life-saving information encoded in them. Their emotional intensity ensures that the memories are preserved, as a protection against potential future danger.

For the trauma therapist, the task of managing nightmares is twofold. First, to educate the patient about how these symptoms and experiences are the result of their nervous system, which is working to protect them (their left hemisphere sense of self) from horrible and overwhelming emotional, somatic, and sensory experiences sitting in the right hemisphere. And second, that these intense somatic and emotional memories can gradually be metabolized into the left hemisphere, with trauma therapy that targets the brainstem activity that is generating the symptoms.

The detailed description of these brainstem response patterns, and how these engage the limbic system, is elaborated in the next chapter. In this chapter the focus is on how the intense brainstem-limbic activation pattern is integrated into right brain implicit memories: initially with overwhelming physiological (autonomic and emotional discharge), and gradually more integrated with imagery that begins to process how the self can manage these challenging experiences.

Overview of the Visual Processing System

By way of general background, visual experiences are processed in complex ways. From the retina the visual signals travel along the optic nerve, with signals crossing at the optic chiasm. At the optic chiasm, some fibers from the optic nerve cross over to the opposite side of the brain, to begin the integration of left and right visual fields. These signals move to the superior colliculus, where integration with auditory information begins, and eye movement responses are determined to focus on objects of most interest from moment to moment.

Visual signals are forwarded to the cortex along the *tectopulvinar pathway*. At the pulvinar nucleus of the thalamus further integration of the visual signal occurs including attention and spatial awareness. These signals are sent to the *primary visual cortex* (V1) and then by two visual processing streams, which complement each other to provide an integrated experience of our current environment.

One pathway identifies *what* you are seeing. This *ventral visual stream* (VVS) processes colors, shapes, and facial features to provide object recognition information to the temporal lobes for processing visual memories. The other pathway, the *dorsal visual stream* (DVS), is the *where and how* pathway. It is responsible for determining the location of objects and their motion and creating a global spatial map of your location with respect to objects in your environment.

Visual information from the VVS is accumulated in the *inferior temporal gyrus* (ITG), features detected, and distinct objects identified and remembered. This allows the categorization of different objects (e.g., faces, tools, pets). It is at this level that we can become conscious of familiar objects and connect them with past experiences. Importantly, the ITG participates in integrating visual information with other sensory and cognitive inputs to provide a felt sense of our current environment.

This information is integrated into the default mode network (DMN). Direct input from the ITG to the DMN is the pathway that allows visual experiences to spontaneously be integrated into our moment-to-moment awareness. With trauma, the ITG provides intense trauma-related experiences to self experience, which intrude repeatedly into experience.

Activation of the Ventral Visual System Is Correlated With Flashbacks and Nightmares

An important part of the answer to what causes posttraumatic nightmares comes from a recent collaborative neuroimaging study, the Advancing Understanding of RecOvery afteR traumA (AURORA) Study. The AURORA study has been investigating the multimodal MRI markers of PTSD. Recently they explored the neural circuits activated in nightmare sufferers. The study included prospective trauma survivors who had experienced a medical accident that required participants to visit the emergency departments of hospitals. The 278 participants came from hospitals across the United States. The cohort was largely female, racially/ethnically diverse, with varying degrees of posttraumatic dysfunction.

The AURORA study published their investigation of intrusion and nightmare experiences (Harnett et al., 2022). The study explored the multimodal magnetic resonance imaging data from these patients. All patients underwent fMRI studies 2 weeks after their traumatic event and again at 6 months. In addition to the fMRI data, participants also completed the PCL-5 to assess PTSD symptoms at 2 weeks and at 6 months, as well as a measure of nightmare intensity, frequency, and severity.

The investigators identified that a visual neural network could be identified by its coordinated activation after trauma. This was the ventral visual stream (VVS). The correlated elements of this system included the inferior fronto-occipital fasciculus, visual cortex, and anterior temporal pole. Together these elements comprised the *structural covariance network* of the VVS (SCN of the VVS).

Higher loadings of this integrated visual SCN network at the 2-week fMRI study was positively associated with immediate (2-week) PTSD symptoms. Specifically, the VVS was related to increased PCL-5 *intrusive* symptoms (e.g., flashbacks, reexperiencing, etc.) ($p = 0.033$), but *not* PCL-5 avoidance, negative cognition/mood, or arousal symptoms (all $p > 0.05$). VVS activation was specifically and only associated with intrusive symptoms and significantly different from all the other posttraumatic symptom experiences (e.g., avoidance, negative cognition/mood, and arousal).

The study also measured nightmare intensity, frequency, and severity independently from PTSD symptoms measured by the PCL-5. Like the SCN relationship with PTSD PCL-5 intrusive symptoms, VVS loadings were significantly related to nightmare intensity ($p = 0.027$), but not significantly related to nightmare frequency ($p = 0.07$). However, nightmare severity (defined as the sum of nightmare intensity + nightmare frequency) was also significantly related to VVS activity ($p = 0.034$). This corroborates that an activated visual system (VVS) provides the neurobiological substrate for flashbacks and reexperiencing symptoms like intrusive thoughts and nightmares.

The study authors also explored the relationship between the activity of the VVS and the salience network by interrogating amygdala-hippocampal connectivity. Interestingly, increased activity of the VVS was found to be associated with reduced resting state connectivity between the amygdala-hippocampus and the inferior temporal gyrus (ITG). This finding indicates that these visual activation patterns are separate from the contributions of the salience system (which has long been found to be associated with PTSD symptoms).

The ITG with other temporal lobe structures like the middle temporal gyrus and the fusiform gyrus, is integral to consolidating visual emotional memories. The ITG may also play a role in envisioning future emotional events. Initially higher structural integrity of the VVS may contribute to greater attention and reactivity to threat-related visual stimuli. This likely leads to formation of stronger, and more enduring, trauma-related visual memories, which can then intrude into consciousness (usually indexed by default mode network activity).

Further investigation revealed that VVS activity at 6 months was no longer associated with ratings of PTSD symptoms at 6 months. However, the *reduction in SCN VVS activity* from 2 weeks to 6 months was also found to be significantly related to development of PTSD symptoms. Those whose VVS loadings decreased more (from 2 weeks to 6 months) had higher 6-month PCL-5 subscale scores for *negative thoughts and feelings* (p = 0.019). Reduction in VVS was not found to be related to any of the other PCL-5 subscale scores (intrusive symptoms, avoidance, or arousal (all p > 0.05).

The authors of the AURORA study opined that the chronic stress of PTSD likely underlie these changes, although it is not clear how this would occur. The data suggest that as VVS connectivity goes down, there has been an underlying increase in the patient's tendency to see themselves more negatively and to feel correspondingly moodier. That might be because some patients' high intrusive experiences begin to internalize the responsibility for what happened, with the result that those negative self-attributions increase, but their negative intrusive symptoms have decreased.

The study authors concluded that, "while greater structural covariance of the VVS facilitates encoding of traumatic memories acutely after trauma, decreased structural covariance over time contributes to negative trauma-related thoughts and feelings" (Harnett et al., 2022, p. 6). The VVS loadings are visual recollections of their trauma, which the person is not in direct control of. However, they are in control of whether they blame themselves for something overwhelming. And these results suggest that initial intensity of the trauma is managed by some patients by blaming themselves.

An earlier report (Harnett et al., 2021) had identified two neural circuits that were related to development of PTSD symptoms by the 3-month time period. One of these, high connectivity between the right ITG and the DMN at 2 weeks, was predictive of both immediate PTSD symptoms as well as persistent aspects of PTSD symptoms. The authors concluded, "one interpretation of the present findings is that greater ITG-DMN connectivity in the early weeks after trauma exposure supports formation, consolidation, and retrieval of emotional, traumatic memories" (p. 1268).

Therefore, treatment that intentionally targets the sensory intensity (visual, auditory, smells, touch) of flashbacks and nightmares related to traumatic experiences that are over (and which aim to reduce the sensory/physiological charge of these implicit memory circuits) are likely necessary to permit the integration of these intrusive right hemisphere memories into left hemisphere episodic memories.

Longitudinal Clinical Studies of Response to Trauma

> Dreams point to issues for therapeutic focus and may portray the child's attempts to recover or repair. (Nader, 2001, p. 22)

Tracking how children's nervous systems respond to overwhelming stress is instructive. As their nervous systems are not fully developed, these developing minds can provide a valuable insight into how the young mind comes to terms with an overwhelming event. Among such events that have been studied are natural disasters or violent events. Such studies have demonstrated that there is a natural sequence to how the mind wraps itself around the event.

The initial reaction often does not include either nightmares or dreams. For example, after a public suicide, children had night terrors for the first year or two. This raw and amorphous emotional state initially prevented REM sleep. Until significant progress had been made in the trauma work, children (and some adults) did not have any dreams or nightmares at all. It is a sign of progress in the clinical work that the raw, amorphous autonomic reactivity has been processed to the point that REM can occur during sleep. Now, a narrative around the emotion is produced in the form of a nightmare.

> In dissociative disorders and other amnestic syndromes, dreams may be the first clue in recovering repressed memories of trauma. . . . and that dreams were one of the modes in which these memories first returned. (Barrett, 2001, pp. 3–4)

In this respect, even the most horrible nightmares provide a clear signal that the mind is now ready to put symbols and a narrative experience to the way in which the traumatic events impacted that person. *Patients need to be advised that the nightmares are a sign of progress in the treatment, not a setback.*

Treatments Targeting Nightmares Specifically

> If a trauma-exposed individual presents with primary difficulties of nightmares and sleep, it may be prudent to start with direct treatment of those problems, followed by, if necessary, components addressing other post-trauma symptoms. (Davis, 2008, pp. 206–207)

Many nightmares continue for decades in patients in the form of repetitive dreams with intense visual imagery. As early as 1987, Gordon Halliday suggested that while nightmares have many causes, mounting evidence suggested they could be effectively treated by changing the nightmare content. In the 35 years since then, an increasing variety of direct treatment approaches have been suggested with clinical evidence that these can be remarkably effective for many nightmare sufferers.

Among the earliest proponents of rescripting nightmares was Rosalind Cartwright's RISC protocol. In *Crisis Dreaming* (Lamberg & Cartwright, 1992), Cartwright provided an easy to understand introduction to using dreams to overcome a range of life challenges. She proposed a 4-step process to rewriting dream scripts that had been overwhelming:

Recognize: that you are having a bad dream.
Identify: what it is about the dream that makes you feel badly.

Stop: the bad dream as soon as you can (there is little benefit from it continuing).

Change: the negative dimensions into positive outcomes.

Barry Krakow and Antonio Zadra (2006, 2010) further refined these principles into the Imagery Rehearsal Therapy (IRT) approach. In particular, they augmented the role of imagery in an intentional way, to create change in the underlying narratives of nightmares. IRT introduced rescripting and practicing the visual imagery of the rescripted dream to resolve the nightmares.

In 2010, the Standards of Practice Committee of the AASM; published a *Best Practice Guide* (see Aurora et al., 2010) for the treatment of nightmare disorder in adults. The *Guide* concluded that there were two level A treatment suggestions: Prazosin for pharmacological treatment of PTSD-associated nightmares and IRT for treatment of nightmare disorder.

In an update of the 2010 *Guide*, the AASM (see Morgenthaler et al., 2018) concluded that only IRT treatment was *recommended* for both nightmare disorder and PTSD-associated nightmares. Among second-line treatments that *may be used* for PTSD-associated nightmares were: CBT, CBTi, EMDR, and exposure, relaxation, and rescripting therapy (ERRT).

In addition to these psychotherapies, the update also mentions that off-label uses of medications are common in the management of PTSD. Prazosin (which is an alpha-1 antagonist) reduces adrenergic activity in the central nervous system. It was initially approved for treatment of hypertension but can improve sleep, reduce nightmares, and reduce overall severity of PTSD symptoms. Atypical antipsychotics, such as Seroquel and Olanzapine, were also included among the treatments that *may be helpful* for insomnia and PTSD nightmares but may cause oversedation during the day. Pharmacological treatments were considered helpful, but RCT evidence for their use in PTSD has been mixed.

For treatment of nightmare disorder, there were additional behavioral treatments suggested based on some level of empirical evidence. Among these was lucid dreaming. Clare Johnson has recently published (2021) a comprehensive treatment protocol for using lucid dreaming in this way, *The Art of Transforming Nightmares*. Joanne Davis elaborated the IRT model into the Exposure, Relaxing, and Rescripting Treatment (ERRT) model, which was described in her book *Treating Post-Trauma Nightmares* (2008). As well, Justin Havens has introduced Dream Completion Therapy, with online videos describing the procedure. These can readily be accessed by the patient and work well for most patients. And most recently, Kristy Pruiksma and her colleagues developed a Cognitive Behavioral Therapy for Nightmares (CBTn). This six session intervention has both a therapist guide and patient manual (Pruiksma et al., 2023).

Overall, there are many good reasons for introducing a nightmare-targeted treatment into trauma treatment of PTSD patients. While these interventions may not stop all nightmares (for reasons that are discussed in the next chapter), it is true that many patients achieve an immediate sense of relief from nightmares, which is empowering in and of itself. Many patients feel more in control when their nighttime arousal system is calming down. And for many, when these nightmares become less persistent there are further benefits to their daytime functioning, including feeling more energetic, improved ability to manage stress, enhanced mood stability, decreased triggering, and better cognitive functioning.

Eye Movements and Treatment of Intrusive Symptoms

There is one additional finding of the AURORA study that Nathaniel Harnett and his colleagues found that relates to the development of PTSD symptoms from the disturbing images of their trauma. Namely, that with the passage of time, those whose visual system connectivity decreased across the next half year were significantly more likely to have higher negative self-beliefs (Harnett et al., 2022). In other words, the distress brought by the original sensory elements (images and somatic distress) may not be as clinically evident, because these may have been transformed into self-criticism and self-blame.

Eye Movement Desensitization and Reprocessing (EMDR) Therapy

In the rest of this chapter, we illustrate how trauma treatment that is based on having the patient reconnect with their past trauma; reactivating those specific images and related emotions can bring the insidious process of self-blame to their awareness. Engaging the visual system in bilateral eye movements helps to reactivate and spotlight many long-forgotten aspects of the experience, to desensitize them. As these emerge while the patient observes these connections from a safe place, they can have powerful ability to bring the patient's awareness to elements of the original trauma that have been long forgotten. This new perspective on what they experienced allows both letting go of the overwhelming implicit memories, as well as a profound new understanding of how they have been relating to themselves.

Introduction of bilateral eye movements creates the opportunity for enhanced associative processes being activated. The bilateral eye movements initially serve to activate the right brain implicit memory circuit of that experience, along with activating the left brain's ability to notice what is being experienced. It also induces faster synaptic and neuronal plasticity. There is evidence that *"EMDR therapy induces faster processing of traumatic memories as compared to other psychotherapies"* (Mattera et al., 2022, p. 12). Research conducted across the past 10 years (Mattera et al., 2022; Pagani et al., 2017) has begun to demonstrate that eye movements have critical importance in deactivating intense right hemisphere negative affective states and their integration into left hemisphere memories. Earlier, Uri Bergmann (2000, 2019) had highlighted how EMDR recruits the necessary brain areas to accomplish this task: "EMDR stimulation and the protocol that anchors it, involves, comprehensively, the pontine brainstem, limbic area, lateral cerebellum, gyral cortical structures, and the neocortex" (Bergmann, 2000, p. 188).

While there are many significant studies that are elaborating the brain mechanisms that support the desensitization and reprocessing of traumatic experiences with bilateral eye movements, we will provide an example of the power of this treatment to help the patient fully grasp the impact of their original trauma.

EMDR TREATMENT OF RECURRENT INTRUSIVE THOUGHTS

What follows is a vignette from the treatment of Julie, a woman in her fifties referred for treatment of sleep difficulties. Julie had had a sleep test demonstrating problems with both apnea and chronic insomnia (a racing mind she could not turn off at night). She had been off work for a decade due to trigeminal neuralgia pain , multiple concussions, and periods of depression. Julie was self-described as of average weight, height, and looks. She was on long-term disability for an invisible illness, the kind she said that medical professionals dismissed. They said her physical pain condition, although the most painful known to the medical community, couldn't be that bad. Diagnosed and treated for depression years previously, despite the stigma involved, she sought treatment again. Here is her description of her life story, the emergence of her negative voice, and its resolution with EMDR.

Julie's Story

Julie: Life happens. Traumas, losses, heartbreaks, physical illnesses, they add up. Because you look well, people often don't know or forget how severe your struggles can be. I have a negative voice that lives in my head, one that is incredibly spiteful and mean. This voice is the nastiest person I have ever met, let alone have to live with. Kinder people in my world would tell me I was pretty, I was kind, I was funny, I was loved, but these felt like whispers compared to the vicious loud voice that I couldn't not hear.

I developed trigeminal neuralgia following a dental appointment. Prior to this I had been enjoying a career, I was on top of my mental health by continuing with preventative therapy, I was at the start of a new happy and healthy relationship, I was maintaining good physical health, I was earning good money, I was traveling on my time off, I had a great social life, I was happy. My negative voice was quieter, but still in the background.

Pain and Depression

Then, my world slowly crumbled. Not knowing what ailed me, not being able to work, living with invisible pain, surviving the day by taking a crazy number of narcotics (all prescribed), combined with experiencing additional traumas, my depression and my negative voice came back with a vengeance.

Mean me started getting louder and louder. Not having short-term disability and having to go on unemployment insurance, she would tell me I was a drain on society. Since my illness started with a simple toothache, she would tell me it was my fault.

I believed every word she said. My world shrank. I had a successful brain surgery and returned to work. I was able to return to work for 4 years but had to have a modified schedule to continue my medication regime, regulate my sleep, and limit the amount of time I was speaking, as I would still get the occasional flare of trigeminal pain and speaking was one of the triggers.

Of course, with my conditions being invisible, no one could see the struggles. They knew I was "different" from before; they knew I had a tooth issue, but most weren't aware of the rare condition I had been diagnosed with, let alone the rest of it. I looked the same and it wasn't terminal, so my negative voice thought they were *all* saying it wasn't real, it was in my head, I was being dramatic. Some of my colleagues most likely really did think that.

More Pain, Depression, and Disability

After what was supposed to be another simple dental procedure turned into a complicated, extensive treatment, my trigeminal neuralgia flared up, and I was off work again, and still am to this day. A second brain surgery that intended to help made it worse, and the downward spiral began again. Let's add in the deaths of multiple people very close to me, sexual assault, multiple physical accidents, COVID, living on a limited income, the breakdown of important relationships and now continued trigeminal pain. I was a mess.

The depths of the depression, the self-deprecation, chronic physical pain, posttraumatic stress symptoms, and chronic sleep issues all led my neurologist to refer me to trauma treatment.

Trauma Treatment

I recognized trauma treatment was different than any other mental health treatment I had ever done. A part of me thought it was a bit "wooeee." I have had some sort of therapy most of my life. I have had awakening moments and been provided some amazing coping tools, but it was all focused on the present crisis.

From my sleep studies, we learned that there were some traumatic events I haven't properly processed that were interrupting, disturbing, and sometimes completely preventing my sleep.

At the suggestion that we had to go back to painful traumas and relive them, I thought, "Hell no! Is this guy crazy?" There's no way to change past experiences, so why revisit them when they aren't on my mind? Why poke the beast if it's sleeping?

He explained how my sleep was being affected, so I jumped in to give it a try. I started listening and doing the work.

I've had a lot of traumas in my life. And I have suffered a lot of losses. So picking a starting point was tough. We started with something emotionally painful that stood out.

We would begin with an incident that I thought was bothering me as I could recall it in my conscious brain. We would delve somewhere deep in my memory and recall the traumatic event.

Grounding and Diaphragmatic Breathing

But, prior to getting too far along, I was taught about diaphragmatic breathing and why it was important. I had always been told deep breathing was good for me and that there was a physiological change that occurred. But it had never been explained how it affected my brain and central nervous system.

I was taught how to ground myself, while I was led through the process of remembering events.

I would ground myself, and we would recall a memory together, and we would stay with that memory. We would begin with what thoughts and feelings came to the surface and discuss them, and then continue deeper into the memory.

We would relive the intensity of the moments. I would physically feel the heartache, the anxiety, my heartrate would increase, my fight-or-flight was on high alert.

We would recall the incident with such intensity that it was like it was happening right then and there. Then somehow, we would hit the emotions attached to the memory, and then . . . they released.

Recalling and releasing the emotions would result in me doing the ugly cry, going through a box of tissues, have a terrible headache and sometimes a flare up of my trigeminal pain and exhaustion. My weekly 1-hour sessions were dreaded. But I could feel something shifting. A change was taking place. So I would sign in and smile for my next session. It was usually a repeat. We would tap into a different traumatic event, guide me to be grounded, and then get into it.

I was introduced to bilateral brain stimulation, which I use as a tool to defuse any emotions that linger during the week. Between this, the grounding, and the breathing, I have managed to make some huge strides. EMDR allowed me to get deeper into the memories with his guidance.

EMDR: Desensitizing and Reprocessing Trauma

I would be adamant every session that there was no way I would be "ugly crying." I am not normally a crier. So, to me, the fact we could get into my brain and get so deep to enable this ugly cry release was new. I thought it must be because I had locked into the memories that my conscious brain knew were there. It was like he had a magic trick, and I was determined to find out how to catch him out on it.

I would start out sessions with a "not today attitude"; then our work would take a different turn and uncover something that I didn't even know was buried in my brain and heart, and he would win again, although ultimately, I was the one winning.

I was asked when the last time was that I felt free of any negative thoughts and feelings, no self-judgment, nor cared about the judgment of others. The answer to this took time. I honestly couldn't remember ever feeling completely free to be me. I assumed the negative voice had been there forever. So, we would go to another trauma, and do the work.

Where Did the Pain Begin?

Then one day, when my pain was bad, we went to the first time I ever felt pain like this. I started with the day when my current pain became an issue. The therapist pushed: "Think harder, you must have felt pain before this." It took a while to get to the first time.

The last time I felt free and the first time I felt pain were the same. I was an 8-year-old child. I was the first kid on my block with a three-speed bike. I was fast and fearless. No hands felt great, like a soaring bird, but I made the mistake of looking back to see where my brother and my friends were, when I looked forward again it was at the back of a parked car, I flipped over my bike, hit the lamppost, then hit my head on the big hydro boxes [power company equipment], then landed on my handlebars . . . with my teeth.

I came to and I remember seeing my mum running toward me. One of my friends had gone to get her. She was in the middle of changing. Someone said, "Here are your daughter's teeth. The rest of her is down the street." As any mother would do, she ran toward me without hesitation.

In my memories before this treatment, this was the whole story. I had extreme pain as I had knocked teeth out and had exposed nerves.

Getting deeper into the memory, so much more became clear. I remembered that my parents had to take two days off work, to take me to medical and dental specialists. That is not something we could easily afford.

I remembered having to go to a dental specialist. As he was looking in my mouth (trying to help me stop feeling the pain from the exposed nerve endings) he said,

> **"Well, I guess you wouldn't do that again.
> You have disfigured yourself."**

There it was. The start of my negative voice! That simple. That unintentional. That seemingly insignificant moment. It was not even in my conscious memory. But I started blaming me. Wow!

Quieting the Negative Voice

Commentary. Julie was a child, and an adult—a figure of authority—told her it was her fault and that she was disfigured. The negative voice came to life, telling her things that were worse than anyone could ever say to her . . . so she could protect Julie from being hurt by others.

Julie: The negative voice stayed a child pretending to be an adult voice protecting me. From that day on, that voice stayed with me throughout my life. Why bother trying to get an education, you're stupid and you'll fail. Why start a weight loss program or exercise program, you'll start, then fail. My fear of failing prevented me from accomplishing things in my life. My fear of failure, that I thought was part of my depressive condition, came largely from the negative voice inside myself.

When we found that voice, the therapist wanted me to bring her to the present day. I was like, "Hell no! She is a vindictive bitch! Leave her there!"

He said no, "We are not leaving her there. We need to bring her to the now and thank her for trying to protect you. We need to acknowledge she is still a child, and that we have grown up now, and you don't need the negative voice to protect you anymore."

I have the skills and tools to protect myself. This realization was overwhelming.

It took days for me to recover from this one session. It took a few more sessions before I could wrap my head completely around this realization. After nearly 2 weeks of deep thought, tears, sadness, grief, working to stay grounded. REM to release more emotions. Deep breathing. I started to feel a shift.

I felt lighter, the sky was bluer, the flowers prettier. I didn't even hide myself to myself when I got out of the shower. I was ok with me. I was good. The world is good, and I am meant to be in it. I matter. I do make a difference.

Since this realization, my life has changed. No longer do I see myself as an ugly four-eyed toothless kid with a tummy. I am a not bad-looking human, with a big heart. I am surrounded by love in my life. I am beyond lucky to have amazing an amazing hubby, along with a great family and friends who love me. I am not a failure for not having kids; I am lucky to be available to many nonbiological children when they need someone other than a parent in their corner. I am not an unemployed lazy person; I am a person with disabilities that are invisible. I have good days, and I have bad days and that is okay.

I love who I have become, and being me, is a great place to be. Understanding where the negative voice in my head came from, why she was there, and that she was actually being protective has, to date, been the biggest, most significant realization in my history of over 30 years of therapy. I continue to grow into a healthier me each day. Friends and family have noticed the positive changes in me, without knowing about the work I have been doing. I stand up for myself more, I create healthy boundaries, I do not beat myself up for things that I have no control over. I have stopped worrying about what other people think and say. I also feel much more gratitude for the people, things, and therapists I have in my life.

If I could reach out to one person, who possibly has a similar story, I would say, "Do the work." It is hard. It is invasive. It is emotional. And the emotions do not necessarily stop when your session ends. Work through them with your grounding, breathing, and bilateral eye movements. It is life changing. I cannot yet say that I completed the work and am at the end of my journey. I am not. I still have much more work to do—but I am not afraid of it. I welcome it because the results, and changes, are worth every tear I have cried, and every fear I have felt.

The Transcript of the Transformative Session in Which the Negative Voice Emerged

The following edited transcript is taken from Julie's 20th psychotherapy session. At that point we were focusing on the traumatic events that had been triggering her serious depressive episodes (about 6 months into our sessions). Trauma treatment was being provided using the standard EMDR protocol (Shapiro, 2018).

After an initial description of how exhausted she had been feeling that week, I asked her what period in her life she had felt that bad. She replied when she had had terrible trigeminal pain that resulted in root canals and surgeries. She added that these dental problems began when she had a bike accident at age eight.

> PATIENT: I had a bike accident when I was eight and I lost all my front teeth. There's that connection. The autoimmune stuff seems to flare up around all of that. Or it flares up any time I get any new trauma.

THERAPIST: Your immune system has a trigger finger. It is ready to find enemies anywhere to attack, including your own body's tissue. That's the auto part of it. It's an overaggressive immune system, looking for a battle. But your exhaustion goes back to the dental work you had as an adult. You said that for two days, you were laid up after the actual dental work.

PATIENT: In agony. I crashed.

THERAPIST: It's worth going to that as our starting point, our target memory, because it is probably loaded with not just emotional pain, but also your body. When you get dental work done, that's not just an emotional situation. It's physical. They are actually drilling. Affecting your nerves. So your whole body and your nervous system are affected.

PATIENT: Prior to that they had suggested it was MS. When I had a toe problem. After that, I was having fluctuations in my blood, but not diabetic. Feeling drunk, or buzzed, or something. And obviously I had not taken anything.

THERAPIST: I would call that dysregulation. Your autonomic nervous system is the central control panel. Every physiological function is regulated by the autonomic. But when the autonomic is dysregulated, meaning that it's not stable, then you're going to get weird symptoms. They pop up because the control panel is short-circuiting. Is there any memory related to what happened when you were getting the dental work done? That could be intensifying that dysregulation? Making it more challenging?

PATIENT: My first memory of traumatic dental stuff was when I was eight.

THERAPIST: Let's go back to that. In a couple of sentences tell me what you are remembering.

PATIENT: I was the first kid on the block with a three-speed bike. I was doing "no hands" and showing off. I hit a car, a curb, and then I flipped up. They used to have hydro boxes on poles. I flipped up on one of them. I hit my head on the pole. I was knocked out. And I then landed on the handlebars of my bike. And then being humiliated because I had hit my head, and I had some other bumps and scrapes. The teeth were the last thing to be checked out at the hospital. And that was like nerves . . . raw nerves.

THERAPIST: I am sure they were touching your mouth and asking, "What does this feel like?" Through the roof pain. Isolate whatever moment stands out. From when you were on the bike, hit the pole, all the way through to when you're in the hospital. Is there one moment that stands out?

PATIENT: The pain. I got released from the hospital, and I had to go to a dental clinic, a dental specialist. And I remember them poking around and feeling sick with the pain.

THERAPIST: That part really stands out. And then they are actively making it worse when they're checking it out. We'll use that.

PATIENT: That is when I found out that my nerves apparently don't freeze. So that memory of going into that building. And not knowing what to expect. At the time I had only ever had like two cavities. Not even.

THERAPIST: We'll use that experience. Particularly as they start poking around. When you bring your full attention to that moment, allowing that experience to sit fully in your awareness, what words go with that? Is it feeling powerless? Or hopeless? What do you think is going on in that 8-year-old's brain as she's being poked?

PATIENT: It's powerless, very powerless. No one is saying, "It's all right. It's going to be okay." Because nobody knew. My mom especially because I apparently had perfect teeth. They were my second teeth, my permanent teeth. And now they are gone!

THERAPIST: There is a huge sense of loss.

PATIENT: Dad was supposed to fly out, like the next day for a business trip, or something. I remember it being chaos and painful.

THERAPIST: Focus on that moment. When you bring your full attention to being in that dental office, and the words, "I'm hopeless and powerless. It is chaos." As you just sit with that experience, on that scale we use from 0 to 10, how disturbing does that feel right now?

PATIENT: At that moment, it was a 10. That was the worst moment I've experienced for pain.

THERAPIST: As you are bringing that image back, how does it feel right now?

PATIENT: 7 or 8.

THERAPIST: That 7 or 8 level, where are you feeling that in your body right now?

PATIENT: My tummy. My anxiety.

THERAPIST: That's what we are going to start with. Notice the memory and the sensations. What is popping up into your awareness?

PATIENT: I can feel the pain in my mouth and my face. It happened almost 45 years ago. And I still really don't have any control over that face pain.

THERAPIST: That would be a reason to feel terrified, right? "That pain is coming back. What am I going to do?" Go with that. Notice the fear, the sensations that you're experiencing in your body. As you notice the experience, see if you can find the part that bothers you the most.

PATIENT: Self-blame.

THERAPIST: Self-blame. Was the 8-year-old you critical of you?

PATIENT: I was just trying to show off. And I caused it. And that wasn't necessarily anyone else telling me that. I knew that.

THERAPIST: Notice that part of you that gets activated: that self-blaming or self-critical part. Whatever way you notice it. It might be the voice. Or the criticism that it might be giving you. And again, once you're aware of that, then I want you to continue with the next set.

PATIENT: This is a big aha moment. I think that's when all my negative self-talk started! I didn't have a weight issue at that time. And then I became the new kid with the accent. And I gained weight because of the teeth. Because everything was soft. To this day ice cream and cake are soft. I felt like those things were treats and I deserved a treat. But then I disfigured myself. I caused it!

THERAPIST: Notice that realization. That is where the negative self-talk started.

PATIENT: There was none of it before.

THERAPIST: As you notice that turning point. There may, or may not, be any feeling that you have about that. How things changed for you. Be aware of that realization. That's an important one. You and I need to help out that 8-year-old girl.

Because that 8-year-old did what most 8-year-olds do. They enjoy riding their bike. They enjoy feeling confident in it. Almost every kid, once they figure it out, wants to show off. Show others how much they've learned. That's what every normal 8-year-old does. We need to get that 8-year-old young girl and bring her to the present. So I'm going to have you go back. Whatever way you picture her. Whether it's getting her from the dental office or getting her from when she crashed her bike. I want you to go back and to tell her that it's really important for her to come with you. Maybe what she needs to be told is her guilt about having the accident, that somehow, she felt she did something wrong. All of this self-criticism comes from a place of, "I screwed up."

PATIENT: How that has carried with me even until today. I'll give you an example. I look at the pictures from Sunday, when we were at the tennis finals with my friends. And *they* looked fabulous. But that's not how I see me.

THERAPIST: That's the 8-year-old. It's important to understand what you're describing. The 8-year-old part of you ended up causing a calamity. Very innocently. But it happened. It was an accident. It was not intentional. We need to help that younger part. As soon as that younger part of you gets activated, starts being self-critical, then the you-of-today, the adult part of you, feels incredibly self-critical. That younger, self-critical part has taken over. That's why we want to bring that younger part to the present. And we need to tell that younger part of you, first of all, that she did nothing wrong! She was just being an 8-year-old. That she matters! Her feelings matter! And so do her thoughts. That she is special. There is nothing that she did that was wrong. She does not have to berate herself! Or criticize herself!

PATIENT: I don't think that that 8-year-old even knew what those feelings were. Because there was pain. There was self-criticism. There was physical pain. Self-criticism like, "You're disfigured." I couldn't get crowns or caps put on. I had to go to school with half my teeth missing for weeks.

In the dentist's chair, at that time, you just want it to stop! Then literally like, "Why did I do that? Why did I do that?" Because you were just being a kid! You were just being a kid: you did not do it!

THERAPIST: That is the message that you need to keep telling her. Over and over. Because she is stuck in that accident moment. She is stuck in the dental office. She is stuck in blaming herself. That she did something horrible. But she didn't.

PATIENT: To this day, like sitting here now, with any pain or exhaustion. I will tell myself, "I did this to myself again."

THERAPIST: No, you did not. That is the way in which the brain functions in trauma. When something awful has happened, there is a part of us that somehow wishes that we could have controlled everything. Or created a different outcome. And it becomes overly critical, incredibly critical. Even mean, in terms of the perfection it expects.

PATIENT: I am the meanest person to myself. What I say to myself I wouldn't say to anybody!

THERAPIST: The root of that self-criticism is an 8-year-old. An 8-year-old who did not understand about accidents, and pain, and teeth. She felt she had created this awful, awful situation. And her way of responding to it was to be like, let's say a super-punitive adult.

PATIENT: It was all me. Maybe the dentist who said I had disfigured myself, but not my parents.

THERAPIST: The first step in that is to understand that 8-year-old. What is she doing when she is becoming self-critical? She is somehow desperately trying to fix the accident. She is trying to somehow make up for what she perceived at the time as some massive oversight or a terrible error that she made. In fact, she has nothing to make up for. That is important for her to know. But we also need to understand her intention in criticizing. It also comes from a place of wanting to make it good. She's not mean-spirited. Or being difficult. She is just trying to make up for something that was too painful. We need to love up that young girl and say, "Look, you are just an 8-year-old girl. Riding a bike and enjoying it. And having a ball. And showing your new friends how much fun it was."

PATIENT: "You are so damn clumsy!" And that sticks with you through the rest of your life.

THERAPIST: You can tell her, "You know what, we really appreciate your intent of trying to fix the accident. But we don't need that criticism or that harsh, perfectionistic voice. We know you were trying your best. That was good enough!"

The self-criticism is not needed. We don't need to erase it. But we do need the level of criticism to change. Because it is what an 8-year-old would imagine an adult to be like. Which would be super strict. Not realistic, strict.

PATIENT: She is just mean!

THERAPIST: We need that part to begin to soften. She can still be critical, but she doesn't have to be so uber-strict. The way to do that is to remind her that the accident is over. Bring her up to date with what has changed. In her mind, she's still living in the accident, in the intensity of what she felt she had done wrong. Still trying to repair it by being critical of herself. Begin to talk to her. See how that works. During this next week, see if you can get her to feel that she's fine as she is. That she doesn't have to make up for anything.

PATIENT: That she doesn't have to apologize for it. I think I might write her a letter.

THERAPIST: Tell her how much the adult you loves her enthusiasm, loves her bravery.

PATIENT: The adult me really wishes she could have fixed it! It's interesting how the self-criticism all started then. And then it developed into weight problems, but the dental stuff never stopped.

THERAPIST: I love the letter idea. That was a brilliant insight, your awareness of how the self-criticism started. That is why I love using EMDR. All these pearls pop up.

The Next Session: Further Integration of the Insight Into Her Self-Critical Thinking

The *awareness* of the self-criticism is only the beginning of the process of changing this self-critical part of herself. At the next session, we explored what she did with this insight.

PATIENT: Honestly, the stuff that comes through my head to myself! I would never say, not even to my worst enemy. It would not happen.

THERAPIST: It is important to understand that she has been doing a really difficult job. She has been doubling down on trying to prevent more pain and humiliation. It is the best way the 8-year-old could find to give herself some assurance that this would not happen again. Of course, she has caused you a lot of hardship. She's been a very tough taskmaster to live with. So the way in which you as the adult—need to begin to think about this young part, is that we are understanding there is a voice, a part of you that came into operation when this accident happened. This protective part has always had the goal of trying to minimize and prevent that intense pain and failure from ever happening again. And the best way that you and I can work with that part is to see whether that part is willing to be a little bit more flexible.

PATIENT: It's a very childish thought process. That voice is mean. It is not who I am. So I think maybe that my negative voice *is* the 8-year-old, pretending to be an adult.

THERAPIST: That is exactly what it is. And because of the trauma, how overwhelming that accident was, and the pain, the voice ups her volume. She has to be louder than the pain.

PATIENT: The younger one did go out of control. For a long time. In many different ways. It would be really nice to have constructive criticism and supportive criticism. I think it will take the young negative, and the older negative time to rationalize.

Because this last week was an amazing, amazing revelation! How it started. It blew my mind that I started it. That my own self started that negative voice. And the only negative comment was from one dentist. Other than the getting picked on and all that. That was after.

Key Messages for Therapists

1. Dreams and nightmares are a valuable entry point for trauma therapy. Many patients achieve an immediate sense of relief from imagery rehearsal therapy (IRT) for nightmares. When nightmares become less persistent, there are benefits to daytime functioning: feeling more empowered, having more energy, having improved ability to manage stress, feeling enhanced mood stability, suffering less triggering, and experiencing better cognitive functioning.
2. Progress in trauma therapy is marked by a shift from the raw, amorphous autonomic response of night terrors, and amnesia for traumatic memories, to conscious narrative based awareness of these terrifying moments in nightmare images and flashbacks. Research shows that the increase in nightmare activity is a sign of progress, not a setback. The implicit traumatic experiences are now coming to explicit memory and consciousness, which allows for therapeutic desensitization.
3. The ANS, at its core, is keeping the person safe. It gets frozen at the time of the trauma. The intensity of the physical and emotional experience keeps it locked up in the right brain (implicit) memory system. As it begins to cross over to left brain (explicit consciousness) it initially overwhelms. Trauma work includes reexperiencing the trauma, validating how the younger self did their best, and guiding that part to see how their life has changed. This allows a gradual, but steady, resolution of these implicit memories.
4. Desensitization of the ventral visual stream (VVS) rapidly, which has activated horrifying imagery kept in the inferior temporal gyrus (ITG), is accelerated by empowering the patient to rehearse visual imagery. This is accomplished through IRT or Cognitive Behavioral Therapy for nightmares (CBTn), but could also include EMDR and DBR therapy, dream completion therapy, lucid dreaming (LD), and exposure, relaxation, and rescripting therapy (ERRT).

5. Flashbacks, intrusive thoughts, insomnia, and nightmares impact the patient's daytime experience in important ways. The circuits involved in these experiences are slowly being identified. The VVS plays a significant part in these experiences, but there may be other circuits that have yet to be identified that are activating other sensory experiences related to the trauma. However, addressing these issues rapidly creates noticeable changes in daytime functioning, which empower the patient and reinforce the value of their trauma therapy.

9

Targeting Restless REM Sleep: From Nightmares to Dreaming

"Dreams [during REM sleep] display images representing the interaction of recent emotional experience and previously associated images. . . . When sampled in sequence across the night, dreams display the progressive down-regulation of disturbing emotion."
—Rosalind Cartwright (2010, p. 165)

"We propose that "instability" of REM contributes to . . . chronic fragmentation of REM sleep lead[ing] to dysfunction in a ventral emotional neural network, including limbic and paralimbic areas that are specifically activated during REM sleep."
—Dieter Riemann, Kai Spiegelhalder, Chris Nissen, et al. (2012, p. 167)

"The Restless REM sleep that is typical of insomnia prohibits a consolidated noradrenaline time-out . . . [interfering with] synaptic plasticity in limbic circuits."
—Eus Van Someren (2021, p. 995)

All of us have experienced insomnia. Anytime our current circumstances have activated either great excitement or great distress, our sleep is interrupted. However, for most of us these periods are brief, and even if they recur periodically, as long as we recover from them quickly, we are able to manage periods of poor sleep with some equanimity.

The difficulty comes in when this pattern of poor sleep continues for weeks, months, and years. For many trauma patients, these bouts of inadequate sleep are persistent. They never let go and give our nervous systems time to recover and recharge. Without recovery time, it feels like our ability to function slowly grinds to a dead stop.

DEFINITION OF CHRONIC INSOMNIA

If you ask anybody to define insomnia, they will tell you it is not getting enough sleep. The *DSM-5* criteria for chronic insomnia go further, clarifying the following specific criteria for insomnia disorder (American Psychiatric Association, 2013):

a. A predominant complaint of dissatisfaction with sleep quantity or quality, associated with one (or more) of the following symptoms:
- Difficulty initiating sleep (i.e., initial insomnia)
- Difficulty maintaining sleep, characterized by frequent awakenings or problems returning to sleep after awakening (i.e., maintenance insomnia)
- Early morning awakenings with inability to return to sleep (i.e., terminal insomnia)

b. The sleep disturbance causes clinically significant distress or impairment in social, occupational, education, academic, behavioral, or other important areas of functioning.
c. The sleep difficulty occurs at least three nights per week.
d. The sleep difficulty has been present for at least three months.
e. The sleep difficulty occurs despite adequate opportunity for sleep.
f. The insomnia is not better explained by and does not occur exclusively during the course of another sleep-wake disorder.
g. The insomnia is not attributable to the physiological effects of a substance.
h. Coexisting mental disorders and medical conditions do not adequately explain the predominant complaint of insomnia.

As with the nightmare disorder discussed last chapter, this definition also excludes coexisting disorders (see h above), which allow insomnia to be considered an integral part of a PTSD diagnosis. However, the fact that a separate diagnosis of insomnia disorder (ID) is possible is significant. It means that there are many who may not have suffered the full PTSD syndrome, but *do* demonstrate all the features of ID.

To add additional complexity to the discussion, there are those who do not suffer from inadequate sleep quantity (they sleep for 8 to 10 hours a night) but still wake up feeling unrefreshed. Their problem is not inadequate *sleep quantity*, but instead they suffer from inadequate *sleep quality*. They are sleeping through the night, but what is happening in their sleep is not rejuvenating their energy, focus, and mood. They struggle with *Nonrestorative Sleep* (NRS).

Behavioral and self-report studies have not been able to shed light on why those with NRS are not recovering with the sleep that they have been getting. It has only been since the advent of neuroimaging studies in the past 20 years that the common cause of both ID and NRS has been appreciated. Van Someren (2021) reviewed neuroimaging studies of the past decade and concluded that it is *restless REM sleep* that is the problem. Van Someren suggested that there is a hyperarousal disturbance that underlies ID and that this may well be a transdiagnostic risk factor for all mental and physical health conditions. NRS is likely to have the same underlying neurophysiological arousal disorder, but with a different clinical presentation, as these patients are not waking up from the underlying restless REM sleep.

In this chapter, we will review the latest neuroimaging findings that provide us with a radically new understanding of the neurophysiological underpinnings of insomnia, nightmares, and other forms of restless sleep. As well, we provide a clinical example of how a psychotherapy, namely deep brain reorienting (DBR), that targets the hyperaroused locus coeruleus-norepinephrine (LC-NE) system can effectively treat ID and nightmares.

What I will learn in this chapter to become a better sleep and trauma therapist:

1. Insomnia disorder (ID) is better understood as an underlying hyperactivation of arousal and emotional circuits, rather than over- or underactivation of sleep circuits. ID is a distinct neuropsychiatric disorder, with a specific underlying brain mechanism, which makes ID a *transdiagnostic primary risk factor* for the development of other common psychiatric conditions (anxiety disorders, depression, and PTSD) and predisposes to physical health issues.
2. The *vigilance system* (i.e., Ascending Reticular Arousal System (ARAS), Locus Coeruleus (LC), Pedunculopontine Nucleus (PPN), Dorsal Raphe Nucleus (DRN), Laterodorsal Tegmental Nucleus (LDT) allows for wakefulness, attention, and alertness and is necessary for a healthy sleep-wake rhythm. In contrast, the *salience network* (i.e., Superior Colliculus (SC), Locus Coeruleus (LC), Periaqueductal Gray (PAG), Dorsal Raphe Nucleus (DRN), Ventral Tegmental Area (VTA) initiates survival responses through the activation of the innate alarm, the LC-NE system and is overactive in PTSD.
3. Intensified LC-NE activation results in mental alertness, physiological arousal, and mobilized bodily sensations. They become recurring internal states that enter conscious awareness as panic attacks or a range of physical symptoms. The intensity of these hyperaroused survival reactions overwhelms the usual shift into sleep at the end of the day and predisposes the individual to disordered sleep.
4. This pattern of early or repeated trauma (evident in repeated activation of the LC-NE system) results in a persistent pattern of disrupted sleep called restless REM sleep. Restless REM sleep is at the heart of ID and most likely also related sleep conditions of night terrors, nightmares, and nonrestorative sleep (NRS). Restless REM sleep impedes the overnight emotional adaptation of the amygdala and results in increased risk of multiple psychiatric conditions, including PTSD.

5. Deep Brain Reorienting (DBR) therapy may be particularly effective in resolving ID, as DBR is the only psychotherapy that targets systematically releasing LC-NE hyperactivation. This hyperactivation is evident from the nonverbal experience of a body shock preparing the body for action prior to emotional defense reactions. These pre-affective shock reactions must be cleared prior to the processing of the periaqueductal gray (PAG) affective responses that follow the pre-affective shock so that the continuous triggering of traumatic memories is resolved.

In this chapter, we will begin with one of the most common disorders found in any clinical population, namely the lack of sleep. Insomnia disorder (ID) is easily evaluated. The sleep condition index provides an assessment of whether a patient meets the criteria for chronic insomnia. It is reliable and easy to administer (see Table 2.2). A total score of 16 or more tells you that your patient has an ID problem.

After considering what research tells us about what gives rise to insomnia, we will explore what the latest neuroimaging studies can tell us about the most likely causes of ID. Following that we will review the implications of these studies for non-restorative sleep, which shares the same daytime consequences as insomnia, but without evidence of the sharp reduction in the quantity of sleep the patient is getting. Once the neurophysiological causes of ID have been described, an effective treatment protocol targeting these neurophysiological underpinnings will be described and illustrated.

What Are the Life Experiences That Lead to Insomnia?

While insomnia disorder has long been understood to be a pervasive, limiting, and difficult-to-treat condition, its causes were not well understood. Through the last 40 years there has been increasing speculation that hyperarousal of the nervous system is a critical factor in precipitating and perpetuating the condition. However, the increasing understanding of both circadian and homeostatic sleep functions did little to add to our treatment options for chronic insomnia.

Sleep studies began focusing on both physiological markers (heart rate, cortisol levels, etc.) and cognitive factors (worry, rumination, and hyperfocus on sleep difficulties). These tended to support the view that the dysfunction in ID is related to arousal, attention, and difficulties with emotional processing among these patients.

What Are the Brain Mechanisms Underlying Chronic Insomnia?

With the advent of neuroimaging, studies began to investigate the brain circuits that were either elevated or suppressed in ID. These have generally found little over- or underactivation in the sleep circuits of the human brain. Instead, *circuits involved in arousal and emotional functions* have been particularly affected. The weight of the evidence supporting this new, neuroscience-based understanding of ID has been summarized by Eus Van Someren (2021), one of the leading neuroimaging investigators of insomnia.

REM Instability: The Origins of The Restless REM Sleep Hypothesis. Dieter Riemann and the sleep research group in Freiburg, Germany conducted a seminal study of the relationship between subjective reports of sleeplessness with the underlying characteristics of the polysomnographic (PSG) sleep characteristics. The study compared 100 chronic insomniacs (ID) with 100 good sleepers (Feige et al., 2008). The study confirmed that the sleep of ID participants was more disrupted on both subjective and PSG measures. Specifically, the arousal index across total sleep time was elevated among ID participants, and this increase was due mainly to a strong increase in REM sleep.

Subsequently, the Freiburg research team sought to identify the specific factors that contributed to participants' estimates of their subjectively reported wake times. Linear regression modeling identified only two PSG factors: (1) their total PSG measured wake time, and (2) the total time in REM sleep. The PSG measure of time awake was related to subjective time awake for all study participants. This was not a surprise. However, for insomniacs (but not good sleepers) time spent in REM was related to more subjective wake experience. As it has commonly been thought that insomniacs have more light (NREM) sleep, this finding of no difference in NREM sleep, and a strong link between REM sleep and increased subjective awake experiences at night, was a surprise (see Figure 9.1).

Further investigation revealed why. Insomniacs had elevated levels of arousals during sleep, and more of these arousals happened during REM. Previous studies had not compared the arousal index across sleep stages, so this finding of increased cortical arousal within the REM period reshaped our understanding of how insomnia differs from healthy sleep. Riemann and his colleagues (Riemann et al., 2012) went on to elaborate on the critical role of REM instability to the experience of disrupted and nonrestorative sleep. They pointed out that REM is the most highly aroused brain state during sleep, and therefore more susceptible to fragmentation. On this basis they proposed that acute or chronic stress were critical factors causing sleep fragmentation.

Supporting this thesis were animal studies in which the activity of the LC-NE was directly stimulated, with the result that REM sleep (REMS) was significantly reduced (Mallick & Singh, 2011). Not only this, but animal studies also demonstrated that such REMS deprivation reduced monoamine oxidase-A (MAO-A) (which degrades NE) *and* increased both intracellular Na-K ATPase activation and tyrosine hydroxylase, both of which support *sustained* NE levels after REMS deprivation. In summary, sustained activation of the LC-NE alarm undermines the normal functioning of REM sleep, and inhibits its role in modulating and integrating emotional arousal. Mallick and Singh concluded that "one of the functions of REM sleep is to maintain brain excitability," and when REM is disrupted we have both chronic insomnia as well as increased risk of a range of emotional and psychosomatic conditions (bipolar disorder, depression, cardiovascular, etc.). In other words, regular periods of REM sleep stabilize the integration of emotional arousal experiences, to maintain amygdala adaptability, resulting in optimized openness to new experiences.

The importance of Riemann's reformulation of the root of the insomnia problem cannot be overstated. Until this time, insomnia was largely conceptualized from a behavioral perspective. Repeated awakenings at night were attributed to light sleep and too much time in bed. Framing sleep fragmentation as a dynamic process, triggered by the underlying hyperactivity of the autonomic system, was new. Earlier reviews of *insomnia as hyperarousal* had been reported, but not with any clarity about how this hyperarousal occurred. Riemann and his colleagues identified this missing link.

Ramifications of the Restless REM Sleep Hypothesis. In a recently published monograph, entitled *Brain Mechanisms of Insomnia: New Perspectives on Causes and Consequences,* Eus Van Someren (2021) provides an extensive review of the clinical and research evidence of ID. He suggests that we should consider ID as a distinct neuropsychiatric disorder, with a specific underlying brain mechanism, which makes ID a *transdiagnostic primary risk factor* for the development of many other common psychiatric conditions (anxiety disorders, depression, and PTSD) and the predisposition to and exacerbation of physical health issues.

Van Someren first considers the evidence for insomnia being a consequence of brain sleep circuits, like the circadian and homeostatic sleep-regulating circuits. Studies examining the structural connectivity of brain centers in those with ID suggest that patterns of connectivity instead support the view that the arousal and emotional brain circuits are more involved in these sleep disturbances. There do not appear to be any characteristic irregularities in the connectivity patterns of sleep-regulating circuits.

A specific brain region found to consistently demonstrate irregularities among ID patients is the right orbitofrontal cortex (OFC) region. The OFC is important for downregulating and reappraising emotional distress. Low gray matter density in the OFC (especially at the border with the insula) increases the risk of fragmented sleep, poor sleep quality, and ID. The area bordering the insula is especially important for the salience network.

There has also been evidence found that those with ID demonstrate reduced connectivity between the orbitofrontal-anterior insula and the anterior cingulate cortex, both structures of importance in the salience network.

Poor sleep quality has also been associated with weaker connectivity between the OFC and the head of the caudate nucleus. The caudate nucleus is important for suppressing cortical excitability. The heightened cortical gamma-wave activity among those with ID may reflect difficulties in inhibiting this cognitive reactivity.

The LC receives extensive input from the ACC and the OFC, providing contextual relevance. The LC is therefore monitoring activity in the salience network and adapting its activity based on this contextual information. If the salience network continues on high alert, the LC will be responsive and continue to work against falling asleep. Even once asleep from exhaustion, the background activity of continuing LC activation causes restlessness in both NREM and REM sleep.

The continuing activity of the LC neurons across the night results in persistently high levels of noradrenaline/norepinephrine (NE) across the night. This is the cause of the restless REM (see the levels for Insomnia in Figure 9.1). In contrast, for the good sleeper (see the Normal sleep levels in Figure 9.1) the silencing of LC activity results in lower levels of NE and LC-NE silencing during REM. This results in normal REM sleep being able to continuously adapt amygdala functions across all REM periods of the night. *With restless REM the amygdala cannot be adaptively modulated with new information from recent daytime experiences. The result is that the amygdala is frozen in trauma time.*

In NREM, restless sleep is evident from continued activation of A2 and A3 CAP subtypes, resulting in multiple brief awakenings from sleep. In REM sleep the continued activation of NE neurons prevents the usual silencing of NE activity that permits the neuroplastic emotional reorganization that happens in REM. For these ID sufferers, there is a failure of the emotional processing aspect of sleep. This results in multiple awakenings from sleep, with both fragmented NREM and REM sleep periods (Figure 9.2).

Some sleepers have the same underlying physiological fingerprint of poor sleep but remain asleep despite the fragmented sleep stages. These are sleepers with nonrestorative sleep (NRS). How to go about educating these NRS patients has emerged from the research and theoretical contributions of Eus Van Someren and his laboratory in Amsterdam (summarized in Van Someren, 2021).

During sleep, memory traces of wake experiences are reprocessed across nightly NREM-REM cycling. The basolateral nucleus of the amygdala is thought to be important for memory processing during REM sleep, involving the amygdala-hippocampus-medial prefrontal cortex (AMY-HC-mPFC) circuit. REM sleep favors selective pruning and consolidation of new synapses, crucial for memory processing. Reduced NE levels during REM sleep are necessary for this synaptic downscaling; sleep-related synaptic plasticity contributes to episodic, semantic, and autobiographical memory consolidation.

Through neuroimaging studies of normal healthy sleepers, Wassing (2019a and 2019b) showed that these subjects, when allowed to sleep after exposure to emotionally distressing material, demonstrated less emotional distress, less autonomic arousal, and less activation of the amygdala on re-exposure to the same stimuli after a night of sleep. This adaptation of the amygdala to the emotional challenge has been attributed to the reductions in NE levels in REM sleep. To summarize, Van Someren proposes that the activity of the LC during the REM sleep period is the critical factor. When the LC is silent, the amygdala can adapt to emotional challenges. When the LC is hyperaroused, distress continues and may be one significant contribution to the development of a variety of neuropsychiatric disorders like depression and PTSD.

Van Someren (2021) recently published an extensive review of chronic insomnia that explicitly explored the brain mechanisms responsible for chronic insomnia. He reviewed the findings of existing neurophysiological and fMRI studies of insomnia and proposed a model of restless REM sleep positing that insufficient LC silencing during REM sleep is the most likely cause of persistent disturbed sleep. *This model can account for both increased occurrence of nightmares and chronic insomnia after trauma.*

Restless REM sleep disrupts the normal emotional adaptation processes of sleep that confer synaptic plasticity. This disruption results in sustained hyperarousal and anxiety. The model proposes that "insufficient overnight adaptation to emotional distress" (Van Someren, 2021, p. 996) is the key common mechanism for insomnia as well as the psychiatric disorders that insomnia spawns (including anxiety disorders, mood disorders, and PTSD). Importantly, the persistence of restless REM supports the continuation of nightmares as well as other intrusive, negative affective, and hyperarousal symptoms of PTSD.

Reviews of brain scan studies demonstrate that insomnia vulnerability is mediated by functional alterations in brain circuits involved in arousal and salience,

FIGURE 9.1 Awakenings from REM Instability in Insomnia vs. Healthy Sleepers (see insert for color)   Source: Reprinted by permission: Eus Van Someren (2021, p. 1000) and Dieter Riemann et al. (2012)

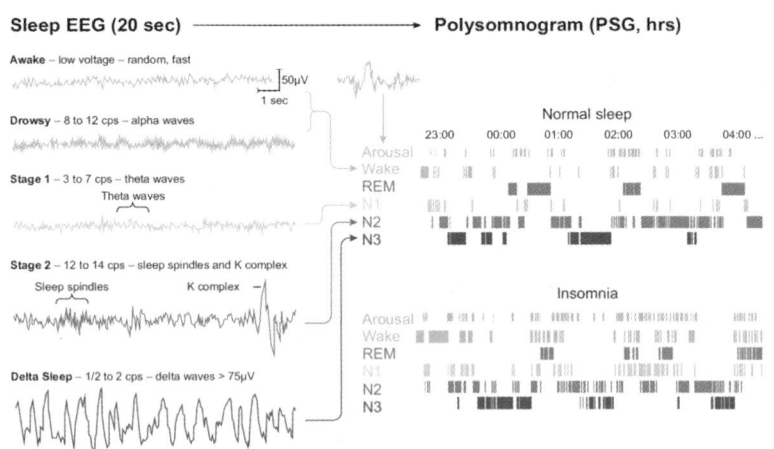

FIGURE 9.2 Normal REM Sleep With Amygdala Adaption vs. Restless REM Sleep (see insert for color) Source: Permission of Eus Van Someren (2021, p. 995) and Rick Wassing et al. (2019)

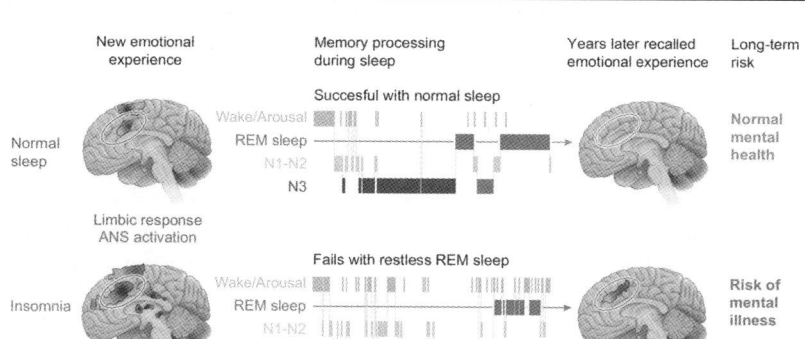

with sustained activity of the salience network leading to difficulties in reaching low arousal levels before sleep. This is also supported by the occurrence of CAP A2 and A3 subtypes in the NREM sleep that follows, which awaken the sleeper (see Chapter 1). Changes in claustrum-initiated activation of the anterior cingulate cortex during REM sleep may also contribute to restless REM.

People with restless REM sleep do not find relief from emotional distress during sleep, which leads to the persistence of their emotional burdens. Van Someren (2021) concluded that people with insomnia are predicted to exhibit features associated with increased LC activity, including higher arousal levels, active cognitive task engagement, and enhanced cortical excitability. They are also more likely to experience repeated nightly disruptions of sleep, with multiple awakenings in response to stressful periods.

Van Someren (2021) concluded that in ID, hyperarousal continues into deepest sleep and the presence of this biomarker of ID (LC-NE activations) provides a theoretical understanding of the brain center creating disrupted sleep, as well as a means of measuring the outcomes of treatments targeting ID specifically.

A Psychotherapy Model That Targets Resolution of Locus Coeruleus Hyperactivation

The central role of the LC and the salience network in the genesis of PTSD symptoms has now been demonstrated in neuroimaging studies as difficulties imaging this small nucleus with earlier fMRI and PET technologies are overcome. In an in vivo ultra-high resolution 7-Tesla study of LC size, Laurel Morris and her colleagues (2020) demonstrated that human patients with anxiety or stress-related disorders had larger LC volumes compared to normal subjects (Cohen's d=1.08). Moreover, larger LC was associated with clinical variables like poorer attentional and inhibitory control and higher arousal transdiagnostically across the entire sample.

In a study directly assessing whether the LC-NE system underlies the hyperresponsiveness of PTSD patients, Christof Naegeli and his colleagues (2018) demonstrated that atypical high phasic noradrenergic activity originating in the LC resulted in hyperactive autonomic alerting/orienting responses. More recently, Clifford Cassidy and his colleagues in Ottawa (McCall et al., 2024) using more advanced neuromelanin sensitive MRI (NM-MRI), demonstrated that the LC signal of veterans with PTSD was elevated, and that this was most pronounced in the caudal LC. The caudal LC signal was also clinically correlated with the CAPS-5 hyperarousal subscale, but not any of the other PTSD subscales.

Craig Berridge (1991, 2012) has long argued that the LC plays a central role in induction of the waking state, including the activation of cortical EEG. What Van Someren has added to our understanding of these processes is that restless REM sleep is a preliminary step that instigates changes in the adaptive response of the amygdala and associated limbic structures. The failure of this adaptive process results in restless REM, which then directly increases the vulnerability for a broad range of neuropsychiatric disorders, including PTSD. It follows from Van Someren's review that any intervention that targets quieting the hyperactivity of the LC will be effective in repairing restless REM, reducing sleep disturbance, restoring adaptive amygdala functioning, and ultimately resolving neuropsychiatric disorders such as PTSD.

Frank Corrigan, a neuropsychiatrist from Glasgow, Scotland, has proposed just such a psychotherapy protocol (Corrigan & Christie-Sands, 2020). The Deep Brain Reorienting (DBR) protocol focuses the patient on identifying the initial orienting tension to danger. The patient then tracks their moment-to-moment physical responses. The shock reactions initiated by the SC-putamen-amygdala-LC pathway are stored in implicit memory in the right hemisphere as body reactions to the trauma.

During DBR therapy, the patient is encouraged to identify the initial aggravating stimulus that triggers their alarm reaction. This stimulus is introduced, and their nonverbal body reactions are tracked. These come as a series of shock reactions as the alarm signal in the brain is sent to the body to prompt action to overcome the danger. The tracking of the pre-affective shock reactions in a DBR therapy session releases the triggered LC neural activity. These are evident to the patient from the shock reactions that follow the orienting response. See the clinical example below for a full explanation.

Unlike other PTSD treatment protocols (like dialectical behavior therapy, EMDR, cognitive processing therapy, and exposure therapy), the DBR protocol focuses on the body's initial reaction to the threat signal, which allows identification of the *orienting response*, followed by the release of the *pre-affective shock responses* activated by the LC. And unlike CBTi and other mind-body treatments of insomnia, DBT targets the neural activity that causes restless REM.

Review of Brainstem Centers Integrating Incoming Sensory Data

Four brain regions respond to a survival challenge: (1) the brainstem nuclei (superior colliculus (SC), locus coeruleus (LC), periaqueductal gray (PAG), and cerebellum), (2) the limbic system (amygdala and hippocampus), (3) the thalamus, and (4) the prefrontal cortices (PFC). First, a brief review of how incoming sensory information is processed and responses to danger are initiated will be discussed next.

The brainstem includes three regions: the medulla, the pons, and the midbrain. The lowest (most caudal) of these is the medulla oblongata, which processes incoming visceral information from the organs, as well as touch, vibration, and proprioceptive cues from the limbs. Signals from the heart, lungs, and viscera are relayed to the nucleus tractus solitarius (NTS) by the vagus nerve. It integrates and relays this information to nuclei in the brainstem (nucleus ambiguus and rostral ventrolateral medulla) and hypothalamus to integrate autonomic functions to regulate heart rate, respiration, and blood pressure.

A structure that spans across the brainstem (from medulla across the pons and up to the midbrain) is the ascending reticular arousal system (ARAS). It participates in attention and arousal responses as well as activating autonomic reactions and sleep-wake cycling. The medulla also coordinates motor signals to the throat, neck, larynx, and tongue.

The pons is where auditory and vestibular information is coordinated. The rostral pons area is where the locus coeruleus (LC) is located. The LC is the brain's primary source of norepinephrine (NE) neurons, which are pivotal to initiating autonomic activation to threat and recruiting additional brain survival responses. Other motor responses that nuclei in the pons activate include eye movements, chewing, and facial expression of emotions.

The midbrain area is located in the upper part of the brainstem and is divided into the *tectum*, located in the dorsal (top) part of the midbrain, and the *tegmentum*, located in the ventral (bottom) of the midbrain. The tectum integrates incoming information in the inferior colliculus (auditory) and the superior colliculus (SC; visual, auditory, and sensorimotor) information. The SC is particularly important as it is the first area in the brain to integrate incoming signals of threat and cross-reference the danger with one's present location.

The Integrative Hub of the Superior Colliculus

Frank Corrigan's deep brain reorienting model provides the following understanding of the cascade of neural circuits recruited to respond to *danger!* How are the various sensory inputs (visual, auditory, and somatosensory) integrated to recognize that there is a *danger!*? Incoming visual signals are first noticed in the *superficial layers* of the SC and relayed to the thalamic pulvinar. The pulvinar directs the visual signals to areas of the visual cortex for further processing. In this way the SC provides a continuous mental map of one's position in space alongside nearby objects and their threat values. The pulvinar also sends the signals to the amygdala, which further evaluates the *danger!* and activates the appropriate level of LC response.

Just inside the superficial layers of the SC are the *intermediate layers* of the SC. These intermediate layers of the SC create the *first integrative hub*, where auditory and somatosensory inputs are integrated with the visual signals. When a serious threat is present, the adjacent *deep layers* of the SC tense muscles of the eye, forehead, and neck to immediately orient to the danger. This *orienting tension* (OT) prepares the organism to respond to danger with a range of cascading responses.

This initial orienting tension recruits the involvement of three nearby brainstem structures (LC, PAG, and cerebellum), as well as the limbic system (amygdala and hippocampus). Once the SC has directed attention to the threat, the other brainstem nuclei act in a coordinated way to mount a *survival response* to the *danger!* Initiation of the fight-or-flight stress response is a coordinated response of all these brainstem and limbic structures. Importantly, the PFC (the seat of our conscious experience) is not aware of, nor involved in, these initial survival responses.

The tegmentum, which is ventral to the SC, plays a crucial role in further sensory processing, motor response, and modulation of consciousness. When the integrated signals from the SC engender *danger!*, rapid motor responses are initiated immediately through the adjacent tegmental structures in the pons (LC) and the midbrain (PAG). The LC initiates active motor response of the body through activation of body muscles. These alarm reactions of the LC were elaborated in detail in Chapter 8. The PAG initiates defensive behaviors by activating emotional response sequences like flight-fight-freeze. Outgoing motor responses are coordinated through connections with the adjacent cerebellum.

The Periaqueductal Gray Recruits Affective Experience and Defensive Responses

At the same time as the SC is alerting the LC to alert all brain areas to the *danger!*, it also signals the PAG to initiate an appropriate emotional-behavioral response to *danger!* The PAG can rapidly change heart rate, blood pressure, and respiration, as well as orchestrate the emotional reactions necessary to coordinate the overall behavioral response to danger. These behavioral responses are also assisted by the cerebellum, which coordinates the body's response to *danger!* by fine tuning autonomic and motor responses.

In the DBR model of survival response, when danger is still avoidable, the dorsolateral PAG (dlPAG) initiates a *fear*, or flight reaction. If the danger is to be confronted, for example, when backed into a corner, the dlPAG can shift to a *rage*, or fight, response. If the danger is inescapable or overwhelming, a *freeze* response is initiated. Here the intense sympathetic fight-or-flight reaction is still active, but a paralyzing response is initiated by recruiting the parasympathetic system, which results in an internally activated but behaviorally frozen state. Each of these three carry a unique emotional-experiential internal state (fear, rage, or freeze). These internal intensely emotional states become a central part of the event memory.

The freeze response is further exacerbated by the simultaneous activation of the ventrolateral PAG. When both dlPAG and vlPAG are coactivated, the result is a state of tonic immobility. When the vlPAG takes over full control of defensive response, the result is a hypotonic freeze with collapsed immobility. The later state can be further exacerbated by the release of dynorphin, a kappa opioid, which activates a *neurochemical dissociative state* that can include physical sensations of nausea, dizziness, heaviness, loss of muscle control, emotional numbness, and cognitive confusion. Exactly how and when the autonomic fight-flight-freeze responses recruit endocrine responses is still not clear.

The Integration of Limbic System Responses of the Amygdala and Hippocampus

As the brainstem nuclei (LC, PAG, and cerebellum) are mounting a response to the *danger!*, the limbic system is also processing the threat. These responses occur in the right amygdala, where the AMPA receptor binding sites are saturated from the intensity of the *danger!* This shifting of the amygdala into high alert causes the sensory and emotional memory fragments to remain unprocessed in the limbic system. In this way, they are perpetually present, ready to be retriggered repeatedly.

Upregulated amygdala responses result in intrusive thoughts or memories. When these happen in daytime, they result in a flashback experiences. When these happen during sleep, the person experiences a replicative nightmare. With the passage of time, replicative nightmares will transition into symbolic reworkings of the original traumatic event. These dreams will retain much of the emotional intensity of the original experience, but not necessarily the same images, context, or participants.

Deep Brain Reorienting: A Neuroscientifically Guided Psychotherapy for PTSD

> These approaches [DBR and other somatic sensory-based treatments] exploit subcortical processes by means of somatic sensory feedback and facilitate awareness and experience of somatic sensations in the present moment of safety as opposed to a past trauma. This process may be the antithesis to dissociative

flashbacks, derealization, and depersonalization and a catalyst for reinstating a sense of agency and trust in the body. (Kearney & Lanius, 2022, p. 21)

Van Someren's review of neuroimaging data highlighted the central role of the LC and concluded that insomnia is not a sleep disorder, but "could be a disorder of overnight emotional memory regulation, originating in a pre-symptomatic vulnerability to have Restless sleep." This same underlying vulnerability is proposed to contribute to the full-blown development of anxiety, depression, and PTSD disorders. It follows from this that psychotherapeutic interventions that effectively resolve LC hyperactivity will reduce restless sleep (in all of its presentations), resulting in reduced sleep disturbances (e.g., insomnia, nightmares, and sleepwalking), improved amygdala functioning, and gradual reduction of PTSD symptoms.

Application and Case Illustration of Deep Brain Reorienting

Frank Corrigan's DBR treatment protocol (Corrigan & Christie-Sands, 2020) focuses on the body's initial reaction to the threat signal, not to the range of daytime symptoms that follow. DBR treatment proceeds in a series of steps (Kearney et al., 2023), which allows the patient to track and release the implicit body-shock responses. Following these steps provides a neuromodulatory intervention that shifts the brainstem functions from a hyperactive state to a more stabilized ANS. The sequence of phases in DBR treatment include:

1. Identifying a target *activating event*, particularly the initial reaction to threat.
2. Orienting the patient to their present *where self* (the attuned moment-to-moment self that attends to one's internal experience).
3. Returning full attention to the attention-grabbing activating stimulus of the traumatic event and inviting the patient to attend to the *cascade of internal sensations*.
4. Guiding the patient to finding the *orienting tension* in the head, face, or neck (this permits anchoring in their initial SC-generated orienting tension.
5. Allowing space, time, and collaborative attention for all experiences of the *shock responses* to surface (this includes all bodily reactions mobilized by the LC).
6. Only after all shock responses are fully experienced does attention shift to *affective responses* (focusing attention to PAG-initiated emotional responses).
7. As tensions and affective responses release, the session closes with the patient invited to reflect on whether a *new perspective* on how the self sees itself is emerging (this engages the deep midline SC-PAG-thalamus-cortex axis).

Clinical Case Applying Deep Brain Reorienting to Chronic Nightmares and Insomnia

These steps will be illustrated with the following case. This is a 36-year-old single male, who I will call Esteban. He has been in weekly psychotherapy with me for 4 years. His presenting problem was repeated nightmares and chronic insomnia that he had struggled with all his life. Getting close to women triggered intense anxiety in him. In the previous year, he had made huge strides in getting into an intimate relationship. However, when he became ill and was hospitalized, his girlfriend left him.

Esteban recovered from his medical setback and resumed his activities. He was socially active with many good friends, and he enjoyed his work. While many areas of his life were going well for him, across the 4 months prior to this session, he was having recurrent nightmares. For example, one recurring theme was him feeling terrified that a nuclear bomb would go off. In the dream, it was his responsibility to find that bomb and prevent it from going off. He was frantic that he would not find it in time.

We had used EMDR repeatedly to desensitize the emotional distress activated by these terrifying nightmares, but the nightmares continued. At the core of these experiences was a terrified feeling rooted in intimate relationships. In the month prior to this session, Esteban had recalled an experience from when he was 5 years old.

His uncle had a girlfriend, who had mental health issues. Babysitting Esteban, his brother, and another cousin, the girlfriend became agitated and intensely terrified that the uncle was coming to kill them all. Her panic and distress overwhelmed the young Esteban, as he and his young mates were told to build a barricade so they would not be killed. They flipped over tables and brought mattresses and other furniture from other rooms to fortify the barricade. For Esteban, it felt like World War III was about to erupt and this explosion was triggered by being in an intimate relationship that could turn on you. The intensity of his terror resulted in repeated dissociative reactions to manage these intense explosions of terror.

Shortly after this sleepover experience, Esteban began having nightmares in which he was frantically looking for a nuclear bomb. He was frantic because if he did not find the bomb, it would explode and destroy everybody. He continued to have this nightmare regularly for the next 30 years. He described it as the same movie, sometimes in different locations, but always with the same intense dread and terror. He added that the only way he could cope with these intense feelings was to dissociate from them.

These moments of being completely overwhelmed persisted despite years of learning and using breathing, progressive muscle relaxation (PMR), meditation, regular exercise, self-compassion exercises, and yoga practice. Esteban had been in psychotherapy twice before with other EMDR therapists. While the

EMDR work we had been doing was helpful in resolving each individual terrifying experience fairly successfully, it had not resulted in halting new episodes of the terror. The session we are going to review was Esteban's first DBR session. Each of the steps in the DBR protocol are illustrated.

> PATIENT: That first week I had nonstop nightmares. Like hardly any sleep. And the nightmares were similarly themed, but they were changing. Every night I was waking up. There were maybe 2 nights where I was just so tired, I don't remember the nightmares. I wrote them all down. Then last week, very strange, I was having wonderful dreams. So when I wake up and, in my dreams, I'm loved. And I feel warm. And I would wake up with enthusiasm. It was like the exact opposite of the previous week. And then I had two triggers. Which I was impressed with how I dealt with. Because I felt it [the anxiety] right away. And then I went into my body. My mind was going a mile a second. I was able to calm my body down, and then the mind went away. It happened a second time. Yesterday I had a trigger that put my brain into full-fledged panic mode. I've had a little bit of everything over the past two weeks. A lot to bring to the table.
>
> THERAPIST: That is helpful. We have been focusing on experiences using the EMDR for many weeks now. But there is something about the experiences that still triggers you. It got activated again. Let's think of it as a cascade. Something happens, a trigger, and then there is a shock reaction in the body. The shock reaction is the basic brain reaction of, "I'm in danger."
>
> Something really dangerous is going to happen. And that shock reaction is then going to mobilize your body's reactions to protect you. And then the emotions (like fear, anger, shame, whatever), all of those happen after. We need to shift, just a little bit earlier, to see if we can get to the starting point.

Commentary. The therapist is highlighting the importance of beginning the DBR therapy at the very moment when the brainstem and body react, which is before the thinking brain is aware.

Phase 1: Identifying the Activating Event

> THERAPIST: To get to that initial moment where you gasp or you hold your breath, when you think about the nightmares, the three triggers, do you have a sense of how that reaction happens in your body?
>
> PATIENT: Do you mean back to the beginning of a trigger?
>
> THERAPIST: You can think of it like a little explosion. We are trying to catch that earliest moment, when the mind is saying, "Oh, shit."
>
> PATIENT: I'll go to the one yesterday, because it was the biggest trigger. And it's the one that I'm still working through. The first thing is dissociation. As with the previous two triggers, I noticed the dissociation, and I went

into my body. And I noticed, "Okay, my heart is beating really quickly. I have tension." So the first two times I was kind of able to ground myself. And then when this thing happened yesterday that little guy was triggered, and I tried to bring him into my body and it actually made things worse. It only made me a kind of rubber band. Where I said, "Okay, Esteban, you're dissociating. Let's listen to your heart." I've been sitting at that high RPM for 24 hours now.

Commentary. As Esteban remembers a particularly intense recent experience, his speech is faster, almost breathless.

THERAPIST: What exactly happened at the very beginning?
PATIENT: The adult can talk to me. But the child feels so much shame and embarrassment. Anyway, I was at school. Next semester I'm teaching a new class. (It's a course I've never taught before.) Another art teacher has been extremely helpful in giving me her materials and whatnot. I asked her, "Oh, do you mind if I ask you some questions and we can do some planning?" And she was like, "Yeah, no problem. No problem at all."

So I met with her yesterday. And she was truly kind, very sweet. Like she had her winter coat on and her bag, and she was walking out the door and I said, "Oh, I was just coming to find you." And she said, "Now is the perfect time." I said, "Oh, you are just leaving." She said, "No, no, like, I have time."

So we find a classroom. She takes all of her stuff off, she takes her laptop out, we're talking. And also, she is very cute. And she's very sweet. And she's very . . . she has been helping me out. And then I saw that she was married. There was a ring on her finger! And that, for whatever reason, that threw me into a complete panic mode! I knew that I was triggered. I tried to put myself in my body. I just totally dissociated. I said, "Oh, you know, I better let you go." And then I just hightailed it out of there. And I'm not sure why seeing a ring on her finger triggered me.

Commentary. Once the trigger is identified, there is no further discussion of why the reaction happened, or what he was thinking could have caused the reaction. Any cognitive, or upper level processing of the experience moves away from the body memories that will be reactivated. Instead, the therapist takes about 5 minutes to ground the patient in their present self, which anchors their perception to their inner states and knowing exactly where they are in this moment. In DBR this is the critical step of grounding in the where self.

Phase 2: Orienting the Patient to Their Present Where Self

THERAPIST: What we are going to do first is set up for the reorienting work. We will come back to that event shortly. First, we will ground you in this moment. Just sit comfortably. And as you're sitting there, I'm going to have you really connect with the part of you that is taking in information. All the information from around you: through your eyes, and through your ears. All that information that's coming in, is *telling you exactly where you are*. So this gives you a sense of being in this moment. Right now.

I want you to notice that without looking anywhere you can tell where your arms are. You can tell where your legs are positioned. You get a real sense of your body and your posture.

You can also clearly feel the sensation of your feet on the floor. You can feel the ground under the soles of your feet. Similarly, you can feel the weight of your body in the chair. That really gives you a sense of being located right here, right now.

And you have the visual field from your left and right eyes. You know, without even moving your eyes, one way or the other, or changing your gaze, you can draw your attention to something in your visual field from one side or the other. And similarly, if there was a sound off to your left, you could tell where it is from your left ear. Or, if there was a sound to the right, you could notice that in your right ear. And this sense of being located right here, right now, also includes a clear sense of being in a space. A room. And without looking around, you already have a sense of the walls. How far behind you the wall might be. The walls beside you, and in front. And that there's a floor. And a ceiling above you. And all of those create boundaries. An envelope of space, within which you are sitting. Fully aware of your presence right here.

The you that knows where you are is also fully aware that if you walk out the door, out of this room, it leads to stairs, or a hallway, or another room. And there are a number of rooms and spaces in the house in which you're in. And you could also, in your mind's eye, picture leaving out the front door. And having a sense of the space outside the house.

So this part of you that is fully conscious of your whereabouts. And is fully in the present. And is always taking in information. That is the part that we're going to start with. That is your where self.

And as you sit there, you may also be aware that there may be some stress in your body. See if you can let that go. There may be some tension around the eyes. See if you can let that go. Similarly in the back of the head, and the back of the neck. You may be noticing some tension there. See if you can release that.

Commentary. The grounding in the where self finishes by taking a moment to feel as relaxed as possible, with as little tension as possible in the body. Once this state has been achieved, it is now time to reintroduce the activating stimulus.

Phase 3: Introducing the Activating Event and Tracking Internal Responses

THERAPIST: Now, with that part of yourself that is fully aware of where you are, I want you to bring back that memory of being with that cute, kind, sweet teacher. As you glimpse the ring on her finger, notice your reaction. What is triggered in you? Allow that to be present.

As you sit with that, notice whatever you're experiencing in the forehead, around the eyes, or the back of the neck.

If you can find words to describe what you are picking up. Tell me what you notice.

PATIENT: It feels like I'm suffocating. Like I can't breathe. Tension in my left arm. Then tension in my legs and my glutes. And my whole body just kind of seizes up. It is like I'm being squished.

Commentary. The activating stimulus has triggered an intense reaction in his body. These sensations are a combination of shock reactions triggered by the LC and a suffocation response triggered by the PAG. The orienting tension would be found around his head. This first noticing of shock or emotional responses is very typical. For most patients it is the intensity of the shock reactions into the body that overpowers the more subtle initial reaction around the forehead, the eyes, or the back of the head. The therapist encourages him to slow down the response cascade and see if he can find the orienting tension. Until the orienting tension is identified the therapist is quite active in guiding the patient. After that he will follow the process as it emerges.

Phase 4: Guiding the Patient to the Orienting Tension

THERAPIST: It is happening really quickly. There is a cascade that runs all the way through to your arms and your legs. If you can, back up the movie to that first moment where you notice the ring. That moment in which you notice a quick reaction. And again, just see if you can begin to detect something early in that sequence. Around the forehead? Around the eyes? Or the back of head? Be curious about what you're beginning to notice.

PATIENT: The first thing I notice is my left arm totally seizes up.

THERAPIST: That's important. You are picking up a strong, very tight reaction. That would not be the first reaction. The beginning is always from the head and out to the body. See if there is anything that you can identify that may have happened before. Any sensation across the forehead? Or top of the head? Eyes?

PATIENT: I noticed tension in my eyes. It's almost like I'm squinting to see something. Like there's that type of tension.

THERAPIST: Just sit with that sensation, the squinting tension. See if there's anything else that you can identify, anything in the head?

Commentary. Esteban has identified the strain in the muscles around the eye as the orienting tension. The therapist is taking a little longer to see if there are any other sensations that he can become aware of in this initial orienting tension.

>PATIENT: I noticed a tension in my jaw.
>THERAPIST: That is part of the shock reaction. These are really powerful, almost like an earthquake inside the body. A quick movement through the muscle systems. As more of this shock reaction begins to come into your awareness, be curious about anything else that you are noticing. Especially the back of the neck, the forehead, or around the eyes.
>PATIENT: I mainly notice the eyes and the jaw.

Commentary. Esteban confirms that the eye strain is the main orienting tension. The jaw tension is part of the shock reaction to the threat. The therapist guides Esteban to deepen into the orienting tension.

>THERAPIST: Let's stay with the eyes. Whatever way you are experiencing that tension, deepen into your connection with it. Notice fully what is happening there. Stay with that.

Phase 5: Allowing Space for the Patient to Track Their Pre-Affective Shock Responses

>THERAPIST: Be open minded. Be curious about any other sensation that may come to your awareness. Some of these may be very fleeting or very quick. Others may stick around.
>PATIENT: I noticed tightness in my cheeks. A little bit in my forehead. But again, I think it's this breathing thing. It's like somebody is . . . something really heavy is on my chest. And I can barely breathe.

Commentary. In DBR processing, Frank Corrigan distinguishes a gasp of shock from the more frightening sense of air hunger felt in panic. The former is a shock reaction from the LC and the latter is activated by the PAG (Corrigan et al., 2024).

>THERAPIST: That commands all of your attention. The fear that you're not getting enough air. If it's helpful, if you can, as you notice the sensation of barely being able to breathe, I want you to do your best to sit with it.
>PATIENT: I'm focused on this tension in the cheeks and the jaw. As well, on the eyes.
>THERAPIST: If it feels a little bit uncomfortable, or you feel stuck with that tension, see if you can remain curious about the sensations that are coming to your awareness.

PATIENT: I noticed my left arm. It was so tense that it started to shake. I could just feel it release a little. I'm breathing again. I don't have that suffocating feeling anymore. And I noticed tension on the left side of my forehead.

THERAPIST: Take a moment to deepen into that sensation. The tension in the left forehead. Notice whatever character it has. Once you've noticed that, be open to any other sensations or reactions that begin to come to your awareness.

PATIENT: My left shoulder, a lot of tension. And with that, I guess the biceps and the triceps. I know I was holding it.

THERAPIST: These are all part of the shock reactions in the body. Any other tension held in the body?

Commentary. Esteban has been able to stay with his physical sensations. Others may shift to their thoughts and ideas. The therapist encourages him to continue to be curious about other sensations that come up.

PATIENT: My fists are clenched up. And my feet, the same thing, that grip to the ground. I'm still noticing tension in my arms and my shoulders as well. And also same thing in my left temple. My eye, and the left side of my head. It all feels very tense.

THERAPIST: You're doing well slowing it down, noticing the waves of tension come. If they linger, that's okay too.

PATIENT: I still notice some tension in my left jaw.

THERAPIST: Just open to your experience. Track it moment by moment.

Commentary. The therapist has been very present with his responses to let Esteban know that he is on the right path. He has now noticed waves of shock into his chest, cheek, shoulders, arms, fists, and left side of his face. Each of these reactions release reactions that were initiated but likely not expressed. For example, a tightening of the arms can follow from an urge to fight or from an urge to attach. The jaw can tighten from bracing against the urge to fight, and so on. The DBR therapeutic stance in treatment is to allow Esteban more space to directly experience all that comes up for him, not to interpret it.

PATIENT: I was clenching my teeth. My jaw relaxed, let up on the pressure on my teeth. I just noticed my left shoulder relax. Because I was holding it tense up here. And this left arm, I just felt that drop a little bit. Relax into place Again, just a little bit more relaxation in my left arm. I feel that I can breathe a lot. My breaths are much deeper. I don't feel that suffocating feeling.

THERAPIST: There's a release that's coming from being attentive and going with the flow.

PATIENT: I still feel tension in my left cheek and my left jaw area. My feet touch the carpet. There was some tension in my right arm. That relaxed a little bit.

THERAPIST: These are waves of tension that come and then begin to relax. All part of the shock response, as the brain reacts. You have slowed it down really nicely to be attentive to what you are feeling.

Commentary. Esteban has experienced the waves of tension that have become clearer in his awareness of his body responses. As he continues to notice more shock reactions, the stance of the therapist is to continue to provide Esteban space to release the shock reactions.

PATIENT: I just noticed a tension in my abdomen. Again tension in my jaw, my cheek, my left eye area. A very long exhale. And then followed by a nice long inhale. That was nice.

THERAPIST: Feeling you're getting your full breath back again. There may still be some aftershocks. Just small, reactive jolts or tensions. See if there's anything else.

PATIENT: Tension in both shoulders. I was really pushing into my thighs instead of just letting my hands rest there. Again a nice big inhale. And a nice long exhale. My shoulders relax. Tension left in my left eye. My abdomen is nicely relaxed. When we started, I constantly had a thought to like, break things. Like I have to slam on the desk. That was extremely fast. And now my body feels nice and relaxed. And I don't really notice that thought anymore.

Commentary. Esteban had an aggressive impulse earlier that he did not tell the therapist about. But he did feel it. In DBR the first task is to allow the shock reactions to be felt. If Esteban had mentioned the rage reaction, he would have been told that it is important, but we first continue attending to the body shock. Only after those have subsided do we turn to the affective reactions.

THERAPIST: That was part of the initial overload and feeling really distressed. Then it would make you want to pound your arms down. There was a real shift that is continuing. Draw your attention back to the head. Notice whatever is still there.

PATIENT: Still some tension in my jaw and eye.

Commentary. The therapist is evaluating whether the orienting tension is still operating. Esteban is noticing both the orienting tension around the left eye, as well as the shock reaction of tension in his jaw. As the eye tension is still there, the attention to emerging shock reactions continues.

PATIENT: Now it's less, but I still notice tension in my left eye and the left part of my jaw.

THERAPIST: That has been the most resistant.
PATIENT: I just noticed that there is a nice release.
THERAPIST: These residual aftershocks are slowly melting away. Continue to be curious.
PATIENT: I feel much more relaxed than I was before. I was just noticing tension in my legs. But I noticed that relax a little bit. The hamstrings in both legs.
   Tension in my right arm just relaxed.
THERAPIST: You are very connected. Attuned to your own body.
PATIENT: My mind is trying to take off, but I'm still scanning my body, trying to stay grounded.
THERAPIST: Your mind wants to go somewhere else. That is okay. You are paying attention and remaining 100% tuned into what is going on inside the body.

Commentary. Esteban has noticed the tendency to go upstairs to his thinking mind. The therapist continues to support his focus on physical sensations.

PATIENT: I take a nice deep breath in and out. And I still notice tension in my left eye. . . . Now I feel relaxation in my left eye. . . . I now have a sense of everything feeling a lot more relaxed in all areas of my body.
THERAPIST: A sense that some of these aftershocks are beginning to diminish, to die down. See if there are any other elements that might pop up.

Commentary. Esteban is approaching the end of the shock reactions. As the orienting tension releases, he is noticing his whole body relax.

PATIENT: I just noticed a nice deep breath in and a nice deep breath out. I feel like my face is pretty relaxed now.
THERAPIST: Anything else? Any residual tension anywhere in the body?

Commentary. The therapist checks for any body tensions that are still present.

PATIENT: I feel a little bit of tension in my fingers. I can feel my legs relaxing. I put them further out. They feel more relaxed.
THERAPIST: They don't feel like they have to run away from the shock.
PATIENT: I cracked my toes. And my feet, which were planted, ready to sprint. My heels are kind of up now. I'm stretching my feet.
THERAPIST: There is a moment now of feeling really comfortable in your skin.
PATIENT: I sat further down in the seat. I'm less upright.
THERAPIST: My guess is that the intensity of some of these shock reactions in the body is probably what has been driving that dissociative reaction: "I've got to get out of my body. I've got to escape." But you were able to ride

through that. And to get to this place where you are now relaxed. You are leaning back in the chair.

Phase 6: Exploring Affects That Arise From the Reorienting

The first priority of DBR is to activate the LC-NE shock reactions and allow space for the patient to feel and track these. Only when these have been exhausted will the affective responses become the focus of the patient's work. They did come to the fore earlier (the impulse to smash his fist down) but these were bypassed so the release of shock could be fully realized.

Phase 7: Exploring Any New Perspectives That Emerge

THERAPIST: Do you have a new perspective? If you begin to think about what has been happening here? Do you have a new sense of how you feel in your body? Or how you were able to manage this internal earthquake?

PATIENT: What I have noticed over the past few sessions, and especially today, is if I can try to focus on the body—I don't want to say ignore, but ignore the thought that is moving a mile a second. And just to stop. To just actually be in my body. Because that is the dissociation. I feel so uncomfortable. Like, my goal is to get out of the body. But if I can try to ground myself, and just sit for 5 or 10 minutes, or 20 minutes, and try to stay in my body. I think that's the key.

THERAPIST: Absolutely. Even while the shock reactions are happening, being able to tune into them to notice them. The orienting tension was the tension right at the start: right around your eye. You have your orienting tension to go back to.

Commentary. Esteban has provided a clear account of how distressing these shock reactions are. In the moment that they hit, there is the overwhelming sense of "I have to go. I cannot tolerate this." That is the trigger for dissociating. He has been in therapy long enough that he is acutely aware of his moments of dissociation. In this session, the orienting tension did provide him with an anchor to stay in his body.

THERAPIST: If the shock reactions stick around for a while, you can sit with them. And then pretty much all of them slowly gave way. Even the stickiest ones that were a little bit harder. Gradually everything began to shift and change. And you got to a place where you can feel the calm through the body. Let's take a moment and really appreciate and enjoy what you have been able to connect with. By watching those shock waves come and go, come and go. And sitting patiently and tuning in to your body. That has now given you this sense of—if you have ever been whitewater rafting—that you have been going through all the turmoil, and then you get down to a nice little pool of water, and sit back in your canoe and enjoy the moment. And enjoy what you have accomplished. That you have navigated through some pretty treacherous and unruly water. But now you're in a place where you can enjoy.

Closure: Highlighting the Role of Pre-Affective Shock: EMDR Versus DBR Processing

THERAPIST: This was different than our usual EMDR reprocessing. We wanted to pay more attention to the body all the way through, without doing the eye movements because the eye movements activate other memories and associations. This is a little bit slower, but it allows you to tune in at a much deeper level. How are you getting the shift? And where do you get to at the end of the process? How would you compare this with the EMDR sessions?

PATIENT: This seems to be a lot more physical, in terms of noticing my body. There were so many times where my mind wanted to talk about my emotions. But none of that matters, really. What matters is what you are feeling in your body. There is a part of me that still wants to say, "Hold on, no! We have to talk about the emotions and all this stuff."

Commentary. On being asked directly for his experience, Esteban explains how the experience of DBR supported stepping back from cognitive analysis to allow him to actually experience what the body has remembered.

THERAPIST: The emotions are also important, but the thing that I'm understanding, and maybe you are also understanding is that we have done some rather good EMDR work around emotions and around events. And it is striking to me that there are still these upheavals. In terms of the repeated nightmares you endured for a whole week.

That is why we have to back up, to get to the shock reaction in the body before the emotions. The shock reaction is pre-affective. It comes before the emotions have been activated. All the talk that we did about the emotions helped a lot to understand your ability to change things. To take that younger part of you under your wing. But it did not stop the shock reactions. These things happen at the brainstem level. This is in the very oldest part of the brain. This is where we begin to get our sense of what is happening. You will be the judge of how our work today has helped. The EMDR, as helpful as it was, was not removing the nightmares. It did not quiet the arousal system.

When we get together next time you can tell me if this created a different sense of inner calm. Or whether you were able to sleep through the night.

Commentary. This session ended with a reflection on change in Esteban's perception of himself. He was better able to stay with his body experiences in the face of his usual dissociative reaction. But beyond this there was no new perspective he noticed. The therapist ends the session by asking Esteban to pay attention to the sleep and nightmare symptoms he had been having.

The next scheduled psychotherapy session was 2 weeks later. We now go to the edited transcript of the beginning of that session.

> THERAPIST: How have things been going since our last meeting?
>
> PATIENT: Our last session we didn't do any EMDR. And I remember after that session, my child self was kind of going a little bit crazy, like, "What are we going to do?" But one of the things I found was that [the DBR] session really helped me. Because we spent a good amount of time just being in my body. Narrating what I'm feeling. I spent the past 2 weeks not doing meditation—or any of these 9000 other practices in which I [usually] partake. I would just sit and feel what was going on in my body. And recognize it. I haven't had a nightmare in 2 weeks, since before our last session.

Commentary. Strikingly, he has not had any nightmares, in contrast with his experiences after the previous session, which he said had triggered a week of nightmares.

> THERAPIST: I think DBR has the same benefits as EMDR; it's just a little bit different. Because, as you put it beautifully, you are really tuning into your body, moment by moment, by moment. In a witnessing way, without preconceptions. You are allowing what is present in your body, to become present in your mind.
>
> PATIENT: There were a few nights where I didn't dream at all. And I had a few dreams that were quite different for me, that were positive. When I came out of the dream, I felt so loved and accepted. And wonderful things were happening in my life.
>
> One of the things I've learned with the DBR technique and sitting is that when I practice that state of being, it is so different from my usual state. My usual state is that I have anxiety.
>
> One of the things that I started to do when I would feel anxious I would say, "What am I doing?. I am practicing anxiety." Then I would take a moment to drop into my body. Because the two states are so different. And it showed me that what I'm practicing now is a pattern. If I can recognize that pattern, and interrupt it, then I will have a new state of being.
>
> Having no nightmares was hugely different. It was great. I find when I don't have the nightmares, I'm a lot more open to connection.

Commentary. Esteban has articulated something I have heard from many nightmare sufferers. It is not just that they had the nightmare. It is that the nightmare sets up a mental attitude that is phobic of approaching the day ahead. Esteban explained how the lack of nightmares allowed him to function differently. *The release of shock reactions has caused a major shift.* The novel experience of positive emotion in his dreams provides evidence this major neuromodulatory shift toward a more stabilized brainstem.

PATIENT: I was very busy the past two weeks. Because when I have not had the nightmares, I wake up and I don't have that fear within my nervous system. That little extra 5% or 10% of confidence allowed me to call up a friend or make plans.

Usually where I would feel anxious and afraid because of what's going on in the dreams. I found the past two weeks I was busy almost every day. "I feel good today, so I'm going to call this friend." As opposed to, "Oh, maybe this person hates me, or I had this dream so I'm afraid to go out."

THERAPIST: Inner confidence that you could feel comfortable in your body. You could feel into the body and allow yourself to move forward.

PATIENT: Absolutely. And then on Sunday, I went on a date. That was nice, to get out again.

THERAPIST: Good for you! Your felt sense of your day-to-day activities is more grounded. There is less intrusion from anxiety. And for the last 2 weeks, the nightmares have disappeared off the landscape. What has begun to appear is those positive dreams, where you felt loved. I think that's a real breakthrough.

We have been working on this for, I would say at least 6 weeks. At least in terms of the nightmares. Then the memories of remembering your uncle's girlfriend. Building the fort so you would not be killed. And your terror about all that. You had to go through all of that. I don't think there was a shortcut. I don't think we could have got to what you felt in the last 2 weeks, in that calm, without first going through all of the shock.

And the EMDR was important in processing that, but I am finding too that using this DBR body-centered focus can be so helpful.

So the DBR has really helped to settle things. What I am getting from you is that you are living your day-to-day life, and your opportunities, the way you want to. You are not feeling crowded out by anxiety, or fears, or worries.

PATIENT: I'm starting to see myself differently, as well. I'm a lot more interactive with people. I feel I do have much more choice. Instead of being bogged down, by trying to recover from last night's nightmare, or by the anxiety. It's a pattern. The anxiety still pops up every now and then. And then I tried to do the grounding exercise. I think the biggest trick for me is not to get caught up in the thoughts. If I can ignore the thoughts for, say, 10 minutes, and do the breathing, I am fine.

I started to do the grounding technique before bed. I would not stop doing the technique until I started to have happy thoughts. I would do it no matter how long it took me. Usually about 10 to 20 minutes. At the start, I would notice my anxiety, my anxious thoughts. "Oh, I have got to do this . . . and this . . . and this."

When I started to think about friends, and loved ones, and the future, and possibilities. I would say, "Okay, I'm going to go to bed now." Rather than using a timer, to make it a certain time, I judged it based on when my body was relaxed.

THERAPIST: Because you now know what it feels like when you feel calm. When you are at peace inside your body. When you said you "did the technique," what were you doing? Thinking about the day's activities? Or is it meditation?

PATIENT: It's very similar. As a joke I called it the *Reitav Technique*. [Both laugh heartily.] Because you have to name it after somebody. I sit down. And I would do about 20 seconds of feeling into my body. Then I would open my eyes and I would and say, "I felt my right toe. I am tense. And my heart is beating fast."

And I would say aloud what my body was experiencing. I would take another 20 seconds to notice tension here and there. I would stop after 20 seconds and narrate what was happening in my body. Almost as if you were in front of me doing exactly what we did last time.

THERAPIST: Oh, fantastic. It's beautiful that your negative thoughts and anxiety begin to evaporate.

And then you get to that core positive experience.

Commentary. Esteban surprised me with this update. I had not thought to suggest that he practice the grounding into the where self at home. He decided to do it because he had found it profoundly helpful. Esteban's experience in the previous session underlined that healing happened when he stayed with his body.

PATIENT: When we started going through the experience, I was very angry inside. We had done all this EMDR work, and I was still having nightmares. And now you tell me we are not doing EMDR!

These thoughts were plowing at me when we started. But toward the end of that session, I didn't even remember what the original [angry] thoughts were! So I went away from that and thought, "Oh, my thoughts are really just a reflection about how my body feels."

So if I can do what we did, then maybe I won't even think about what my thoughts thought (even 20 minutes ago).

THERAPIST: You took what really resonated deeply with you. You could feel the shift.

PATIENT: I have all these books, different meditations, hypnosis, and whatever. And it allowed me to get rid of all of those ideas. And just sit and be with myself.

And I think at the end of the day, that is the most important thing.

Commentary. During the last session, Esteban had felt a surge of anger early in the session, and could not remember it at all by the end of the session. This made a big impression on him and he was persuaded to use the grounding exercise himself. It helped in turning off his nightmares, which may have been fueled by his previous pattern of nightly worries.

> THERAPIST: You resonate with how it begins to change your way of relating to yourself: your body, your feelings, your thoughts. It begins to be experienced in a different way.
>
> PATIENT: The no-nightmare thing is a pretty big deal! I still wake up in the mornings surprised, because I've had them for so long. There is no screaming. It's different! I can get used to that.
>
> THERAPIST: I hope you do. And I hope you continue with that. Does that mean that once you do get to bed, it's easier? Are you noticing any difference in terms of how long it takes you to fall asleep? Or awakenings in the night? Or how long you're sleeping?
>
> PATIENT: I tend to fall asleep pretty quickly. The first week I was not sleeping longer. Before, I would wake up before my alarm. Now my alarm goes off and it takes me about 10 minutes to get up. My sleep is a little bit longer. And it takes longer to move from the sleeping state to the waking state.
>
> THERAPIST: As you're sleeping, you're probably getting into deep sleep. And that anxious brain that was creating those nightmares that used to wake you up has settled down.
>
> When the alarm goes in the morning, you're down in a much deeper REM sleep. You are not as close to being in an awake state.

Commentary. Everything Esteban describes is consistent with the recovery of undisturbed REM sleep, in which his dreaming occurs with a silenced LC-NE system. That dampened alarm reaction permits deeper sleep through the night as well as the initiation of truly adaptive amygdala reorganization during REM. Esteban's increased difficulty in waking up in the morning is actually a sign of deeper sleep.

Summary of Session and Clinical Implications

Esteban's descriptions of how his nightmares disappeared, his daytime experiences were more engaging, and his sleep was deeper (especially that he finds it harder to wake up out of sleep) all are consistent with a reset of the background LC-NE arousal system.

The striking thing for me, as his therapist, was that he had been fully trained in using diaphragmatic breathing, yoga, and progressive muscle relaxation, yet none of these skills were of much help to reset his LC-NE hyperarousal. *The release of the autonomic shock reactions he experienced in the DBR session were turning points in his treatment.* We continued to meet monthly about other triggers, with each of these being resolved with DBR.

As the changes in autonomic reactivity reported here are for a single patient, they certainly require confirmation in a randomized trial with insomnia and nightmare patients with appropriate control groups. However, there is little doubt that Esteban's experience was significantly shifted by the combination of the DBR session and his spontaneous adoption of grounding in the where self exercise.

In the next chapter we will explore in greater detail the use of DBR with patients who have significant medical comorbidities.

APPLICATION

To make effective use of the information you have been reading, we invite you to apply the concepts described in this chapter by engaging patients with these important steps in exploring their sleep:

Assess Insomnia Disorder (ID) Routinely in Trauma Patients: Use the Reitav-Thirlwell Trauma Sleep Inquiry (Table I.3) and the Sleep Condition Indicator (Table 2.2) to evaluate the degree of insomnia symptoms present in your trauma patient. When sleep is disrupted, conduct a short inquiry to determine how long the disturbance has been present, how it impacts daytime functions, and how severe it is presently.

Determine What Difficulties Are Most Disturbing to the Patient Currently: If insomnia or nonrestorative sleep is present, also evaluate whether the patient has nightmares, night terrors, or sleepwalking. Collaborate with the patient to find the most difficult experience for them across the past week. It can be used as an activating stimulus for DBR therapy.

Contact the Deep Brain Reorienting Website to Register for Training Sessions: Contact www.DeepBrainReorienting.com to find information on training sessions to learn how to use this form of psychotherapy. Manualized treatments follow a fixed protocol of steps. DBR is not a manualized treatment. DBR therapy uses the therapist's understanding of brainstem functions to respond to the patient's emerging experiences in a *systematic* way. The goal is activation of a traumatic memory system, and then resolution of shock reactions, affective responses, and distortions in attachment patterns.

Key Messages for Therapists

1. Insomnia disorder (ID) is defined by an underlying hyperactivation of arousal and emotional circuits, rather than over- or underactivation of

sleep circuits. ID and NRS are a distinct neuropsychiatric disorders, with a specific underlying brain mechanism, which makes ID and NRS transdiagnostic primary risk factors for the development of other common psychiatric conditions (anxiety disorders, depression, and PTSD) and predisposes/exacerbates physical health issues.

2. The vigilance system (i.e., ARAS, LC, PPN, DRN, LDT) allows for wakefulness, attention, and alertness and is necessary for a healthy sleep-wake rhythm. In contrast, the salience network (i.e., SC, LC, PAG, DRN, VTA) initiates survival responses through the activation of the LC. Early or repeated trauma results in restless REM and related sleep conditions of night terrors, nightmares, ID, and nonrestorative sleep (NRS). Restless REM sleep, caused by a hyperactive LC, impedes the overnight emotional regulation of the amygdala.

3. In trauma, the hyperactivated LC is continuously activating the norepinephrine (NE) circuits of the whole brain, recruiting the brain into a hyperaroused state. Intensified mental alertness, physiological arousal, and mobilized bodily sensations become recurring states that can enter conscious awareness as panic attacks or as a range of physical symptoms.

4. The intensity of these hyperaroused survival reactions overwhelms the usual shift into sleep at the end of the day and predisposes the individual to long sleep latencies, sleepwalking, night terrors, nightmares, insomnia, and nonrestorative sleep.

5. EMDR therapy targets resolving PAG-activated affective states (to desensitize emotions), to finally resolve the traumatic memory state and allow cognitive reprocessing. Completion of the reprocessing of a traumatic memory means that there is a date stamp on the memory, integrating right brain emotional experiences into a functional left brain episodic memory.

6. DBR therapy activates the initial orienting tension (OT) to provide an anchor point from which to reorient to both body shock reactions and reexperiencing overwhelming emotional distress. DBR targets release of LC hyperactivation (critical in development of restless REM and ID), evident from pre-affective shock reactions. This is completed prior to the processing of the PAG affectively laden memories. If emotional reactions begin flooding in to trigger dissociation, returning to the OT provides a brake to prevent derailing the therapeutic process. Returning to the OT improves the patient's ability to stay with their body state experiences. In this way the patient begins to live in their bodies and move forward from their disembodied emotional state.

10

Somatic Distress and Self-Regulation

"The brain and peripheral bodily organs continuously exchange information. . . . Stress responses involve a neurobehavioral cascade."
—Andre Schulz, Dana Schultchen, and Claus Vogele (2020, p. 132)

"The mammalian stress response is a multicomponent response that includes an endocrine limb, an autonomic limb, an immunological limb, a behavioral limb, and a cognitive limb."
—Elisabeth Van Bockstaele and Rita Valentino (2009, p. 1669)

"The higher incidence of disease states following a period of severe stress . . . is due to the link between the hypothalamus and the immune system. . . . Feeling one's pain or fear in the subjective emotional present activates the homeostatic recovery system of the body."
—Alan Fogel (2013, pp. 159–161)

Somatization is the word that describes the universal and normal experience of feeling the body whenever there is some kind of arousal in the nervous system. We all feel our bodies as we go about our activities during the day. Somatic disorders refer to the disturbances in that background felt sense of the self, in which some somatic symptoms become prepotent and dominate one's consciousness. In the *DSM-5*, these conditions are under the heading of somatic symptom disorders. In earlier versions of the manual they were called somatization disorder, and in even earlier times, hysteria.

Hysteria, as a diagnosis, is no longer a part of our vocabulary as a clinical description of a patient's somatic symptoms. However, the clinical picture of multiple somatic complaints from early trauma is still very present. Vague

Somatic Distress and Self-Regulation 229

somatic complaints frequently do not have a diagnosis, other than a medically unexplained disorder (MUD), but are etched in the neurophysiology of trauma reexperienced by the client. Bessel van der Kolk's *The Body Keeps the Score* (2015) details the evolution of clinical thinking about early trauma from Pierre Janet to the present. The main takeaway is that somatic symptoms are integral to trauma work. What is not as clear is the source of these symptoms.

In this chapter, we will explore the neurobiological roots of how somatic symptoms are intertwined with trauma and sleep disturbance. We will then focus on cardiovascular distress particularly and how trauma treatment can be used to resolve the intense and disabling effects of psychophysiological distress triggered by cardiac events.

What I will learn in this chapter to become a better sleep and trauma therapist:

1. Early childhood trauma can cause distressing somatic experiences related to not having needs met. When these happen repeatedly [adverse childhood experiences (ACEs)] the child's bodily sensations become overwhelming, and they will disconnect from their bodily sensations. These reactions continue into adulthood and can be the cause of multiple somatic symptoms and/or hypersensitivity to such sensations.
2. Acute traumatic events trigger the *endocrine limb* of the stress response with release of corticotropic releasing factor (CRF), and CRF receptors (CRFr2) are immunoreactive. The stimulation of these receptors not only accelerates the stress cascade (release of cortisol) but also increases the level of serotonin (resulting in intensified anxiety experiences) and activates the *immunological limb* of the stress response with pro-inflammatory responses including the release of inflammatory cytokines, macrophages, and other immunological responses. The pro-inflammatory response can be further intensified as CRFr2 receptor sites are also located on immune cells and tissues throughout the body. Depending on context, activation of these sites can either be pro-inflammatory or anti-inflammatory.
3. Many neurons in the LC integrate receptors for CRF and endogenous opioids. The interplay of these two endocrines allows for immediate responsiveness to threat as well as feedback loops to stabilize LC-NE tonic activation. However, these feedback loops can become dysregulated, with the result that LC-NE activity becomes chronically hyperaroused.
4. Somatic symptoms triggered in the trauma-stress cascade will not improve until the underlying role of the dysregulated ANS is addressed in therapy. This is critically important for understanding how health psychology can contribute to the resolution of these symptoms in medical patients. Understanding these symptoms as caused by a dysregulated ANS opens up the possibility of effective treatment through application of trauma treatments to the physical symptoms themselves.

5. Treatment of the traumatic consequences of cardiovascular events includes introduction of agency back into the patient's response to psychophysiological distress. Deep Brain Reorienting (DBR) provides an effective and targeted way of: (1) reducing the activation of *autonomic limb* pre-affective shock, (2) managing the PAG-mediated *behavioral limb* affective responses, and (3) returning interoceptive signaling back to pre-traumatic event levels by engaging the attentive where self. The neurobiological processes engaged during DBR treatment modulate the LC-NE system's hyperarousal response, which is at the heart of dysregulation of the ANS, whether the threat came from the environment (a predator) or from within the body itself (a heart attack).

ROLE OF EARLY ATTACHMENT EXPERIENCES FOR SOMATIC SYMPTOMS

Ruth Lanius and her colleague Brianne Kearney (2022) highlighted the presence of somatic co-embodiment of the young child with the mother. They suggested that this co-embodiment "forms the basis for an emerging sense of self embodiment in the young child. *It is through this physical and physiological attunement that children sense that they are protected, cherished, and safe*" (Kearney & Lanius, 2022, p. 10). This concept is an important contribution to understanding the roots of the development of physical symptoms. In a paper entitled *The brain-body disconnect: A somatic sensory basis for trauma-related disorders*, these researchers integrated research from child development and developmental psychopathological studies to propose a central role for the early attachment experience of the child as the crucible in which distressing somatic symptoms begin. They compare the developmental path of a securely attached infant with that of an insecurely attached infant. The former leads to an *embodied* experience of self (Figure 10.1 top panel), while the later creates the psychophysiological substrate for a *disembodied* self (see Figure 10.1 bottom panel).

Since most research into interoception in trauma and somatic symptoms occurs after the trauma has happened, it is difficult to know for certain whether these suppositions about the underlying physiological mechanisms are accurate. What we do know for sure is that the earliest memories of the child are somatosensory. We also know that unlike trauma that happens in adulthood, childhood trauma results in restless REM (Van Someren, 2021).

Restless REM is a biomarker of an impaired ability of the amygdala to adapt. The adaptive functions of REM sleep may extend well beyond the regulation of affective experience, which is, of course, a bodily experience. Ivan Pigarev (2014) presented evidence that the insula appears to play a significant role in communicating critical somatic signals back to organ systems, to effectively regulate their internal functions. Although the role of REM sleep in regulation of somatic experience is not well studied to date, it is well known that children

FIGURE 10.1 Impact of Secure (top) vs. Insecure (bottom) Attachment on Somatic Sensory Integration (see insert for color)   Source: Reprinted by permission: Kearney & Lanius (2022, p. 11)

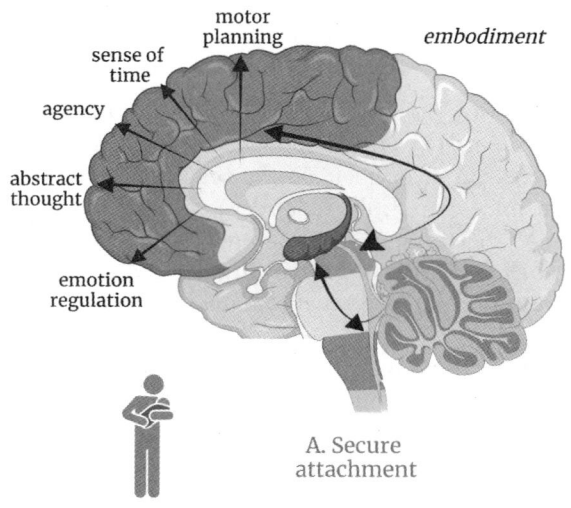

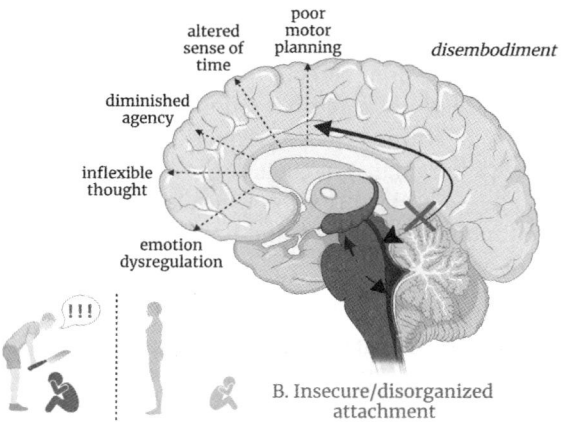

with persistent somatic distress are vulnerable to a persisting disembodied self. As a result, later life experiences that flood the body with distressing signals cannot be processed, and the adult is more vulnerable to develop the full PTSD trauma syndrome.

An important part of trauma work is therefore helping the trauma patient face these overwhelming somatic experiences and integrate them into their autobiographical memory. This chapter will provide a review of the neurobiological bases for these conditions and examples of how to resolve these challenges through DBR treatments. We begin with a review of how normal development proceeds.

Positive Caregiver Experiences

The regular and responsive presence of the caregiver is critical for the normal development of the infant. The attuned presence of the caregiver is felt by the infant through the release of oxytocin in the brainstem and throughout the brain. Studies with mice (Yu et al., 2022) demonstrated that pleasant touch stimulation promoted social interaction and preference for the touch context. *These touch stimuli elicited firing of neurons in the PAG, which enhanced oxytocin firing in paraventricular (PVN) hypothalamic oxytocin neurons, releasing more oxytocin into the body.*

Studies with children in orphanages (Linden, 2015) where there had been a deprivation of touch found a similar outcome. Twenty to 60 minutes of daily touch resulted in babies sleeping better, crying less (protest behavior), and developing better motor, attention, and cognitive skills. Connecting the two studies allows us to infer that, for mice and men, the PAG functions as a critical hub for detecting and responding to positive and negative touch sensations.

In the brainstem, the presence of oxytocin has a very salutary impact on the raphe nuclei. Oxytocin increases the firing rate of serotonergic neurons, resulting in increased release of serotonin in many areas of the brain. Alongside the increase of oxytocin, there is a simultaneous reduction of corticotropic releasing factor (CRF), a key signal activating alarm responses in the brain and body. The repeated experiences of an attuned caregiver and the positive balance between oxytocin and CRF helps the infant engender feelings of safety, emotional connection, and trust. The result of this virtuous cycle is an enhanced sense of well-being, improved mood, better sleep and dreaming, and most likely more prosocial engagement with others.

Negative Caregiver Experiences

In contrast, early life experiences in which there is a lack of touch, connection, and attunement results in palpable distress in the infant. Gina Forster and her colleagues conducted a study of early life neglect/stress by isolating young rat pups post weaning for 21 days (Lukkes et al., 2009). Twenty days later these isolated pups demonstrated higher anxiety behaviors than normal, which persisted as the pups were reintroduced into normal social contexts. The authors concluded that the 3-week social isolation experience in the early developmental period resulted in persisting anxiety-like behaviors long after their experience of isolation. More interestingly, these were directly related to the effect of CRF on the CRFr2 receptors (but not CRFr1) of the dorsal raphe nucleus (DRN). We explore the role of the DRN in somatic symptoms next.

The Raphe Nuclei Regulate Mood, Sleep-Wake Rhythms, and Inflammation

The raphe nuclei are a series of eight component subnuclei located in the brainstem. The neurotransmitter that is expressed by the raphe nuclei is serotonin, or 5-HT. Among the critical functions regulated by the raphe nuclei are:

1. Regulation of mood, emotion, and sleep-wake cycles (dorsal and medial raphe).
2. Regulation of mood, emotion, and sleep-wake cycles (caudal linear nucleus).
3. Regulation of autonomic cardiovascular and respiratory activity (superior central raphe nucleus)
4. Generation and regulation of REM sleep and modulation of muscle tone during REM (raphe pontis).
5. Modulation of pain by release of serotonin in the spinal cord (raphe magnus).
6. Control of heart rate, blood pressure and respiration (raphe obscurus).
7. Regulation of body temperature in response to ambient temperature changes (raphe pallidus).
8. Coordination of motor movements like walking (Bungner's nuclei).

The pathways by which trauma impacts the serotonergic raphe nuclei are complex but among the most important of these is the role of *touch, connection,* and *bonding.* When these are present in a securely attached child, the raphe nuclei not only amplify the sense of general well-being and calm autonomic and cardiovascular reactivity, but also regulate sleep-wake rhythms and promote the generation of REM sleep for amygdala adaptation, which better modulates emotional regulation.

When infants have few, inconsistent, or painful interactions with the caregiver, there is a profound increase in physiological distress around the attachment drive. Connecting with the other now has a distinctly aversive flavor. The infant, and later the adult, feels the need for connection and support, while at the same time feels it is dangerous. Attachment itself feels dangerous and not safe. The infant has increased internal distress and a sense of isolation and abandonment, with the result that they have no way to regulate that physiological distress.

Conflicted attachment urges can operate at the same time and are evident in the SC, which can activate both pathways for facilitating approach as well as pathways triggering defensive responses of recoil and withdrawal from engagement. The danger triggered by the unresponsive caregiver activates SC defensive signals to the LC (the pre-affective shock reactions into the body) and the PAG (defensive responses of fight-flight-freeze). Together the LC, DRN, and PAG initiate an intense cardiovascular response to prepare for an integrated behavioral response to threat.

Pre-affective shock is experienced as distressing tension and bracing reactions in the body. The further activation of the PAG and its defensive responses of fight-flight-freeze further accentuates somatic distress. The concomitant release of adrenaline in these states means that the somatic memory of distress is locked into the memory circuits of how one feels in one's body. In a particularly intense reaction, the child might collapse in a distressed state and not be able to reach out to the caregiver for necessary comfort.

Stress-induced activation of the dorsal raphe nucleus (DRN) is thought to be driven by the CRF type 2 receptor (CRFr2). This stress-enhancing reaction is facilitated by signaling from the bed nucleus of the stria terminalis, part of the memory of past distressing events, triggering stress responses in the extended amygdala.

The work of John Donner and his associates (2018) clarified that CRFr2 receptors are immunoreactive, meaning that the stimulation of these receptors not only accelerates the stress cascade (release of cortisol), but also intensifies anxiety experiences and activates pro-inflammatory responses including the release of inflammatory cytokines, macrophages, and other immunological responses. The pro-inflammatory response may be intensified as CRFr2 receptor sites are also located on immune cells and tissues throughout the body. Depending on context, activation of these sites can either be pro-inflammatory or anti-inflammatory.

Donner and colleagues (2018) conclude that inescapable or uncontrollable stressors lead to two critical outcomes. First, they activate a pro-inflammatory cascade. Second, they increase neuronal tryptophan hydrolase-2 (tph2) mRNA expression in the DRN neurons, with known behavioral consequences of increased anxiety-related and depressive-like behavior.

Clinically this finding is important; the autopsied brains of depressed suicide patients demonstrate elevated tph2 mRNA expression and immunoreactivity. These findings place the DRN at the center of the critical emotional and sleep-wake functions that intersect with inflammatory reactions. The interaction of these systems can create perfect storms of emotional distress, dysregulated sleep, and physical symptoms like fatigue, dizziness, panic, and loneliness.

Ruth Lanius and her colleagues in London, Canada, conducted a meta-analysis of studies (Tursich et al., 2014) examining the importance of inflammatory processes in traumatized individuals. Across the 15,000 participants in the aggregated 36 studies they found that trauma exposure was positively correlated with increased levels of C-reactive protein (CRP), and the pro-inflammatory cytokines IL-1β, IL-6, and TNF-α. Regression analyses indicated that the presence of psychiatric symptoms was a significant predictor of increased effect sizes for IL-6 and IL-1β.

Lanius concluded that chronic inflammation represents one potential mechanism underlying the risks for health problems among trauma survivors (Tursich et al., 2014). They noted that in those studies that tracked the presence of trauma in patient histories there were significantly elevated levels of inflammatory biomarkers among those with early trauma compared to those without. They also raised the more important question of whether such consequences of trauma can be ameliorated with trauma treatment. They cited preliminary evidence that trauma treatment had led to improvements in chronic immune dysregulation, even though results to date have been contradictory and unclear. This suggests a three-way clinical interaction among trauma, inflammation, and sleep.

The impact of trauma on the development of somatic symptoms is present throughout one's lifespan. The widespread clinical impact of early trauma on later life physical and mental health was dramatically highlighted by the results of the ACEs study of 30 years ago (Felitti et al., 1998). Among the most significant impacts of trauma on health were increases in: chronic pain problems, sleep disturbances, cardiovascular conditions, as well as gastrointestinal issues, immune system dysfunction, and a range of psychiatric disorders. In a more recent study of older adults, Pietrzak et al. (2012) found that traumatic experiences were associated with cardiovascular conditions (angina, tachycardia, and hypertension), as well as arthritis and digestive conditions.

Research Perspective Into Somatic Symptoms in Psychiatric Conditions

While the body and brain are in constant communication, most of these bidirectional signals occur below the level of conscious awareness. Most of us have the option of focusing our attention on a part of the body and begin to experience the physical sensations present there, but we rarely attend to these.

Perception of physical experience is integrated in the insula. The posterior insula is engaged with the subconscious physical experiences from all organ sources. The anterior insula is focused on the physical sensation of emotional and prominent physical sensations.

In the previous chapter, we elaborated on the important function of the LC in intensifying both the physical sensations in the body in the form of shock reactions, as well as the impact of these distress reactions in amplifying the memories of these bodily states. As these persist or are further aggravated by additional distress, they can easily become ongoing bodily symptoms. Such stress-related symptoms include chronic pain, dizziness, nausea, weakness, shortness of breath, tinnitus, fatigue, unsteadiness, and likely dozens more. To better understand how this can happen, we turn to a research-based model of the process of interoception itself.

FIGURE 10.2 The Schulz and Vogele Process Model of Interoception
Source: Reprinted by permission of Schulz, Schulchen, and Vogele (2020, p. 134)

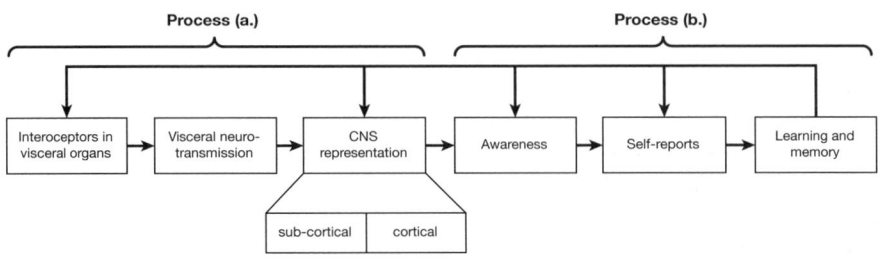

The process model of interoception (as modified by Andre Schulz & Claus Vögele, 2015) is helpful here (see Figure 10.2). The model identifies each step that participates in the process of interoception. These authors have suggested that the 7 steps that underpin a subjective awareness of a physical sensation can be divided into two groups, based on the factors that impact on the generation and amplification of the physical sensation. Process (a.) includes the nonconscious signal generation and amplification activity in the subcortical domain, and process (b.) the conscious, perceptual processes.

Process (a.) reflects the 4 nonconscious steps that are triggered by the somatic signal. *Step 1* is the visceral sensations that are recorded in the visceral organs. *Step 2* is the neurotransmission of those signals to the subcortical brainstem area. The spinothalamic tract relays pain and temperature information from end organs to the thalamus. The vagus nerve (10th cranial nerve) is 80% afferent, relaying cardiovascular, respiratory, and gastrointestinal visceral signals to the brainstem.

In *Step 3* of interoception, visceral signals are integrated as *subcortical* CNS representations. The subcortical aspect tracks how vagal input is relayed to the nucleus tractus solitarius (NTS), which in turn relays these to the nucleus ambiguus, solitary nucleus of the hypothalamus, parabrachial nucleus, and rostral ventrolateral medulla. These nuclei form an integrated cluster of nuclei at the subcortical level ensuring that visceral states are represented, but also that the reticular activating system can participate in orchestrating appropriate autonomic responses to threats.

In *Step 4*, the *cortical* aspect of CNS representation, thalamic nuclei project these internal states to three main cortical areas, where these visceral signals can be effectively experienced: the insular cortex, the cingulate cortex, and the somatosensory cortex. *Step 5*, marks the first point at which the conscious awareness of body states happens. It involves the anterior insula (for awareness of the felt experience of bodily states) and the cingulate cortex (for discerning emotional and pain-related aspects of internal states).

What happens to interoception when you are confronted by a threat, like seeing a snake on your morning walk? As the visual cue of the snake is perceived in the superior colliculus (SC), it immediately orients to the threat by activation of the deep layers of the SC. This permits ongoing tracking of the snake with integration of head and eye movements. The SC continues tracking the threat, while activating the reticular activating system (RAS), and the amygdala-LC circuit to activate the *endocrine and cardiovascular axes* of the stress response. It quickly produces a racing heart rate and shortness of breath. This happens automatically, with no conscious awareness.

The SC also initiates the *behavioral axis* of the stress response, through PAG activation of the defensive fear response (tightness in your gut and the urge to instinctively move away from the snake). All of this happens in the brainstem (SC-RAS-Amy-LC-PAG) without any conscious awareness or verbal articulation. Both the physiological signals and the attention that is placed on them are instinctive reactions in our nervous system.

The intensity of these reactions in the visceral organs is amplified by the LC-NE nucleus, which makes the subcortical responses more visible as these responses are transmitted as a palpable experience to the cortical area (*Step 4*) through activation of the *cognitive axis* through innervation of LE-NE to mPFC neurons. This triggers the conscious activity of searching for an escape from the snake threat.

In addition, when stresses become repetitive or chronic, the central NE system is *sensitized* and later hyperactivated. All of this underlines the importance of chronic stress as a major risk factor for the development of physical symptoms alongside mental symptoms.

Process (b.) reflects how much, or how little, you consciously focus on these sensations subsequently. In the above snake example, *Step 5* of the stress reaction amplifies your awareness (cortical cognitive readiness to pay attention to that signal) due to RAS-LC-mPFC activation. Whatever you may have been thinking before you saw the snake disappears from consciousness as your SC-LC-mPFC places 100% of your conscious attention on the snake threat. When threatened, you are immediately aware of these physical sensations because the subcortical alarm reaction of RAS-LC-NE-mPFC activation has amplified the physiological shock signal for you.

In the absence of threats, verbalizing your experiences and sensations (*Step 6*) means that more of these experiences can be integrated into your conscious memories (*Step 7*). However, in the presence of threat (e.g., the snake threat), you may be left speechless (no verbalization or self-reports). The LC-NE will activate the central amygdala nucleus (CAN) to further accentuate the fear response. And these threat experiences are then locked into the implicit right hemisphere as implicit sensory and somatic memories, with no context and without a date stamp. This raw, amorphous autonomic body arousal (Step 5) has no narrative component, and therefore is not put into words (Step 6) or remembered as an integrated memory (Step 7). As a result, this autonomic reactivity remains out of consciousness and can be elicited by any future trigger that even remotely resembles a snake.

LC-NE Activation and the Cardiovascular Axis of Stress

Sustained activation of the LC-NE system can be considered a hallmark of the stress system. Activation of the noradrenergic system results in surging activity in both the cardiovascular and cognitive arms of the stress system. This intertwined physiological substrate is also likely at the heart of the comorbidity of cardiovascular and affective symptoms of trauma (Wood & Valentino, 2017, p. 2).

How Does the LC-NE Activate Cardiovascular Reactivity?

Tonic activation of the LC-NE immediately activates cardiac activity through two channels that remove the brakes from cardiovascular activity. The two braking systems are: (1) the rostral dorsal motor vagal nucleus (DMV) and (2) the nucleus ambiguus (Amb). For the former, the LC-NE directly inhibits the DMV to remove the DMV's vagal inhibition at the A/V node on the heart, increasing heart rate. For the latter, the Amb usually inhibits the sympathoexcitatory rostroventrolateral medulla (RVLM), but when the LC-NE suppresses the Amb this results in increased RVLM cardiovascular excitatory input, further accelerating heart rate.

To summarize, LC-NE inhibits the DMV and Amb parasympathetic braking systems, which directly innervates the preganglionic sympathetic neurons in the intermediolateral nucleus of the spinal cord, to activate stress-induced cardiovascular reactivity. Finally, additional projections back into the central nucleus of the amygdala (CNA) further accelerate cardiovascular activation. In summary, the LC exerts both simultaneous inhibitory regulation over the parasympathetic system, as well as excitatory regulation over the sympathetic system, resulting in immediate surges in heart rate, blood pressure, and respiration.

What Increases the Tonic Activation of LC-NE?

Acute stress exposure results in release of CRF into the LC from two sources: (1) the primary CRF afferents to the peri-LC come from the CNA and the bed nucleus of the stria terminalis (BNST) and (2) secondary afferents to the LC core come from autonomic-related brain areas including the PVN in the hypothalamus, Barrington's nucleus, nucleus paragigantocellularis (PGi), and nucleus prepositus hypoglossi (PrH). These inputs to the peri- and core LC increase LC tonic activity to an alarm level for as long as required to respond behaviorally to the acute stressor.

The increased activation of the LC-NE core activates the *cognitive axis* of the stress system by release of NE in the medial PFC (LC-mPFC), which activates thinking processes to disconnect from previous activities and focus on the threat and how to overcome it. Increased LC tonic firing causes both stress-induced anxiety and aversive behaviors (McCall et al., 2015).

Pain-Induced Aversive Withdrawal Responses

Visceral sensory afferents bringing pain signals from the body come to the nucleus tractus solitarius (NTS), which relays these to the amygdala, which in turn relays them to the LC and PAG. The LC activates a general shock alarm and the PAG generates aversive emotional and behavioral responses to the pain signals.

LC projections to the amygdala and mPFC are central to both promoting aversive learning and of extinguishing aversive responses. Aversive responses are initiated through Pavlovian conditioning when LC-CAN and LC-BLA (basolateral nucleus of the amygdala) microcircuits are engaged. Overactivation of the LC-BLA pathway is particularly important for pain-induced anxiety, which enhances aversive learning responses.

In contrast, extinguishing aversive responses involves the participation of the hippocampus, Amy, mPFC, vmPFC, and basal ganglia. The mPFC and ACC are key to inhibiting emotional responses and activating the hippocampus to facilitate extinction. The vmPFC participates by inhibiting fear responses from the PAG during the extinction process. With the ventral striatum involved in integrating the reward/aversive valence and the dorsal striatum involved in the initiation and execution of goal directed behavior, the basal ganglia participate to overcome aversive behaviors. To successfully overcome the aversion, the intensity of the aversive shock response must first reduce so that dopaminergic reward signals can be restored and goal-directed behavior initiated.

Stabilization of LC-NE Tonic Activation

At the LC-NE core, influx of intracellular calcium levels stimulates the activity of the endocannabinoid system (eCB), which synthesizes and releases eCB 2-AG. eCB 2-AG crosses the synaptic channel and binds to the presynaptic CB1r present in the amygdalar-CRF afferents, which results in deceased release of CRF, with the result that LC-NE activity is suppressed and begins to return to normal.

With chronic stress, especially in vulnerable populations, the eCB response is overexpressed. This increases LC-NE activity, instead of decreasing it. Hyperactivity of the eCB system will also interfere with the inhibitory interneurons in the LC-NE, further aggravating the unopposed LC-NE core activity. The resulting dysregulation of the LC-NE core cascades to aberrant influx of NE into the mPFC, which results in increased activity of the cognitive stress axis, and more anxiety- and depression-like behaviors, including avoidance behaviors and increased distress.

Evidence of Resilience to Chronic Stress from Animal Studies

What are the other mechanisms that help to stabilize LC-NE hyperactivation when stress is constant? Rodent studies with the *resident-intruder* model of human social stress have provided an insight into another opioid-based signaling system that modulates and stabilizes LC hyperactivation. In these studies, an intruder rodent is placed into the cage of an aggressive conspecific who will attack the intruder. Repeatedly placing the naïve animal into this context results in progressive dysregulation of the autonomic system, including HPA dysfunction, decreased social interaction, anxiety-like behaviors, anhedonia, self-administration of drugs, decreased heart rate variability, alterations in circadian rhythm amplitudes, and long-lasting pro-arrhythmic effects (Wood & Valentino, 2017).

Most interestingly, the naïve intruder animals can be sorted into two populations: one group with short defeat latencies and the second with long defeat latencies. Defeat latency refers to the length of time it takes the intruder rodent to submit with a defeat posture. The increase in defeat latency across exposures occurs with the emergence of a parallel, active coping, upright posture in the intruder rat.

In the first exposure to the resident stressor, both short- and long-latency groups were similar on functional neuroanatomical studies. Two pathways activated the LC: (1) the CRF afferents from the CNA and (2) the delta opioid pathway of ENK-PGi afferents to the LC. By the fifth intruder exposure, the two groups began to diverge. The CRF-CNA afferent activation was only evident in the short-latency group. In those traumatized rodents, the activation of the ENK-PGi afferents had been silenced with repeated resident rodent stress exposures. The long-latency group showed the opposite effect. Activation of the ENK-PGi afferent was maintained and the CRF-CNA pathway to immediate submission was lost!

Susan Wood and her colleagues (Wood et al., 2010; Wood et al., 2012; Wood & Bhatnagar, 2015; Wood & Valentino, 2017), concluded that it is the ability to respond to the threat with an active coping response (e.g., the rats adopting an upright posture in response to the threat), that supports and is supported by the shift in the balance of LC afferent regulation from CRF-CNA to ENK-MOR inhibitory influence.

Wood and her many colleagues (2010, 2012, 2014, 2015, 2017) also elaborated on the long-term consequences of the passive-coping responses of the social-defeat group. Repeated social defeat stress, with its exaggerated CRF-CNA afferent regulation, disrupted the circadian rhythm of the heart rate, increased arrhythmias (by 30-fold), and promoted cardiovascular dysfunction, including maladaptive cardiac hypertrophy and cardiac fibrosis (see Sgoifo et al., 2014, for a review). Wood and Valentino (2017) conclude, "these studies indicate that the [passive] behavioral coping response is associated with cardiovascular susceptibility to stress" (Wood & Valentino, 2017, p. 397). In contrast, they say:

> In active coping rats, the afferent regulation of LC that is biased toward PGi-ENK would translate to decreased activity of the LCs cardiovascular efferents. This would reduce inhibition of the parasympathetic DMV and Amb and suppress excitation of PVN, promoting resilience to stress-related cardiovascular pathology. (Wood & Valentino, 2017, p. 398)

Wood and Valentino conclude that the LC plays a central role in determination of cardiovascular vulnerability conferring an added risk to passive copers for adverse cardiac events going forward. Further support for this conclusion comes from Susan Wood's earlier data (Wood, 2014) showing that the activity of the LC was negatively correlated with HRV, a robust measure of cardiovagal output and health. In patients suffering from PTSD, HRV is reduced compared with non-PTSD controls, contributing to the increased risk of developing cardiovascular disease in these psychiatric disorders.

Implications for Patients Vulnerable for Suffering Cardiac Events

> Repeated re-consolidation of fear memories coupled with an inability to extinguish aversive memories due to hyperactivation of the limbic circuitry and decreased cognitive flexibility contributes heavily to the pathophysiology of PTSD and other anxiety disorders. Both the amygdala and mPFC are targeted by LC-NE afferents. (Wyrofsky et al., 2019, p. 9)

Alarm reactions of LC-NE activation of the brain are central to understanding traumatic memory, sleep disruption, and physical (somatic) symptoms. The important point here is that when bodily symptoms are related to the dysregulated activity of the autonomic nervous system (caused by traumatic events), the ANS can be stabilized through trauma treatment. This has an important consequence for health psychology and the treatment of a broad range of medical conditions, including cardiovascular, respiratory, gynecological, gastrointestinal, and urological conditions.

The course of such somatic conditions is often chronic, leading to disability or early retirement. Figure 10.3 illustrates the impact of chronic stress on the cardiovascular system. Chronic stress creates a state of persistent dysregulation of the physiological stress axis (arrows 1. and 3.), resulting in chronic awareness of cardiac symptoms (upper right panel of Figure 10.3, process b.). The symptoms will not improve until the underlying role of the dysregulated ANS (loop 1 to 3) is addressed in therapy. This is critically important for understanding how health psychology can contribute to the resolution of these symptoms in many medical patients. Understanding these symptoms as caused by a dysregulated ANS opens up the possibility of effective treatment through application of trauma treatments to the physical symptoms themselves.

FIGURE 10.3 Positive Feedback Looping of Chronic Stress, Dysregulated ANS, Altered Interoception, and Physical Symptoms that Amplify Cardiovascular Distress
Source: Reprinted by permission of Schulz, Schulchen, and Vogele (2020, p. 143)

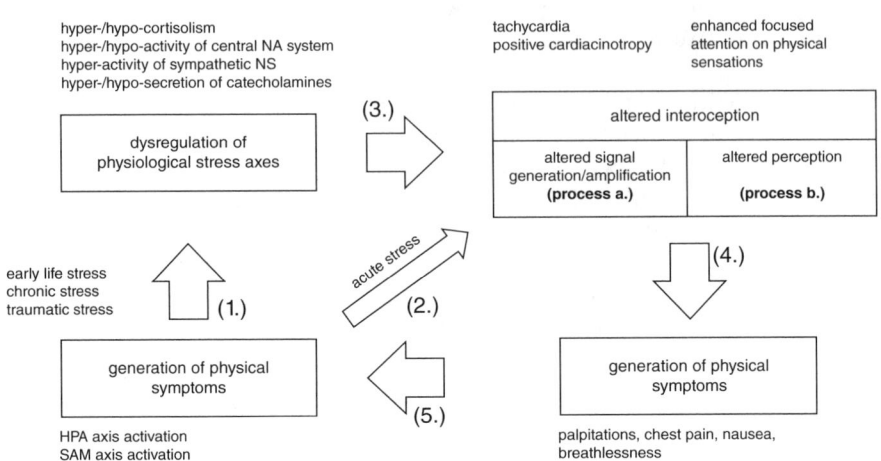

Physical sensations provide ongoing important feedback about the status of our body. These sensations are intended to come into our awareness so we can take action to prevent damage or injury. For example, if you feel pain from a burr in your sock, to prevent possible injury you find the burr and remove it.

The body generates physical signals from every muscle and organ system on a continuous basis. Most of the time we ignore these interoceptive signals. What can't be ignored are signals of impending danger. These capture our attention, obliterating every other concern. The unintended problem with these signals activating survival behavior is that they are stored in order to prevent future problems. However, these memories are not protective but become land mines that can be triggered by the most innocuous experience, like seeing a wedding ring on a colleague's finger (see previous chapter).

The major difficulty in managing these land mines is the power of these abreaction responses. It is overwhelming for the patient and can be overwhelming for the therapist as well. The fact that cardiovascular distress is an important part of these explosive psychophysiological experiences means that the trauma patient is also vulnerable to being disabled from physical symptoms.

In the remainder of this chapter we will focus on the disabling effects of cardiovascular events on patient recovery from heart attacks and demonstrate, with an example from a clinical treatment session, how DBR trauma treatment reduces autonomic and emotional distress to help the patient recover from these often disabling conditions.

Cardiovascular Reactivity and Social Connectedness

Considerable evidence exists to demonstrate that the existence of positive social relationships is related to lower cardiovascular risk. As more negative social relationships are present, the reactivity of the cardiovascular system increases. A study by Jeffrey Flinders and his colleagues enrolled healthy adults with no cardiovascular or mental health conditions into a study of cardiovascular reactivity (Uchino et al., 2001). Subjects were then given two stressful tasks: one was giving a speech and the other doing mental math. They found that the subjects who had positive social relationships exhibited more of a buffer against heart rate reactivity to stress compared to those with negative social relationships. Those with negative social relationships had more reactivity, and those with ambivalent social relationships (meaning having both positive as well as negative social relationships) demonstrated gradually increased heart rate reactivity with increased age. These results demonstrate that cardiovascular reactivity is positively affected by positive attachments.

Chronic Stress as a Cardiovascular Risk Factor

As cardiovascular disease is the largest cause of mortality in the western world, a group of Canadian researchers were interested in identifying the factors that increased the risks associated with having a first heart attack. The INTER-HEART Study (Yusuf et al., 2004), was the first international case-controlled study into factors related to first heart attacks. Over 1000 cardiac patients were enrolled, all of whom were having their first cardiac event. This study recruited subjects from six continents, including both developed countries as well as underdeveloped countries.

To control for factors related to aging and illness, these cardiac subjects were yoked with patients from the same hospital facilities as the cardiac patients, but not patients with cardiac complaints. The case-controlled feature allowed the study to determine what factors were specifically important to increasing cardiovascular risk.

Among the factors that were tracked were a range of medical and lifestyle factors that could be related to increasing cardiovascular risk. For example, among the medical factors that were tracked were blood cholesterol levels, hypertension, and diabetes. Among the lifestyle factors were sedentary lifestyle, smoking, and poor diet, and among the psychosocial factors were chronic stress, depressed mood, external locus of control, financial stress, and the occurrence of major life stresses in the past year.

The two most common factors related to prevalence adjusted risk (PAR) for having a heart attack were high cholesterol and smoking. This was not a surprise to the researchers or anyone else who had been aware of the cardiovascular literature to the early 2000s. However, what was a surprise was that chronic stress (operationally defined as five specific factors) was the third most important risk factor for the incidence of heart attacks worldwide.

Strikingly, the increased risk of heart attacks from chronic stress was more important than the risk conferred from diabetes and hypertension put together! Similarly, it was more important than sedentary lifestyle and poor diet combined. Overall, what the study brought to the attention of the health care community was the unexpectedly caustic impact of chronic stress on the cardiovascular system.

INTERHEART defined stress as a composite of five measurements: (1) chronic stress at home, or work, or both, (2) persistent financial stress, (3) clinical depression, (4) three or more major life events in the past year, and (5) losing the internal sense of control in life. Each of these five factors contributed about 10% to the overall 50% level of prevalence adjusted risk from stress.

In addition, across the first decade of the new millennium, the increased risks for cardiac events from sleep disorders like insomnia and sleep apnea were becoming more apparent. A review by Michelle Miller and Francesco Cappuccio (2007) highlighted the confluence of four factors that significantly increasing cardiovascular risk. These four were inflammation, sleep disturbance, aging, and obesity. While each of the four clearly impacted the risks of adverse cardiac events, it was not possible to disentangle the impact of each of them individually.

Miller and Cappuccio (2007) outlined numerous ways that sleep increased the possibility of cardiac events. Short sleepers (less than 5 hours a night) had increased blood pressure. The intermittent bouts of hypoxia in patients with sleep apnea result in significantly elevated levels of inflammatory cytokines TNF-α and IL-6, as well as hsCRP and adhesion molecules. CPAP therapy has been demonstrated to normalize TNF-α levels.

The risk from sleep disturbances was considered significant and the 2009 edition of the *Canadian Guidelines for Cardiac Rehabilitation and Disease Prevention* (Prior et al., 2009) included the assessment and treatment of sleep disorders as recommended risk-prevention strategies for cardiac patients. Jaan Reitav (2012) elaborated on the clinical management skills necessary to manage reductions of sleep risks in the cardiac population. In this chapter, we will focus on management of the risks associated with chronic stress, trauma, and PTSD.

Chronic Stress Continues to Be Ignored As a Treatment Target

One would have expected that the dramatic demonstration of the critical role of autonomic distress by INTERHEART would have led to major changes in how cardiovascular rehabilitation would be conducted. However, stress as a target of clinical intervention for cardiac patients has remained a largely ignored aspect of clinical treatment options for this population. Part of the reason for this is that there is not a quick solution, like medications, to resolve the difficulty. Another part of the reason has been that the traditional psychotherapeutic strategies like psychoeducation and talk therapy have been of little value in reducing the risks of future cardiac events (Linden et al., 2007; S. H. Richards et al., 2018).

However, not all of the news has been negative. For example, in the metanalysis Wolfgang Linden and his colleagues (Linden et al., 2007) conducted, there was clear evidence that to the degree that therapeutic interventions were able to reduce the physiological distress of cardiac patients, risks for future events were reduced. As sleep can be viewed as a barometer of underlying distress and autonomic reactivity, this led us to investigate whether the presence of significant underlying sleep disorders was in any way related to the benefits obtained by patients learning stress management skills. As all patients were receiving the same stress management training (SMT) for improving their skills in boosting their parasympathetic activation and modulating their sympathetic distress, we predict that all patients should benefit to the same degree, regardless of underlying sleep disturbances.

However, what we found was that the amount of underlying sleep disturbance was a latent factor in undermining the benefits of SMT (Reitav et al., 2019). If we take the extent of the sleep disturbance as a measure of the dysregulation of the autonomic system, this suggests that greater levels of underlying autonomic distress do not respond to simple teaching of SMT skills to reduce physiological distress, as Linden (2007) had predicted. The most likely cause of inconsistent results is the underlying level of autonomic dysregulation, which in many cases is traumatic in origin and not as responsive to teaching skills alone.

Trauma-Informed Treatment of Cardiovascular Stress Symptoms

Traumatic experiences, which negatively impact cardiovascular outcomes, need to be included in patient management, but are often overlooked. As Andre Schulz and his colleagues have highlighted, "The aims of health psychology should be to promote adequate interoception in cardiovascular diseases (1) to prevent mental disorders associated with fear of cardiac symptoms and (2) to potentially enhance the course of the chronic condition itself . . . [through] the modification of interoception" (Schulz et al., 2020, p. 145).

They conclude their review of the challenges of treating patients with comorbid medical and psychiatric conditions with the suggestion that protocols for interventions that enhance interoception be developed. Such opportunities to retrain the interoceptive system, by explicitly targeting the brain-body communication pathways, could reduce physical symptoms in both mental disorders and chronic physical conditions. In the earlier example of the snake (see Figure 10.2), we noted that an overwhelming intense subcortical fear response in the body (Step 5), prevented an integration of this experience in conscious memory (Steps 6 and 7).

Schulz and colleagues list some treatment options that could meet that goal. These include: (1) transcutaneous vagal nerve stimulation (tVNS), (2) transcranial magnetic stimulation (TMS) targeting inhibition of the anterior insula, (3) heartbeat perception training (HBPT), and (4) neurofeedback targeting cortical representation of heartbeat electrocortical potentials (HEPs).

Not included in their list of possible treatments are eye movement desensitization and reprocessing (EMDR) and deep brain reorienting (DBR). EMDR directly targets the behavioral limb of the stress cascade by desensitizing emotional distress of the cardiac event. DBR directly targets the autonomic limb first (the LC-NE circuit that initiates the alarm—pre-affective shock reaction). After pre-affective shock has been cleared, then the behavioral limb (the PAGs affective responses) is addressed. Sequencing the intervention in this way prevents the dysregulation of the ANS. When these ANS responses are not addressed, they can become overwhelming and magnify the feedback loop that transforms physical sensations to chronic physical symptoms. We will illustrate how both of these trauma-informed treatments can effectively reduce the significant burden of traumatic symptoms in patients experiencing heart attacks.

Case 1: Trauma Treatment of Takotsubo Heart Attack With EMDR

Takotsubo cardiomyopathy is also known as *broken heart syndrome*, or stress-induced cardiomyopathy. It was first described as a unique heart attack in 1990 by cardiologist Hikaru Satow, who published a series of six cases with the same clinical findings. All patients had experienced a severe emotional or physical stressor. The clinical signature of the condition includes all the features of a heart attack: shortness of breath, severe angina, and often pain in the shoulder or left arm. Test findings include a distended left ventricle (the main pumping chamber of the heart), which looks like an octopus trap on imaging. In Japanese, the word for an "octopus trap" is "takotsubo."

More than 90% of takotsubo patients are women between 58 and 75. Almost 5% of all women having a heart attack are having a takotsubo heart attack. In all heart attacks the symptoms come on because the heart is being deprived of needed blood supply. When this happens, the brain receives signals of intense distress from the heart muscle, called angina. Intense angina pain signals activate the survival alarm reaction, including PAG-activated shortness of breath.

In traditional heart attacks the reason for the deficient blood supply is a physical blockage in the artery, usually caused by atherosclerosis (plaque buildup in the artery wall). In takotsubo, the deficient blood supply occurs because an intensely stressful life event causes the sudden release of adrenaline into the blood, which constricts the arteries to such an extent that blood flow to heart muscles is compromised. Both types can lead to some degree of heart muscle damage. The left ventricle muscle becomes extended under this intense, dire predicament. It can take a year or longer for the symptoms of a takotsubo heart event to remit, longer if the life stresses that caused the event are still active.

The case material that follows highlights the treatment of Angela, a female in her 70s. She had a heart attack when her 25-year-old niece, Clarissa, jumped to her death off Angela's 15th-floor balcony. (Both names are pseudonyms.) On Christmas day, Clarissa came over for a visit. On arriving Clarissa said she had gotten warm on the walk over and went out onto the balcony. Angela went to the kitchen to make some tea for her visitor. When Angela came out to look for Clarissa, she could see Clarissa's coat and bag, but no Clarissa.

Angela was gripped by horror and first looked around the apartment. To no avail. At first, she was in denial, not wanting to look over the balcony to the ground below. Angela then went to the balcony and peered over the railing apprehensively. Her worst fears were confirmed. Far below she could see a body sprawled on the ground. Angela rushed downstairs, her heart beating out of her chest. By the time Angela got there, a police officer was preventing anyone from getting to the scene. Angela began to experience an intense chest pain. She remained calm and conversed with police, who called the ambulance. With a portable ECG they diagnosed a heart attack and took her to the hospital.

Angela was brought to the same hospital to which Clarissa's body was brought. Angela began to recover. An angiogram determined the attack was takotsubo, as Angela had no arterial blockages. She was treated, stabilized, and released. At home she was preoccupied by the image of Clarissa's coat and bag, but no Clarissa. Her chest pain and shortness of breath continued. Her ruminative thoughts about Clarissa's death interfered with her ability to sleep. She continued to have angina with any level of exertion. Angela felt overwhelmed by the combination of physical and emotional symptoms she was experiencing.

Angela's husband had had cardiac problems 10 years earlier, so she knew about cardiac rehabilitation (CR). While her cardiologist had not recommended CR, Angela arranged for a referral to the CR program. She began with her exercise prescription, which meant going for a daily walk. She kept up with the walks, even though she felt angina coming on each time she began the walk. She pushed through this and gradually it decreased in intensity. What she could not shake was the image of Clarissa's coat and bag with no Clarissa. And as these images came to her mind, there was noticeably increased physical and emotional distress that would not go away.

Angela found the support and guidance provided by the CR program helpful. She was given lots of advice about not overdoing it and taking it easy. She followed this advice carefully, but the psychological distress did not decrease. When her cardiac supervisor suggested that she have a consultation with a psychologist, Angela reflected on her persistent unhappiness after her niece's suicide and quickly agreed.

Angela was open to EMDR as a trauma therapy. We identified three specific memories that stood out as flashbacks for her: (1) Clarissa's coat and bag but no

Clarissa, (2) the image of Clarissa's body in the garden 19 floors below, and (3) Angela being held back from getting to Clarissa's body by the police.

Angela described the treatment sessions as difficult. She said she felt like a sleepwalker, going back to relive the experience in a very emotional way. Initially, she had the sense that something important was happening, but she did not notice any change in the worst symptoms. Each of the EMDR sessions were intense. She would feel her heart racing, and she felt shock and horror, with waves of tension and shallow breathing. Gradually, the intense physical symptoms began abating, usually with the sensation of feeling cold and then tingling in her hands and feet.

After three EMDR sessions, she reported that her mind was not going back as often to the traumatic memories. After five sessions she noticed that her angina was easing up, but she still felt a terrible dread around the memories. There was also intense fear and waves of grief and sadness. However, between sessions she reported that she felt that she had now worked through what she termed "an important layer" of the memories, as she felt more settled. Also, when she awoke during the night, she said that Clarissa was not the first thought on her mind any longer. On nights that she awoke with chest pain, she would start diaphragmatic breathing and do some meditation. She said this helped her enormously.

Within 2 months she noticed that she was sleeping better. Other changes started to occur. The pressure in the chest under physical or emotional stress was letting up. While reliving the memories during the EMDR sessions she continued to actually feel the chest pressure she had at the time of the trauma. There were many other physical symptoms that arose as well, including fluttering sensations in the chest, a tight throat, the instinct to run, and tension all over. These physical symptoms gradually gave way to intense grief and sobbing.

By 3 months into treatment Angela began to realize that the one thing that she most needed to happen had started to happen. Angela could think about Clarissa, a person whom she had loved so dearly, without only thinking about her in what she termed that "capsule environment of her death." She began to start remembering a lifetime of wonderful memories, as opposed to just that one horrible defining event. Angela felt encouraged to continue with the treatment until she had resolved the emotional and physical symptoms.

In total, Angela was seen for 12 EMDR treatment sessions across a 4-month period. During those sessions we reprocessed the shock and horror of her niece's suicide. After 10 weeks of treatment she said she did not have as many sad thoughts. As we moved to the memory of Clarissa's body in the garden, Angela related that Clarissa had been diagnosed with schizophrenia over 10 years previously. Since that day, Angela's greatest fear had been that Clarissa might take her life. During this phase of treatment Angela reflected on the bad periods that Clarissa had gone through, and how Angela was always there for Clarissa, and how Clarissa always trusted Angela. These memories of how close the two were consoled Angela. She had recovered her special bond with her niece.

Angela also said that she and her husband were now able to go out on the balcony without distress. At night she was beginning to dream a lot. She added that she had always been a "gifted sleeper" who usually had lots of dreams. The work in reprocessing the traumatic images was easier, as both the intensity of her emotions was much reduced and so was the tension in her throat, chest, and body.

Between sessions Angela said she was getting her joy back. By the end of the treatments, Angela could empathize fully with how tormented Clarissa's life had been and could understand Clarissa's decision. Angela was at peace with the events that happened and was back to living her life again.

Angela had a consultation appointment with her cardiologist about a month after the completion of the EMDR treatments. The cardiologist said that looking at the imaging of her heart, one would not have known that she had had a heart attack at all. The apical distension and swelling characteristic of the takotsubo heart attack were fully resolved. Angela still had a lingering pinch of pain in her chest as she went for her walks, but other than that she felt that she had fully resolved the emotional and physical symptoms from the heart attack.

In summary, this case of a takotsubo heart attack demonstrates that the intense overwhelming autonomic stress response to a catastrophic event can, by itself, result in a heart attack with persisting cardiovascular symptoms. This heart attack was activated by the shock and horror of the unthinkable: the suicide of her niece at her apartment. There was no preexisting cardiovascular disease, and once the dysregulated ANS was treated, there were no residual cardiac symptoms or disease evident on imaging of the heart. This case also demonstrates that trauma therapy, which targets the dysregulated autonomic nervous system and the collateral impact of surging PAG emotional distress, is effective in resolving the psychophysiological crisis that triggered the cardiac event.

Case 2: DBR Treatment Following a Heart Attack at Home

DBR provides an effective and targeted way of: (1) reducing the autonomic limb of activation of pre-affective shock, (2) managing the behavioral limb of PAG-mediated affective fear responses, and (3) by activating the where self, being attentive to current bodily sensations to return interoceptive signaling back to pre-cardiac-event levels. In the review article by (Kearney & Lanius, 2022) the authors note that DBR:

> exploits subcortical processes by means of somatic sensory feedback and *facilitates awareness and experience of somatic sensations in the present moment of safety* as opposed to a past trauma. This process may be the antithesis to dissociative flashbacks, derealization, and depersonalization and a catalyst for reinstating a sense of agency and trust in the body [emphasis added]. (p. 21)

The edited transcript that follows highlights the introduction of DBR principles with a 38-year-old man we'll call Allan. Allan had a heart attack while working from home. The average age of females having a first heart attack is in their 70s, and for males it is in their 60s. For this young man to have a first heart attack almost 30 years earlier is likely due to excessive stress he experienced prior to his cardiac event. His preexisting conditions included a diagnosis of ADHD and major depression after his mother's unexpected passing 3 years earlier. Also, he was a lifelong smoker, primarily to help manage his anxiety.

His mother's passing was particularly distressing to him, since he talked to her daily. In the period prior to her passing, he was particularly busy at work and could not take his mother's calls. After she died, he blamed his company for putting a lot of pressure on him to work extra hours. These events continued to distress him and led to his depression.

On the day he had the heart attack, he felt he had an elephant on his chest. He could not breathe. He experienced cold sweats and nausea. But he did not suspect a heart attack, as he was so young. He decided to lie down and see if the symptoms disappeared. They did not. In the next 3 days he experienced these symptoms coming and going. As they did not disappear, he went to the hospital and was finally diagnosed as having had a heart attack.

He was given three stents to improve the blood flow to his heart. This ended the angina, which had been severe. However, he continued to have multiple symptoms. He felt tired all the time, numb, and disconnected. He described himself as an anxious worrier and said he was very scared about what would happen to him, his work, and his ability to look after his family.

In particular, he was panicking about his ability to return to work. During COVID he had begun working from home. The heart attack happened in the room where he routinely worked. Returning to the job meant having to work in the same room. After his heart attack he was so panicky he could not even enter that room. He avoided it completely.

He came for cardiac rehabilitation 6 months after his cardiac event. He responded well to the physical exercise prescriptions he was given and recovered enough that he would be able to return to work on the basis of his physical recovery. However, there was no change at all to his psychiatric symptoms of feeling tired, disconnected, nauseated, and panicky. He was referred for psychological treatment of his PTSD symptoms (reexperiencing, hyperarousal, avoidance and numbing, negative cognitions) a few months after starting his cardiac rehab.

He was seen for 16 psychotherapy sessions, the first 12 with EMDR, and the last 4 with DBR. The edited transcript that follows is the 14th psychotherapy session, in which DBR is used to identify and release the shock reactions that the heart attack triggered.

Step 1: Identifying the Activating Event

PATIENT: What I'm scared of is facing another heart attack. Anything like angina. I fear that my panic is going to be much higher. The first time around, I was calm. But next time I probably won't be as calm. I will just go into full-on panic.

My wife and daughter left to visit her parents. When they were on the flight, I had chest discomfort, like a muscle twitch, on the right side, but not left. I was scared because there was nobody here. I felt that sensation coming back. What's going to happen? The house was empty.

When the heart attack happened, I was by myself as well. But then I was able to calm myself. This time it was only on the right side. Nothing else. Probably I sat differently, and I had been picking up luggage. This could be just a muscle thing. And I was able to calm myself down. But that fraction of 3 to 4 seconds, I was panicking. "What is happening?" That was overwhelming.

THERAPIST: Was there a trigger?

PATIENT: Being at home alone was the trigger. I felt helpless, just as I felt when the heart attack was happening. "Oh no." Like something is not right. It was just those muscle memories. I did not panic to a point. It was just a span of 2 to 4 seconds, and then I was able to calm myself down. I used sensory things like pressing my arms so that I am in the moment. I was able to use that to calm myself down. I distracted myself. I started watching a funny show, diverting my mind.

THERAPIST: You managed it extremely well. We want to go back to what I call automatic triggers. Because they are happening in the body, in the brainstem. And they are automatic. We want to go back to the trigger for those automatic responses, that sense that you had when you had your heart attack. Where you felt helpless. You recognized, as it was happening, that something wasn't right. You had that thought, "I may not live. I may not make it."

We will go back to what happened in a few minutes. Notice what you felt. And begin to allow the different waves of feeling or sensations to come and go.

Step 2: Orienting the Patient to Their Present Where Self

First, the therapist grounds the patient in the present moment. The therapist takes the time to orient the patient fully to their present where self. This step took about 5 minutes (see Chapter 9 for a full description of Orienting to Where Self).

Step 3: Introducing the Activating Event and Tracking Internal Responses

THERAPIST: Bring your full attention back to that moment when you were in the bedroom where you were working and you felt that chest pain. It kept getting more and more tight. In that moment when you felt helpless. You knew something was not right.

Bring that moment to your awareness right now. I want you to pay attention to any experience that you notice around your head. It could be around the forehead, or around your eyes, or toward the back of your neck. Tell me what you are noticing.

PATIENT: I am feeling there is a pull on the back of my left neck.

A bit stiff, when I think about it. In terms of muscles, on my chest, on the left-hand side. I feel like a hawk is trying to grip it. That is the feeling that is coming.

Commentary. His first physical sensations are shock reactions that go down into the body. This is very typical, as these shock reactions are the intense physical activation during this life-or-death threat situation.

Step 4: Guiding the Patient to the Orienting Tension

THERAPIST: Focus on the head sensation first. That is really important. There is a pull at the back of the neck. Are there any other sensations? Anything else around the forehead? Or around the eyes?

PATIENT: The forehead, when I go back to look at it, it is just that pressure. If I go back—I am visualizing—at that particular point when I got up, I felt the pressure and the loss of breath. I wasn't able to breathe. So when I bring back that memory, it also triggers, "Okay, am I breathing right now?" Like I have to push my breath, the air, out and see if everything is fine. Like that reaction is coming in. At the same time I am feeling my left neck, and my shoulder, get stiff. Like it carries a lot of tension. When I am breathing, that is where the tension goes.

THERAPIST: Let's focus on the tension that you are noticing around the head. Definitely, there is some pressure around the forehead. I want you to deepen into those feelings. Stay with the way in which you are noticing that tension around the forehead. Allow your full attention to sit with that.

Step 5: Allowing Space for the Patient to Track Their Pre-Affective Shock Responses

THERAPIST: And now just pay attention. Just be curious about any other sensations that come to your awareness. Some might be very fleeting.

Or they may stick around for a while. Tell me what you are becoming aware of.

PATIENT: That is where, as I am feeling it, I am also noticing how easily I'm breathing. And that gives me a relief. I can breathe properly. Air is coming in and out. And that is actually calming me down. In terms of anything in my forehead and neck. Just closing my eyes is actually relaxing me.

THERAPIST: You're noticing how there is a shift as you make a small change. I want you to notice any residual tension, any other ways in which your body may be holding onto some of the tension triggered by your heart attack. Sit with those tensions. We are not trying to make them go away. We are trying to sit with them, to allow them. Just notice what else comes up in your awareness.

PATIENT: I just noticed when I am keeping my eyes open I can feel more pressure in the back of my neck. Leading up to the back of the head. Like there's a pressure. Like something stings. Something pulled or cracked. When I notice the sensation that came with the heart attack, it is keeping me away from that. At the same time I am focusing on the memory, my mind is putting out a "Stop!" That is a danger sign. I am feeling that it is not letting me go back. Like probably this is not the right setting, or something.

Commentary. This is a critical observation by the patient. He is beginning to be aware of the recoil away from the overwhelming body experience. The therapist responds by encouraging him to stay with the feelings as best he can.

THERAPIST: Your job is only to notice where the tension is coming. And you described it beautifully. How it is coming up from the neck and the shoulders. What waves of physical experience come?

PATIENT: Like somebody massaging me, but instead of the massage, it is like a wave of shock going through. It's hard to describe. It is like a blood flow, like, if it is a pipe, somebody is pressing it, and the pressure goes up. You feel that in your body. The pressure is shifting. Going from my back to the back of my neck, to the shoulders. It's moving up the left side of my body. Like somebody is pressing. It is a massage, but it is not a comfortable press. It is like somebody is trying to push the blood out.

Commentary. What is most striking about his descriptions is that they are very specific, and he is noticing how they shift and change, as he tracks the movement of the tension through his body.

PATIENT: Now at the back of my head there is a weight created with all the stiffness. In the back, that is what I am feeling.

THERAPIST: Sitting with these sensations. Noticing. Tracking whatever way they come up. Anything else that begins to happen?

PATIENT: The stiffness in the back of my head is pressuring. There is a spasm now. It is moving to my neck. So I am focusing more on that. The funny part is that everything is happening on the left side. I am trying to feel something on the right side. It is coming up a bit vacant. Like my focus has all been going on the left side. In terms of shocks, the forehead becomes lighter when I close my eyes. But as I try to open my eyes and try to go back into the position that I was in then, it is a bit hard. I don't see myself as an observer. Rather, I am feeling it. Anytime I am trying to go back, close my eyes and go back, I feel that my throat is getting dryer on the side. That is when I start breathing heavily, and say, "Okay, now I can pass the air."

Commentary. From his description it is clear that he is reexperiencing the event, not just remembering it. That is what is needed for the reorienting work to change the memories. Notice how the sensations are very specific, not vague.

THERAPIST: It is changing how you are breathing,. the breathing reactions that you had at the time. Any other experiences?

PATIENT: Now, as we are speaking, it is going to the right. As if it is pouring down on the right from my head down to my body. But the talk that brought that up, I would say that it is not as unpleasant. It is getting down to a 5 or 4. Before I felt that "This is going to happen" and it was a 6 or 7. It is not bad going back to it now. But the fear that I am getting is, "What if it comes back again?"

I try to work out every day. But it is not up to the mark that I want. And eating healthy. I am eating well, but still question, "Am I doing it right?" Based on the blood work, and everything that I do. It is just that worry, "Am I doing everything properly?"

THERAPIST: That is important. As you hear those words, "What if I am doing it wrong", notice the physical sensations you begin to have.

PATIENT: When I think about that, that I am not doing the right thing, I feel, just behind, on top of *my left eyebrow, gets heavy*. There is a pressure in it. At the same time, I can feel that agitation. I feel the cold sweats around my shoulder. There is panic, like something is going to happen. It does come in.

Commentary. As he reflected on this thought, a more intense autonomic reaction triggered. This is the activation of the PAG, which initiates behavioral responses of flight-fight-freeze to escape from the danger. There is a noticeable increase in his distress. The *heaviness of his left eyebrow* suggests the beginning of an opioid-based neurochemical dissociative reaction. If we go directly to the affective reaction, he will likely be flooded with this experience, and the good work he has been doing to this point may be in jeopardy.

THERAPIST: It sounds like it is different from when you were having your heart attack. Let's stay with the sensations that we were working through today. Go back to anything you are aware of around your head. Are you aware of any tension in the back of the neck, or around the forehead?

PATIENT: In terms of tension, it is shifting now that I am focusing a lot on the back. It shifted from the left side to the right side. And I feel that a headache is coming in my forehead. But it is not a headache.

THERAPIST: There is still some tension there. But it has moved more to the right side. Just sit and notice that tension. And even if it has gone down. Not a 6 or 7. Any other sensations that pop up?

PATIENT: I am trying to go back into it. Not recreate, but to go back into it. The only change that I see that is coming, is me making sure I can breathe again. That is the point that the chest came in. I wasn't able to actually breathe out properly. So I am making sure that I'm able to do it.

Commentary. Part of the intensity of the terror response during a heart attack comes from angina, the extreme constriction of the chest wall. He had described the experience when he stood up as "an elephant" on his chest. The simultaneous restriction of breathing along with reduced cardiac output made this experience the absolute worst part of the event. This reaction occurs because of an extreme life-or-death arousal response, in order to respond to the dire life challenge. The patient is fixated on being able to follow the instructions of tracking his physical responses, even as he is making certain that he can keep breathing.

PATIENT: I wasn't able to take the air in or let it out. That effect keeps on coming. The body memories triggering . . . "Okay, you can breathe now. So be relaxed."

THERAPIST: Right now the body memories are that you can breathe, but when you go back to the memory in your bedroom, standing up. In that moment you couldn't.

I feel like I might not be able to take the air in. Because the pressure was so high that I could not breathe in. Instinctively, a part is coming back and saying, "Okay, you can breathe."

Commentary. The patient beautifully describes the intensity of the terror that can be an integral feature of many heart attacks. Because this is a "normal" psychological reaction of the endangered autonomic system, it is not included in most medical treatment plans for cardiac patients.

THERAPIST: There may still be some of the tension that goes with that memory. That experience that you had that day when you had your heart attack. The brain may still be holding on to some of that fear: "I can't breathe." The chest feels heavy. Like an elephant is sitting there.

If there is any of that residual tension, we want to invite any reactions, anything else the body is still holding onto. We want to allow the body to bring those feelings and sensations back, so that you can begin to see, "Okay, that is now over. We don't need to hold on to those memories of when we couldn't breathe."

Commentary. The therapist returns to the resolution of the shock memories that were activated in this DBR session.

> PATIENT: It is going down to the chest. Like how I felt on the left side. When I'm feeling like somebody is trying to grab it or do something. But it is not there. It is like a shadow. Like somebody is just brushing it. In terms of the agitation, it is just a stiffness. When I go back to that memory, the important part is, "Okay, I am able to do it!" I am able to breathe. It is the fact that I am able to relax. "You don't have to worry too much about it." When I'm going back, that is the big change I'm noticing today.

Commentary. The patient is continuing to track his physical sensations and he is particularly happy that the treatment can be slowed down, so the intensity of the terror is not overwhelming. The therapist continues to encourage tracking of all residual shocks.

> THERAPIST: Again, you are tracking and noticing your physical sensations. Some of these waves of physical sensations are what your body actually experienced back then, when you had the heart attack. It is like your brain kept some of these physical sensations. Now you are able to begin to let go of them.
> PATIENT: Exactly. It is not happening now. It is giving a cool, calming effect. You create a panic it is finding a way to soothe.
> THERAPIST: You are noticing what is happening moment to moment. You are also seeing how things are different now for you today. compared to when you are witnessing the physical experiences. And your witnessing brain is beginning to say, "That was back then. Right now we are sitting and talking to the therapist."
> PATIENT: It is actually out of fear. It could be that since I am alone in the house, my mind is probably going to do more to put me into that position where there is danger. Because I know that there is limited help. It probably will shadow it. That is what I feel.
> THERAPIST: It is important that your wife and child are away.
> PATIENT: I am extremely cautious, more cautious in exploring things. The way I could go in and see for myself is different. I am trying to do the

same thing as before. It is showing me a curtain, a white curtain. It is a see-through curtain. I see it, but just a glimpse of it.

Commentary. The complexity of the underlying feelings is now beginning to emerge. He is aware of how the presence of his wife is calming, and her absence makes the feelings more threatening. As he has continued his tracking, he is now more conscious that his effort to connect fully with his physical sensations is automatically activating a nervous system recoil reaction from them. He describes this as a see-through curtain. He is consciously open to feeling what happened, but he now feels "the curtain," an automatic reaction deeper in his nervous system, which protects from its intensity. This is the dissociative process distancing from the more intense *affective* terror reactions that had just begun to emerge a few moments ago.

THERAPIST: That makes complete sense to me. What are you noticing in your body right now?
PATIENT: That is the focus. The back and the back of the head. They are carrying a weight. That is what I can feel. As we are talking, I am trying to be in that moment, like when the heart attack happened. I feel a twitch coming into my forehead. And then it goes away. As if I am going to have a headache. But it is just blood flow, or something.
THERAPIST: How much stress, tension, or distress do you feel at this moment?
PATIENT: I would say it is significantly less.

Commentary. As the patient actively returns to his heart attack, to notice any residual orienting tension, he experiences only a temporary twitch. The therapist is satisfied that the reorienting from this session's activating stimulus has been largely resolved. We move on to asking the patient to reflect on how today's experience may have shifted his perception of himself and how he is relating to his body.

Step 6: Exploring Affects That Arise From the Reorienting

The patient had noticed a significant PAG fear response beginning earlier in the reorienting. He was redirected back to the physical shock reactions. In DBR, these LC-NE shock reactions are first fully addressed and released. If they are not, the intensity of the PAG affective reactions becomes overwhelming. Emotional reactions are processed in subsequent sessions.

Step 7: Exploring Any New Perspectives That Emerge

THERAPIST: You notice that the tension has come down. Do you have a new perspective about yourself based on allowing these sensations and energy to be released? Does that help you understand yourself in a different way?

PATIENT: Yes, it does. With the breathing I noticed that I was able to breathe. My mindset is saying, "You are not in harm's way." I had felt, "The world is closing in, and you are about to die." But now, "Look, you are breathing easier." And there has been an effect like, I know that you are my safety net, and it is going to go away. I felt, "Okay, I am hopping on that." My body calms down. Nothing is happening, nothing to be worried about. I have things in control.

Commentary. The patient draws together three important observations from today: (1) he could now breathe, while during the heart attack he was terrified ("about to die"), (2) he felt the "safety net" of the therapist, which helped face the physical shock of that experience, and (3) he now felt "in control," to begin to revisit those feelings in subsequent therapy sessions. He goes on to make other associations about other current experiences.

PATIENT: I am trying to eat healthy. It is tempting, when you are upset, to open up some ice cream. But I have not! Because I am trying to do my best. I am going to have grapes or a plum.
THERAPIST: You have that perspective that things are different today.
PATIENT: I have made changes. And I have been talking to people. Yesterday, my friend asked, "What's wrong? Why are you so closed? You don't mix with anybody. You don't see us. You talk about health and say you are tired and fatigued." He probed. And there is a lack of confidence that I feel. That I have for myself. That is probably what brings up a lot of anxiety.

Commentary. The patient now divulges deeper worries, which are also extremely common among cardiac patients: (1) the urge to withdraw from others, which is part of that PAG fear-avoidance response and (2) the subsequent internal awareness of this recoil response, resulting in a significant reduction in his self-confidence. Both of these are linked to the intensity of the earlier awareness of the overwhelming PAG terror response, which was not addressed in today's session. In subsequent sessions, therapist and patient will revisit those deeper affective experiences to resolve the withdrawal and lack of confidence.

THERAPIST: That feeling of being alone is intensifying the vulnerability. Because the heart attack happened when you were alone. You did not have anyone else you could turn to. Because of that, your anxiety shoots up.

Commentary. He is now no longer alone, as he is in a therapeutic relationship. The safety of the therapeutic relationship is critical to give the patient the strength to face the intensity of these affective responses. Without it, no amount of the passage of time will normalize these recoil responses. They are locked into the nervous system.

PATIENT: I have given that a lot of thought. I am less confident that I'll be able to achieve something in the future. But in terms of managing the heart, and health wise, I know if it comes back, I know how to manage it. I am not going to die. At least I will seek help.

Commentary. The patient is confident in knowing what to do to get help for any future heart problems (external resources), but tentative about his self-confidence (internal resources).

THERAPIST: You now have tools to manage your heart problems. But in the brain, we have learned that your nervous system has kept these internal physical maps. "This feels like how it was when I had my heart attack." Today we activated your memory of being in your bedroom, standing up, and being out of breath. The brain had locked in that file. That activated a memory sequence. That file included these physical sensations. You had the shock waves coming up on the left and later on the right. We have been letting go of that. Allowing that energy, those old maps to emerge and to be experienced. And then to let them go. You will see if that changes your anxiety.

If I were to ask you to summarize what you learned today?

PATIENT: Those are just muscle memories. And when that comes in, I am in the moment, and I can follow the sensation. I am in a safe setting. I am able to calm myself now.

Summary of Session and Clinical Implications

This session illustrates some critical issues in the treatment of cardiac patients who have experienced an intense, life-threatening heart attack. The most important of these is that the subjective experience of the chest tightening and not allowing the body to breathe in or out is traumatizing. This sensory signal activates the suffocation alarm system located in the PAG (Graeff, 2012, 2017). Electrical stimulation of the dlPAG in human patients undergoing neurosurgery evokes feelings of dread and symptoms of panic. Strikingly, activation of the mPFC is related to the existence of anticipatory anxiety about panic attacks, while activation of the dlPAG is related to the panic itself. Graeff notes that "anxiety is mainly integrated in the forebrain, whereas panic is chiefly organized in the midbrain [PAG]" (2012, p. 368). Specifically, the dlPAG activates the sympathomotor control areas of the rostral ventrolateral medulla (RVLM).

Once the dlPAG has been activated in the cardiac patient, the fight-or-flight reaction initiated by the removal of the parasympathetic buffer provided by the nucleus ambiguus, which was suppressing the RVLM's excitatory input, instantly and decisively follows. However, the irony is that there is neither a predator to run away from, nor to turn and battle. When it is your own body that is choking the life out of you, you are paralyzed in a frozen state of helplessness.

Allan's descriptions of his moment-to-moment experiences provide ample evidence of how overwhelming these physical sensations are and how terrified this leaves even the most capable person. When the dlPAG flooded the patient with shock and affective terror, he was paralyzed. Also important in Allan's descriptions is the presence or absence of another person. His isolation during his heart attack aggravated the intensity of his panic and pain and made him feel more vulnerable on his family's leaving him. The role of attachment in initiating panic on initial separation and depression if the attachment need is not re-established was elaborated by Douglas Watt and Jaak Panksepp (2009). Allan demonstrated all of these reactions in his sensitivity to being alone, his panic about returning to work, and his earlier depression on his mother's passing.

Panksepp and colleagues' studies (1978) with animals have demonstrated that opioids regulate the distress of social isolation on young animals. Low doses of opioids reduced the crying and motor agitation of the pups during isolation. Based on these observations, Graeff (2012, 2017) investigated how serotonin and mu and delta opioids interacted in the dlPAG to determine whether panic attacks could be attenuated. He found that *the anti-panic effect of the serotonin in the dlPAG required the presence and activation of local endogenous opioids for the panic to be suppressed.*

Previously, Preter and Klein (2014) demonstrated that the prolonged physiological effects of childhood parental loss (CPL) include compromise of the endogenous opioid system in these CPL individuals. Preter and Klein "objectively, experimentally showed a physiological link between endogenous opioid system deficiency and panic-like suffocation sensitivity in healthy adults" (p. 9). As a result, we can predict that a subgroup of patients with early life-attachment challenges (like separation, aloneness, or deaths) are more vulnerable to panic disorder in adulthood.

In DBR treatment, the protocol calls for a series of steps that help provide a sequenced and scaffolded approach to resolving these symptoms. In today's session, the therapist first took pains to ground Allan in the where-ness and now-ness of the present moment. After introducing the activating stimulus that needed resolution, the psychophysiological orienting response is identified to provide an anchor that both provides an impetus for the physical shock responses of the LC-NE and the PAG-triggered affective reactions.

The therapist's stance is then of allowing space for the shock reactions to manifest and release, while being attentive to delay the important processing of affective responses for later. In this example, it was evident that Allan was managing the pre-affective shocks quite well. He experienced intense shock reactions on the left side of his face, chest, and back. After these waves of pressure passed, he felt similar, weaker sensations on the right side.

It was only when the PAG-affective panic reaction was triggered by the thought that he "might be getting it wrong," that he got a clear sense of the more intense and overwhelming feelings. These remained hiding "behind the curtain" as the full experience of these emotional sensations were too terrifying. One of the benefits of using DBR with cardiac patients is that the shock reactions can be cleared first, before the panic reactions are approached and resolved. Sequencing treatment in this stepped approach allows targeted resolution of a troubling symptom that impairs many cardiac patients and pressures them to repeatedly visit the emergency rooms of local hospitals.

While DBR helps to make the task of facing the unimaginable more manageable, it does not reduce the courage that the patient must demonstrate in facing each of these phases of psychotherapeutic treatment. Certainly not simple, or easy, by any metric. But the necessary presence of the therapist, collaborating actively with the patient, makes it more possible to titrate the sessions to move toward total resolution of these autonomic-based symptoms. Allan noted this when he said that the safety that the therapist provided was essential for him to remain calm.

If cardiac patients are sent home with the expectation that they conquer those feelings on their own, continued overwhelming distress and the inability to accommodate back-to-work responsibilities will persist. Ongoing long-term disability is inevitable. At this point in the evolution of cardiovascular rehabilitation, there is no systematic recognition of such challenges in the cardiac rehabilitation treatment guidelines and protocols that exist anywhere in the world.

Adding to the challenge is that identifying patients with such reactions is difficult for at least two reasons: (1) patients themselves avoid thinking or talking about these experiences, and (2) health care providers and family are usually quick to point out to the patient that they are so lucky to be alive. It is certainly not wrong to guide patients to appreciate the positive and to motivate them to do their best in their active recovery, but not at the cost of overlooking a land mine that will repeatedly undermine their recovery.

For example, the intense dread that Allan felt as the panic and terror of not being able to breathe came up for him is likely the same internal distress that brings hundreds of cardiac patients who have had heart attacks back to the emergency room (ER). They are having the experience of going past that curtain and being swallowed up in the terror of dying again. If Allan's experience is indicative of what can be done for these patients, thousands of ER visits can be avoided by identifying and treating such patients during their CR.

Mental health professionals should be available at every cardiac rehab program to make pointed inquiry into the residual symptoms of these cardiac patients. The diagnostic categories that must be considered go beyond anxiety disorder and depression. Many cardiac patients have full blown panic disorder and/or PTSD symptoms. Again, it is worth noting that none of the existing international cardiac rehabilitation guidelines suggest that this be an essential part of the assessment function of cardiac rehab programs.

The final question to be answered is the question of whether it makes any difference to the outcomes our patients achieve, if such difficulties are or are not identified. This is a critical clinical question that calls for research to evaluate whether the benefits of DBR for cardiovascular patients recovering from heart events extends to others with such challenges. And if it does, what is the effect size of such treatment outcomes? An RCT study would be needed to provide these answers.

What we can report on is Allan's outcome. Allan reported feeling better after this session. Even so, in this session he described two aversions: (1) going into the room in which he had the heart attack, and (2) going out to socialize with friends. These avoidance patterns are directly related to the intensity of the terror of the heart attack itself. In Allan's case, this autonomic response was particularly intense. In this 14th session, we noted that Allan reoriented to a significant amount of the physical shock reactions in his body. However, the more intense PAG panic reactions were not processed in this session but were addressed in the two additional psychotherapy sessions that followed. At the conclusion of the 16th psychotherapy session with Allan, he was back to full-time work and continuing with his recovery journey.

Sleep and Increased Risk of Cardiovascular Events

Prospective studies of adults at risk for cardiovascular events are not very common. One notable exception is the Sleep Heart Health Study (SHHS; Bertisch et al., 2018) which has followed almost 5000 adults in their sixties for over 10 years. The study measured sleep of all community-dwelling adults with a polysomnographic sleep test at the outset of the study, as well as evaluating whether participants described themselves as having insomnia or poor sleep at the outset.

Based on these evaluations, the authors described three phenotypes among those with poor sleep: (1) short sleepers on polysomnogram (PSG) studies, (2) self-rated insomnia or poor sleep, and (3) insomnia or poor sleep plus objectively short sleep on the PSG. Their research tracked the occurrence of cardiovascular events across the following 12-year period.

While insomnia alone, or short sleep duration alone, did not confer increased risk for having a cardiovascular event in the follow-up period, the phenotype with both short sleep as well as insomnia (daytime distress from the lack of sleep) increased risk of having a cardiovascular event in the follow-up period by 30%. These findings are particularly compelling as this was a prospective study with a community sample. None of the participants had been identified as having preexisting risks for cardiovascular events prior to enrolling in the study. In Chapter 12, we present treatment of a case with short sleep and daytime insomnia symptoms with DBR.

APPLICATION

You did not start reading this book for academic reasons. *To make effective use of the information you have been reading, we invite you to engage yourself and the patients you work with in a brief opening dialogue about their sleep:*

Identify Patients With Trauma and Somatic Symptoms: When you go back to the traumatic event you just told me about, reflect on what you remember feeling in your body. Tell me what you notice.

Was Your Sleep Restorative at That Time? When you went through that difficult time, what happened to your sleep pattern?

Explore the Trauma, Somatic Symptoms, and Sleep Patterns: Did the trauma make your sleep worse? When you have a bad night of sleep, what happens to your physical symptoms?

Identify a Starting Point: As you think about what has happened to you, what would help you the most in getting your life back to normal? If it is sleep, what one important change would you want to make to improve your sleep?

Key Messages for Therapists

1. Early childhood trauma can cause distressing somatic experiences related to not having needs met. When these happen repeatedly (adverse childhood experiences; ACEs) the child's bodily sensations become overwhelming, and they disconnect from their bodily sensations. These reactions continue into adulthood and can be the cause of multiple somatic symptoms and/or hypersensitivity to such sensations.
2. Acute traumatic events trigger the *endocrine limb* of the stress response. Release of CRF activates CRF receptors (CRFr2), which are immunoreactive. The stimulation of these receptors not only accelerates the stress cascade (release of cortisol), but the receptors also increase the level of serotonin (resulting in intensified anxiety experiences) and activate the *immunological limb* of the stress response. Immunological inflammatory responses include the release of cytokines, macrophages, and other immunological responses. The inflammatory response can be further intensified as CRFr2 receptor sites are also located on immune cells and tissues throughout the body. Depending on context, activation of these sites can either be pro-inflammatory or anti-inflammatory.
3. Many neurons in the LC integrate receptors for CRF and endogenous opioids. The interplay of these two endocrines allows for immediate responsiveness to threat as well as feedback loops to stabilize LC-NE tonic activation. However, these feedback loops can become dysregulated, with the result that LC-NE activity becomes chronically hyperaroused.

4. Somatic symptoms triggered in the trauma stress cascade will not improve until the underlying role of the dysregulated ANS is addressed in therapy. This is critically important for understanding how health psychology can contribute to the resolution of these symptoms in medical patients. Understanding these symptoms as caused by a dysregulated ANS opens up the possibility of effective treatment through application of trauma treatments to the physical symptoms themselves.
5. Treatment of the traumatic consequences of cardiovascular events includes introduction of agency back into the patient's response to psychophysiological distress and also requires the presence of an attuned therapist responding actively to the patient's shock and affective responses. Deep brain reorienting (DBR) provides an effective and targeted way of: (1) reducing the activation of autonomic limb pre-affective shock, (2) managing the PAG-mediated behavioral limb affective responses, and (3) returning interoceptive signaling back to pre-traumatic event levels by engaging the attentive where self. The neurobiological processes engaged during DBR treatment modulate the LC-NE system's hyperarousal response, which is at the heart of dysregulation of the ANS whether the threat came from the environment (a predator) or from within the body itself (a heart attack).

11

The Life-or-Death Crisis and Neurochemical Dissociation

> "Chronic pain engages brain stress circuits and increases secretion of dynorphin . . . [which] decreases the amount of NREM and REM sleep and increases sleep fragmentation . . . revealing a pathophysiological role of [dynorphin] that promotes vigilance."
> —Hisakatsu Ito, Luiz de Souza, Barbara Vagnerova, et al. (2022, p. 1186)

> "[Dynorphin] inhibits the release of dopamine in various midbrain efferents . . . contributing to negative affective states in mood disorders and addiction."
> —Hugo Tejeda and Antonello Bonci (2019, p. 91)

Dissociation is defined as the failure to integrate consciousness, perception, emotion, memory, body, behavior, and identity into an integrated whole experience. A dissociative reaction can happen whenever the experiential impact of an event overwhelms the person's ability to process the event. Dissociation triggers the underlying brainstem mechanism for creating a disconnect between the nonconscious memories of the experience and the conscious representations of the event. The result is a failure to create an integrated (left and right brain) memory of the experience. This process is not restricted to those who have a diagnosis of a dissociative disorder. We can all dissociate when an experience has overwhelmed our ability to integrate it with our long-term memories.

The *intensity* of an overwhelming experience will decide whether a dissociative disconnect is activated. The larger the intensity of the overwhelm, the larger the disconnected memory system. There are at least two mechanisms that can activate these disconnected states in our memories.

The first is the intensity of the neural responses in the brainstem. While there is some controversy about the source of the disconnecting stimulus, the leading contender for this disruptor of the memory system is the LC-NE initiation of the alarm response. An overwhelm response to an event will activate the dlPAG, which will prompt the fight-or-flight response. Both of these are active response patterns. When these defensive responses are not adequate to resolve the problem, the activation spills over to the vlPAG, which prompts the collapse of the active response strategies.

If the active fight-or-flight response does not resolve the crisis, neurotransmitters that specifically reduce pain experience are recruited. These include endocannabinoids and enkephalin, which can be recruited to cap the intensity of the emotional responses activated by the PAG. In such cases the emotional responses (e.g., fear or grief) become overwhelming, and the person begins to experience a numbing of the emotions as well as bodily sensations of feeling cold or a tingling experience in their bodies. In many situations, an endocannabinoid or enkephalin cap is all that the nervous system needs to begin to feel it is back in control of the experience.

LIFE-OR-DEATH CRISES ACTIVATE DISSOCIATIVE RESPONSES

Life-or-death experiences completely overwhelm the defensive responses of the PAG. In addition, the mu and delta receptor capping responses from endocannabinoids and enkephalin are not enough to obviate the physical and emotional pain. In these more extreme situations, the dlPAG shift to the vlPAG shuts down active responses and recruits dynorphin, an endogenous kappa opioid, to manage the overwhelm.

Released dynorphin moves to the kappa opioid receptors (KOR), which result in multiple responses of muscle inactivation, impaired cognitive functions, emotional numbing, and dampening the reward (dopamine) system. This results in common symptoms of muscle weakness, overwhelming exhaustion, inability to think, plan, concentrate, or remember, and a pervasive sense of nausea, dizziness, and physical distress.

If the dynorphin release persists, this will shut down the mesocortical and mesolimbic dopaminergic pathways. This shutdown produces both sleeplessness and depressive states. In the clinical cases we will review, we will track how intense pain results in the release of dynorphin, which undermines active responses to the challenge. We will also see how DBR therapy provides both the collaborative therapeutic support necessary for the patient to return to these crippling psychological states, and a clear therapeutic target, focusing on releasing the shock reactions that trigger these dysphoric dissociative states.

What I will learn in this chapter to become a better sleep and trauma therapist:
1. Review the brain mechanisms activating the dissociative response.
2. Heart attacks can be exquisitely painful, and can result in the release of

dynorphin, an internally produced opioid, which results in immediate psychophysiological changes in the brain's sensations of the body. When the intensity of the internal somatic sensations becomes intolerable, release of dynorphin shuts down the subjective sensation of distress in a neurochemical dissociative response.
3. The clinical features of neurochemical dissociation include analgesia (lack of physical pain), an intense internal dysphoria (emotional distress, dizziness, and discomfort), aversion and recoil reactions, and an overwhelming sedation or inability to move (heaviness in the limbs), and cognitive confusion (brain fog).
4. Treatment of the traumatic consequences of cardiovascular events includes introduction of agency back into the patient's response to psychophysiological distress. Deep Brain Reorienting (DBR) provides an effective and targeted way of reducing the pre-affective shock that triggers depersonalization and derealization, the psychological mechanism causing dissociation. The neurobiological process of reorienting to the intolerable chest pain during DBR treatment releases the LC-NE shock reactions to the heart attack (even when the heart attack was a year or more previously).

The Neuroendocrine Response to Overwhelming Cardiac Angina

One of the central functions of the PAG is regulation of both emotional and physical pain sensations. As the intensity of emotional and physical pain experiences escalates to an inescapable and uncontrollable pain, a breaking point is reached at which internal body sensations are intolerable. At that point, the PAG shifts from a dlPAG behavioral response of hyperactivation to a vlPAG-mediated freeze response (Fanselow, 1994). In this moment of freeze, the parasympathetic system surges to overwhelm the sympathetic activation. In the freeze state, both the sympathetic and the parasympathetic systems are in hyperdrive, but the parasympathetic dominates and the person goes into a collapsed state.

In parallel with this, the PAG expresses dynorphin (DYN, a kappa opioid) to provide neurochemical dissociation from the body's pain. The release of DYN, an internally produced opioid, results in immediate psychophysiological changes at the synaptic level in other brain centers above and below the brainstem. Dynorphin is expressed at the spinal cord level, making limbs heavy and numb, as well as in the amygdala, hippocampus, striatum, and cortex, numbing sensations and impairing cognitive functions. Muscles go flaccid. Mental concentration evaporates or the person faints.

The dynorphin and orexin neuropeptide systems are also intricately interrelated at the hypothalamic levels (Ito et al., 2023). Orexin neurons also express dynorphin suggesting that they work together to regulate broad behavioral responses, particularly sleep-wake behavior. Many orexin synapses have collocated glutamate and dynorphin receptors to modulate sleep-wake responses. Activation of the glutamate receptors keeps the sleep-wake switch open to wakefulness. The release of dynorphin in the paraventricular nucleus of the hypothalamus further amplifies the vigilant response, fragmenting sleep and reducing NREM and REM sleep (Ito et al., 2023).

This orexin-gating switch can be considered an important part of the stress system's ability to modulate the sleep-wake response to extreme danger. When the intensity of the internal somatic sensations becomes intolerable, release of dynorphin shuts down the subjective sensation of distress, in a *neurochemical dissociative response*. The features of this response include analgesia (lack of physical pain), an intense internal dysphoria (emotional distress, dizziness, and discomfort), aversion and recoil reactions, and an overwhelming sedation or inability to move (heaviness in the limbs).

The immediate impact of activation of the kappa opioid receptors (KOR) is to shut down the hyperactivation of the autonomic nervous system. It also impacts the dopamine system, shutting down the brain's reward system (Tejeda & Bonci, 2019). There are two pathways supported by dopamine: the *mesolimbic system* (the ventral tegmental area and the nucleus accumbens, which modulate the experience of pleasure), and the *mesocortical system* (prefrontal cortices that support the regulation of attention and cognitive and executive functions).

When these two systems are dysregulated by dynorphin, the result is a disturbing internal state of dysphoria, poor motor control, lack of motivation, and confused cognition. Moreover, as these states are highly relevant to the life-or-death status of the individual, they are locked into memory and can return as flashbacks or symptoms triggered by subsequent life events. The person is haunted for months or years by the continuing shadowy presence of a dysphoric state of malaise and helplessness. These effects are magnified by disturbed sleep, and for many, this results in a full depressive condition (Baglioni et al., 2011). We will illustrate the impact of dynorphin release on the subjective experience of a cardiac patient with the following clinical vignette.

A Case of Neurochemical Dissociation After a Heart Attack

The edited transcript that follows builds on the themes introduced in the last case study. When the more intense PAG-initiated panic reactions were triggered in that session, a clear dissociative response was noted. In the last chapter we saw that Allan's brain automatically disconnected from the intensity of the physical experience, providing him with what he called a curtain to place that unwanted and overwhelming physical sensation behind. What is critical to understand about these dissociative reactions is that they are not voluntary changes. In fact, while there is a decision being made ("this is too terrible"), it is being made at the brainstem level, not by the conscious brain.

The following case illustrates in more detail how these intense dissociative reactions emerge, and how they can be managed with DBR therapy principles. Nancy (not her real name) experienced a heart attack at age 53. (She asked that her actual age be used as her cardiac event at such an early age confused doctors in the ER.) In the year after her heart attack, she struggled with an extremely poor memory, low motivation, and a high level of tension in her body. Despite this, she was determined to return to her work. She was working full time when she sought treatment for these symptoms. She had previously attended the cardiac rehab program, which was helpful in her physical recovery from her heart attack.

However, despite these gains, Nancy was plagued by a persistent feeling of distress, constant angina (at a 4/10 level), periods of dizziness, and a poor memory. She had none of those problems before her heart attack. She attended stress management training classes, as well as a sleep workshop and a group EMDR trauma-treatment program. Despite her enthusiasm and dedication to all those efforts, a year after her cardiac event her symptoms still persisted.

Nancy was offered individual treatment with DBR therapy. The DBR treatment was explained to her, and she was seen for 14 DBR psychotherapy sessions. As there had been no previous empirical study of the use of DBR for these difficulties, this exploratory treatment was offered to see if this would provide her with any relief from the distressing symptoms she had been struggling with for over a year.

Like Allan, Nancy's heart attack also happened at home. In her case the intensity of the pre-affective shock reactions activated neurochemical dissociation from the release of dynorphin, resulting in intense sensations of dizziness, weakness, and nausea. The transcript is from the sixth DBR session with this patient. In the preceding sessions she had been able to tolerate increasing sensations of the crushing pain she experienced during the heart attack. In this session we continued with this focus.

Review of Events Since Previous Week's Session

THERAPIST: Last time we met we continued with the DBR reorienting work, focusing on your reactions during your heart attack. Did you experience any cardiac symptoms this past week?

PATIENT: Yes. I had to write it down because otherwise I will forget. I guess it's that everything is overwhelming.

Commentary. The patient has had persistent memory problems. There are many root causes of such difficulties. As this session unfolds it will become more apparent how memory functions can be compromised by the autonomic (stress) system and the release of dynorphin.

> PATIENT: Last Thursday, after our session, I went upstairs and fell asleep. I could not believe that. I mean, I usually don't take naps. I drink a lot of coffee. I just took a nap for about half an hour. I'm quite sure I slept very deeply. I got disconnected completely, like shut down.
> THERAPIST: The body got into a deep state of relaxation. That's good news.
> PATIENT: The next night I had a lot of dreams. Even last night I had dreams.
> THERAPIST: Even though you don't usually nap, your nervous system changed. It began to be more relaxed. That tells me you were able to let go of some of that tension the brain was holding onto. Our work resulted in some of that experience being released, even if it is just 10%. If we continue, step by step, we will release more.

Commentary. Traumatic events automatically trigger a persistent red alert reaction in the LC-NE alarm system. This means the background level of brain hyperactivity is well above what would be typical for Nancy. Until the traumatic events have been fully resolved, the brain is in a perpetual state of readiness, waiting for the other shoe to drop. The brain is locked in trauma time. The change that Nancy noticed is highly significant. Having a nap is impossible with hyperarousal. The fact that she was able to nap is evidence of a reduction in the sympathetic arousal present for her that day. During the preceding year she had never been able to nap. The second observation, the appearance of dreams, can be understood similarly. As was discussed in the last chapter, activity of the LC-NE system during the night interferes with entry into REM sleep. If the LC-NE system is beginning to downregulate, then REM dreaming can begin.

> THERAPIST: Were there any negative feelings like the chest pain for you this past week?
> PATIENT: It is the same. Sometimes it is more. My job is stressful, and pretty much everything is in my brain, because I let them stress me. I actually care about my work. I want my work to be meaningful for everybody. Some of my coworkers think that I am overthinking, that I am not doing my work fast enough.
>
> I am trying to sleep, but I sleep less than 6 hours. The best would be 7 hours, but I don't want to give up on anything. I do my meditations in the morning. I have my CPAP machine, so I have the exact time. Last night I slept 6 hours and a bit. But it is not enough, I was able to sleep 6 hours a night in the past week. By the morning I was dreaming. Even though I am not sleeping 7 hours, I still dream. Am I sleeping deeply enough?
> THERAPIST: That is a very good sign. It means that your brain is going through the right stages and is getting into REM sleep. And even if you

don't remember the dreams, that is perfectly fine. The brain is reorganizing itself in that time.

PATIENT: When I am walking on the treadmill, and I am very sleepy, sometimes I get a headache. Last night I walked for 30 minutes. I felt a sharp pain in my eyes. Maybe it was because of tiredness.

THERAPIST: I would say, frankly, take a break. You have been exercising 7 days a week for 7 months. There is never a day where you relax?

PATIENT: Oh, I am relaxing. I am just not running. Since we started the deep brain reorienting I feel very tired. I am not able to run. I used to put the treadmill to 5.5 or 5.0. Now I barely go to 4.5. Usually I am at 3.5 or 3.7. I start at those for 3 minutes, and then I increase to a maximum of 4. I am just walking.

Commentary. The patient is confusing relaxation with intensity of the exercise. Reducing the intensity of exercise to walking, but continuing to walk every day for months, is not providing the cardiovascular and musculoskeletal systems with time off. Such breaks are necessary to release the tension in the musculoskeletal system. Continuous strain results in vulnerability to increased headaches. The fact that the DBR treatment is making her feel tired suggests that she is downregulating the intense SNS surge she felt when she had her heart attack. Allowing more space for the PNS to relax the body and brain is essential for recovery. In the next passages the therapist makes the effort to bring the importance of such breaks to her attention.

THERAPIST: Even athletes training for a race will take off the whole week before the event. For the body to relax and restore its energy. Training always has to be in balance. You push your body, and you let it recover. You are doing some recovery on the 30-minute days where it's a slower walk. But there is also a place for you to rest for at least a day or two every week. Where you take one or two days off and just relax. Just step back for a couple of days. See if you can let the body heal. Resume your 7-day program after that.

PATIENT: I will do that one day, just for you. I'm scared that if I stop doing it every day, it will be hard for me to get back into this routine.

Commentary. The patient is compliant but explains why she has been reluctant to do this earlier. Her fear is that if she stops doing the exercises she will not start them again. This is a common fear among many patients who have begun doing something (exercising) they have never done before. The motivation for exercising does not come from her internal affective system; it comes from her fear of not doing what her doctors have told her. If she stops, she fears falling back into old habits. She does not feel any emotional need to continue with her exercises. This is consistent with the absence of a connected dopaminergic system, which is the source of our internal motivational responses.

Step 1: Identifying the Activating Event

THERAPIST: Go back to your memory of what happened. Tell me what moment is standing out. Where do you begin to feel that surge of sensation, the chest pain? How are you remembering when you first felt your reaction?

PATIENT: I was lying on the bed, face down. I calmed myself, and then everything is a blur. I do remember when I got the chocolate with aspirin in my mouth I was actually walking. I don't know why. I think the doctor from the ambulance said that I needed to walk. Maybe she gave me a reason, but I don't remember. Then I went back to lying down. Nothing stands out, other than the crushing chest pain. That's all I remember. My husband told me that the first to arrive were the firefighters. Maybe they took my blood pressure. I don't remember them. It's the brain erasing the memory.

Commentary. The extent of the patient's difficulty in remembering anything about the heart event is clinically important. It suggests that the memory-encoding function of the brain was compromised. There are two possible reasons for this. The most likely one is that a compromised heart (during the heart attack) is not supplying enough blood to the hippocampus and prefrontal cortex for those structures to be able to encode events. The second reason is that release of dynorphin, an opioid, shuts down the dopamine system and impairs the neurotransmitter support necessary for memory formation. In Nancy's case, both of those physiological functions seriously compromised her memory.

THERAPIST: I don't know that your brain erased the memory. Remember, when we did therapy last week, at first you had the chest pain; then the dizziness came. The dizziness is important because the brain is not getting enough blood and so you feel dizzy. It's a marker. If you don't supply the parts of the brain that would create the memory with blood, they don't work. You probably didn't make a memory of the firefighters being there. That's the importance of the dizzy spell. It's taking offline that part of the brain. That part of the brain is still there. When you don't give it enough oxygen and glucose it can't do its memory making. But that is a different kind of memory than your body memory, your physical sensation of what your body is feeling, where the chest pain is and how crippling that pressure is. The body part of the memory is very clear. That memory is stored on the right side of the brain.

The firefighters coming in is an event memory and that is kept more on the left side of the brain. There are two different memory systems. And there is no blood supplied to the *events around you* memory, because the *how your body feels* memory, is the total focus of your brain.

Step 2: Orienting to Safety and the Where Self

The activating event for this patient was the experience of her heart attack. We took 5 minutes to orient her to her present "where self." After grounding her in the present moment we follow the patient's reactions. We will move directly to step five, her tracking of her physical sensations through the heart attack.

Step 5: Allowing the Patient Space to Track Pre-Affective Shock Responses

PATIENT: I'm not breathing so deeply. Still very, very dizzy, and my arms are getting numb.

THERAPIST: The numbness is coming from the opioids. The brain recognizes that this is profoundly serious, that the pain is too much. It dumps the opioids to kill the pain. Dynorphin is the opioid. It is like your body is releasing its own morphine. Dynorphin does two things. It dulls the pain sensations and makes your head very heavy. So it's hard to keep it up.

Notice that the opioid is there. See if it's possible to still move your head just a little bit.

That is very important. The opioid is protecting you. Mainly from the pain.

What we want to do is stay in that witnessing part of you. See if you can remain focused. Right now, it is just replaying that movie. You are remembering. It is activating the same cascade. The same sequence of responses. Notice how the heaviness comes in.

PATIENT: The pain is more intense. And I have another witness. My husband just got home.

Commentary. Nancy heard her husband come in the house. Her noticing the sound of his entrance tells the therapist that she is fully in her where self, noticing all that is present in the here and now. With the where self fully present, the attention to the intensifying angina can continue.

PATIENT: The most important thing was that I knew I was not alone. I had all of my family around.

If I lost my senses, if I fainted. I would have been safe. They would take care of me.

Commentary. The presence of others in life-or-death situations is critical to reducing the risk for enduring psychiatric problems. Unlike Allan, who had been completely alone and felt terror at the prospect of nobody being there to help him if he fainted, Nancy does not experience the same sense of terror from isolation. Her challenge is to tolerate the pain that increases as the dynorphin levels subside.

> THERAPIST: You would have been well taken care of. It is important for your witnessing where self, right now. Because it is fighting the memory map that was made, noticing that even back then when the body signal was very overwhelming, you had family there. You were safe. Even when you were groggy and struggling to remember things.
> Your where self is present. And reliving what happened allows you to integrate a narrative memory and release the body memory. It is starting to understand at a deeper level that you were still safe. That you had many allies. People who cared deeply about you.
>
> PATIENT: Time was passing without me realizing that it was 1 hour after, then 2 hours. I lost track of time. Everything started around 4 or 5 p.m. And I remember it was about 9 p.m. when we left for the hospital. So that is 5 hours.

Commentary. The duration of time that the opioid brain bath is present is critical to how long treatment of the condition will take. For this state of neurochemical dissociation to continue for 5 hours increases the treatment correspondingly.

> THERAPIST: In those 5 hours, if you were having the chest pain, and there was that opioid dump, then you would be very hazy. You would not remember very much at all. That is normal. If there are any other sensations that come up to your awareness, let me know. How things are changing.
>
> PATIENT: When my husband came in the house, it brought me back to the present. And I wasn't feeling that dizzy. Now I can hold my head. It is fine.

Commentary. The sensory information telling her that her husband was home was a powerful stimulus grounding her firmly in the present again. The fact that she noticed this shift provides her with additional important information that regression back to these overwhelming memories is temporary. Exiting the difficult experience can be initiated by refocusing on present sensory signals. Awareness of these moments of relief help to bring a better sense of control to the patient.

> THERAPIST: You were in that memory. You were literally back in that moment, having a heart attack. And then the sound of your husband's feet coming up the stairs brought you to the present. And your brain instantly knows, "There is no heart attack here."
>
> PATIENT: Everything is good. Life is good. Still here.
>
> THERAPIST: You are doing a really good job of going back to that map with your witnessing self.
>
> PATIENT: [After 1 minute of reorienting] Now I feel some pressure on my

head. Maybe it's because you told me I am supposed to, because it is the normal way things happen.

THERAPIST: I think the alarm center is catching up.

Commentary. The patient is able to reconnect with the overwhelm easily and she is encouraged to sit with it. She is given more space to follow the body memories, time spent on reorienting.

PATIENT: The chest pain is not that intense now. It is getting a bit lighter.
   I am getting some pressure here, between the eyes. And I'm doing the breathing with exhaling through my mouth.

THERAPIST: That pressure that you are beginning to feel between the eyes.
   Just sit with that. That pressure could be an orienting pressure. It is telling you that you are here. That something serious is happening. But that you can pay attention to it. You can observe it. That tension is your friend. Just notice exactly where that is. If you can, deepen into the sensation.

PATIENT: I am getting the back of my head being a bit numb.

THERAPIST: Kind of a numbness? Or tightness? Or achiness?

PATIENT: I think it is just numbness. My witnessing self, I guess it's confused. I am not sure what is happening.

THERAPIST: Again you are witnessing and noticing, moment-to-moment. Exactly what is there.
   Sometimes the words can't even capture what the feeling is. You're doing a good job of just paying attention to it.

PATIENT: My face is getting numb. My chest is getting numb. I think it's confusion and numbness.

THERAPIST: The opioids are circulating. And are getting to your face.

PATIENT: My arms are numb. My upper body is numb. What is happening? Can I come back? Can I please come back?

THERAPIST: Yes, you can. Yes, absolutely.
   So that witnessing part of you can just begin to be aware of . . . maybe there is a sound on the stairs. Or maybe you can hear my voice.

Commentary. The increased distress in the patient's voice is palpable. The therapist is checking to see if she can hear him and direct her attention to sensory signals that convey safety. As long as her where self is present, she is safe.

PATIENT: I do hear your voice, but I am all numb. My legs are numb, and I am confused. What is happening?

THERAPIST: The confusion is because the opioids are messing up your ability to think. It dulls your perception of the pain, and it dulls your thinking. That is okay. It is just a normal part of what the body has released. Keep that witnessing part of you noticing how the numbness comes like a big

wave. On the arms, the face, the throat. It's okay. You're doing a good job paying attention to it.
PATIENT: I don't like it.
THERAPIST: Is there a part of you that is also beginning to feel some fear?

Commentary. The patient's reaction escalated, and the therapist is checking to see if the PAG has been activated.

PATIENT: A big pressure on my chest. How can I come back?
THERAPIST: Right now it is like a war in your body. Between the pressure in the chest, the pain. That is on one side. Numbness is on the other. It is doing its best to minimize the pain.
PATIENT: My, my upper brain. is like controlling, but everything else is numb. And it is hard to breathe.

Commentary. The patient's whole body has become unavailable to her. She still feels a tiny island of being present and feeling in control, but the sense of losing control of her body entirely is beginning to activate PAG terror response. She is being encouraged to continue to stay in her where self by staying connected to the therapist's voice.

PATIENT: How can I come back?
THERAPIST: Stay in touch with my voice. You can hear my voice.
   The witnessing where self is still fully present. It is noticing—as your memory bank is playing this map—how overwhelming it was for you. That numbness is probably what happened in those 5 hours that the opioids were fighting the pain for you. Doing its best to kick the pain out.
   The numbness will pass. You are just going to sit with it. And you are going to listen to my voice. As you notice any change of where the numbness is or where it moves to. Where it moves away from.
PATIENT: It's all over.
THERAPIST: The numbness is all over now. And you were saying that at the top of the head it felt a little different?
PATIENT: I thought I could control it, but I can't.

Commentary. The feeling of complete loss of control is the trigger for the PAG response.

Step 6: Affects Arising From the Reorienting

THERAPIST: That is the scary feeling. Just think of it as your body taking over. There is a kind of wisdom in your body. And the wisdom is trying to make the pain go away.

But it is also frightening you. It is also scary because we want to be in control all the time. We want to manage what our body is doing.

Right now what are you noticing?

PATIENT: My hands are getting numb. . . . it's . . . I can't breathe.

This is what happened when I had my panic attack years ago. Can I come back?

I can't move my hands.

THERAPIST: Yes, move your hand. Notice whatever sensations you can control. Again, we are going to be patient. We know that this will pass. We know that it is going to be fine.

Right now we are replaying a very scary movie. The most difficult experience your brain experienced and is now reliving.

PATIENT: I don't know how to describe it. My breath is very shallow. Can I open my eyes? Come back?

THERAPIST: I can hear you. I am here. Is your where self still present?

Commentary. At this exact point in the treatment, the video call link got dropped. Technical difficulties while doing trauma therapy are never helpful. In this case, the dropped call could not have happened at a more inopportune time. The therapist waits while the patient's service reconnects with the session.

THERAPIST: What happened is that our video link somehow got dropped.

PATIENT: This was like how it happened when I had the panic attack 16 years ago. Oh, my goodness! That happened in February as well. Okay, maybe February is not my month! [She starts laughing.]

Commentary. The therapist is relieved that the patient is laughing about the experience now. He is also very curious about what happened during those few minutes that allowed her to have a fresh outlook. This shifts the focus of the session from active processing of internal sensations to reflecting on what happened.

Step 7a: Reflecting on the Therapeutic Experience

THERAPIST: Can you tell me what happened? I had some trouble hearing you. And then the call got dropped. You were experiencing the numbness, and it was terrifying. And you were worried about how to get out of it. What exactly happened?

PATIENT: I was very scared. I opened my eyes and I noticed that you were frozen. And I tried to come back to the present. I was still numb.

THERAPIST: That is the opioids.

PATIENT: But the controlling part of me tried to take over. That was scary!

THERAPIST: I could tell. You were actually in touch with what your body and brain were feeling through those 5 hours when you had your heart attack. Those intense feelings linger because the brain does not want to let go of the terrifying memory; it locks in the memory of going numb to prevent it from happening again. Also, as you were going numb, the brain began to get confused. You began to lose your sense of who was there with you, and what was happening. That is what you were reliving. When you bring those memories back, what happens is your brain begins to experience it fully and releases that terror.

Commentary. Very important in DBR trauma work is the shared understanding of both patient and therapist that what emerges during the reorienting work is *reliving the experience*, as opposed to *remembering the experience*. Reliving these sensations allows the mind to then reflect on the experience afresh and to arrive at a new perspective.

> THERAPIST: What would you call it?
> PATIENT: Phantom maps.
> THERAPIST: Those things have just been sitting in the brain, and now you have the strength and the courage to allow those experiences to come back. And as you do it, allowing the brain to let go of those moments. I don't think "fear" is the right word. It is terror. It is absolute terror. "What is happening? Will I be okay?"
> PATIENT: I was very scared.

Commentary. Allowing space for the patient to begin to put words to these visceral and physical sensations is an especially important aspect of DBR. This is where the patient can begin to know their internal experiences more directly and to notice changes and shifts in those experiences. She is now beginning to link her right hemisphere body experiences with what her observing self can put into words.

> THERAPIST: If you can, put into words what you understand about it. How has it felt from the inside? As you were going back to that experience.
> PATIENT: There was the chest pain, and then everything gets numb. Inside, it was the witnessing part that got very, very scared and confused. I didn't know what to do. I heard your voice, and I knew, "I am safe." But my brain was not getting the safe part. Then when my hands got cramped into a fist. It was terrifying!

Commentary. The patient is able to remember exactly how it felt. She now uses the word terrified (before she was saying only that she had been scared). Hearing the therapist's voice was very reassuring, but as soon as the total numbness and total disconnect from her body hit, the sense of knowing where she was melted away. It was as if her sense of self was melting away. The combination of total disorientation with the feeling of complete isolation triggered the intense vlPAG freeze response with global opiod release disolving her sense of her body.

> THERAPIST: The numbness, you said that you noticed it first in your hands and your arms. And then from there, it came up to the back of your head, and then to your face. And that happened pretty quickly. You could feel it like a wave coming over you. When did you notice that moment of panic, the "Uh-oh, what's happening? Can I get out of this?" When did you notice that That was the witnessing where self?

Commentary. The therapist is providing the opportunity for Nancy to reflect on the experience again and put words to how her sensations came and went.

> PATIENT: I was getting numb, and the witnessing part was like, "I don't like it!" [She chuckles.] Not noticing anything. I was unable to function. Like not even the witnessing part. Everything!
> THERAPIST: Was it for a few minutes that the numbness actually drowned out the witnessing part? Did it feel like that?
> PATIENT: Cloudy. I felt like when you are in fog, and you . . . you don't know which way is what.

Commentary. Nancy is now really understanding how disorienting and how disembodied she felt at the heart of this experience. It is as if your entire being has been swallowed up into a fog from which there is no escape. Resolution of these experiences requires working within the safety of a therapeutic alliance. No patient's nervous system will allow them to venture into that internal space alone. The terror that emerges immediately dissociates them from the experience.

> THERAPIST: The "where" self knows which way is down and up. When we start the session, I point out the feeling of your body sitting in the chair. You feel the gravity and it tells you which way is up and down. But when you get into the numbness, it takes away the body sensation. Then you are lost. You don't know where you are or what is happening.
> PATIENT: I was, like [chuckles], lost! Lost and in a fog. You do not know anything!
> THERAPIST: And when you had that experience, when you were lost and, in a fog, could you still hear my voice?
> PATIENT: Yes.
> THERAPIST: And was that still grounding? You knew that you are still here. You are not actually in the heart attack. It is just we are reliving these maps the "phantom maps." But you can see how terrifying that was.
> PATIENT: To the point where my hands were cramped! That did not happen

to me when I had my heart attack. It happened only when I had a panic attack 15 or 16 years ago. Before that I had two moments when I got this, the cramps. And I said, "Okay, that is a panic attack. It will go. It's okay."[She is laughing.]

Commentary. Ironically, it was the cramping of her hands, which was a familiar feeling experienced during two previous panic attacks (but NOT part of her heart attack), which settled her down. This relieved the sense of terror, and allowed her to exit the "phantom map" of the heart attack.

> PATIENT: Ignorance is bliss. If I would have known that it was a heart attack . . .
> THERAPIST: You would have called the ambulance and been on your way, right?
> PATIENT: Or maybe I would have just said, "Okay. It is my time. Good-bye."
> THERAPIST: No, you are a fighter. And you have proved it today. Because that wave, the battle between the pain, the huge pain. that you said felt like three elephants, and then that opioid, the part that will wash away all the sensations in the body. They were battling. When your brain loses all sensation of the body, that activates the terror, right? That is a huge insight into how desperate you must have felt at the time. And how you felt, "I am losing consciousness." Maybe even the thought, "I am about to die." Or something like that.
> PATIENT: Yes! [Laughing now.]

Step 7b: Exploring Any New Perspectives That Emerge

Before the DBR session draws to a close, the patient is engaged in reflection on whether their experiences during the session have begun to change their perspective about their self experiences. This patient had earlier mentioned that she planned to take a trip to her homeland. The therapist follows up on this theme.

> THERAPIST: If that memory is sitting in your brain, I am not surprised at all that you want to go back to your homeland, to say some goodbyes. Because that memory is telling you, "Look how close you came!" You are doing exactly the right thing.
> How are you feeling right now? What's happening in your body? What are you noticing?
> PATIENT: I get a lot of great feedback from you. Telling me what we did was an important part of it. So, I am happy! I am so happy. And also happy that this kind of therapy is actually working for me.
> THERAPIST: It is working. We are peeling different levels of the onion. Getting deeper and deeper, to the heart of what happened.

I know. *But we have to track exactly what's going on in the body. Right? You could feel the numbness coming in the arms. You could feel it coming to the back of the head and around to the face, and to the throat and then all over the body. Almost drowning you in that numbness. But your witnessing side was still noticing. It was terrified, but it could still hear my voice. It still noticed what was going on.*

I guess that moment when you felt the cramping in your hands. That triggered for you. "Okay, I want to come back to real life. Enough of playing this movie again." Right?

PATIENT: Yes.

THERAPIST: That was an amazing session. Just really, immensely powerful. And taking a lot of courage. You can be very proud of yourself. You are a fighter. And I think we've done really well.

And if I asked you does this start to give you a new perspective, just a new way of thinking about how the heart attack affected you?

What do you think? What are your thoughts about yourself?

PATIENT: I survived. That is in the past. This was like a challenge.

THERAPIST: Like probably the biggest challenge. The biggest thing that you have had to face. A major life-changing moment.

PATIENT: Like going over a fence. . . . I was able to go over.

THERAPIST: You overcame it. You transcended a massive challenge or roadblock. An obstacle.

PATIENT: Yes, an obstacle! [She exclaims with delight.]

THERAPIST: The obstacle was this memory. We knew it was sitting there, in the back of your brain. Before today, it was really impossible to allow your witnessing self to wander into that experience. But today, you had the strength. You had the conviction, "I think I can do this." And you stayed with it. And you overcame that obstacle. Your witnessing self is much stronger than this terrifying movie. This part of you that was still buried somewhere in the back of the brain.

PATIENT: I realized that maybe it was a traumatic experience for my son as well. And I asked, after last week, "When I called you, and you didn't answer." He started to apologize. "I'm sorry I didn't answer the phone. Sorry you had to call the landline." And I told him, "Don't apologize. You did come. You did help me. I am here. So it is fine."

But I hope I didn't cause any trauma to my family.

Commentary. Nancy's reliving her heart attack (across the past few weeks of our sessions) has made her aware of others' reactions. This is another indication that she has been able to put the heart attack into the past and understand that others may have had their own reactions to what happened. One year after the heart attack, she is realizing how it may have affected her son, for the first time.

THERAPIST: I am glad you are talking to him and asking him about what he felt. It is important to communicate. That is activating his witnessing self, too, so he can notice what he felt. How scary that might have been. You have a good instinct.

PATIENT: It is almost a year after my heart attack. It never crossed my mind before.

THERAPIST: I take that as another sign that you are putting the memory of the heart attack into the past. Now your witnessing self is more in the present. Both for yourself, but also noticing your son, and what his reactions are. That's a big shift. Letting go. Because these traumatic experiences grip us. They hold on to us. And we literally get stuck in the past. You're doing really well.

Enjoy the fact that you are now through. You are now in your present, your witnessing self.

This case illustrates how terrifying the internal experience of losing all sensation in the body and any sense of being in control of your limbs is. When the corrosive impact of that experience dissolves your conscious self experience, that fog encircles body and mind, and an absolute terror emerges that cannot be faced alone. Nancy did not have any developmental trauma, so she was able to sit with the intensity of the experience. Working with those who have dissociative disorders involves the same process, but the pace will be more graduated.

A Pathway From Neurochemical Dissociation, Through Sleep, to Depression

While the outcome in this case was positive, the larger issue is how these observations can be helpful to the many thousands who remain on medical disability because they continue with severe sleep disturbance, in a brain fog, exhausted and unable to focus their mental or physical energy enough to return to a productive life. Many become depressed, because the opioid activation impairs the mesocortical and mesolimbic dopaminergic circuits, resulting in severely disturbed sleep, lack of physical energy, and cognitive impairment (Tejeda & Bonci, 2019).

The pathway from brainstem activation of the opioid response (the nervous system's way of quickly protecting from overwhelming emotional and physical pain) through a cascade of brainstem responses that fragment and dissolve sleep often results in clinical depression (Baglioni et al., 2011). Here is how it happens. The first step is release of dynorphin, which numbs pain, initiates brain fog, makes the body heavy and lethargic, and suffocates the release of dopamine from the VTA. As well, release of dynorphin activates the lateral habenula (LHb), which enhances aversive signaling by inhibiting neuronal activity. An activated LHb provides additional indirect suppression of dopaminergic activity which suppresses NREM sleep.

As this dysphoric state persists, the HPA axis becomes increasingly engaged and the release of cortisol, the stress hormone, contributes to further circadian dysregulation (Ito et al., 2023). The background activation of both the vlPAG (feeling terror) and dynorphin-KOR receptors (numbness, heavy limbs, inability to think) also leads to parallel changes in neuronal plasticity in brainstem neurotransmitter systems. For example, there is a carryover effect that impacts the eight raphe nuclei (the serotonergic centers in the brainstem), which play a dual role in maintaining feelings of wellness and regulating REM sleep. In addition, there is some evidence that dynorphin may activate release of pro-inflammatory cytokines in the brain, resulting in increased inflammation of the brain itself, triggering depression (Dantzer et al., 2008).

Importantly, all of the above shifts in brainstem dynamics directly impair sleep and dreaming states through synergistic and mutually reinforcing mechanisms of:

1. a surge in the alarm reaction (RAS-LC-Amy-vlPAG),
2. reduced activation of DRN centers that activate REM sleep,
3. increased brain inflammation, and
4. reduced dopaminergic signaling, eliminating much of the NREM sleep prior to REM sleep, and reducing REM latency.

The impairment of dopaminergic signaling during sleep undermines the normally effective capacity of NREM and REM sleep to adaptively modulate amygdala functioning. As this state persists, the sleep disturbance continues and the ability of sleep to regulate emotional distress evaporates, and a full-blown clinical depression ensues.

While the above account is based mainly on animal studies of brainstem dynamics, the profound impact these underlying brainstem circuits have on our mental and physical states is not in doubt. As studies into these dynamics in PTSD patients follow, the broad strokes of this thesis may be revised and clarified. The variety of possible brainstem nuclei contributing to these clinical outcomes will be revised, but what will not be revised is where these dynamics play out: these clinical syndromes are rooted in the brainstem.

More important than whether dynorphin release plays a central role in the cascade leading to depression is whether such powerful brainstem responses can effectively be treated with psychotherapy. While the case presented in this chapter had an encouraging resolution, this does not constitute conclusive evidence that such outcomes are routinely possible.

However, bolstering this argument, a recent RCT conducted by Ruth Lanius and her colleagues in London, Canada, provides additional support (Kearney et al., 2023). The study recruited patients with PTSD. Exclusion criteria included bipolar disorder, substance use, and major medical condition, but not dissociation. Patients were randomized into a wait-list control or provided with eight sessions of DBR therapy. Results confirmed a large-effect size in reduction of trauma symptoms that increased by the 3-month follow up period. Further research is needed to demonstrate the advantages and limitations of this treatment in managing the particularly troubling symptoms of neurochemical dissociation, both in psychiatric clinics as well as in medical settings in which cardiac events and surgical procedures can precipitate similar neurochemical dissociative reactions.

Key Messages for Therapists

1. Dissociation occurs when overwhelming experiences disrupt the integration of consciousness, perception, and memory, causing a disconnect between implicit (nonconscious) memories and conscious representations, affecting both psychological and physical states.
2. The dissociate response occurs in the brainstem. The SC integrates sensory signals about threats with visceral bodily states and activates LC responses. When these signals are inescapable or overwhelming, the LC activates intense shock responses to body and mind, triggering depersonalization and derealization. Active dlPAG responses quickly shift to a passive vlPAG shutdown freeze response, often supplemented by release of dynorphin (an endogenous kappa opioid). For example, the hours of unrelenting chest pain during a heart attack can trigger this *neurochemical dissociative response*.
3. The clinical features of neurochemical dissociation include immediate analgesia (lack of physical pain), an intense internal dysphoria (emotional distress, nausea, dizziness, and physical discomfort), aversion and recoil reactions, brain fog (inability to focus thoughts or think), and an overwhelming sedation or inability to move (heaviness or weakness in the limbs). The heightened autonomic vigilance state also undermines restorative sleep. Dynorphin also actively sabotages the dopaminergic system resulting in anhedonia, depressed mood, lethargy, and for some, extended periods of despair and suicidality.
4. Treatment of dissociation includes reintroduction of safety and agency in the context of an attuned therapeutic alliance, grounded in the present. DBR activates the memory and anchors the person in the orienting response. This permits an effective and targeted way of releasing pre-affective shock. The collaborative process of jointly reorienting to the intolerable chest pain releases the LC-NE shock reactions to the heart attack (even when the heart attack was a year previously).
5. Developmental trauma is more complex than a heart event in adulthood. However, the DBR therapeutic process is the same. The patient is encouraged to return to intolerable feelings and/or pain, and pendulate (from the pain to the orienting tension). The orienting tension provides the patient with an anchor, and the presence of the therapist and the patient grounded in their where self provides the necessary safety to help the patient begin to tolerate pain and overcome the dissociative response.

12

Putting Trauma to Sleep

"Any patient presenting with autonomic dysfunction should be queried about their sleep patterns, and close attention should be paid to symptoms of autonomic dysfunction in patients with sleep disorders."
—Mitchell Miglis (2016, p. 40)

"Trauma is first, and last, biological. That is why it occurs in all cultures. Everyone is vulnerable to trauma." —William Nash (2022)

The goal of psychotherapy is to restore the patient to normal functioning of their sense of self, along with the ability to look forward and to create the life that they want for themselves. This forward-looking capacity requires an intact autobiographical memory system. In this chapter, we will explore the ways that the brain prioritizes the brainstem response on the body's memory of the traumatic event. The intensity of these body-shock responses dominates the brain's activity going forward, fueling higher levels of cognitive activation in which the primary objective mentally is continuous surveillance for dangers. This state of brainstem hyperarousal maintains a cognitive state that is frozen in a past life-threat moment.

These experiences will be evident in the bodily sensations that the patient experiences as they track their reactions to reliving the moment that the trauma is activated. Before going to the clinical case material, it is necessary to review the brainstem systems that collaborate to keep these neural circuits active and in the process cause the sleep pattern to be fragmented by repeated disruptions and curtailed to prevent any sense of renewal or recovery from the trauma.

LIFE-OR-DEATH EXPERIENCES ACTIVATE SURVIVAL RESPONSE CENTERS

In normal waking life our daily experiences are tagged by the experience of a positive or negative emotion. In life-or-death experiences, the positive or negative dopamine tags are suffocated. This happens through two pathways. The innate alarm system, triggered by SC-amygdala-LC activation, creates an intense shock reaction into the body. The intensity of these activating signals spills over into overwhelmingly intense emotional defensive reactions (activated by the dlPAG, vlPAG, and DRN), which then dominate the experience of the person. The second pathway opens when these bodily reactions of intense emotion or physical pain are too overwhelming. At this point, the opioid system releases dynorphin A to manage the pain. We reviewed this in the last chapter, and the same process applies to the clinical case we will review this chapter.

The net effect of overwhelm and shutdown is that the cascade of brainstem activation overwhelms the autobiographical memory system. A narrative memory is now impossible; replacing it is a felt self that experiences splinters of sensory, affective, or procedural memories. With these experiences there is no presence of an observing self; instead, there is a vigilant, vulnerable, sleepless, and tenuous self waiting for the other shoe to drop. This self is not living life. This self is the cognitive sentry stuck in trauma time. This self is unable to feel feelings or to make new memories. This self exists in order to preserve its existence. Nothing more.

In extreme duress, the activation of the innate alarm system is amplified by feedback loops through the nucleus gigantocellularis (NGC) in the ARAS, the hypothalamic orexin nucleus, and the thyroid system. These positive feedback loops effectively magnify a danger signal 10-fold. The resulting state of affairs includes an *amplification of cognitive reactivity: a constant ruminative circuit that keeps looking for the source of the danger*. As well, it amplifies the NGC-LC-orexin-thyroid circuit, which fuels an elevated full-on 24-hour state of wakefulness: sleep cannot be allowed, as it will leave the person vulnerable to the death they just escaped.

The Fragmented Short Sleep Phenotype of Insomnia

The activation of the amplified NGC-LC-orexin-thyroid circuit creates a specific phenotype of sleeplessness: chronic insomnia with repeated awakenings from sleep, resulting in difficulties returning to sleep, few, or no, REM (or dream) periods, and early morning awakening. This insomnia phenotype carries the double burden of fragmented sleep throughout the night as well as short total sleep time (usually less than 5 hours).

The occurrence of high levels of cognitive activation among those with little or no sleep was central to early formulations of chronic insomnia. Insomnia was attributed to the intense cognitive arousal in most of these patients. Nicole Tang and her colleagues (2023) recently published a systematic review of 40 years of psychological theorizing about the relationship entitled "Cognitive Factors and Processes in Models of Insomnia." Their review identified nine distinguishable models that have been advanced across four decades, that as a group identified 20 cognitive factors and processes included in these nine models. The article is thoughtful and accurately captures how important cognitive activation is in insomnia, as well as how embedded it is with related processes like attachment, autonomic arousal, beliefs, and safety behaviors. What is not always appreciated is that insomnia is not a single disorder in which every insomniac has the same cognitive activation.

Earlier reviews have proposed that insomnia is not a single sleep disorder, but a prominent feature of six (van Someren, 2021) to eight (Aellen et al., 2024) different sleep disorders. What is needed to clear up the ambiguities of insomnia theorizing is not more theories, but treatments based on targeting specific neurophysiological models of what causes these various cognitive activations. Specifically, what brainstem centers are causing the cognitive arousal seen in chronic insomnia? How can we silence the centers perpetuating chronic insomnia, *if* they can be silenced?

Targeting Brainstem Centers at the Heart of Cognitive Arousal

In this chapter we review the features of chronic insomnia with fragmented short sleep, the probable brainstem centers perpetuating this pattern, and an example of how psychotherapy targeting these brainstem centers can silence persistent insomnia. Finally, we consider how the responses of the brainstem overwhelms normal autobiographical memory processes.

The radical response of brainstem structures to life-or-death situations creates a locked-in response, which freezes that past life-threat moment, impairing both sleep and the dynamic process of shaping our autobiographical memory. We review how the hyperactivation of the innate alarm response in a concussed patient triggers a cascade of responses that recruit the orexin nucleus in the lateral hypothalamus. The result is severely compromised sleep, characterized by frequent awakenings and little total sleep time.

We first elaborate the nature of these deep brainstem processes that hijack normal life experiences and then provide a clinical example of how these can be resolved. We then return to the broader question of how resolution of all trauma-induced dysfunctional implicit memory systems is necessary to reactivate the person's ability to recover their episodic memory and use this subjective system to orient toward the future and gain control of their lives.

**What I will learn in this chapter to become
a better sleep and trauma therapist:**
1. Review of brainstem regions that support wakefulness.
2. Understand the contribution of the orexin nuclei of the lateral hypothal-

amus to maintaining prolonged wakefulness and persistent fragmented sleep.
3. Presentation of a persistent postconcussive syndrome (PPCS) case that demonstrates that these disabling psychological symptoms of autonomic activation and dysregulation can be treated with the neuromodulatory approach of stabilizing the brainstem with DBR treatment.

HOW THE BRAINSTEM SUPPORTS WAKEFULNESS

The Brainstem's Medial Medullary Reticular System Activates Wakefulness

In the 1940s, sleep was still considered a passive state. Sleep began when daytime interests faded. You *fell* asleep until the brain again received enough sensory input in the morning to reactivate it and start another day. This perception of sleep as a passive brain state needing no explanation beyond increased sensory stimulation from the environment in the morning was shared by physicians, neurophysiologists, and biologists. All of that changed with the neurophysiological studies by Giuseppi Moruzzi, Horace Magoun, and Donald Lindsley into the neural basis of wakefulness.

In 1949, Moruzzi and Magoun discovered that stimulation of the medullary brainstem instantly awoke a sleeping cat. This source of waking activation was named the reticular activating system (RAS). These researchers conducted further studies leaving the sensory nerves intact but transecting the reticular formation. The result was a comatose cat that could not respond to increasing sensory input. This demonstrated that wakefulness did not just happen, it was actively turned on by the brainstem. And when that "on" switch was removed, no amount of sensory input will awaken the animal.

Moruzzi and Magoun's discovery, that stimulating the core of the medullary brainstem resulted in activating all the electrocortical arousal activity evident in daytime waking EEGs, was groundbreaking. Over the next 70 years our understanding of the role of the medullary reticular activating system has deepened.

The master neurons responsible for the brain's *generalized activation* (GA) are the large medullary neurons of the nucleus gigantocellularis (NGC) located just above the spinal cord. They have both extensive inputs as well as extensive outputs in both ascending and descending directions. They "provide the essential driving force for elevating GA for entry into consciousness, for the initiation of behavior" (Pfaff, 2019, p. 28).

Donald Pfaff and his colleagues proposed that the NGC neurons in the ventral and medial reticular formation initiate arousal of both the autonomic limb and the cortical limb. They demonstrated in studies with mice that stimulating these neurons at either 200 or 300 Hz resulted in both cortical as well as autonomic activation (Wu et al., 2007). On the cortical side, they noticed a significant reduction of both delta and theta waves and a corresponding increase in gamma-wave power. In another study in which NGS neuron activity was slowed pharmacologically, a corresponding slowing of activity in the cerebral cortex was observed (Gao et al., 2019).

On the autonomic side, these stimulation experiments also demonstrated raised heart rates. And these physiological shifts were present even in deeply anesthetized animals, demonstrating a powerful biological effect overwhelming even intensely soporific states.

In addition to autonomic and cortical activation, these NGC neurons are described by Pfaff as "leaders in the initiation of behavior" (2019, p. 31). Activation of these glutamatergic or glycinergic neurons is essential for the initiation of movement as well as the intensity of movements In addition to motor responses, these glutaminergic neurons also influence cortical and autonomic responses. Pfaff set five criteria for determining that the NGS neurons are a critical factor in generalized CNS arousal. Specifically, higher NGC activity should be correlated with generalized arousal in cortical (more gamma high-frequency activity and less delta and theta low-frequency activity), motor (increased muscular discharge), and autonomic (increased heart rate) responses.

All five criteria were met, indicating that NGC neurons have a central role in generalized activation of the nervous system. Moreover, NGC neurons responded to inputs from all sensory channels: tactile, visual, auditory, vestibular, and olfactory. And excitation of NGC was directly related to observed increases in neck muscle tension and cortical arousal. The combination of being able to respond to multiple sensory channels, with increased excitation resulting in initiation of behavior, led Pfaff to conclude that these NGC neurons are a critical component of the "first responder" (Pfaff, 2019, p. 32) circuits, for response to danger or life threat.

This leads to the important question of what the inputs to this critical central station are? Pfaff points out that the dendritic tree that collects incoming signals fans out widely including ascending signals from the spinal cord and a range of descending inputs. These include the vestibular nuclei, the midbrain reticular formation, the PAG, and the deep layers of the superior and inferior colliculi (SC and IC). Also the NTS receives input signals from the cardiovascular, respiratory, and digestive systems. In summary, the diverse inputs from multiple sensory and somatic channels that can detect early danger to the organism are here combined with the capability to initiate motor responses to alarming stimuli.

The range of outputs for these NGC neurons is as dense and integrated as the inputs. They project to the pons to the pontine reticular formation (to increase the alarm signal), the vestibular nuclei (for coordinating posture and action), and the locus coeruleus (to engage norepinephrine neurons to further intensify the alarm response). They also project to the midbrain reticular formation, the PAG, and the deep layers of the SC and the cerebellum.

The configuration of the NGC cells—collecting information from a broad range of sensory processing centers and then sharing the state of alarm from one center to all of these integrative nuclei—has the effect of creating a feedback loop that can amplify the individual sensory inputs. The converging inputs and diverging outputs in a bidirectional "fan in—fan out" connection pattern is highly effective in activating the entire brain.

A metaphorical parallel for the divergent output would be the difference in impact between a single bomb exploding, contrasted with a cluster bomb exploding. Both are destructive, but the impact of the cluster bomb multiplies the effect of the single bomb. Similarly, the neuronal architecture of the NGC, its dense input tree, and its similarly dense output tree, make the intense activation of this brainstem medullary reticular center highly reactive and a persistent threat to usually quite balanced sleep-wake rhythmicity.

The arousal outputs upward into the brain follow two pathways, both critical for cortical activation. Donald Pfaff calls the first the "low road" (Pfaff, 2019, p. 33) that ascends to activate the hypocretin-secreting orexin system in the lateral hypothalamus and the cholinergic-secreting neurons of the basal forebrain. Each further amplifies the alarm signal and activates brain reactivity and is discussed shortly.

The other pathway, "high road" innervates the central thalamus, which can both increase sensitivities to sensory signals, like sounds and smells, and increase motor activity. Pfaff concludes that this second arm of brain activation "support[s] attention and direct[s] motor acts through a forebrain 'mesocircuit'" (Pfaff, 2019, p. 33).

Importantly, the activation of the central thalamus will strongly excite cortical activity, which, in turn, relays that excitation to the striatum the subcortical motor control center, which then fuels the continuing background activity in the central thalamus.

Pfaff (2019) also notes that these powerfully activating NGC neurons are usually kept under inhibitory control by nearby GABAergic neurons: "the most powerful and crucial neurons should be silent when there is nothing important to signal" (p. 31). But, at least in theory, if the multiple low road and high road pathways of activation from the NGC break free from this inhibitory control, these multiple channels could amplify the danger signal and create an extreme awake state. What are not clear are the conditions that could precipitate this loss of inhibitory control and how it could be restored.

How these low road output signals to the orexin and basal forebrain centers amplify the signals from the medullary reticular system is reviewed next.

HOW THE LOCUS COERULEUS AMPLIFIES THE SURVIVAL RESPONSE

The Locus Coeruleus Initiates the Innate Alarm System

In Chapter 8, we highlighted the important role of the LC in initiating the innate alarm response. The LC is the hub of the largest collection of norepinephrine cells, supplying norepinephrine to the entire forebrain. Increasing the activity of the neurons in the LC causes activation of cortical EEG patterns of high frequency, low amplitude waves (Berridge & Foote, 1991).

We now consider the range of inputs into the LC, and how these modify its activity. Pfaff (2019) highlights three primary inputs: (1) the paraventricular nucleus (PVN) of the lateral hypothalamus, (2) cardiovascular and visceral inputs, and (3) the orexin-hypocretin system inputs. This range of inputs lead Pfaff to conclude that the LC must play a role in both behavioral arousal as well as autonomic regulation.

The Locus Coeruleus–Paraventricular Feedback Loop

The paraventricular nucleus (PVN), located in the anterior hypothalamus, gives rise to an extensive projection system, which plays a major role in management of energy expenditure. The PVN provides stimulation of the hypothalamic-pituitary-thyroid pathway, to stimulate the production of TSH by the anterior pituitary, which activates the release of T3 and T4 by the thyroid. Upregulation of thyroid release can contribute to metabolic hyperarousal that would make sleep more difficult to engage.

The PVN neurons innervating the core LC were found to express stress-related corticotropic releasing factor (CRF). As the primary hormonal input to the core LC is CRF, it is important to note that CRF increases the discharge rate activity of LC neurons in a dose-dependent way. A major stress event will release major amounts of CRF.

The Locus Coeruleus: Cardiovascular and Visceral Inputs

Important visceral input signals come from cardiovascular and vagal inputs, as well as the amygdala. The cardiovascular signals come from the nucleus of the tractus solitarius (NTS), the dorsal motor nucleus of the vagus (DMV), and from the hypothalamic preoptic areas (POA) that regulate sleep and temperature.

A cardiovascular phenomenon that has an immediate activating effect on the LC is reduction in blood volume. A hypotensive event causes the LC to increase its firing rate, as does distention of any visceral organ such as the bladder, colon, rectum, and stomach (Elam et al., 1986). These reactions to visceral states are mediated by the central nucleus of the amygdala, which is the primary source of CRF, activating the LC from hypotensive stress as well as other visceral signals. Importantly, these inputs underline that LC hyperactivity can be triggered by extreme visceral stress, not only psychosocial stress. Hypersecretion of CRF can maintain LC hyperactivity for extended periods of time.

The Orexin Pathway and the Locus Coeruleus

The orexin-hypocretin system forms an important hub that is responsible for maintaining the sleep-wake state without frequent shifts back and forth between states. Orexin neurons are located in the lateral hypothalamus but have extensive outputs throughout the brain in order to support its role in maintaining wakefulness. This includes dense projections to the serotonergic dorsal raphe nucleus (DRN), the norepinephrinergic LC, and the histaminergic tuberomammillary nucleus (TMN). All of these outputs promote arousal.

Certain orexin neurons have been shown to be able to coexpress dynorphin and glutamate alongside orexin. That capacity to release multiple signaling molecules simultaneously increases its ability to regulate arousal. For example, releasing dynorphin will suppress arousal and facilitate sleep, while releasing orexin and glutamate will facilitate wakefulness, increasing the potency of the dynorphin/orexin balance to regulate sleep and wakefulness. The important role of dynorphin will be returned to later in this chapter.

There are multiple inputs to the orexin neurons. These include cholinergic neurons of the basal forebrain, which provide input promoting wakefulness. Also, GABAergic neurons of ventrolateral preoptic area promote transition into NREM sleep as well. Serotonergic neurons of the median and paramedian raphe promote wakefulness. Finally, the many limbic nuclei that process emotional responses (from amygdala, infralimbic cortex, nucleus accumbens shell and bed nucleus of the stria terminalis [BNST]), also stimulate wakefulness. The diversity of inputs indicates that orexin nuclei integrate cognitive and emotional functions to determine whether to stay awake or to transition into sleep.

One indication of the potency of the orexin nuclei in activating the awake state comes from studies of optogenetic stimulation of the orexin neurons in the sleeping mouse. When orexin nuclei were stimulated in either SWS or REM sleep there was an increased probability of awakening (Carter et al., 2013). In addition, orexin itself excites orexin neurons, forming a positive feedback circuit through indirect and direct pathways, resulting in an elevated and sustained level of hyperactivation for long periods. In addition to this pathway, orexin is highly responsive to levels of CRF, ATP, neuropeptide Y, and fluctuations in levels of acid and CO_2 in the blood (Inutsuka & Yamanaka, 2013).

Studies using optogenetics, in which specific nuclei are stimulated or inhibited, have demonstrated that the awakening from sleep by stimulation of the orexin nucleus is mediated by the activity of the LC. This is because when the orexin nucleus is stimulated, while at the same time the LC is inhibited, no awakening occurs. Carter and colleagues' (2013) further experiments in which both LC and orexin neurons were stimulated or inhibited led them to conclude that, "noradrenergic neurons in the LC are particularly important for mediating the effects of hypocretin neurons on arousal" (Carter et al., 2013, p. 1).

The pedunculopontine tegmental nucleus (PPT) further activates cortical arousal through its glutamatergic and cholinergic neurons, which provide excitatory arousal to both the central thalamus and cortical centers. Orexin nuclei are thought to play a role in generating physiological responses to emotional stimuli. For example, local injections of orexin in the PPT nucleus strongly inhibited REM-related atonia in the cat, indicating that orexin undermined the conditions necessary for REM sleep (Mieda et al., 2013; Takakusaki et al., 2005).

How Is Tonic Locus Coeruleus Activation Downregulated?

This raises the question of how the hyperactivity of the LC could be controlled. There are two main inhibitory mechanisms. One is the nearby GABA neurons in the dendritic field of the LC. When activated, these inhibitory neurons can downregulate LC activation. The other pathway is activation of the mu opioid receptors in and around the LC. In a study in which enkephalin, an opioid, was microinfusions into the LC (Kreibich et al., 2008), the discharge rate of the LC was not altered, but responses to various stimuli were attenuated, as was the normal neuronal hypotensive stress response in which heart rate goes up when blood pressure goes down.

More recently, Ryan Wyrofsky and his colleagues (2019) at Drexel University in Philadelphia reported on a series of experiments with rats that explored the impact of acute and chronic stress on LC-NE activity. Their working model of stress demonstrated how endocannabinoid (eCB) activation regulates the output of the LC-NE system.

Acute stress causes a high-frequency (5–10 Hz) tonic limbic reaction in the central amygdala (McCall et al., 2015) releasing CRF into the peri-LC, while autonomic activation through the PVN provides CRF activation of the LC core. The result is a surge in tonic LC-NE activity including a release of NE into the mPFC. The increase in LC activity causes the synthesis of eCB in the amygdalar-CRF afferents, leading to decreases in CRF release and subsequently attenuation of LC-NE activity.

However, in other situations in which eCBs are overexpressed, the heightened level of eCBs supports continued elevated LC-NE activity. While moderate increases in eCB modulate LC activity, large increases further inhibit the GABAergic neurotransmission with the LC, preventing the usual habituation response and a return to normal LC functioning. This would continue the LC-NE activation of mPFC with the resulting continuation of the mPFC-central thalamus circuit and persisting symptoms of hyperarousal.

HOW BRAINSTEM SURVIVAL RESPONSES CAUSE COGNITIVE AROUSAL
Clinical Features of Fragmented Short-Sleep Insomnia

The NGC-LC-orexin-thyroid system is an integrated network in which positive feedback loops serve to push the system toward hyperactivation and persistence of the waking state. As a core survival system, once activated there are no physiological systems that will bring this system back into balance and stability. It will continue to function aggressively, as it has the one and only goal of survival. No other neurobiological system has a more system-critical task, so the cycle once activated will remain in place. The main features of this phenotype are cognitive arousal, repeated awakenings, little or no REM (or dreaming) sleep, and a short sleep duration.

Fragmented short sleep has particularly corrosive impact on the restorative qualities of sleep. Among the casualties of fragmented sleep are: (1) slowed processing speed, difficulty concentrating, and memory problems; (2) impaired mood; (3) increased inflammatory and hormonal dysregulation; (4) physical symptoms including musculoskeletal pain (including fascia and myofascial); and (5) a lack of interest in social interactions.

Cognitive activation is among the first functional changes to emerge, as norepinephrine hyperactivation of the LC-mlPFC and LC-ACC circuits increase cognitive activation but modulate and suppress emotional awareness. Cognition is hijacked to a primary role in scanning the environment for danger, as opposed to integrating with internal emotional states, as this shift to scanning for danger serves the critical goal of survival. This suppresses any integrated responsiveness between cognition and emotional states necessary for adapting to new situations and forming autobiographical memories.

Sleep fragmentation occurs across both the NREM and REM states of sleep. We review the mechanisms that undermine both states next. Jennifer Smith and her colleagues (2023) at the University of Pennsylvania found there is a synchrony during NREM sleep between infra slow rhythms in the spindle bands of the EEG and activated glutamatergic neurons of the preoptic area (POA) of the hypothalamus. Optogenetic stimulation of these glutamatergic neurons during NREM resulted in increased microarousals and awakenings from NREM sleep. In addition, when the subject animals were subjected to social defeat stress, the frequency of these microarousals as well as the number of awakenings from sleep increased. Smith and her colleagues further demonstrated that these POA neurons are innervated by glutamatergic neurons in the lateral hypothalamus (LH), a brain region known to regulate stress and sleep. The authors concluded that this represents "a novel circuit mechanism by which POA excitatory neurons regulate sleep quality after stress" (Smith et al., 2023, p. 1).

Vladyslav Vyiazovskiy and Russell Foster and their colleagues in Oxford had previously shown that photoactivation of the inhibitory fibers of the lateral preoptic area (LPO) not only triggered a state switch from sleep to awakening, but also increased the EEG indices of cognitive arousal (Yamagata et al., 2021). In contrast, when the same neurons were photo inhibited, arousal levels were reduced but without a switch in state from awake to sleep. Arousal of the same neurons during REM also led to awakenings, but it took longer for animals to awaken from REM than NREM.

In addition to these disruptions to the continuity of sleep, recent studies of individuals with PTSD by Anne Richards and her colleagues (Natraj et al., 2023) demonstrated shifts in the adaptive functions of NREM. Sleep spindles are a prominent feature of N2 sleep. Spindles play an important role in consolidation of memory. However, in PTSD, increases in spindle activity have been found to be positively associated with higher intrusive memories of trauma (van der Heijden et al., 2022). Richards's PTSD participants viewed neutral and stressful pictures and then napped for two hours. After the stressful pictures spindle rates in N2 were increased in all participants.

The PTSD group was divided into those with low versus high CAP scores. The group with lower symptoms demonstrated higher memory accuracy on retest after the nap, while those with higher stress had less anxiety. The increased spindle activity for those with high PTSD symptom burden favored emotional recalibration over memory consolidation. An earlier study of intercranial recordings of human subjects had discovered ripple activity in the amygdala in NREM, and found that these ripples co-occurred with hippocampal ripples, and both were associated with sharp waves linked to sleep spindles (Cox et al., 2020). Based on the dialogue within this hippocampal-amygdala-neocortex network, Richards proposed that cortical NREM spindles had a role in anxiety regulating dynamics, based on the "sleep dialogue" (p. 906) of these three brain structures. What is not yet clear is whether this anxiety regulating effect operates at the limbic level (amygdala), or reaches below that (LC level) to release pre-affective autonomic shock. Importantly, short, fragmented sleep would also undermine this reparative sleep function.

We have already reviewed Eus Van Someren's review of how LC-amygdala circuits continue to be active into REM sleep in people with insomnia, NRS, and PTSD. The continuation of LC-NE activity in REM resulted in restless REM, which disrupts the nightly adaptive remodulation of the amygdala in REM sleep. As a result, mood is not adequately regulated across the nightly shifts between NREM and REM sleep periods. The effect of not silencing the LC during REM prevents the nightly REM based stabilization of the amygdala's affective system.

Fragmentation of sleep and reducing total sleep time has also been shown to impact physical well-being. Harvey Moldofsky and Phillip Scarisbrick (1976) demonstrated that disrupting healthy subjects from sleeping for a few nights, resulted in increased bodily aches and pains in muscles, fascia, and myofascial tissues. Even a few nights of sleeplessness are enough to cause variable musculoskeletal pain. These can present as headaches; neck, shoulder, and back pains; and carpal tunnel syndrome.

Finally, lack of sleep can impact interest in social interaction. Activation of the NGC-LC-orexin-thyroid system will tend to favor withdrawal from possible stress and danger. When we suppress oxytocin release, the stress cascade that releases CRF in the PVN is activated, resulting in increased defensiveness and a social withdrawal pattern.

CLINICAL CASE PRESENTATION OF A FRAGMENTED SHORT SLEEPER

Persistent Post-Concussive Syndrome: Insomnia Returns After Successful Treatment

In the Introduction, we read about Mike's successful EMDR treatment of his insomnia, which had been triggered by a head-on traffic collision. He sustained whiplash and postconcussive symptoms. He was treated with 16 EMDR sessions targeting three specific traumatic memories, described previously. At the time, he said his sleep pattern improved back to about 90% of his pre-accident levels and we terminated treatment.

Figure I.2 in the Introduction documents his sleep in the first 4 months after his accident. In the first month post-accident, his sleep increased to an average of 10.3 hours a night, with little variability in TST. During this time he experienced dizziness and nausea. In the last chapter, we saw the way that intense pain activates a neurochemical dissociative response (release of dynorphin) to disconnect from the pain experience. The hallmark signs of this kappa opioid were dizziness, heaviness, and cognitive confusion.

Mike, like Nancy, noticed that when the dizziness passed, the pain intensity increased. Where would this dynorphin release happen? While there are multiple brain structures in which KOR receptors are expressed, the most important one for maintaining arousal is the PVT. The PVT receives dense projections from both OrxA and DynA neurons (Matzeu et al., 2018). The PVT is mostly a glutamatergic system that promotes wakefulness. Alessandra Matzeu and her colleagues (Matzeu et al., 2018) demonstrated that DynA and OrxA modulated glutamate signaling in opposite directions: DynA decreased glutamate transmission, and OrxA increased glutamate transmission of the PVT. Both neuropeptides solely target glutamate release; however, the Orx system regulates glutamatergic release by modulating a synaptic network, while DynA acts locally on presynaptic networks. Importantly, the Orx inputs to the PVT facilitate cortical arousal that potentiates general arousal and prolonged wakefulness.

In Mike's case, the immediate goal of suppressing pain most likely activated a combination of increased dynorphin to the PVT, suppressing cortical activation and general arousal, resulting in increased sleep. As this modulating effect broke down, the dizziness disappeared, and arousal, headaches, and insomnia increased. While the mechanism for this shift is clearer, what is not clear is what factors led to the fatigue of this modulating effect of dynorphin.

While it is not certain that the above account of dynorphin activity accurately captures the precipitous decline in his total sleep time from 10.3 to less than 3 hours a night, these brainstem structures are the most likely candidates. In addition, there was more variability in his sleep, night to night, with about 5 nights a month in which he did not sleep at all. The other way of stating this is that in the first month of his recovery, the brain injury caused a biologically driven increased need for sleep. Once that underlying restorative physiological repair milieu was no longer available or needed as brain tissues had healed—and was abruptly withdrawn—the brainstem centers driving alarm and defensiveness reasserted themselves. This sharp transition is seen clearly in his sleep data.

The drastically restricted level of TST in the next few months likely has multiple causes. For example, the traumatic memory encoded at the time of the accident (procedural, sensory, and affective responses) would all still be present and actively fueling arousal systems. These memory circuits would continue to activate brainstem NGC-LC-orexin-thyroid responses that were locked in during the traumatic accident, even if these circuits were initially suppressed in an intermediary period by the numbing effects of dynorphin and other reparative immune and neurotransmitter activity.

The drastic effect of the shift in the underlying dynamics is very clear from the sleep data. In Figure I.4, we see the state of Mike's sleep in April, just prior to entering EMDR treatment. In the previous few months, his sleep had improved from 2.8 to 3.5 hours a night, or a very modest improvement of about 13 minutes a month. At this rate, it would take 14 months to get above 6 hours a night.

From April to July, his EMDR treatment continued with weekly meetings. Mike's sleep started improving about 6 weeks into the EMDR sessions, with the inflection point occurring about mid-June. Mike had been taught diaphragmatic breathing in early May, and in early June he was shown the yawning breath and the progressive muscle exercises. Neither of these strategies and tools made a big difference in his TST.

However, Mike had identified three target memories to reprocess, and it was only as we were transitioning into the reprocessing of the second (extreme pain) memory that he reported a felt sense of relief. The third traumatic memory target (of helplessness and hopelessness) was reprocessed a few weeks later. Mike reported that his sleep improved through this latter half of his treatment. EMDR is a very effective treatment in relieving the PAG-affective charge from trauma memories. However, it does not target pre-affective shock specifically as EMDR targets the affective memory system. The effect of releasing these emotional circuits was the accelerated improvement of his sleep from 3 to 6 hours TST at the end of active EMDR treatment.

FIGURE 12.1 Total Sleep Time Between EMDR and DBR Treatments

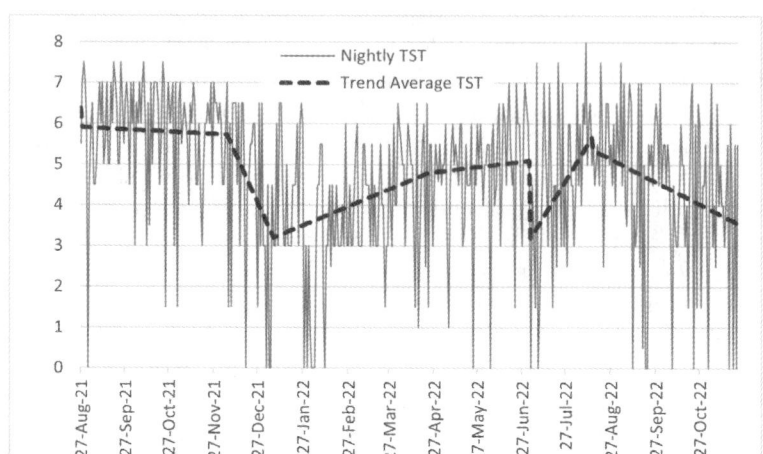

After mid-June there were no nights with no sleep at all, and sleep variability was improved. The last EMDR session was 6 weeks later on July 28th. Across the 3 months of treatment his TST improved from 3.5 to 5.5 hours. In the month after ending active treatment his sleep continued to improve. When he came in for a follow-up meeting on August 25th, his TST was now over 6 hours (Figure I.4). His sleep had continued to improve, which gave us a positive outlook. We both agreed that Mike had reached his treatment goals. He was quite appreciative of the result and treatment was terminated.

Later that year, in November, at about the 1-year anniversary of his accident, his sleep began to deteriorate again. He reached out to me a few months later, as his sleep had continued to steadily deteriorate. I suggested that he go for a sleep test, to rule out sleep apnea. I also wondered whether the return of his insomnia might be due to dysregulation of brain hormonal levels. He went for a full blood screen and received suggestions for modifying his diet and taking supplements.

Figure 12.1 demonstrates the challenges to maintaining the restorative sleep pattern across the year following the completion of the EMDR therapy. There were three times at which his sleep pattern deteriorated noticeably. The first was at the end of November at the anniversary of his accident. His recovery from this setback was slow and incomplete, continuing across the next 6 months. He had COVID at the end of July, and that again impacted his sleep, although he made a reasonable recovery. The third setback reflects his return to full-time work. He had been working 4-day weeks, using his vacation days to take each Wednesday or Thursday off. However, he used up his vacation days at the beginning of August and he began working 5-day workdays. This led to the third deterioration of his sleep. It was at this point that Mike returned for active treatment.

Insights From His Sleep Test

The sleep test showed mild apnea but exceedingly fragmented sleep. The dietary suggestions helped him lose weight, but with no change in his sleep pattern. In addition, his work was particularly difficult, with long hours, impossible demands, and no ability to control his workflow.

We met seven times across the next 9 months, following up with assessing the possible reasons for the setback in his sleep, outlined above. His sleep test result reinforced that he was indeed experiencing severely disrupted sleep. He fell asleep in 46 minutes, supporting the view that his nervous system was hyperaroused. Although he was in bed for 8.5 hours during the test, he only slept for 4.5 hours of that time. Adults his age get over 6 hours of sleep a night. His sleep efficiency was 55%, compared with an age norm of 84%. In short, the increased SNS tone of his autonomic system was only allowing him to sleep just over half the time that he should be sleeping. All of this indicated a sleep-wake system that was skewed toward vigilance and awakening.

The latency to sleep was 46 minutes, or twice as long as normal (<30 min). Once asleep, the latency to his first REM period was 173 minutes, also twice the normal. His hypnogram (a measure of his brain-wave activity) showed: N1 was 7% (the age norm is 12%); N2 78% (age norm is 53%); N3 3% (age norm is 15%); REM 12% (age norm is 20%). Overall, he had plenty of time to sleep, but had difficulty getting to sleep and staying asleep. In addition, once asleep, his brain waves demonstrated that his deepest sleep (both his SWS and REM sleep) were both severely compromised. Most of his sleep period was spent in N2, which is not restorative sleep.

Mike's sleep was fragmented. The number of times he was awakened each hour of his sleep is measured by the arousal index. Mike's arousal index was 13 (age norms are less than 5), of which 3.3 were respiratory-related and 9.8 were spontaneous awakenings. He did not have any periodic leg movements.

Overall, the sleep test allowed us to conclude that his apnea was mild. An AHI of 7.2, with oxygen saturation remaining above 90%, indicates some mild apnea with little clinically relevant desaturation. Although his overall AHI across the night was low (7.2), apneas in REM sleep (34) were severe, while those in NREM (3.5) were not a problem. This high concentration of apneas in REM sleep suggests that Mike may be routinely awakened from REM by these stoppages in breathing. This would explain both the long latency before his first REM period and also lower levels of REM sleep (12% vs. 20%) across the night.

While apneas were not disrupting his total sleep time (TST), Mike's TST was clearly severely disrupted. What was elevated across the night was a hyperactive

SNS autonomic stress system. This was evident in 9.8 spontaneous awakenings each hour.

To summarize, significant and disruptive autonomic hyperarousal was evident in Mike's sleep test, from his long sleep latency (46 vs. <30 min), sleep fragmentation (arousal index of 9.8 vs. <5), short sleep (TST of 4.5 vs. 7+ hours) and low sleep efficiency (55% vs. 84%).

Mike confirmed that he was not experiencing any emotionality or nightmares. We reviewed the sleep test results and I suggested that the autonomic hyperarousal could best be treated with psychotherapy. Neuromodulation of the brainstem through DBR could target the NGC-LC-orexin-thyroid system and might possibly help him in dampening this source of sleep disruption. The rationale for a course of DBR treatment was deduced from these clinical formulations. However, DBR had not previously been used as a treatment for chronic short, fragmented sleep. While DBR has proven effective in a clinical trial for PTSD (Kearney et al., 2023), no RCT for chronic insomnia has yet been conducted. Mike understood the rationale and was open to the treatment. Here is the transcript of his first DBR session.

Transitioning From EMDR to DBR for Postconcussive Syndrome

> THERAPIST: The DBR deals with the initial shock reaction after a traumatic event. It is different from EMDR as it focuses mostly on the body's reaction. That horrifying moment in which you realize something terrible is going to happen. The brain shoots off a message that alerts the whole body. For the whole system to be on the alert. Within milliseconds.
>
> It's pure shock. That file hasn't even made its way up to the thinking brain to be cognizant of it. It is being responded to at the brainstem level. It is a basic instinct for survival.
>
> In our last session you realized the importance of that third visual frame before you hit the other car and blacked out. We did some EMDR reprocessing of that image last time.

Commentary. The first active treatment session in this second block of treatment was a month prior to this appointment. It was an EMDR session. During that session Mike realized that he had had a third "flash" of a visual image before he lost consciousness. The first two (a van pulling out directly in front of him and then seeing the windows right in front) he had remembered in the first block of EMDR treatment a year ago. The new memory that emerged from the previous session was a third image from right before the crash. This he describes as a flat gray screen that he realized was the air bag exploding.

> PATIENT: That was one of the biggest differences that I noticed. My sleep has gone down over December. But it's up over an hour from where I was last

year at this time. So I see it as quite a positive. On top of that, I have not had any headaches this month. The last two years, from late November right through until May it was a nonstop headache. I feel blessed a little that something is correcting itself. It's a sign of getting back to normal.

Sleep has been fluctuating a lot. I had a couple of days in January where I didn't have any sleep. I don't know why. Everything seemed to be okay workwise. My diet was okay.

I didn't sleep the first night after our last session. I don't know if you call it a flashback or if I just thought about that first scene. About the accident.

Previously, it didn't seem to matter how much I wanted to get my mind onto something else. It would keep going to the same loop. Over and over again. Whereas this time, I would go through the loop maybe five or 10 times. And then I would think about something else. And then I would go through the loop again.

But I haven't had that since. I saw that as a positive. It didn't seem to be as overwhelming in terms of taking over my thoughts. That was good.

Commentary. These communications about the discontinuation of both the headaches and ruminative thoughts are important. They are a measure, from one session to the next, of what is changing and what is not changing yet. The fact that the headaches have stopped suggests a decrease in physical tension. What he called flashbacks reflect cognitive intrusions. These reflect increased cortical gamma-wave activity. Persistent gamma waves will prevent shifting into sleep. He noticed that previously these looping thoughts had been outside his conscious control. No matter what he tried, he could not divert his attention from them. After the last session, an EMDR session, he was able to divert into other thoughts, but these thoughts are still disruptive to sleep. We surmise that what has changed is a reduction of the LC-NE activation of the mPFC. That is what was previously fueling the hypervigilant cognitive ruminations.

PATIENT: Sleep for the rest of the month fluctuated between 3 and 6 hours a night. It's unusual. Literally, day-to-day, up and down, night to night.

Just over 4.6 hours a night for the month. That is a big improvement over where it was last year!

THERAPIST: The trend is in the right direction, but with variability. The way I understand it is that the EMDR we did around that third frame before the crash was beginning to relieve the stress that the brain is still carrying. Think of it as a circuit that has gotten supercharged. This rogue circuit in the brain is firing away. One night it has more of an impact, kicking you out of sleep. Another night it prevents you from getting to sleep.

But it does not have anything to do with your work situation, or day-to-day activities. Something is happening deeper down that is destabilizing the autonomic nervous system. When your sleep goes up and down, that is destabilization.

The additional reprocessing we did last month has begun to take some energy out of that circuit.

PATIENT: That was probably one of the two big improvements last year. The other big one was, as silly as it sounds, having a bath and going back to the progressive muscle relaxation exercises. I have cut back on those, but I still do them two or three times a week.

I got to the point where there was nothing left of me. I would work all day, have dinner, and then it was a bath and muscle relaxation, bed, trying to sleep, and then up and go to work again.

Around Christmas time, I found it more emotionally draining. Normally, I would at least get together with some friends, or something. This year, I actually found myself saying, "I've got to pass. Let's just have a phone call, or something." And then I thought, "This is silly." These are my friends, my family; that was tough throughout the holidays. I still had a couple of get-togethers. I saw some good long-term friends.

It is that balance. Knowing you have to heal, but at the same time not going crazy in the process. Or letting your emotions get too down because you're just so isolated, at a time when you really would like to be with your family and friends. That is what Christmas is about for me.

Commentary. This is the first time he has alluded to feeling emotionally drained and feeling detached from others. Previous to the holidays, his normal workweek cycled between work and home repeatedly, so he was not as aware of how he was isolating himself. This is not at all who he is. Both the exhaustion and the isolation reflect the effects of a chronic lack of REM sleep. My hypothesis was that the heightened flashbacks (cognitive gamma-wave activity) reflected a hyperactivated LC-NE-orexin complex, resulting in intermittently fragmented NREM and REM sleep. This would undermine mood, concentration, memory, and interest in social interactions.

PATIENT: It makes you feel a little bit down. But I got through it. My energy level is up. It is not where I'd like it to be. But it's certainly higher than it has been in quite a while. Despite my sleeping being down, I have more energy this month than I did last month. Maybe I am just catching up, recharging or something. I don't know what it is. But it seems to be going in the right direction.

Commentary. Improving energy suggests that sleep quality may be beginning to improve. This combined with the relief from headaches suggests that the last EMDR session helped desensitize the affective intensity of his memories, but may not have reduced the pre-affective shock reactions to any great degree.

PATIENT: The other thing I've noticed this past month is my memory seems a little better. Back in October every time I had a conversation with my son, 5 minutes later he would have fun with me. He'd ask me, "What were we just talking about?" And nine times out of 10, I would have absolutely no clue. It was fun for him. But for me, embarrassing. I couldn't remember what I was talking about.

This month it has been better. I've been involved in a fairly large project at work. Overall I think I've done okay. A lot better than the previous few months. That's another positive sign.

Commentary. Another indicator of less hyperarousal and better cognitive focus. While improvements from the EMDR were encouraging, we continued with our plan of switching to DBR, to target the LC-NE system more directly. With the update completed the therapist moves to identify a target for DBR reorienting.

Step 1: Identifying the Activating Event

THERAPIST: I want you to go to all three visual pre-accident images to see what is present. What way are they activating for you?
PATIENT: When I think about the first frame, it is consciously knowing and feeling, "I'm going to hit" and wondering how hard? I go to the second frame, and now I can feel my body tensing up. When I go to the third frame, which I didn't notice back in December, I notice the back of my neck tensing up. I have no idea why.
THERAPIST: What we are going to try to catch is the first moment of realization, of "I am going to hit." That is where we will go, to see what is going on in the body. Before we go back to that we will do some grounding.

The DBR stages 2, 3, and 4 (of grounding and activating the memory circuit) were done with the standard DBR protocol, as described in Chapter 9. We move to the tracking of the shock reactions into the body.

Step 5: Allowing Space for the Patient to Track Their Pre-Affective Shock Responses

The following edited transcript skips about 20 seconds of silence between each patient response as the patient silently processes his experiences.

PATIENT: My stomach feels like it is in a knot. The lower back of my neck is almost a band or strain. That got stronger. I had the odd little strain in my arms and toward the end a strain in my right leg as well. But the dominant strain was definitely in the back of my neck and in my stomach.

THERAPIST: You're picking up some additional aftershocks in certain muscle groups. You are feeling it, particularly in the stomach. That's the beginning of the emotional response. But before we get to the emotions, we want to make sure that all of these physical tensions, these bands of strain, are clear. Notice if you can go back to the tension in your neck, because that's the initial signal. Notice whatever way it's still there. As things pop up in your awareness, tell me what you're noticing.

PATIENT: The back of my neck feels not only strained but it feels heavy, if that makes any sense. Almost like there's a weight pushing down on the back of my neck. And I'm still feeling little spasms in my arms.

Now there is a slight strain going up from the back of my neck up into my head; very slight. A heavy load on the back of my neck.

THERAPIST: As you're noticing it, particularly if it feels like it's increasing or getting uncomfortable, you can breathe. Just do some nice slow releasing breaths to see if anything changes in terms of that tension.

PATIENT: It's pretty tense.

THERAPIST: Just sit with the tension. This is slow motion, noticing where the nervous system is holding this tension.

PATIENT: It feels like the longer I'm focusing on it, the more pervasive it is. Not only the lower back band of my neck but almost into my neck then. If that makes any sense. It's not a surface pain. It's deep in my neck as well.

THERAPIST: It's recruiting muscles deeper in the neck. Go with that. Allow your awareness to sit with what's coming up.

PATIENT: My neck area is the part that is strained, almost feels like it's growing. It's expanding. Slightly up. Deeper into my neck, almost into my throat. And only two thirds, three quarters of the way up the back of my neck. But still strongest around that bottom band and inwards.

THERAPIST: You're noticing how it's beginning to shift and where it's going to. Just noticing, being curious, witnessing.

PATIENT: It's slowly creeping up to my lower head at the back. Also even more strain toward the middle of my neck or toward my throat, to the front. Nothing on my shoulders, or arms, or legs. It's all in my neck, and then sort of drifting into the lower part of my head. Now even toward the bottom of my ears, I almost feel it in my teeth. I can't quite explain that one but literally it's sort of a strain going into my teeth. I don't know if this makes any sense to you.

THERAPIST: It may be it's tracking the progression, the kind of flow of the nervous energy through the nervous system from the moment you recognize the impact to when you did make impact and your head, and your teeth, hit the airbag. There would have been some pretty intense signals going back to the brain. But we're not judging anything and we're not looking for any logic. We're allowing the nervous system to release the energy. It's made a map of where all of this impacted you, and how intense the impact was. We're allowing that map to rise up to your awareness. The same as with the EMDR, once you become aware of it, you feel the sensations, the actual experience can begin to melt away and no longer be kept in storage.

PATIENT: It's continuing to creep up. It's in the upper part of the back of my head and it's even coming around to the front of my forehead. Still strong with the lower neck though, probably still the strongest part.

Now the strain is starting in the front of my head. Also increasing in the back of my head quite sharply. Pain is now almost behind my eyes. Still at the back of the head, too, at the back of the neck.

Now a strain up the side of my neck up toward the back. Right up to my ears, the bottom of my ears. Evolving almost to the point of my whole head feeling like there's pressure inside my head. And almost feels warmer, or hot. Now I am very strained up by my spine in my neck. Particularly at the bottom of the neck.

Now a stiffening feeling in my neck. Not just the pain but it almost feels like the ability for my neck to move is locked.

Moving toward the front of my eyes, my eyebrows. Movement of pain, or strain, seems to be stabilized, where it just feels like my head is under a lot of pressure. Like from the inside out.

Now definitely seems to have stabilized. Pressure inside my head. And it literally feels warm.

THERAPIST: That might be from the stress reaction. The body heats up. So it's stabilized, and it's stopped changing now?

PATIENT: I still have a band of strain at the back of the bottom of my neck. My head itself feels like it's under a state of internal pressure.

THERAPIST: What do you make of that? What do you think is going on? It's very much a slow-motion kind of watching as things change. But what's changing? These are all maps that your brain has made of body sensations. So all of this is below your thinking brain level. That's the way we understand it. Is it a somatic memory? It's a real memory the same as, for example, "I was holding a ball in my hand" is a memory. Only this is a physical sensation. Something that's stored in the body or the body's memory. We began with the accident. You laid out that initial map. That brought up other maps that the brain has made. What was your experience of tracking it and watching it?

PATIENT: If I were to try to make sense of it, it's tracking the strains in my head and neck as it was going through the motions of the collision. I don't know why the back of my neck hurt the most. Except maybe my head swung forward.

THERAPIST: It comes forward first, and then it swings back into the headrest.

PATIENT: Maybe just the jolt forward, but then the fact that it went around my eyes was kind of weird. If you have an air bag exploding in front of you then that makes sense. That would probably hit your whole head. Or the better part of it. The stress around my throat was interesting. Stress, or strain, deep into my neck as opposed to just surface stress. That was unexpected.

THERAPIST: What it tells me is that this is all of the muscle groups tensing, engaging, all of the muscles, not just superficial, but the deepest level of the muscle. All of those being activated with this kind of surge of bracing, holding, trying to protect the brain and body from collision. As you got to the end, and you said it felt like pain inside the head, I thought after the whiplash back and forth, inside the head there's going to be some swelling, some inflammation. Or the warmth from the adrenaline spike.

PATIENT: Makes sense. The temperature was odd. Even now I feel my head is quite warm. I guess I never even thought of it that way.

THERAPIST: The body is smarter than you and I put together. It doesn't throw random sensations at you. This is what it remembers. Because it made the map when you were unconscious. And if the theory of what's happening is right, what's happening is that you witness what the brain saved. The right side of the brain is where body memories are saved. And now that you're engaging your left side, you're witnessing the brain. That conscious reflection allows the left side to integrate the experience. At least in theory, the brainstem should now be able to begin to let go of those stored maps: of tension in the neck, in the head, around the eyes, in the face. That's the theory. You'll tell us what happens in real life.

PATIENT: Do we go through multiple iterations of this? Or do we try it for a few weeks to see what happens?

THERAPIST: Try for a few weeks. You've been really good at tracking, so let it tell its story. We can meet again, in 3 or 4 weeks and see where your sleep got to, and if we need to do more work.

Now the question is, how does that release of those memories translate into the brainstem and the brain actually now being able to get into a deeper rest without that kind of background irritation from these circuits that have been holding on to the pain and tension? So, we'll see. You're part of a real-life investigation.

PATIENT: Even as I was going through the exercise, there were no emotions to it. It was just purely trying to follow where the strain was moving around in my head. It was just interesting.

THERAPIST: Frank Corrigan, who developed deep brain reorienting, calls it "pre-affective shock." "Affects" of course are the emotions: like fear, happiness, anger, sadness, guilt, grief, all of those are affects. But this is all pre-affective shock. It is real. It is held in the body. It is a big disruptor of sleep. So you are a kind of guinea pig. I am hoping this therapy works. You have done your part by doing such a good job of tracking what your body experienced. Now we will wait to see what your sleep is like.

Email Describing His Experiences After the First DBR Session

Before the next session, the patient sends this email:

> Our last session was one of the most powerful ones I have had with you yet.
>
> It was an experience that left me with a deepened sense of reality as to what happened to me physically during the collision. I left our meeting believing that perhaps we have unlocked another key piece of the puzzle.
>
> While the night right after our session, I obtained zero sleep (go figure!?!), the following four nights I had 6 hours per night! This month so far, I am at about 4.7 hours per night, which is more than 1.5 hours better than both of the past 2 years. Significant progress.
>
> I have more stability in my sleep patterns. My sleep was up and down from one night to the next. Now I'm up for 3 or 4 nights, then down for 3 or 4 nights. It's easier to manage. My short-term memory has improved, a big win, as long as that continues.
>
> No resurgence of headaches. I had nonstop headaches for months. Their absence makes a huge difference. My energy level is still low, albeit a slight improvement (maybe topping off at 50%?). I also had an odd incident just over a couple of weeks ago—a lack of strength and a numb feeling or pain in my left arm, from my shoulder down to a tingling feeling in my fingertips. I went to a clinic and then the ER. A CT scan turned out negative; however, they would still like to do an MRI, which is scheduled for next week. They have asked me to take aspirin and Plavix, but somehow, I don't think it was a stroke. I still have a tingling feeling in the fingertips of my left hand. I would think that should have gone away by now (?).
>
> Otherwise, all okay.
> Mike

Transcript of the Therapy Session Later That Day

THERAPIST: You said that the last session was one of the most powerful ones that you've had.

PATIENT: When you think of a collision and hitting an airbag, you think of your forehead hitting something hard, whether it's the airbag or the steering wheel, but the feelings that I went through during that session we of pain in my teeth, and right around my eye sockets. I thought, "Wow! It is not just your forehead. It is clearly probably your whole head and your upper body." It gives you a different perspective.

THERAPIST: You can't make that stuff up. You are tuning into what your where self is giving you as a flow of information. It comes from inside. From the way your body memory was registered.

PATIENT: It was very pronounced, considering this is more than 2 years later.

I'm very surprised how something that is so relatively simple in terms of therapy can evoke such a very strong feeling physically.

THERAPIST: It is harnessing the power of the mind and the brain to work for your recovery, for integrating your experience. That means going back to what happened. Being open to it is like opening a file to what experiences and sensations come up.

Your email said the night after the session, you didn't sleep at all.

PATIENT: I went to bed, and I thought, "I'm going to have a great night's sleep." Then I lay awake the entire night. Completely wide awake. That was the exact opposite of what I was expecting after having had a really good session. But the following 4 nights I had 6 hours of sleep each night.

Commentary. Since this session, I have found that an activated night of little sleep is a common experience after sessions releasing pre-affective shock. *There is a lightness and energy that seems to be available, energy that is no longer being drained by dread and fear.*

PATIENT: During our last session I said that in January I was literally up and down every night. One night would be okay and the next night would be very poor. Then the next night would be okay. The last three weeks, it's been three or four nights good and then three or four nights bad. Then back to good. It has been much more moderate, much more stable. Not necessarily all good, but more stable. I find much easier to navigate through my day. I don't have to worry about, "Am I going to have a good night's sleep, or a poor night's sleep?" There is now some predictability, that if I have had a bad night, I'll probably have two or three more bad nights. I can plan around that. That helps.

My energy is still low. M headaches have been gone for a while. It is mainly just the sleep. I was hoping my energy would pop up more. I am still having many days where I just want to go hibernate somewhere. Go to bed in the late afternoon.

I had a strange, not bad pain. It was a numbing pain in my left arm. I thought, "Okay, this is odd." Pain in my left arm is usually never a good thing. I thought it might be linked to how I use my computers. I work on my laptop, and I've been working at home for almost 3 years now. Maybe it was an awkward position. Many years ago I had carpal tunnel in my right arm. But after a while, I shook it off. I did some stretching exercises.

But this was different. The carpal tunnel was just sort of in my forearm and my wrist. This was all the way from my shoulder down to my fingertips. I went to a clinic, thinking they're going to tell me, "It is just carpal tunnel." And they said, "No, you better go to Emergency and get it checked out."

Nine hours later, they said, "The CT scan came back negative, but we'll send it to the neurologist and see what they say." Last week I went to a neurologist. He said, "I am not really sure. So we'll do an MRI just to be on the safe side." That is next.

THERAPIST: From everything you have noted, the changes have been positive. It did not cure everything. It is definitely trending in a way that we want.

I don't know for sure about the experience you are describing in the left arm. You said numbness was a part of it. It could be something your autonomic system is doing.

It could be related to a surge in sympathetic activity, where there is an increase in bracing or activation. And then it creates different spin-off sensations. It might be related to the accident itself.

If we learned anything from our last session, it is that the brain has kept very close internal record of how things felt 2 years ago. Moment by moment, for example, as you hit the airbag with your teeth. Who knows where this kind of feeling down the left arm may come from? It may be another piece of those memory fragments that relate to what happened back then.

And so it can be something that you and I can do another round of DBR with.

PATIENT: I didn't even think it was related to our last session.

I thought if it is something to do with me working on my computer, why now? All of a sudden. I've been doing this for 3 years the same way. It has been a couple of weeks, but I can still feel tingling in my fingers.

I don't think it was a stroke. I didn't feel any traditional stroke symptoms other than a weird feeling in my head and my left arm.

THERAPIST: With a stroke, you are going to feel weakness on one side. Or you might also notice that there's some slurring if you're speaking.

PATIENT: No slurring. The weakness was definitely in my arm, but only in my left arm. The rest of me was fine. They did the normal tests. All that was fine.

But even now, 2 weeks later, my fingers are still tingling. I have no idea what is causing it.

THERAPIST: How did you first notice it?

PATIENT: I usually start work 7:30 to 8 o'clock in the morning. Actually, now that you mention it, the prior week I noticed discomfort in my left arm.

But I thought, "Okay, it's probably just because I've been cramped up working on my laptop." On top of a dining room table is never ideal. When your hands are up. Doing that all day long.

The weekend came around and it was fine. On Monday maybe an hour after I started working I noticed it again. It came along fairly quickly and was much more pronounced than it had been previously. The previous week it was almost nothing. On Monday, I really noticed something wrong with my left arm. To the point where I was even typing incorrectly. You know, when you type and all of a sudden, your letters don't work between your right hand and your left hand.

Weakness and numbness, and my typing on the left hand was lagging by two or three characters to my right hand. The left hand was not keeping up with the right hand. What I was reading as I was typing did not make sense.

THERAPIST: A difference in terms of the reaction time: you are sending the information down to your fingers to type the word, say banana. But your left hand isn't typing the letters at the right time. The right hand is jumping ahead. So that is like there is a transmission problem, from the brain to the fingers. The tingling is another feature, or another part of what you felt.

PATIENT: I still feel the tingling in my fingers now. I have most of the strength in my left arm, but it's not 100%. I am thinking, "They asked me to take aspirin and Plavix." Normally, I would have taken that. I would think there was some sort of blockage, or something. So why am I still feeling the tingling in my fingers?

THERAPIST: Let's work on the hypothesis that there is still something else. That it will be beneficial to do more of the deep brain reorienting work. It seemed to create some positive changes.

When you think back about that whole sequence (and I know some of it happened pretty quickly), there may not be any distinct images. But as you allow your mind to go back to the things that happened, what exactly is grabbing your attention? A moment of maybe holding your breath? Or noticing that something dangerous or difficult is happening.

PATIENT: The whole thing still gives me that feeling that all of a sudden out of nowhere, this minivan decides to turn in front of me! I think about it now fairly calmly, but it still evokes some emotions in me.

THERAPIST: See if there is a moment that stands out for you. That something is activating for you. Attention grabbing. Anything in particular that is standing out for you right now?

PATIENT: Most of all the first frame. Where I saw the front corner of the minivan all of a sudden turn in front of me. That triggered a very fast response in my body. Maybe not fast enough.

Everything was going along smooth and steady. Keeping an eye on someone that I thought might turn in front of me. Or are they not going to turn? Okay, they are not going to turn. I am just continuing along. And then, all of a sudden . . .

THERAPIST: Surprise, right?

PATIENT: There they were!

THERAPIST: That is where we will go. But before we get to that, I am going to walk us through connecting in with your where self. Then we can see how the reactions unfold. Sit comfortably, while noticing your sense of being here.

And so that session continued with another round of deep brain reorienting. After this session, we met for another nine sessions, seven of which included DBR reorienting to the body memories stored in his right brain. With each session, Mike tracked his sleep and other symptoms. He continued to notice changes in his sleep. Our last follow-up meeting was 6 months after his first DBR session.

DISCUSSION OF MANAGEMENT OF FRAGMENTED SHORT SLEEPERS

Resolution of Implicit Memories of Accident-Related Autonomic Arousal

In that follow-up meeting in July, Mike related that he had been on a kayaking trip in the wilderness. A supercell storm had hit him and his group. Intense winds and hail pummeled them. He said he did not fall asleep that night, but the next night he slept 5 hours, and after that has been sleeping 7 hours a night. In that month, his total sleep time averaged 6.2 hours a night.

This suggests that his stress system responded to the unexpected and intense storm with an alarm response. However, his autonomic system was able to reset properly after the event, without evidence of continued activation and looping of the LC-NE with the orexin-thyroid systems and resulting in chronically restricted sleep.

Let's now consider the implications of this successful treatment of a particularly protracted and severe case of persistent postconcussive syndrome (PPCS). The first important point to make is that this patient had no preexisting psychiatric symptoms. The traumatic accident resulted in particularly intense physical postconcussive symptoms. His sleep was severely disrupted for many months. In addition, he felt easily fatigued, struggled with recurrent headaches, and had noise sensitivities. However, he did not develop any psychiatric symptoms. The successful outcome of Mike's neuromodulatory DBR treatment indicates that this treatment may be equally effective for psychiatric as well as PPCS patients.

On the PCL-5 his score at the very beginning of the first round of treatment was 11, which was largely accounted for by three items: severe problems with sleep, moderate difficulties with hypervigilance, and feeling distant and cut off from other people. His SCI score was 6/32, suggesting chronic insomnia since the accident. His PSAS scores were high in the cognitive arousal domain (21/40) (consistent with intrusive cognitive ruminations), but not in the physical arousal scales (11/40). The only items endorsed on the later scale were moderate levels of cold feelings in hands, feet, and body, and a slight sensation of dry feelings in the mouth and throat. Both the activation of cognitive arousal as well as the two physical symptoms are consistent with a continued alarm response in the LC-NE nucleus.

Considering his lack of psychiatric symptoms pre- or post-accident, as well as the absence of any significant level of physiological arousal (which would be more typical of a patient with developmental PTSD), this case represents a rare situation. The main issue is severe sleep disturbance, perpetuated by the underlying activation of the autonomic alarm response (LC-NE) and most likely augmented by hyperactivated looping through orexin-thyroid signaling.

With such a specific, uncomplicated target for treatment, the outcome achieved both in the first round of EMDR treatment as well as this second round of DBR is instructive. We can conceptualize the overall treatment as having three phases. A first block of active treatment of emotional dysregulation (13 EMDR sessions across 3 months). The desensitization of emotional distress was very helpful, and his sleep pattern improved to the point that active treatment was discontinued (see Figure I.4).

This was followed by a period of no treatments, during which symptoms returned as Mike coped with three different stressors (see Figure 12.2). The first was the anniversary of the accident in November. This anniversary reaction hit him as hard as the accident itself had the year before: TST dropped from 5 hours a night down to 3 hours in a month's time. He recovered slowly across a 6-month period, with TST going back up to about 5 hours a night.

Mike contracted COVID in July and his TST again bottomed out at 3 hours a night. This time he recovered to 5.5 hours TST within 6 weeks. However, the serious and persistent background workplace stress gradually overwhelmed him. He had returned to work on modified hours, working 4 days a week. He had financial support from his short-term disability plan. This support allowed him to work 2 days, take Wednesday off, and then work another 2 days. This made it possible for him to focus and be productive.

This financial support ran out in July, and Mike had to return to a full-time, 5-day workweek. He appealed the insurance decision, but it was denied. With the stress of the added work hours, no midweek recovery time, and added workplace responsibilities from new projects and attrition of team members, his sleep began another gradual downhill slide.

Mike contacted me seven months later and we met monthly for eight visits. We considered whether he had apnea. He went for a sleep test, which was negative. Mike was also referred to a neurologist for further tests and diagnostics. These did not yield any results. His sleep problems remained and were getting more serious. By the end of that year, we decided on a second course of treatment.

His response to DBR treatment is documented in Figure 12.2. Despite beginning treatment in February, his sleep was unchanged for 6 weeks and then deteriorated till early May. In May, Mike had had enough of the work stress and handed in his resignation. He said he slept 7.5 hours that night! From that point on, his sleep continued to consolidate.

Figure 12.1 illustrated the impact of three life stresses on his sleep. Overall,

Putting Trauma to Sleep

these setbacks underline that after a traumatic event (whether it be physical, mental, or emotional) the mind becomes vulnerable to other stresses. The therapeutic perspective is that treatment of sleep difficulties in trauma is synonymous with treatment of autonomic dysregulation. All stresses currently impacting the person must also be addressed (along with the trauma work) if full resolution of the sleep disturbance is to be achieved. *The important message here is that trauma increases the vulnerability to chronic insomnia because of the unresolved implicit memories of the shock reactions.*

The modulation of the brainstem, achieved through DBR treatments con-

FIGURE 12.2   Total Sleep Time Before and During DBR Treatment

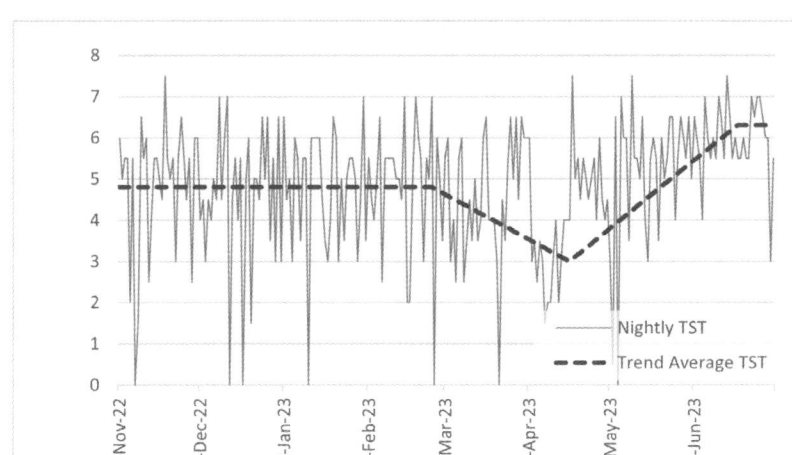

tinued through June and were effective in continuing to release the shock responses around the accident memories. After the turning point of Mike's resignation from his highly stressful workplace, his sleep continued to improve, reaching an average of just over 6 hours a night. It was only when the background pre-affective shock reactions were resolved, *and* his highly stressful current job ended that the brainstem autonomic system was able to stabilize to a restorative sleep-wake pattern.

A follow-up session 2 months later confirmed that his sleep was continuing to improve. Mike has continued to track any changes. He provided the data in Figure 12.3, which tracks his TST since the end of his DBR treatment. For the first time in 2 years, Mike was able to maintain a TST above 6 hours per night. In early November he attended a court hearing about his motor vehicle accident. Unsurprisingly, this stressful event resulted in his TST dropping. However, it did not drop as much (only 4 hours vs. 3 on all previous setbacks). In addition, he recovered again to above the 6 hours TST within a 6-week time period.

Finally, it should be noted that the change across treatment was not only in the average TST. It was also evident in the variability of his sleep each night. For example, up until the midpoint of his DBR treatments, he was still experiencing at least one night each month of no sleep at all. Since he resigned his job, there has only been one night with no sleep at all. In addition, the variability of his nightly TST times have been increasingly tighter around his mean sleep time. Even when he had his recent court stress, there were no nights of no sleep. Both the total sleep has improved and so has the consistency of his sleep.

Resolution of Autonomic Arousal in PTSD and PPCS

FIGURE 12.3   Total Sleep Time After DBR Therapy: 5 Month Follow-Up

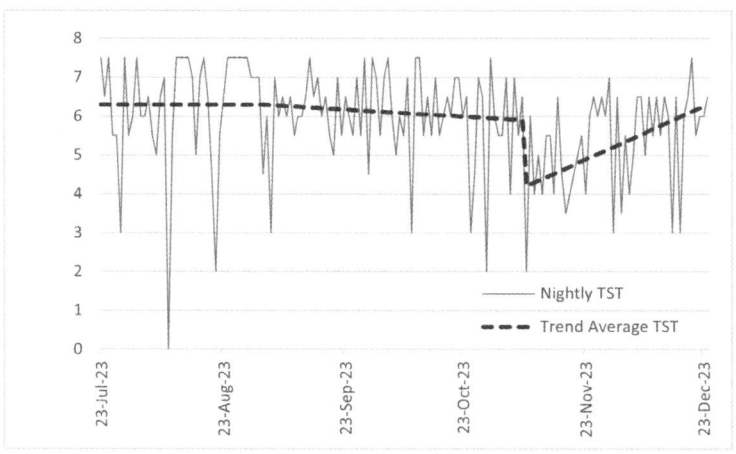

Often PTSD and persistent postconcussive syndrome (PPCS) coexist. Many PTSD patients have suffered undiagnosed concussions in the traumatizing situations they have encountered from abusers who have punched, slapped, kicked, or beaten them. Mike's case provides some evidence that for both conditions; a hyperaroused NGC-LC-orexin-thyroid system may be the root cause of sleep disturbances in both conditions. PPCS-related chronic insomnia has been a particularly difficult condition to treat, and outcomes have not been very encouraging for patients. When Mike met with concussion specialists, he was given antidepressant medications and was told there was not much that could be done.

This case demonstrates that neuromodulation through DBR therapy may successfully resolve at least the sleep disruption present in many PPCS patients. As well, in this case other PPCS symptoms like headache and sensitivities to noise and smells were resolved as sleep improved, and presumably the brainstem hyperactivity patterns stabilized. This outcome is very encouraging as a novel and new treatment option for postconcussive patients. While it is not expected that all patients with postconcussive symptoms can be treated within 10 sessions, it is encouraging and should be submitted for further clinical testing.

More important than the number of sessions is the fact that any treatment at all was of value in resolving persistent symptoms of PPCS such as chronic insomnia and sensory sensitivities. There are thousands of patients suffering with these symptoms after accidents of various types. That there could be an effective treatment targeting the brainstem region (similar to MIke's condition) causing such treatable autonomic hyperarousal is potentially a game changer for these patients.

Key Messages for Therapists

1. Wakefulness is mediated by the NGC and medial reticular formation working in concert with the LC. Many neurons in the LC integrate receptors for CRF and endogenous opioids. The interplay of these two endocrines allows for immediate responsiveness to threat as well as feedback loops to stabilize LC-NE tonic activation. However, these feedback loops can become dysregulated from trauma, with the result that LC-NE activity becomes chronically hyperaroused, disrupting normal cognitive and sleep functions.
2. The short, disrupted sleep phenotype of chronic insomnia, characterized by fragmented sleep and high cognitive arousal, results from amplified brainstem circuits (NGC-LC-orexin-thyroid) synergistically reinforcing each other, causing impaired sleep, and increasing risks for cognitive and physical symptoms.
3. Trauma-induced brainstem activation floods the right hemisphere with raw, amorphous arousal, its intensity threatening to overwhelm the integrity of the left hemisphere autobiographical memory system. These memory fragments remain dissociated, preventing integration of coherent narrative memory. The therapeutic attachment bond allows the patient courage to face these fragmented sensory and procedural memories (pre-affective shocks). As these shock reactions and emotions are experienced, the LC is silenced and the autonomic engine to persistent insomnia is gradually resolved.
4. Neuromodulation through DBR therapy targets brainstem processes specifically by reactivating traumatic memories and tracking the body's locked-in shock reactions that maintain autonomic hyperarousal. The release of these memory fragments through DBR therapy results in resetting of the autonomic system by dampening SNS tone, improved sleep, and reduction in trauma symptoms.
5. DBR has potential as a novel treatment for chronic insomnia as well as persistent postconcussive syndrome. DBR is a promising new neuroscientifically guided psychotherapy for trauma triggered by physical (heart attacks and PPCS), mental (nightmares and cognitive intrusions), and emotional (terror, rage, grief, guilt, or shame) events.

Epilogue: Integrating Sleep Repair Into Your Trauma Treatment

"We can see the characteristics of sleep and dreams that work well in managing changes to the cognitive and emotional organizational schemas that guide behavior. . . . There is a continuity of our mental lives across the 24-hour cycle. . . . The mind keeps working throughout the cycles of changes in brain activity, with only a hint of some 'time off' in the deepest of slow wave sleep."
—Rosalyn Cartwright (2010, p. 178, italics added)

"In my opinion dreams can be immensely useful in what is our most important task—self-knowledge."
—Ernest Hartmann (1999, p. 16)

This book has focused its discussion on how the four TABS (trauma, attachment, body symptoms, and sleep) are interrelated aspects of traumatic experiences, and how each of these four elements must be addressed to successfully resolve trauma. Of these four elements, it is sleep that has been universally neglected in trauma treatment guidelines that currently exist, and so it has been elaborated in this text to demonstrate how it is a necessary part of trauma treatments.

Specifically, a traumatic experience has activated an autonomic sympathetic storm with implicit memory fragments of procedural, sensory, and emotional bodily states. Our survival demands that these fragments be locked into implicit traumatic memories (most of them out of our conscious view), and safely apart from the nightly emotional repair machinery of restorative NREM-REM sleep, which Rosalyn Cartwright describes. The dissociative impact of dynorphin is particularly well suited to exclude these traumatic wounds from our reparative sleep, as restorative sleep would quickly dissolve these fragments into our integrated self.

The range of sleep disturbances (from most to least intense) include night terrors, sleepwalking, intrusive thoughts/replicative nightmares, insomnia, nonrestorative sleep, symbolic nightmares, and finally dreams of decreasing emotional intensity. As we help our trauma clients heal, we reintroduce them to the integrative, healing, psychophysiological balm of stable NREM-REM sleep. As Ernest Hartmann points out, only healthy sleep, with its NREM-REM restorative integrative capability, gives us the dreams through which we truly know ourselves. These allow the continuous digestion of our procedural, sensory, and emotional experiences, to provide a solid pathway towards self-knowledge rooted in our embodied self.

Part II of this book has highlighted how sleep interventions can be incorporated into the trauma treatments being provided by trauma therapists. This material is meant to show trauma therapists how they can become more effective in treating all of their trauma patients. Among the skills identified in Part II is the clinical identification and management of major roadblocks to trauma treatment (like sleep apnea) that will seriously undermine the progress of the client regardless of what trauma treatment, modality, or technique is being administered. Guiding your client by synchronizing sleep-wake rhythms of the dysregulated trauma patient is as vital as basic CBTi interventions. Furthermore, the resolution of the underlying dysregulated autonomic nervous system, which has been elaborated in the last four chapters of Part II, requires addressing within trauma therapy, as the root cause of the dysregulation.

The autonomic dysregulation begins in the brainstem, with the neurological cascade initiated by the LC-NE system. Without directly addressing this root cause, the sleep disturbances and traumatic symptoms can repeatedly return. This was illustrated by the case example of Mike. EMDR is highly effective in reducing the affective distress of trauma survivors, and it did so for Mike as well. Mike had completed a successful EMDR treatment and his sleep and trauma problems remitted.

However, addressing the affective circuits alone was not enough to insulate Mike from subsequent autonomic dysregulation that reactivated the brainstem arousal system (NGC-LC-orexin-thyroid complex), thus reactivating his sleep problems. Similarly, talk therapy and treatments that focus on the higher level cognitive functions, like the linguistic narrative left-brain circuits, also are not going to turn off the LC-NE. Mike's experience was similar to the phenomenon of a delayed onset of PTSD symptoms after an initial traumatic event.

We surmised that the underlying shock reactions initiated in the autonomic circuits reactivated Mike's sleep disturbance, and we treated this putative target with DBR psychotherapy. DBR was developed to explicitly activate those autonomic circuits and release the *shock reactions* initiated by the LC-NE. The interventions with Mike were successful, which underlines the critical importance of integrating such treatments into the skill set of both trauma and sleep therapists.

Focusing trauma treatment on the shock reactions generated by the LC-NE is not exclusive to DBR treatment. Peter Levine has provided the same rationale for first addressing and releasing the shock reactions of procedural memories (Levine, 2015, Chapter 6, Ray's Epilogue), before affective experiences are addressed in treatment. Moreover, this issue is not merely a difference of tactical strategies in doing successful treatment. *It is a matter of first resetting the autonomic dysregulation before addressing the other affective issues in treatment.*

The cases presented in this book were chosen to also demonstrate the value of resolving LC-NE dysregulation in patient populations that have not generally shown good outcomes to other treatment modalities. In particular, these are postconcussive symptoms, the disabling symptoms of neurochemical dissociation, which are part of the sequalae of both medical events like heart attacks and childhood traumatic experiences. These case studies demonstrate that some of these patients can be helped to overcome their disabling symptoms. These insights will have to be demonstrated in proper clinical trials and corroborated by other trauma therapists with their work.

Integrating Sleep Into Trauma Treatment Is Essential for a Successful Resolution

Returning now to where this book began, we can provide a deeper, clearer answer to Bonnie Badenoch's question, "What can happen in the interpersonal system and in the individual mind to encourage integration to emerge?" (Badenoch, 2008, p. 51) All psychotherapists assist in this integrative process by providing a safe, attuned environment in which the patient can revisit and make sense of their lives. Their shared goal is assisting the patient in better integrating their experiences. In all clinical cases reviewed in this book, this meant returning to the most difficult moments in their lives. Revisiting these moments and allowing the patients to remember what their bodies experienced was critical in the process of silencing the core arousal system, the LC-NE, and the cascade of brainstem, thalamic, and cortical systems that this alarm center activates after trauma. All the clinical cases presented throughout Part II demonstrate that this revisiting provides the necessary neuromodulatory experiences to reset the brainstem.

These brainstem reactions constitute the brain's primary survival system. Trauma and sleep go hand in hand. The traumatized brain will not let a person sleep deeply, and they cannot experience restorative NREM and REM sleep. In trauma, the activated LC-NE alarm becomes the day and night vigilance system that tries to keep a person safe from danger. Neither the daytime trauma symptoms nor the hyperactivated brainstem circuits disturbing sleep are erased with time. They might slowly become attenuated but can easily become retriggered by future stressful events and traumas. In some cases we can remove ourselves from environments in which they may be triggered. But they do not silence themselves on their own, even after decades.

Relief can only come with the difficult task of revisiting these traumatic moments. The case examples provided in this book are meant to underscore that such relief does not come from thinking about the past or talking about experiences. Relief comes from the direct bodily experience of what the nervous system was doing, moment to moment, during the traumatic experience. When the patient realizes that they can do this, with the attuned presence of the therapist, the underlying shock responses are silenced; the activated emotional responses are fully experienced; and all three elements (procedural, sensory, and emotional) are integrated into a coherent episodic memory. At this point, the brainstem structures can stabilize and support ongoing integration of new experiences.

When these LC-NE brainstem-initiated reactions are silenced, the restorative processes of NREM and REM sleep can resume and restore the brain's natural tendency to explore the world, integrate experience, and make meaning of one's life. This outcome is evident from the patients' renewed ability to identify and manage emotions, develop and improve relationships, control behavior, and imagine and plan a future for themselves.

Trauma Dysregulates the Autonomic System

We have highlighted in this book that explosive traumatic events dysregulate the autonomic system. It does not matter whether the traumatic events are recent (like Mike's motor vehicle accident; Nancy, Mary, and Allan's heart attacks; and Sally's painful experience of her husband's tortured final months), or whether they happened decades ago (like Esteban's terror of being killed, or Julie's horror that she had deformed herself). In all cases, *the effects of these events are cumulative*, and they trigger an intense alarm reaction in the LC-NE. The LC-NE sets off a cascade of other brainstem physiological responses, which get permanently locked into brain circuits that have the aim of protecting the individual from such overwhelming dangers occurring again.

This intense autonomic dysregulation from trauma undermines both NREM and REM (Antila et al., 2022). The disruption occurs with fragmentation of NREM sleep through activation of POA glutamatergic neurons that increase microarousals and awakenings from NREM sleep. It is also evident in the disruption of REM sleep, replacing it with a restless REM sleep that is repeatedly fragmented by persistence of LC-NE activity. This prevents the remodeling of the amygdala and limbic responses to environmental conditions and full recovery from trauma.

Targeting the Dysregulated Autonomic System in Psychotherapy

Only after the LC-NE alarm system is silenced can the restorative physiological process that the mind and body rely on be renewed—to restore energy, to update long-term memory maps, and to provide new emotional experiences to the amygdala to habituate and revise earlier emotional reactivity. All of that is necessary to prepare for a future not subjugated by a dysregulated autonomic nervous system.

We have proposed that sleep is that latent background physiological, restorative process that provides a foundation for all of these developments. Beginning to be able to think about a future, and decide to move toward that future, requires a deep connection with one's embodied sense of self. As Rosalyn Cartwright highlighted in her book *The 24-Hour Mind* (2010), one of the important roles of dreaming is to allow our deeper autobiographical schemas to be updated every night. By definition, this means the connection of right brain somatic and emotional memory with left brain narrative memory.

Negotiating a Diversity of Distinct Memory Systems

Successful treatment means resuming the never-ending task of the patient actively resuming pursuing the life they want. This forward-looking capacity requires an intact autobiographical memory system. What makes trauma treatment endlessly challenging and complicated is that the memory circuits we usually expect to be functioning are not present or lead to hugely different internal experiences. These include flashbacks that intrude into daytime activities, nightmares that terrify patients from going to sleep at night, intrusive self-critical voices, and bouts of little to no sleep. Because the engine to all of these experiences lies in the brainstem, talk therapy with the patient may provide only temporary relief but not correct the brainstem dysregulation at the root of their symptoms.

In the verbal interactions of talk therapy we are engaging the narrative mind. These processes are located in the left hemisphere, in Broca's area for understanding language, and Wernicke's area for expressing language. However, all the autonomic, somatic, and affective experiences of trauma are stored on the right side of the brain. This creates an impasse for therapy. How can you resolve the problems that exist in the traumatized right brain by engaging the other side, which has no actual experience of the event?

Research reported by Bessel van der Kolk (Rauch, van der Kolk, et al., 1996) illustrated this conundrum beautifully. He demonstrated that the brain response to focusing on a traumatic experience was activation of the right amygdala, accompanied by the silencing of the left brain Broca's area. This finding, that reactivating traumatic experiences often suffocates our ability to put words to our experiences, partly explains why doing trauma therapy can be so difficult. The other reason is that the patient does not want to go back to those memories to begin with. That is essentially how the brain has protected the mind from overwhelming bodily responses. The brain's protective circuits are not ready to give up just because the patient has stepped into a therapist's office.

Implications for Autobiographical Memories

> Episodic memory . . . is more vulnerable than other memory systems to neuronal dysfunction. . . . It makes possible mental time travel through subjective time, from the present to the past, thus allowing one to re-experience, through autonoetic awareness, one's own previous experiences. (Tulving, 2002, p. 5)

All memory processes require encoding, to put the experience into memory somewhere; and retrieval, to access it the memory after it was encoded. Endel Tulving (1972) made the then radical suggestion that there was more than one form of memory. He distinguished *episodic memory* from *semantic memory*. Semantic memory is all the information that we know about the world around us: the capital of France, the size of a watermelon, what a bear looks like, etc. These facts are all known to us without any involvement of us actually experiencing any of them.

An episodic memory is a memory about something that we actually experienced ourselves. For example, how delicious that strawberry that we picked at the farm we visited in the summer was. Episodic memories include our *self* in the memory. Across any given day, we have hundreds of these episodes, each of which can be remembered or reconstructed. Whether a given moment is actually important enough to be remembered is reliant on whether it is tagged with enough of a positive or negative valence and integrated into the nightly REM dream reorganization of long-term memory. All of these individual episodic memories, when we bring them together, create our autobiographical memory: who we are, what we have done, etc.

Sleep Consolidates Autobiographical Memory

The tag that is attached to an experience during normal everyday life occurs through the activity of the VTA dopamine-reward system. Autobiographical memory is consolidated at night. Then these dopamine-tagged experiences are reactivated and replayed in the hippocampal short-term memory so they can be moved to long-term memory in the cortex during the resonant NREM delta sleep period. In subsequent REM sleep, these new experiences (along with their updated emotional experiences) are integrated into a revised cortical schema of the self with corresponding adaptive changes made to the amygdala.

Trauma Undermines the Autobiographical Memory System

In life-or-death experiences, these tags are overpowered by the innate alarm system, triggered by the SC-amygdala-LC and intense emotional defensive reactions activated by the dlPAG, vlPAG, and DR. Furthermore, the activation of the innate alarm system is amplified in extreme duress by feedback loops through the ARAS and the hypothalamic orexin system. The example of Nancy illustrates the power of opioid release (dynorphin) to create a completely dissociative state, overwhelming the integrity of the sense of self.

These brainstem storms create practical challenges for doing trauma therapy. By definition, these experiences were overwhelming at the time they occurred, or they would not have been shut down and avoided. The authors of this book concur with many other schools of trauma treatment that have proposed that the resolution of right brain amygdalar hyperactivation requires attention to the intense body sensations that the brain has locked into memory. Integrating the right brain memories with left hemisphere activation becomes the important task and goal of all trauma treatment.

Hemispheric Encoding, Retrieval Asymmetry Model of Autobiographical Memory

A series of neuroimaging studies conducted by Endel Tulving and his colleagues in the 1990s (Kapur et al., 1994; Moscovitch et al., 1995; Tulving et al., 1994) confirmed that semantic memories and episodic memories were functionally different in how our brain encodes and retrieves these experiences. Semantic memories are encoded by the left prefrontal cortex *and* retrieved by it. Most of these memories are based on language: having words that help us describe the memory to ourselves.

Episodic memories require the left prefrontal cortex to encode the memory, but in contrast to semantic memories, episodic memories are accessed through activation of the right prefrontal cortex. To highlight this critical difference between episodic or autobiographical memories and semantic memories, Tulving called this the hemispheric encoding/retrieval asymmetry (HERA) model of episodic memory.

Tulving added that the right hemisphere is not only activated when an actual memory exists, but it was also activated when the person was trying to remember, even when they may have done something but didn't. This right hemisphere activation signals *seeking to remember* anything that one has experienced, not just memory traces of actual experiences that one has had. But the intensity of traumatic experiences shuts down this gateway to knowing ourselves.

From this we can see that the formation of an autobiographical memory requires a number of steps. The first is to actually permit the felt experience of an event. This requires activation of the right hemisphere. Next, the left hemisphere then begins to attach words and significance to these felt experiences. Without the narrative attached to the experience, the memory remains as the sensory, emotional, or procedural engram in the right brain, disconnected from our sense of self.

Deep Brain Reorienting Psychotherapy Resets Autonomic Dysregulation to Allow for the Reactivation of Autobiographical Memory

Traumatic experiences such as the overwhelming shock and fear that was embedded in Mike's accident memory are locked in right brain memory but unavailable to left brain self-awareness. Initially, that was the tension in his body, the persistent headaches these brought on, the background effects of dynorphin (nausea and dizziness), cognitive hyperarousal, as well as that single looping thought-image that remained with him all night. He was powerless to get that fragment of his lived experience out of his head or to slow down his nervous system so he could get to sleep.

Neither of those pre-affective experiences (headaches and cognitive arousal) were connected with any narrative. They remained as intense signals that continued to activate the NGC-LC-orexin-thyroid system. It was only with the neuromodulatory effects of DBR therapy that these memories could be reactivated and brought to the attention of Mike's current observing where self. Combined with the safety of the therapeutic dyad, he was able to begin to consciously notice the body experiences, feel them, and put these into words. In doing so, he transformed these sensory, emotional, and procedural engrams into autobiographical memories. Once this happens, the NGC-LC-orexin-thyroid system no longer has an external life threat to remain on guard against. It is now an internal experience that poses no threat at all.

Furthermore, now this new autobiographical memory can be retrieved through accessing the right-sided emotional and physical experiences brain. The intense shock and horror of the event have now been released. Not only does this allow Mike to talk about the accident calmly, recalling all that happened, but it also allows his sleeping brain to pass into NREM and REM sleep. Without the underlying LC-NE activated by the unprocessed shock and horror, which had been fragmenting sleep, the normal restorative pattern of sleep is restored. Now, the daily dopamine-tagged experiences of the day can be activated in NREM sleep, moved to long-term memory, and integrated into Mike's ongoing and developing sense of self.

THE ONGOING PARADIGM SHIFT IN TRAUMA TREATMENT

It has been nearly a decade since Anne Germain declared a "paradigm shift reconceptualizing sleep disturbances as biologically relevant and modifiable predisposing, precipitating, and perpetuating factors of PTSD" (Germain et al., 2017, p. 84). However, her call for change has gone unheeded. Treatment Guidelines have yet to incorporate sleep repair into their protocols.

In the interim, there has already been a major paradigm shift in the trauma field: transformational brain imaging studies of both daytime and sleep symptoms in humans and animals. These have revealed insights into the role of deeper brainstem nuclei in triggering the activation that results in disrupted sleep *and* daytime symptoms in PTSD.

The common roots of both are in autonomic dysregulation of the arousal functions of the NGC-LC-PAG-VTA-DRN complex. This neurobiologically active core of our survival system drives all symptoms. This book was written because sleep disturbances were not integrated into trauma treatment guidelines. In making the case for including sleep disorders, we discovered that review of brain imaging studies led to Van Someren characterizing insomnia as a "transdiagnostic primary risk factor" for the development of psychiatric conditions, including anxiety, depression, and PTSD.

Furthermore, our clinical work found that not all trauma treatments effectively resolved these sleep disturbances. Only the intervention targeting the autonomic activation of the locus coeruleus successfully resolved the sleep problem, and also reduced the trauma symptoms. Top-down cognitive approaches (CBTi) and affective desensitization interventions (EMDR) did not. These nuances in trauma treatment are critical for characterization of what treatments work for PTSD, and how they work. While our results require confirmation with RCT studies, if they do have the same outcome as we achieved, the next generation of trauma Treatment Guidelines will need to identify autonomic dysregulation (i.e. sleep disturbances) as core targets for the resolution of trauma.

How to Include Sleep Awareness in Your Trauma Treatments

We wrote this book for one main purpose. To make all health providers aware of the powerful impact sleep has on biopsychosocial health and wellness. Any interventions that help your traumatized patients sleep better will improve their outcomes in the treatment you provide. In exploring the roots of what fragments sleep, we found that they were the same brainstem centers that are simultaneously responsible for dissociative responses.

We understand that the brain is wired to continue on the path that it has found and many therapists might be tempted to continue to ignore the sleep component (the best predictor of future behavior is past behavior). However, changing how you practice, in order to begin to include the sleep sensitive component will take time initially, as with learning any new skill. For that reason, this book is organized to first provide information about how the interventions work. They can be learned and mastered. Each of the chapters includes ideas for beginning to apply what you have learned to your practice.

All therapists are somewhat uncomfortably aware of how difficult change can be. We deal with it every day. What patient would benefit most from what I am learning? We suggest that you start with the patients who have been stuck.

Focus on those whose therapy has not been proceeding as expected. In almost half of trauma patients, there is an underlying sleep apnea problem that has not been diagnosed. Ask these patients some questions about their sleep. How long do they sleep? Do they wake up feeling rested? Be curious. Table I.3 provided a practical overview to starting your sleep inquiry. Once you are comfortable with what to ask and look for, you will be able to identify sleep issues more readily in your trauma clients.

The next step is to read Chapter 1 again, a few times, so you can easily educate your patient about the value of restorative sleep. Only when the patient is aware that they have an internal process to help them in their healing will they begin to pay more attention to sleep. Remember that in the broader culture, the general ethic is that sleep is a waste of time. It takes some effort to overcome that attitude. I often suggest that clients read Matthew Walker's book, *Why We Sleep* (2017).

Finally, readers are encouraged to go to our website (www.PuttingTraumatoSleep.com) to find other resources and ideas for integrating sleep repair into their trauma treatments. Those are our suggestions for ways to begin to use these ideas and to embrace them in your practices. After you are conversant with describing the value of sleep to your trauma patient, you will want to learn to use the Clinical Choice Points roadmap (Figure 2.1) to have a systematic approach to introducing sleep interventions into your practice. Continue your learning from the book to expand your clinical toolkit, in order to more deeply explore trauma (physical, mental, and emotional) and sleep management. We are sure you will find ways to build on them once you have started.

Thank you for taking the time, having the interest in reading, and thinking about how sleep can help you and your patients in your work. We are certain that this will reward both you personally and your patients.

Conducting trauma therapy by embracing the 24-hour TABS model with an attachment based approach, rooted in intersubjective collaborative attunement allows for a safe space in which neuromodulation of the brainstem can occur. Always remember, great trauma therapists can become accomplished sleep therapists!

Acknowledgments

JAAN REITAV

No book springs into existence out of a vacuum. As readers of any book deserve a glimpse behind, to understand the story behind the story, here is how *Putting Trauma to Sleep* came into being. There were many foundational attachments that converged to create this book you are holding. I will frame these as critical attachment moments that will tell that story.

My parents, Adele and Martin, two Estonian émigrés fleeing war, instilled in me the desire to learn and to help others—my father, by telling me about his uncle Karl, the philologist who was learning his sixteenth language when he died, and my mother, the nurse, by stressing that nothing was more important in life than helping bring another person a feeling of joy.

I grew up in the "Estonian Houses," an enclave of two apartment buildings housing thirty Estonian families in Toronto. From the comfort of that enclosed village that was my extended family, I arrived at school without a word of English. My enduring memory is of sitting in Ms. Lang's lap, crying. I felt utterly and completely alone. Her comforting smile and protective hugs gradually helped me make the transition. But this experience left an indelible mark. In my bones, I know that essential human presence is necessary to overcome isolation and pain.

Since then I have been fortunate to have many more caring and compassionate teachers, mentors, and role models. Among these is Endel Tulving, the chairman of our Estonian Houses. He led me to be curious about psychology. What can we really know about how our minds work? Other teachers and role models supported me in finding my career. Among those were Peter Baron, Frank Robinson, Charles M. T. Hanly, Diane Syer, Morris Eagle, Jeffrey Moussaieff Masson, and David Iseman.

Then came my fascination with the enigma of sleep. As I began designing my doctorate study of dreaming and psychological defenses, I enrolled in the

1981 sleep conference in Hyannis Port, Massachusetts. There I met Harvey Moldofsky. Harvey and I were among the few Canadians attending. Harvey was welcoming and encouraging of my interests, so I gladly volunteered at Harvey's sleep clinic. I attended his rounds and began learning about the mysteries and complexity of sleep. Harvey, your gift of approaching sleep with curiosity and wonder is instilled in these pages.

Twenty-five years later, I returned to Harvey's rounds and met his resident, Celeste Thirlwell. Celeste and I share a commitment to healing. Our relationship evolved through presentations at trauma conferences, where we met Robin Shapiro. We told Robin of our plan to write a book on trauma and sleep. She introduced us to her editor, Deborah Malmud at Norton. Deborah, Mariah Eppes, and countless other Norton staff have been the committed and professional force that pushed this book into your hands. My huge appreciation for all that Norton does every day. Thank you!

What I hope the reader can hear in each of the chapters is my passion for what my mother instilled in me: "How can we use our knowledge to change lives?" Clinical work is complex and learning our craft takes decades. Among the behavioral sleep medicine colleagues who I have had the pleasure to learn from are Charles Morin, Duane Johnson, and Dieter Riemann. There were also years of learning about psychodynamic psychotherapy from Habib Davanloo, with my colleagues Gregory Hamovitch, Marvin Skorman, and Allan Kalpin.

Finally, we come to where the magic happens: my daily work with the patients who come for treatment. I am blessed to be able to come into work each day and collaborate with patients who are committed and do what they have to do to heal the wounds of their lives. You will meet many of them in the pages of this book. In forty years of doing this work, I have discovered that they are the true teachers.

This book is anchored in what they have taught me, and I especially thank those who have agreed to tell their stories in this book. Some readers might criticize characterizations of certain schools of therapy. This book is not about schools of therapy. It is about what my patients have told me that helped them in their recovery. In the fullness of time, our theories and our guidelines evolve. Celeste and I hope this book contributes to that evolution.

To do the work I do with my patients, I have needed the support of my team. For almost twenty years I have had the immense satisfaction of working and learning from patients with serious, chronic medical problems. Under the mentorship and guidance of Dr. Paul Oh, our director at the University Health Network's cardiac rehab program, I have had the opportunity to learn from the challenges of our cardiac, cancer, stroke, and diabetes patients. All of them have reported sleep disturbances as central to their distress. Paul has provided leadership and support, to challenge us to do our best. Thank you, Paul, for your integrity, guidance, and support.

The most recent decade of my clinical work has been spent immersing myself in trauma and its treatment. Here I have to thank Barbara Horne, Jeremy Tomlinson, Ruth Lanius, Frank Corrigan, and Cindy and Tina Shrigley. And for years now, I have had the pleasure of sharing this passion for transforming lives with Clare Peddle: we are a small but mighty team. And rising above all grad students I have had the pleasure to work with is Pouria Saffaran. Your presence and contributions were both enormous and essential.

Finally, we get to the emotional foundation of this book: I thank my wife Anu and my son Marty. For forty years, Anu, you have been my companion, my muse, my solace, and my inspiration. You brought me back from despair when an earlier manuscript of this book was lost. I could not have recovered and done this without your love and nurturing. And Marty, my Viking! You have a way of pushing me to understand myself more deeply: no bullshit. Had the two of you never come into my life, this book would never have been written. Thank you both for being who you are.

CELESTE THIRLWELL

I would like to dedicate this book to all the people I have met in this journey, who have dared to come back into wholeness after traumatic events, and to those who continue to search for innovative ways of healing, in order to help keep humanity humane.

I want to thank Gweneth Gordon and Clotilde Celeste, my two intrepid grandmothers, who taught their lineages to dance and play together in the world, as well as triumph over illness, inhumanity, and the ravages of World War II; my parents, Gweneth and Michael Thirlwell, who taught me that living a life at peace in one's heart by being of service to others is the key to sleeping well at night; my sisters, who live their lives with commitment, compassion, and integrity; my children, who have guided me in an ever-unfolding journey into expanded consciousness and embodied love; and Baba, my cheat sheet, who schooled me in learning how to walk out of the tornado of PTSD.

The workings of the brain and the human spirit have been my lifelong passions. Psychiatrist Dr. Harvey Moldofsky, one of the grandfathers of sleep medicine, was my seminal guide into the expansive world of sleep medicine, which spans from bench top to bedside and from cradle to grave. He introduced me to my psychologist coauthor, Dr. Jaan Reitav, a clinician dedicated to neuroscience, learning, his patients, and most importantly, his wife Anu. Anu's steadfast educator spirit ensured the triumphant completion of this book. In addition, psychology PhD candidate, Pouria Saffaran, has dedicated his time and acute mind to the basic neuroscience and diagrams in this book. Finally, I am thankful for the magical, mystical presence of Shakti, Sofia, Alexandra, Anna, Inga, Roman, and the Golden Dragon.

Both Dr. Reitav and I hope that this book brings healing and inspiration to all those who read it.

References

Adams, G. C., Stoops, M. A., & Skomro, R. P. (2014). Sleep tight: Exploring the relationship between sleep and attachment style across the life span. *Sleep Medicine Reviews*, 18(6), 495–507). W.B. Saunders Ltd. https://doi.org/10.1016/j.smrv.2014.03.002

Aellen, F. M., Van der Meer, J., Dietmann, A., Schmidt, M., Bassetti, C. L. A., & Tzovara, A. (2024). Disentangling the complex landscape of sleep–wake disorders with data-driven phenotyping: A study of the Bernese center. *European Journal of Neurology*, 31(1). https://doi.org/10.1111/ene.16026

Aloia, M. S., Arnedt, J. T., Riggs, R. L., Hecht, J., & Borrelli, B. (2004). Clinical management of poor adherence to CPAP: Motivational enhancement. *Behavioral Sleep Medicine*, 2(4), 205–222. https://doi.org/10.1207/s15402010bsm0204_3

American Academy of Sleep Medicine. (2014). *International classification of sleep disorders* (3rd ed.; ICSD-3).

American Psychiatric Association. (2013). *Diagnostic and statistical manual of mental disorders*.

Ammaniti, M., & Gallese, V. (2014). *The birth of intersubjectivity: Psychodynamics, neurobiology, and the self*. Norton.

Antila, H., Kwak, I., Choi, A., Pisciotti, A., Covarrubias, I., Baik, J., et al.. (2022). *A noradrenergic-hypothalamic neural substrate for stress-induced sleep disturbances*. https://doi.org/10.1073/pnas

Aserinsky, E., & Kleitman, N. (1953). Regularly occurring periods of eye motility, and concomitant phenomena, during sleep. *Science*, 118(3062), 273–274. https://doi.org/10.1126/SCIENCE.118.3062.273

Aurora, N., Zak, R. S., Magnati, R. K., Auerbach, S. H., Casey, K. R., Chowdhuri, S., Karippot, A., Ramar, K., Kristo, D. A., & Morgenthaler, T. I. (2010). Best practice guide for the treatment of REM sleep behavior disorder (RBD). *Journal of Clinical Sleep Medicine*, 6(1).

Badenoch, B. (2017). *The heart of trauma: Healing the embodied brain in the context of relationships*. Norton.

Baglioni, C., Nanovska, S., Regen, W., Spiegelhalder, K., Feige, B., Nissen, C., Reynolds, C. F., & Riemann, D. (2016). Sleep and mental disorders: A meta-analysis of polysomnographic research. *Psychological Bulletin*, 142(9), 969–990. https://doi.org/10.1037/bul0000053

Baglioni, C., Regen, W., Teghen, A., Spiegelhalder, K., Feige, B., Nissen, C., & Riemann, D. (2014). Sleep changes in the disorder of insomnia: A meta-analysis of polysomnographic studies. *Sleep Medicine Reviews*, 18(3), 195–213.

Barrett, D. (2001). *Trauma and dreams.* Harvard University Press.

Bergmann, U. (2000). Further thoughts on the neurobiology of EMDR: The role of the cerebellum in accelerated information processing. *Traumatology*, 6(3), 175–200.

Berridge, C. W., & Foote, S. L. (1991). Effects of locus coeruleus activation on electroencephalographic activity in neocortex and hippocampus. *Journal of Neuroscience*, 11(10), 3135–3145. https://doi.org/10.1523/JNEUROSCI.11-10-03135.1991

Berridge, C., Schmeichel, B., & Espana, R. (2012). Noradrenergic modulation of wakefulness/arousal. *Sleep Medicine Reviews*, 16(2), 187–197.

Bertisch, S. M., Pollock, B. D., Mittleman, M. A., Buysse, D. J., Bazzano, L. A., Gottlieb, D. J., & Redline, S. (2018). Insomnia with objective short sleep duration and risk of incident cardiovascular disease and all-cause mortality: Sleep Heart Health Study, *Sleep*, 41(6). https://doi.org/10.1093/sleep/zsy047

Blaustein, M., Cook, A., Cloitre, M., DeRosa, R., Ford, J., Henderson, M., Hubbard, R., Jentoft, K., Lanktree, C., Levitt, J., Liautaud, J., Olafson, R., Kagan, R., Mallah, K., Medeiros, D., Pelcovitz, D., Pagones, P., Putnam, F., Silva, R., . . . van der Kolk, B. (2003). *Complex trauma in children.*

Borbély, A. (2022). The two-process model of sleep regulation: Beginnings and outlook. *Journal of Sleep Research*, 31(4). John Wiley and Sons Inc. https://doi.org/10.1111/jsr.13598

Born, J., Rasch, B., & Gais, S. (2006). Sleep to remember. *Neuroscientist*, 12(5), 410–424. https://doi.org/10.1177/1073858406292647

Brooks, A., & Lack, L. (2006). A brief afternoon nap following nocturnal sleep restriction: Which nap duration is most recuperative? *Sleep*, 29(6), 831–840.

Brownlow, J. A., Miller, K. E., & Gehrman, P. R. (2020). Treatment of sleep comorbidities in posttraumatic stress disorder. *Current Treatment Options in Psychiatry*, 7(3), 301–316. https://doi.org/10.1007/s40501-020-00222-y

Carletto, S., & Borsato, T. (2017). Neurobiological correlates of post-traumatic stress disorder: A focus on cerebellum role. *European Journal of Trauma & Dissociation*, 1(3), 153–157. https://doi.org/10.1016/j.ejtd.2017.03.012

Carletto, S., Borsato, T., & Pagani, M. (2017). The role of slow wave sleep in memory pathophysiology: Focus on post-traumatic stress disorder and eye movement desensitization and reprocessing. *Front. Psychol.*, 8, 2050. https://doi.org/10.3389/fpsyg.2017.02050

Carney, C. E., Buysse, D. J., Ancoli-Israel, S., Edinger, J. D., Krystal, A. D., Lichstein, K. L., & Morin, C. M. (2012). The consensus sleep diary: Standardizing prospective sleep self-monitoring. *Sleep*, 35(2), 287–302. https://doi.org/10.5665/sleep.1642

Carter, M. E., de Lecea, L., & Adamantidis, A. (2013). Functional wiring of hypocretin and LC-NE neurons: Implications for arousal. *Frontiers in Behavioral Neuroscience*, 7(May), 43. https://doi.org/10.3389/fnbeh.2013.00043

Cartwright, R. D. (2010). *The twenty-four hour mind: The role of sleep and dreaming in our emotional lives.* Oxford University Press.

Chu, C. S., Huang, K. L., Bai, Y. M., Su, T. P., Tsai, S. J., Chen, T. J., Hsu, J. W., Liang, C. S., & Chen, M. H. (2023). Risk of suicide after a diagnosis of sleep apnea: A nationwide longitudinal study. *Journal of Psychiatric Research*, 161, 419–425. https://doi.org/10.1016/j.jpsychires.2023.03.028

Collen, J. F., Lettieri, C. J., & Hoffman, M. (2012). The impact of posttraumatic stress disorder on CPAP adherence in patients with obstructive sleep apnea. *Journal of Clinical Sleep Medicine*, 8(6), 667–672. https://doi.org/10.5664/jcsm.2260

Colvonen, P. J., Straus, L. D., Acheson, D., & Gehrman, P. (2019). A review of the relationship between emotional learning and memory, sleep, and PTSD. *Current Psychiatry Reports*, 21(1). https://doi.org/10.1007/s11920-019-0987-2

Cook, A., Spinazzola, J., Ford, ; Julian, Lanktree, C., Blaustein, M., Cloitre, M., Derosa, R., Hubbard, R., Liautaud, J., Olafson, E., Kagan, R., Mallah, K., & Van Der Kolk, B. (2005). Complex trauma in children and adolescents. *Psychiatric Annals*, 35(5). http://www.traumacenter.org.

Corrigan, F. M., & Christie-Sands, J. (2020). An innate brainstem self-other system involving orienting, affective responding, and polyvalent relational seeking: Some clinical implications for a "Deep Brain Reorienting" trauma psychotherapy approach. *Medical Hypotheses*, 136. https://doi.org/10.1016/j.mehy.2019.109502

Corrigan, F., Young, H., & Christie-Sands, J. (2024). *Deep brain reorienting: Understanding the neuroscience of trauma, attachment wounding, and DBR psychotherapy*. Routledge.

Cortoos, A., Verstraeten, E., & Cluydts, R. (2006). Neurophysiological aspects of primary insomnia: Implications for its treatment. *Sleep Medicine Reviews*, 10(4), 255–266. https://doi.org/10.1016/j.smrv.2006.01.002

Cox, R., Rüber, T., Staresina, B. P., & Fell, J. (2020). Sharp wave-ripples in human amygdala and their coordination with hippocampus during NREM sleep. *Cerebral Cortex Communications*, 1(1). https://doi.org/10.1093/texcom/tgaa051

Damasio, A. (1999). *The feeling of what happens: body and emotion in the making of consciousness*. Harcourt Brace.

Dantzer, R., O'Connor, J., Freund, G., Johnson, R., & Kelley, K. (2008). From inflammation to sickness and depression: when the immune system subjugates the brain. *Nat Rev Neurosci*, 9, 46–56.

Daulatzai, M. A. (2012). Pathogenesis of cognitive dysfunction in patients with obstructive sleep apnea: A hypothesis with emphasis on the nucleus tractus solitarius. *Sleep Disorders*, 2012, 1–18. https://doi.org/10.1155/2012/251096

Davis, J. L. (2008). *Treating post-trauma nightmares*. Springer.

Davis, J. L., & Wright, D. C. (2007). Randomized clinical trial for treatment of chronic nightmares in trauma-exposed adults. *Journal of Traumatic Stress*, 20(2), 123–133. https://doi.org/10.1002/jts.20199

Dietch, J. R., Taylor, D. J., Pruiksma, K., Wardle-Pinkston, S., Slavish, D. C., Messman, B., Estevez, R., Ruggero, C. J., & Kelly, K. (2021). The Nightmare Disorder Index: Development and initial validation in a sample of nurses. *Sleep*, 44(5). https://doi.org/10.1093/sleep/zsaa254

Donner, N. C., Kubala, K. H., Hassell, J. E., Lieb, M. W., Nguyen, K. T., Heinze, J. D., Drugan, R. C., Maier, S. F., & Lowry, C. A. (2018). Two models of inescapable stress increase tph2 mRNA expression in the anxiety-related dorsomedial part of the dorsal raphe nucleus. *Neurobiology of Stress*, 8, 68–81. https://doi.org/10.1016/j.ynstr.2018.01.003

Dornelas, E. A. (2012). *Stress proof the heart: Behavioral interventions for cardiac patients*. Springer.

Elam, M., Thorén, P., & Svensson, T. H. (1986). Locus coeruleus neurons and sympathetic nerves: Activation by visceral afferents. *Brain Research, 375*(1), 117–125. https://doi.org/10.1016/0006-8993(86)90964-9

Fanselow, M. S. (1994). Neural organization of the defensive behavior system responsible for fear. *Psychonomic Bulletin & Review, 1*(4).

Feige, B., Al-Shajlawi, A., Nissen, C., Voderholzer, U., Hornyak, M., Spiegelhalder, K., Kloepfer, C., Perlis, M., & Riemann, D. (2008). Does REM sleep contribute to subjective wake time in primary insomnia? A comparison of polysomnographic and subjective sleep in 100 patients. *Journal of Sleep Research, 17*(2), 180–190. https://doi.org/10.1111/j.1365-2869.2008.00651.x

Felitti, V. J., Anda, R. F., Nordenberg, D., Williamson, D. F., Spitz, A. M., Edwards, V., Koss, M. P., & Marks, J. S. (1998). Relationship of childhood abuse and household dysfunction to many of the leading causes of death in adults: The adverse childhood experiences (ACE) study. *American Journal of Preventive Medicine, 14*(4), 245–258. https://doi.org/10.1016/S0749-3797(98)00017-8

Fogel, A. (2013). *Body sense*. Norton.

Freud, S. (1909). Analysis of a phobia of a 5 year old boy. In *Standard edition of the complete works of Sigmund Freud* (trans. James Strachey, 1955 ed., Vol. 10, pp. 3–152). Hogarth Press.

Gao, S., Proekt, A., Renier, N., Calderon, D. P., & Pfaff, D. W. (2019). Activating an anterior nucleus gigantocellularis subpopulation triggers emergence from pharmacologically-induced coma in rodents. *Nature Communications, 10*(2897). https://doi.org/10.1038/s41467-019-10797-7

Germain, A. (2013). Sleep disturbances as the hallmark of PTSD: Where are we now? *American Journal of Psychiatry, 170*, 372–382.

Germain, A., McKeon, A. B., & Campbell, R. L. (2017). Sleep in PTSD: Conceptual model and novel directions in brain-based research and interventions. *Current Opinion in Psychology, 14*, 84–89. Elsevier B.V. https://doi.org/10.1016/j.copsyc.2016.12.004

Gilbert, K. S., Kark, S. M., Gehrman, P., & Bogdanova, Y. (2015). Sleep disturbances, TBI and PTSD: Implications for treatment and recovery. *Clinical Psychology Review, 40*, 195–212. https://doi.org/10.1016/j.cpr.2015.05.008

Graeff, F. G. (2012). New perspective on the pathophysiology of panic: Merging serotonin and opioids in the periaqueductal gray. *Brazilian Journal of Medical and Biological Research, 45*(4), 366–375. https://doi.org/10.1590/S0100-879X2012007500036

Graeff, F. G. (2017). Translational approach to the pathophysiology of panic disorder: Focus on serotonin and endogenous opioids. *Neuroscience and Biobehavioral Reviews, 76*, 48–55. https://doi.org/10.1016/j.neubiorev.2016.10.013

Hamblen, J. L., Norman, S. B., Sonis, J. H., Phelps, A. J., Bisson, J. I., Nunes, V. D., Megnin-Viggars, O., Forbes, D., Riggs, D. S., & Schnurr, P. P. (2019). A guide to guidelines for the treatment of posttraumatic stress disorder in adults: An update. *Psychotherapy, 56*(3), 359–373. American Psychological Association Inc. https://doi.org/10.1037/pst0000231

Harnett, N. G., Finegold, K. E., Lebois, L. A. M., van Rooij, S. J. H., Ely, T. D., Murty, V. P., Jovanovic, T., Bruce, S. E., House, S. L., Beaudoin, F. L., An, X.,

Zeng, D., Neylan, T. C., Clifford, G. D., Linnstaedt, S. D., Germine, L. T., Bollen, K. A., Rauch, S. L., Haran, J. P., . . . Stevens, J. S. (2022). Structural covariance of the ventral visual stream predicts posttraumatic intrusion and nightmare symptoms: A multivariate data fusion analysis. *Translational Psychiatry, 12*(1). https://doi.org/10.1038/s41398-022-02085-8

Harnett, N. G., van Rooij, S. J. H., Ely, T. D., Lebois, L. A. M., Murty, V. P., Jovanovic, T., Hill, S. B., Dumornay, N. M., Merker, J. B., Bruce, S. E., House, S. L., Beaudoin, F. L., An, X., Zeng, D., Neylan, T. C., Clifford, G. D., Linnstaedt, S. D., Germine, L. T., Bollen, K. A., . . . Stevens, J. S. (2021). Prognostic neuroimaging biomarkers of trauma-related psychopathology: Resting-state fMRI shortly after trauma predicts future PTSD and depression symptoms in the AURORA study. *Neuropsychopharmacology, 46*(7), 1263–1271. https://doi.org/10.1038/s41386-020-00946-8

Hartmann, E. (2000). *Dreams and nightmares: The origin and meaning of dreams.* Perseus.

Hasegawa, E., Miyasaka, A., Sakurai, K., Cherasse, Y., Li, Y., & Sakurai, T. (2022). Rapid eye movement sleep is initiated by basolateral amygdala dopamine signaling in mice. *Science, 375*, 994–1000. https://www.science.org

Hughes, D. (2017). Dyadic developmental psychotherapy (DDP): An attachment-focused family treatment for developmental trauma. *Australian and New Zealand Journal of Family Therapy, 38*(4), 595–605. https://doi.org/10.1002/anzf.1273

Insana, S. P., Kolko, D. J., & Germain, A. (2012). Early-life trauma is associated with rapid eye movement sleep fragmentation among military veterans. *Biological Psychology, 89*(3), 570–579. https://doi.org/10.1016/j.biopsycho.2012.01.001

Inutsuka, A., & Yamanaka, A. (2013). The physiological role of orexin/hypocretin neurons in the regulation of sleep/wakefulness and neuroendocrine functions. *Frontiers in Endocrinology, 4* (Mar). https://doi.org/10.3389/fendo.2013.00018

Ito, H., Navratilova, E., Vagnerova, B., Watanabe, M., Kopruszinski, C., Moreira De Souza, L. H., Yue, X., Ikegami, D., Moutal, A., Patwardhan, A., Khanna, R., Yamazaki, M., Guerrero, M., Rosen, H., Roberts, E., Neugebauer, V., Dodick, D. W., & Porreca, F. (2023). Chronic pain recruits hypothalamic dynorphin/kappa opioid receptor signalling to promote wakefulness and vigilance. *Brain, 146*(3), 1186–1199. https://doi.org/10.1093/brain/awac153

Johnson, C. R. (2021). *The art of transforming nightmares: Harness the creative and healing power of bad dreams, sleep paralysis, and recurring nightmares.* Llewellyn.

Kanady, J. C., Talbot, L. S., Maguen, S., Straus, L. D., Richards, A., Ruoff, L., Metzler, T. J., & Neylan, T. C. (2018). Cognitive behavioral therapy for insomnia reduces fear of sleep in individuals with posttraumatic stress disorder. *Journal of Clinical Sleep Medicine, 14*(7), 1193–1203. https://doi.org/10.5664/jcsm.7224

Kapur, S., Craik, F. I. M., Tulving, E., Wilson, A. A., Houle, S., & Brown, G. M. (1994). Neuroanatomical correlates of encoding in episodic memory: Levels of processing effect. *Proc Natl Acad Sci U S A, 91*(6), 2008–2011. https://www.pnas.org

Kearney, B. E., Corrigan, F. M., Frewen, P. A., Nevill, S., Harricharan, S., Andrews, K., Jetly, R., McKinnon, M. C., & Lanius, R. A. (2023). A randomized controlled trial of Deep Brain Reorienting: A neuroscientifically guided treatment for post-traumatic stress disorder. *European Journal of Psychotraumatology, 14*(2). https://doi.org/10.1080/20008066.2023.2240691

Kearney, B. E., & Lanius, R. A. (2022). The brain-body disconnect: A somatic sensory basis for trauma-related disorders. *Frontiers in Neuroscience, 16*. https://doi.org/10.3389/fnins.2022.1015749

Kitchur, M. (2005). The strategic developmental model for EMDR. In R. Shapiro (ed.) *EMDR solutions: Pathways to healing* (pp. 8–56). Norton.

Kobayashi, I., Sledjeski, E. M., Spoonster, E., Fallon, W. F., & Delahanty, D. L. (2008). Effects of early nightmares on the development of sleep disturbances in motor vehicle accident victims. *Journal of Traumatic Stress, 21*(6), 548–555. https://doi.org/10.1002/jts.20368

Koffel, E., Khawaja, I. S., & Germain, A. (2016). Sleep disturbances in posttraumatic stress disorder: Updated review and implications for treatment prevalence and impact of self-reported sleep disturbances in posttraumatic stress disorder. *Psychiatry Ann, 46*(3), 173–176. https://doi.org/10.3928/00485713-20160125-01

Krakow, B. (2006). Nightmare complaints in sleep patients. *Sleep, 29*(10). https://academic.oup.com/sleep/article/29/10/1313/2709189

Krakow, B., Tandberg, D., Scriggins, L., & Barey, M. (1995). A controlled comparison of self-rated sleep complaints in acute and chronic nightmare sufferers. *Journal of Nervous and Mental Disease, 183*(10), 623–627.

Krakow, B., & Zadra, A. (2006). Clinical management of chronic nightmares: Imagery rehearsal therapy. *Behavioral Sleep Medicine, 4*(1), 45–70. https://doi.org/10.1207/s15402010bsm0401_4

Krakow, B., & Zadra, A. (2010). Imagery rehearsal therapy: Principles and practice. *Sleep Medicine Clinics, 5*(2), 289–298. https://doi.org/10.1016/j.jsmc.2010.01.004

Kreibich, A. S., Reyes, B. A. S., Curtis, A. L., Ecke, L., Chavkin, C., Van Bockstaele, E. J., & Valentino, R. J. (2008). Presynaptic inhibition of diverse afferents to the locus coeruleus by κ-opiate receptors: A novel mechanism for regulating the central norepinephrine system. *Journal of Neuroscience, 28*(25), 6516–6525. https://doi.org/10.1523/JNEUROSCI.0390-08.2008

Kushida, C. A., Littner, M. R., Morgenthaler, T., Alessi, C. A., Bailey, D., Coleman, J., Friedman, L., Hirshkowitz, M., Kapen, S., Kramer, M., Lee-Chiong, T., Loube, D. L., Owens, J., Pancer, J. P., & Wise, M. (2005). Practice parameters for the Indications for PSG-AASM Practice Parameters SLEEP Practice Parameters for the Indications for Polysomnography and Related Procedures: An Update for 2005 (Vol. 28, Issue 4). https://academic.oup.com/sleep/article/28/4/499/2696969

Lahousen, T., Unterrainer, H. F., & Kapfhammer, H. P. (2019). Psychobiology of attachment and trauma—Some general remarks from a clinical perspective. *Frontiers in Psychiatry, 10*. https://doi.org/10.3389/fpsyt.2019.00914

Lamberg, L., & Cartwright, R. (1992). *Crisis dreaming: Using your dreams to solve your problems.* iUniverse.

Lancel, M., van Marle, H. J. F., Van Veen, M. M., & van Schagen, A. M. (2021). Disturbed sleep in PTSD: Thinking beyond nightmares. *Frontiers in Psychiatry, 12*. https://doi.org/10.3389/fpsyt.2021.767760

Lanius, R. A., Hopper, J. W., & Menon, R. S. (2003). Clinical case conference individual differences in a husband and wife who developed PTSD after a motor vehicle accident: A functional MRI case study. *Am J Psychiatry, 160*. http://ajp.psychiatryonline.org

Lanius, R. A., Williamson, P. C., Densmore, M., Boksman, K., Neufeld, M. R., Gati, J. S., & Menon, R. S. (2004). The nature of traumatic memories: A 4-T fMRI functional connectivity analysis. *Am J Psychiatry, 161*(1). http://ajp.psychiatryonline.org

Levine, P. A. (2015). *Trauma and memory: Brain and body in a search for the living past: A practical guide for understanding and working with traumatic memory.* North Atlantic Books.

Lewis, K. E., Seale, L., Bartle, I. E., Watkins, A. J., & Ebden, P. (2004). Early predictors of CPAP use for the treatment of obstructive sleep apnea. *Sleep, 27*(1).

Linden, D. J. (2015). *Touch: The science of hand, heart, and mind.* Viking.

Linden, W., Phillips, M. J., & Leclerc, J. (2007). Psychological treatment of cardiac patients: A meta-analysis. *European Heart Journal, 28*(24), 2972–2984. https://doi.org/10.1093/eurheartj/ehm522

Lukkes, J. L., Watt, M. J., Lowry, C. A., & Forster, G. L. (2009). Consequences of post-weaning social isolation on anxiety behavior and related neural circuits in rodents. *Frontiers in Behavioral Neuroscience, 3*(AUG). https://doi.org/10.3389/neuro.08.018.2009

Luyster, F. S., Buysse, D. J., & Strollo, P. J. (2010). Comorbid insomnia and obstructive sleep apnea: Challenges for clinical practice and research. *Journal of Clinical Sleep Medicine, 6*(2).

Lydiard, R. B., & Hamner, M. H. (2009). Clinical importance of sleep disturbance as a treatment target in PTSD. *Journal of Lifelong Learning in Psychiatry, 7*(2).

Mäkelä, T. E., Kylliäinen, A., Saarenpää-Heikkilä, O., Paavonen, E. J., Paunio, T., Leppänen, J. M., & Peltola, M. J. (2021). Signaled night awakening and its association with social information processing and socio-emotional development across the first two years. *Sleep, 44*(12). https://doi.org/10.1093/sleep/zsab179

Mallick, B. N., & Singh, A. (2011). REM sleep loss increases brain excitability: Role of noradrenalin and its mechanism of action. *Sleep Medicine Reviews, 15*(3), 165–178. https://doi.org/10.1016/j.smrv.2010.11.001

Mattera, A., Cavallo, A., Granato, G., Baldassarre, G., & Pagani, M. (2022). A biologically inspired neural network model to gain insight into the mechanisms of post-traumatic stress disorder and eye movement desensitization and reprocessing therapy. *Frontiers in Psychology, 13.* https://doi.org/10.3389/fpsyg.2022.944838

Matzeu, A., Kallupi, M., George, O., Schweitzer, P., & Martin-Fardon, R. (2018). Dynorphin counteracts orexin in the paraventricular nucleus of the thalamus: Cellular and behavioral evidence. *Neuropsychopharmacology, 43*(5), 1010–1020. https://doi.org/10.1038/npp.2017.250

McCall, A., Forouhandehpour, R., Celebi, S., Richard-Malenfant, C., Hamati, R., Guimond, S., Tuominen, L., Weinshenker, D., Jaworska, N., McQuaid, R. J., Shlik, J., Robillard, R., Kaminsky, Z., & Cassidy, C. M. (2024). Evidence for locus coeruleus–norepinephrine system abnormality in military posttraumatic stress disorder revealed by neuromelanin-sensitive Magnetic Resonance Imaging. *Biological Psychiatry.* https://doi.org/10.1016/j.biopsych.2024.01.013

McCall, J. G., Al-Hasani, R., Siuda, E. R., Hong, D. Y., Norris, A. J., Ford, C. P., & Bruchas, M. R. (2015). CRH engagement of the locus coeruleus noradrenergic system mediates stress-induced anxiety. *Neuron, 87*(3), 605–620. https://doi.org/10.1016/j.neuron.2015.07.002

Merker, B. (2013). The efference cascade, consciousness, and its self: Naturalizing the first person pivot of action control. *Frontiers in Psychology*, 4(AUG). https://doi.org/10.3389/fpsyg.2013.00501

Mieda, M., Tsujino, N., & Sakurai, T. (2013). Differential roles of orexin receptors in the regulation of sleep/wakefulness. *Frontiers in Endocrinology*, 4(MAY). https://doi.org/10.3389/fendo.2013.00057

Miller, M. A., & Cappuccio, F. P. (2007). Inflammation, sleep, obesity, and cardiovascular disease. *Current Vascular Pharmacology*, 5.

Moldofsky, H., & Scarisbrick, P. (1976). Induction of neurasthenic musculoskeletal pain syndrome by selective sleep stage deprivation. *Psychosomatic Medicine*, 38(1), 35–44.

Morgenthaler, T. I., Auerbach, S., Casey, K. R., Kristo, D., Maganti, R., Ramar, K., Zak, R., & Kartje, R. (2018). Position paper for the treatment of nightmare disorder in adults: An American Academy of Sleep Medicine position paper. *Journal of Clinical Sleep Medicine*, 14(6), 1041–1055. https://doi.org/10.5664/jcsm.7178

Morgenthaler, T., Kagramanov, C., Hanak, V., & Decker, P. A. (2006). Complex sleep apnea syndrome: Is it a unique clinical syndrome? *Sleep*, 29(9).

Morris, L. S., Tan, A., Smith, D. A., Grehl, M., Han-Huang, K., Naidich, T. P., Charney, D. S., Balchandani, P., Murrough, J. W., & Kundu, P. (2020). Sub-millimeter variation in human locus coeruleus is associated with dimensional measures of psychopathology: An in vivo ultra-high field 7-Tesla MRI study. *NeuroImage: Clinical*, 25. https://doi.org/10.1016/j.nicl.2019.102148

Moscovitch, M., Kapurtt, S., Köhler, S., & Houlet, S. (1995). Distinct neural correlates of visual long-term memory for spatial location and object identity: A positron emission tomography study in humans (visual cortex/hippocampus). *Proc Natl Acad Sci U S A*, 92(9), 3721–3725. https://www.pnas.org

Mysliwiec, V., Brock, M. S., Creamer, J. L., O'Reilly, B. M., Germain, A., & Roth, B. J. (2018). Trauma associated sleep disorder: A parasomnia induced by trauma. In *Sleep Medicine Reviews* (Vol. 37, pp. 94–104). W.B. Saunders Ltd. https://doi.org/10.1016/j.smrv.2017.01.004

Mysliwiec, V., Matsangas, P., Gill, J., Baxter, T., O'Reilly, B., Collen, J. F., & Roth, B. J. (2015). A comparative analysis of sleep disordered breathing in Active Duty Service Members with and without combat-related Posttraumatic Stress Disorder. *Journal of Clinical Sleep Medicine*, 11(12), 1393–1401. https://doi.org/10.5664/jcsm.5272

Nader, K. (2001). Children's traumatic dreams. In D. Barrett (ed.), *Trauma and dreams*. Harvard University Press.

Naegeli, C., Zeffiro, T., Piccirelli, M., Jaillard, A., Weilenmann, A., Hassanpour, K., Schick, M., Rufer, M., Orr, S. P., & Mueller-Pfeiffer, C. (2018). Locus coeruleus activity mediates hyperresponsiveness in posttraumatic stress disorder. *Biological Psychiatry*, 83(3), 254–262. https://doi.org/10.1016/j.biopsych.2017.08.021

Nash, W. P. (2022). *Treating moral injury, identity wounds, and complex PTSD, by strengthening the self.* Training Webinar.

Nasreddine, Z. S., Phillips, N. A., Bédirian, V., Charbonneau, S., Whitehead, V., Collin, I., Cummings, J. L., & Chertkow, H. (2005). The Montreal Cognitive Assessment, MoCA: A brief screening tool for mild cognitive impairment. *Journal of the American Geriatrics Society*, 53(4), 695–699. https://doi.org/10.1111/j.1532-5415.2005.53221.x

Natraj, N., Neylan, T. C., Yack, L. M., Metzler, T. J., Woodward, S. H., Hubachek, S.

Q., Dukes, C., Udupa, N. S., Mathalon, D. H., & Richards, A. (2023). Sleep spindles favor emotion regulation over memory consolidation of stressors in posttraumatic stress disorder. *Biological Psychiatry: Cognitive Neuroscience and Neuroimaging*, 8(9), 899–908. https://doi.org/10.1016/j.bpsc.2023.02.007

Nestor, J. (2020). *Breath: The new science of a lost art*. Riverhead Books.

Ogden, P., Minton, K., & Pain, C. (2006). *Trauma and the body: A sensorimotor approach to psychotherapy*. Norton.

Oikonomou, G., Altermatt, M., Zhang, R.-W., Coughlin, G. M., Montz, C., Gradinaru, V., & Prober, D. A. (2019). The serotonergic raphe promote sleep in zebrafish and mice. *Neuron*, 103(4), 686–701.e8. https://doi.org/10.1016/j.neuron.2019.05.038

Osorio-Forero, A., Cherrad, N., Banterle, L., Fernandez, L. M. J., & Lüthi, A. (2022). When the locus coeruleus speaks up in sleep: Recent insights, emerging perspectives. *International Journal of Molecular Sciences*, 23(9). MDPI. https://doi.org/10.3390/ijms23095028

Pacheco, D., & Rehman, A. (2023, December 22). *What makes a good night's sleep*. Sleep Foundation.

Palagini, L., Drake, C. L., Gehrman, P., Meerlo, P., & Riemann, D. (2015). Early-life origin of adult insomnia: Does prenatal-early-life stress play a role? *Sleep Medicine*, 16(4), 446–456. https://doi.org/10.1016/j.sleep.2014.10.013

Panksepp, J., Herman, B., Conner, R., Bishop, P., & Scott, J. (1978). The biology of social attachments: Opiates alleviate separation distress. *Biological Psychiatry*, 13(5), 607–618.

Parrino, L, Milioli, G., Melpignano, A., & Trippi, I. (2016). The cyclic alternating pattern and the brain-body-coupling during sleep. *Epileptologie*, 33, 150–160.

Parrino, L., Thomas, R. J., Smerieri, A., Spaggiari, M. C., Del Felice, A., & Terzano, M. G. (2005). Reorganization of sleep patterns in severe OSAS under prolonged CPAP treatment. *Clinical Neurophysiology*, 116(9), 2228–2239. https://doi.org/10.1016/j.clinph.2005.05.005

Pascua, J., Blanco, M., Ernst, G., Salvado, A., & Borsini, E. E. (2021). Compliance to continuous positive airway pressure therapy in patients with obstructive sleep apnea – long-term assessment. *Sleep Science*, 14(4), 385–389. https://doi.org/10.5935/1984-0063.20200118

Perlis, M. L., Giles, D. E., Buysse, D. J., Tu, X., & Kupfer, D. J. (1997). Self-reported sleep disturbance as a prodromal symptom in recurrent depression. *Journal of Affective Disorders*, 42.

Pfaff, D. (2019). *How brain arousal mechanisms work*. Cambridge University Press.

Pietrzak, R. H., Goldstein, R. B., Southwick, S. M., & Grant, B. F. (2012). Physical health conditions associated with posttraumatic stress disorder in U.S. older adults: Results from Wave 2 of the National Epidemiologic Survey on Alcohol and Related Conditions. *Journal of the American Geriatric Society*, 60(2), 296–303. https://doi.org/10.1111/j.1532-5415.2011.03788.x

Pigarev, I. N. (2014). The visceral theory of sleep. *Neuroscience and Behavioral Physiology*, 44(4), 421–434. https://doi.org/10.1007/s11055-014-9928-z

Pigeon, W. R., Crean, H. F., Cerulli, C., Gallegos, A. M., Bishop, T. M., & Heffner, K. L. (2022). A randomized clinical trial of cognitive-behavioral therapy for insomnia to augment posttraumatic stress disorder treatment in survivors of interpersonal violence. *Psychotherapy and Psychosomatics, 91*(1), 50–62. https://doi.org/10.1159/000517862

Prather, A. A., Hall, M., Fury, J. M., Ross, D. C., Muldoon, M. F., Cohen, S., & Marsland, A. L. (2012). Sleep and antibody response to hepatitis B vaccination. *Sleep, 35*(8), 1063–1069. https://doi.org/10.5665/sleep.1990

Preter, M., & Klein, D. F. (2014). Lifelong opioidergic vulnerability through early life separation: A recent extension of the false suffocation alarm theory of panic disorder. *Neuroscience and Biobehavioral Reviews, 46*(P3), 345–351. https://doi.org/10.1016/j.neubiorev.2014.03.025

Prior, P. L., Francis, J. A., Reitav, J., & Stone, J. A. (2009). Behavioural and psychological issues in cardiovascular disease. In J. Stone (Ed.), *Canadian Guidelines for Cardiovascular Prevention and Cardiac Rehabilitation - Translating Knowledge into Action* (3rd ed., pp. 107–202). Canadian Association of Cardiac Rehabilitation.

Pruiksma, K. E., Davis, J., Taylor, D. J., Miller, K., Dietch, J. R., Balliett, N., Wilkerson, A., Harb, G., & Wardle-Pinkston, S. (2023). *Cognitive behavioral therapy for nightmares: Therapist guide and patient materials.* http://cbtnightmares.org.

Pruiksma, K. E., Taylor, D. J., Ruggero, C., Boals, A., Davis, J. L., Cranston, C., DeViva, J. C., & Zayfert, C. (2014). A psychometric study of the Fear of Sleep Inventory-Short Form (FoSI-SF). *Journal of Clinical Sleep Medicine, 10*(5), 551–558. https://doi.org/10.5664/jcsm.3710

Pruiksma, K. E., Taylor, D. J., Wachen, J. S., Mintz, J., Young-McCaughan, S., Peterson, A. L., Yarvis, J. S., Borah, E. V., Dondanville, K. A., Litz, B. T., Hembree, E. A., & Resick, P. A. (2016). Residual sleep disturbances following PTSD treatment in active duty military personnel. *Psychological Trauma: Theory, Research, Practice, and Policy, 8*(6), 697–701. https://doi.org/10.1037/tra0000150

Rauch, S. L., van Der Kolk, B. A., Fisler, R. E., Alpert, N. M., Orr, S. P., Savage, C. R., Fischman, A. J., Jenike, M. A., & Pitman, R. K. (1996). A symptom provocation study of posttraumatic stress disorder using positron emission tomography and script-driven imagery. *Archives of General Psychiatry, 53*(5), 380–387. https://doi.org/10.1001/ARCHPSYC.1996.01830050014003

Reitav, J. (2012). Managing sleep problems among cardiac patients. In E. A. Dornelas (Ed.), *Stress Proof the Heart: Behavioral Interventions for Cardiac Patients* (pp. 281–317). Springer. https://doi.org/10.1007/978-1-4419-5650-7_13

Reitav, J. (2016). *A better you: Your guide to enjoying less stress, more sleep, and relationship renewal.* Self-published.

Reitav, J., Thirlwell, C., Casselman, T., & Oh, P. (2019). The presence of either insomnia or sleep apnea attenuates the benefits achieved from stress management training for reducing daytime symptoms of hyperarousal by cardiovascular patients. *Sleep Medicine, 64*(S1), S316.

Richards, D., Bartlett, D. J., Wong, K., Malouff, J., & Grunstein, R. R. (2007). Increased adherence to CPAP with a group cognitive behavioral treatment intervention: A randomized trial. *Sleep, 30*(5), 635–640. https://academic.oup.com/sleep/article/30/5/635/2709221

Richards, S. H., Anderson, L., Jenkinson, C. E., Whalley, B., Rees, K., Davies, P., Bennett, P., Liu, Z., West, R., Thompson, D. R., & Taylor, R. S. (2018). Psychological interventions for coronary heart disease: Cochrane systematic review and meta-analysis. *European Journal of Preventive Cardiology*, 25(3), 247–259. https://doi.org/10.1177/2047487317739978

Riemann, D., Benz, F., Dressle, R. J., Espie, C. A., Johann, A. F., Blanken, T. F., Leerssen, J., Wassing, R., Henry, A. L., Kyle, S. D., Spiegelhalder, K., & Van Someren, E. J. W. (2022). Insomnia disorder: State of the science and challenges for the future. *Journal of Sleep Research*, 31(4). John Wiley and Sons Inc. https://doi.org/10.1111/jsr.13604

Riemann, D., Spiegelhalder, K., Nissen, C., Hirscher, V., Baglioni, C., & Feige, B. (2012). REM sleep instability - A new pathway for insomnia? *Pharmacopsychiatry*, 45(5), pp. 167–176). https://doi.org/10.1055/s-0031-1299721

Rogers, C. (1951). *Client centered therapy*. Houghton Mifflin.

Saper, C. B., Cano, G., & Scammell, T. E. (2005). Homeostatic, circadian, and emotional regulation of sleep. *Journal of Comparative Neurology*, 493(1), 92–98. https://doi.org/10.1002/cne.20770

Sateia, M. J. (2014). International classification of sleep disorders-third edition highlights and modifications. *Chest*, 146(5), 1387–1394. https://doi.org/10.1378/chest.14-0970

Scheer, F. A., Cajochen, C., Turek, F. W., & Czeisler, C. A. (2005). Melatonin in the regulation of sleep and circadian rhythms. In *Principles and Practice of Sleep Medicine* (pp. 395–404). Elsevier Inc. https://doi.org/10.1016/B0-72-160797-7/50039-2

Scheer, F. A. J. L., Morris, C. J., Garcia, J. I., Smales, C., Kelly, E. E., Marks, J., Malhotra, A., & Shea, S. A. (2012). Repeated melatonin supplementation improves sleep in hypertensive patients treated with beta-blockers: A randomized controlled trial. *Sleep*, 35(10), 1395–1402. https://doi.org/10.5665/sleep.2122

Schore, A. (1994). *Affect regulation and the origin of the self: The neurobiology of emotional development*. Psychology Press.

Schore, A. N. (2012). *The science of the art of psychotherapy*. Norton.

Schore, A. N. (2019). *Right brain psychotherapy*. Norton.

Schulz, A., Schultchen, D., & Vögele, C. (2020). Interoception, stress, and physical symptoms in stress-associated diseases. *European Journal of Health Psychology*, 27(4), 132–153. https://doi.org/10.1027/2512-8442/a000063

Schulz, A., & Vögele, C. (2015). Interoception and stress. *Frontiers in Psychology*, 6. https://doi.org/10.3389/fpsyg.2015.00993

Sgoifo, A., Carnevali, L., & Grippo, A. J. (2014). The socially stressed heart. Insights from studies in rodents. *Neuroscience and Biobehavioral Reviews*, 39, 51–60. https://doi.org/10.1016/j.neubiorev.2013.12.005

Shapiro, B., Fang, Y., Sen, S., & Forger, D. (2024). Unraveling the interplay of circadian rhythm and sleep deprivation on mood: A real-world study on first-year physicians. *PLOS Digital Health*, 3(1), e0000439. https://doi.org/10.1371/journal.pdig.0000439

Shapiro, F. (2018). *Eye movement desensitization and reprocessing (EMDR) therapy: Basic principles, protocols, and procedures* (3rd ed.). Guilford Press.

Shah, A. J., Vaccarino, V., Goldberg, J., et al.,. (2024). Posttraumatic Stress Disorder and Obstructive Sleep Apnea in Twins. *JAMA Network Open*, 7(6), e2416352. https://doi.org/10.1001/jamanetworkopen.2024.16352

Siegel, D. J. (2015a). *Brainstorm: The power and purpose of the teenage brain*. TarcherPerigee.

Siegel, D. J. (2015b). *The developing mind: How relationships and the brain interact to shape who we are*. Guilford Press.

Sinha, S. S. (2016). Trauma-induced insomnia: A novel model for trauma and sleep research. *Sleep Medicine Reviews, 25*, 74–83. https://doi.org/10.1016/j.smrv.2015.01.008

Smith, J., Honig-Frand, A., Antila, H., Choi, A., Kim, H., Beier, K. T., Weber, F., & Chung, S. (2023). Regulation of stress-induced sleep fragmentation by preoptic glutamatergic neurons. *Current Biology, 34*(1), 12–23. https://doi.org/10.1016/j.cub.2023.11.035

Solms, M. (2021). *The hidden spring: A journey to the source of consciousness*. Norton.

Spiegel, K., Sheridan, J., & Van Cauter, E. (2002). Effect of sleep deprivation on response to immunization. *JAMA, 288*(12), 1471–1472.

Spoormaker, V. I., & Montgomery, P. (2008). Disturbed sleep in post-traumatic stress disorder: Secondary symptom or core feature? *Sleep Medicine Reviews, 12*(3), 169–184. https://doi.org/10.1016/j.smrv.2007.08.008

Stepanski, E., & Perlis, M. (2003). Introduction to behavioral sleep medicine: A historical perspective and commentary on practical issues. In M. L. Perlis & K. L. Lichstein (Eds.), *Treating Sleep Disorders: Principles and practice of behavioral sleep medicine*. John Wiley and Sons.

Stepnowsky, C. J., & Dimsdale, J. E. (2002). Dose-response relationship between CPAP compliance and measures of sleep apnea severity. *Sleep Medicine, 3*, 329–334. www.elsevier.com/locate/sleep

Stern, D. (1985). *The interpersonal world of the human infant*. Basic Books.

Takakusaki, K., Takahashi, K., Saitoh, K., Harada, H., Okumura, T., Kayama, Y., & Koyama, Y. (2005). Orexinergic projections to the cat midbrain mediate alternation of emotional behavioural states from locomotion to cataplexy. *Journal of Physiology, 568*(3), 1003–1020. https://doi.org/10.1113/jphysiol.2005.085829

Tamanna, S., Parker, J., Lyons, J., & Ullah, M. (2014). The effect of continuous positive air pressure (CPAP) on nightmares in patients with posttraumatic stress disorder (PTSD) and obstructive sleep apnea (OSA). *Journal of Clinical Sleep Medicine, 10*(6), 631–636.

Tang, N. K. Y., Saconi, B., Jansson-Fröjmark, M., Ong, J. C., & Carney, C. E. (2023). Cognitive factors and processes in models of insomnia: A systematic review. *Journal of Sleep Research, 32*(6). https://doi.org/10.1111/jsr.13923

Tejeda, H. A., & Bonci, A. (2019). Dynorphin/kappa-opioid receptor control of dopamine dynamics: Implications for negative affective states and psychiatric disorders. *Brain Research, 1713*, 91–101). Elsevier B.V. https://doi.org/10.1016/j.brainres.2018.09.023

Terzano, M. G., Parrino, L., Spaggiari, M. C., Palomba, V., Rossi, M., & Smerieri, A. (2003). CAP variables and arousals as sleep electroencephalogram markers for primary insomnia. *Clinical Neurophysiology, 114*(9), 1715–1723.

Tulving, E. (1972). Episodic and Semantic Memory. In E. Tulving, & W. Donaldson (Eds.), *Organization of Memory* (pp. 381–402). Academic Press.

Tulving, E. (2002). *Episodic memory: From mind to brain. Ann Rev Psychol, 53*, 1–25. www.annualreviews.org

Tulving, E., Kapur, S., Markowitsch, H. J., Craik, F. I. M., Habibt, R., & Houle, S. (1994). Neuroanatomical correlates of retrieval in episodic memory: Auditory sentence recognition. *Proc Natl Acad Sci U S A, 91*.

Tursich, M., Neufeld, R. W. J., Frewen, P. A., Harricharan, S., Kibler, J. L., Rhind, S. G., & Lanius, R. A. (2014). Association of trauma exposure with proinflam-

matory activity: a transdiagnostic meta-analysis. *Translational Psychiatry*, 4, e413. https://doi.org/10.1038/tp.2014.56
Uchino, B. N., Holt-Lunstad, J., Uno, D., & Flinders, J. B. (2001). Heterogeneity in the social networks of young and older adults: Prediction of mental health and cardiovascular reactivity during acute stress. *Journal of Behavioral Medicine*, 24(4), 361–382. https://doi.org/10.1023/A:1010634902498
Van Bockstaele, E., & Valentino, R. (2009). Corticotropin-Releasing factor and the brain norepinephrine system. In D. W. Pfaff, A. M. Etgen, R. T. Rubin, A. P. Arnold, & S. E. Fahrbach (eds.), *Hormones, brain and behavior* (2nd ed.). Academic Press.
Van Der Heijden, A. C., Hofman, W. F., De Boer, M., Nijdam, M. J., Van Marle, H. J. F., Jongedijk, R. A., Olff, M., & Talamini, L. M. (2022). Sleep spindle dynamics suggest over-consolidation in post-traumatic stress disorder. *Sleep*, 45(9). https://doi.org/10.1093/sleep/zsac139
van der Kolk, B. (2015). *The body keeps the score: Brain, mind, and body in the healing of trauma*. Penguin Books.
Van Someren, E. J. W. (2021). Brain mechanisms of insomnia: New perspectives on causes and consequences. *Physiological Reviews*, 101(3), 995–1046. https://doi.org/10.1152/physrev.00046.2019
van Wyk, M., Thomas, K., Solms, M., & Lipinska, G. (2016). Prominence of hyperarousal symptoms explains variability of sleep disruption in posttraumatic stress disorder. *Psychological Trauma: Theory, Research, Practice, and Policy*, 8(6), 688–696.
Walker, M. (2017). *Why we sleep*. Scribner.
Wang, C., Ramakrishnan, S., Laxminarayan, S., Dovzhenok, A., Cashmere, J. D., Germain, A., & Reifman, J. (2020). An attempt to identify reproducible high-density EEG markers of PTSD during sleep. *Sleep*, 43(1). https://doi.org/10.1093/sleep/zsz207
Wassing, R., Benjamins, J. S., Talamini, L. M., Schalkwijk, F., & Van Someren, E. J. W. (2019). Overnight worsening of emotional distress indicates maladaptive sleep in insomnia. *Sleep*, 42(4). https://doi.org/10.1093/sleep/zsy268
Wassing, R., Lakbila-Kamal, O., Ramautar, J. R., Stoffers, D., Schalkwijk, F., & Van Someren, E. J. W. (2019). Restless REM sleep impedes overnight amygdala adaptation. *Current Biology*, 29(14), 2351-2358.e4. https://doi.org/10.1016/j.cub.2019.06.034
Watt, D. F., & Panksepp, J. (2009). Depression: An evolutionarily conserved mechanism to terminate separation distress? A review of aminergic, peptidergic, and neural network perspectives. *Neuropsychoanalysis*, 11(1), 7–109. http://www.neuropsa.org
Werner, G. G., Danböck, S. K., Metodiev, S., & Kunze, A. E. (2020). Pre-sleep arousal and fear of sleep in trauma-related sleep disturbances: A cluster-analytic approach. *Clinical Psychology in Europe*, 2(2). https://doi.org/10.32872/cpe.v2i2.2699
Werner, G. G., Riemann, D., & Ehring, T. (2021). Fear of sleep and trauma-induced insomnia: A review and conceptual model. *Sleep Medicine Reviews*,55. https://doi.org/10.1016/j.smrv.2020.101383
Wood, S. K. (2014). Cardiac autonomic imbalance by social stress in rodents: Understanding putative biomarkers. *Frontiers in Psychology*, 5(Aug). https://doi.org/10.3389/fpsyg.2014.00950
Wood, S. K., & Bhatnagar, S. (2015). Resilience to the effects of social stress: Evidence from clinical and preclinical studies on the role of coping strategies. *Neurobiology of Stress*, 1(1), 164–173. https://doi.org/10.1016/j.ynstr.2014.11.002

Wood, S. K., McFadden, K. V., Grigoriadis, D., Bhatnagar, S., & Valentino, R. J. (2012). Depressive and cardiovascular disease comorbidity in a rat model of social stress: A putative role for corticotropin-releasing factor. *Psychopharmacology, 222*(2), 325–336. https://doi.org/10.1007/s00213-012-2648-6

Wood, S. K., & Valentino, R. J. (2017a). The brain norepinephrine system, stress, and cardiovascular vulnerability. *Neuroscience and Biobehavioral Reviews, 74*, 393–400. https://doi.org/10.1016/j.neubiorev.2016.04.018

Wood, S. K., Walker, H. E., Valentino, R. J., & Bhatnagar, S. (2010). Individual differences in reactivity to social stress predict susceptibility and resilience to a depressive phenotype: Role of corticotropin-releasing factor. *Endocrinology, 151*(4), 1795–1805. https://doi.org/10.1210/en.2009-1026

Wu, H. B., Stavarache, M., Pfaff, D. W., & Kow, L. M. (2007). Arousal of cerebral cortex electroencephalogram consequent to high-frequency stimulation of ventral medullary reticular formation. *Proc Natl Acad Sci USA, 104*(46), 18292–18296. https://doi.org/10.1073/PNAS.0708620104

Wyrofsky, R. R., Reyes, B. A. S., Zhang, X. Y., Bhatnagar, S., Kirby, L. G., & Van Bockstaele, E. J. (2019). Endocannabinoids, stress signaling, and the locus coeruleus-norepinephrine system. *Neurobiology of Stress,11*. https://doi.org/10.1016/j.ynstr.2019.100176

Yamagata, T., Kahn, M. C., Prius-Mengual, J., Meijer, E., Sabanovi, M., Guillaumin, M. C. C., van der Vinne, V., Huang, Y. G., McKillop, L. E., Jagannath, A., Peirson, S. N., Mann, E. O., Foster, R. G., & Vyazovskiy, V. V. (2021). The hypothalamic link between arousal and sleep homeostasis in mice. *Proc Natl Acad Sci U S A, 118*(51), e2101580118. https://doi.org/10.1073/PNAS.2101580118/-/DCSUPPLEMENTAL

Yu, H., Miao, W., Ji, E., Huang, S., Jin, S., Zhu, X., Liu, M. Z., Sun, Y. G., Xu, F., & Yu, X. (2022). Social touch-like tactile stimulation activates a tachykinin 1-oxytocin pathway to promote social interactions. *Neuron, 110*(6), 1051-1067.e7. https://doi.org/10.1016/J.NEURON.2021.12.022/

Yusuf, P. S., Hawken, S., Ôunpuu, S., Dans, T., Avezum, A., Lanas, F., McQueen, M., Budaj, A., Pais, P., Varigos, J., & Lisheng, L. (2004). Effect of potentially modifiable risk factors associated with myocardial infarction in 52 countries (the INTERHEART study): Case-control study. *Lancet, 364*(9438), 937–952. https://doi.org/10.1016/S0140-6736(04)17018-9

Zayfert, C., & De Viva, J. C. (2004). Residual insomnia following cognitive behavioral therapy for PTSD. *Journal of Traumatic Stress, 17*(1), 69–73. https://doi.org/10.1023/B:JOTS.0000014679.31799.e7

Zhang, Y., Ren, R., Yang, L., Zhou, J., Sanford, L., & Tang, X. (2019). The effect of treating obstructive sleep apnea with continuous positive airway pressure on post-traumatic stress disorder: A systematic review and meta-analysis with hypothetical model. *Neuroscience and Biobehavioral Reviews, 102*, 172–183.

Index

Note: Page locators in italics refer to figures; tables are noted with a *t*.

AASM. *see* American Academy of Sleep Medicine (AASM)
abdominal core muscles
   diaphragmatic breathing and, 94, 95–96
   mobilizing exhalation and, 106
   yawning breath and, 113
abreaction responses, power of, 242
ACC. *see* anterior cingulate cortex (ACC)
ACEs. *see* adverse childhood experiences (ACEs)
acetylcholine (Ach), xi, xii, xxv, 14, 104
actigraphy, 59–60
activating event, identifying in DBR treatment, 210, 212–13, 251, 272, 303
active attunement
   to breathing, summary of clinical issues for, 98–99
   as catalyst for internal psychic change, 86–88, 101
   definition of, 100
   knowing what is meant by, 86
   managing sleep disturbances and role of, 99
adrenaline, 17, 131, 132, 133, 161, 171, 176, 234
   breathing when in danger and, 105
   REM sleep and, 14
   takotsubo heart attacks and, 246
adverse childhood experiences (ACEs), 229, 235, 263
affective responses, shifting attention to, in DBR treatment, 210, 220, 257, 276–77
affective state of patient, maintaining goal of synchronizing with, 62–64
affirmations, 166
agency, 284
   pathway to change and, 65, 83, 94
   patient's response to heart attack, DBR, and, 267
aging, cardiovascular risk and, 244
AHI. *see* Apnea-Hypopnea Index (AHI)

alcohol use, sleep disturbances and, 64, 142, 143, 162
alignment
   definition and function of, 87
   safety and, 99
   see also therapeutic alliance
alpha activity, relaxation, drowsiness, and, 10
alpha-delta sleep, 16, 24
alpha waves, 24
Amb. *see* nucleus ambiguus (Amb)
American Academy of Sleep Medicine (AASM)
   Best Practice Guide for Treatment of Nightmares, 182
   International Classification of Sleep Disorders (ICSD, 3rd edition), 59
   nightmares as described by, 172
American Association of Sleep Medicine, 59
American Family Physicians Association, 147
Ammaniti, M., 58
amygdala, 117, 149, 175, 176, 199, 239
   adaptation, restless REM sleep and failure in, 230
   basolateral nucleus of, 203
   central nucleus of, 291–92
   chronic obstructive sleep apnea and, 135
   downregulation of tonic LC activation and, 293
   dynorphin release and, 267
   frozen in trauma time, restless REM and, 203
   integration of limbic responses of, 209
   survival challenge and response by, 207
amygdala-hippocampus-medial prefrontal cortex (AMY-HC-mPFC) circuit, memory processing during REM sleep and, 203
amygdalo-hippocampal transition area (Ahi), 176
anchor times, consistent sleep times and, 153, 156
angina, 250, 251, 269
   overwhelming cardiac, neuroendocrine response to, 267–68
   takotsubo cardiomyopathy and, 246, 247, 248

anhedonia, 14
ANS. *see* autonomic nervous system (ANS)
anterior cingulate cortex (ACC), 176, 202, 203, 205
anti-inflammatory response, 229, 234
anxiety, 123, 140, 176, 259
A1 cycles, 12, *12*, 13, 16, 19, *19*, 27, *27*, 30
apnea, meaning of, 26, 125. *see also* sleep apnea (SA)
Apnea-Hypopnea Index (AHI), 125, 126, 132, 134, 144
Apple watches, 168
ARAS. *see* ascending reticular activating system (ARAS)
arousals from sleep, as measured in sleep test, 130
arthritis, trauma and, 235
Art of Transforming Nightmares, The (Johnson), 182
ascending reticular activating system (ARAS), 199, 207, 227
  pain and activation of, 166–67
  signaling of muscular tension and, 117–18
Aserinsky, E., 146
assessments
  behavioral, of breathing pattern, 89–90, 89*t*
  breathing, relaying results of, 93–94
  breathing, reviewing results of, 100
  of current breathing pattern, 90–93
  of sleep in trauma patient, 42–43, 43*t*
atenolol, 167
atherosclerosis, 246
A3 cycles, 12, *12*, 13, 16, *19*, 20, 27, *27*, 30
atonia, aging and loss of, 33
atrial fibrillation, 28, 126, 132
attachment
  strengthening between child and caretakers, 61
  style, sleep difficulties and, 37
  unresolved conflicts about, 48
attachment-based approach to sleep repair, 37–57
  application, 56–57
  becoming a better sleep and trauma therapist, 39
  clinical application of relational work with insomnia, 45–53
  collaborative intersubjective clinical inquiry part I, 39–40
  part II, 62–64
  exploration of multiple sleep concerns: TABS model, 40–45
  five-level pyramid of CCPs in TABS model, 38, 38, 39, 57
  key messages for therapists, 57
  sleep evaluation in trauma, complex issues in, 53–56
attachment experiences, somatic symptoms and role of, 230–35
  impact of secure *vs.* insecure attachment, 230, *231*
  negative caregiver experiences, 232–33

positive caregiver experiences, 232
raphe nuclei and, 233–35
Attachment Interview protocol (Siegel), 38
attunement
  active, internal psychic change and, 86–88
  to breathing patterns, 88–99
  see also active attunement; therapeutic alliance, active attunement and
A2 cycles, 12, *12*, 13, 16, *19*, 20, 27, *27*, 30
AURORA Study, 178–80, 183
autobiographical memory, 175, 285
  brainstem activation and overwhelmed system of, 286, 287
  creation of, 322
  DBR and reactivation of, 324
  hemispheric encoding, retrieval asymmetry model of, 323
  sleep and consolidation of, 322
  sleep-related synaptic plasticity and, 203
  trauma and undermining of, 322–23
autogenic training, 107, 118
automatic triggers, 251
autonomic nervous system (ANS), xxvi, *xxvi*, 64, 65, 119, 229
  as central control panel, 190, 195
  dysfunction/dysregulation of, xxv, xxx, 155, 156
  dysregulated, targeting in psychotherapy, 320–21
  educating patient about, xxv, 82
  four TABS disrupting harmony in, xii
  internal level of distress and, 88
  as the master of sleep, 17
  nightmares and hyperactivation of, 173
  pre-sleep wind-down and, 118
  retraining and reorganizing, 83
  sleep apnea and, 26
  sleep duration, depth, and continuity and, 148
  sleep-wake rhythms and, 156
  targeting sleep problems and, xxiv
  trauma and dysregulation of, 320
  traumatic danger and flooding of, 176
  trauma treatment and stabilization of, 241, 264
  two branches of, 156
  vagal brake and, 103
aversive withdrawal responses, pain-induced, 239
AV node, diaphragmatic breathing and, 111
awakenings
  normal morning, visceral integration and, 15–16
  normal state transitions and, 14–15
  see also sleep-wake rhythms and patterns
awareness, safe therapeutic environment and, 48

Badenoch, B., 319
Barrington's nucleus, 238
basal ganglia, extinguishing of aversive responses and, 239
basolateral nucleus (Bn), 176
Beck Depression Inventory (BDI), 22

Index 347

bed nucleus of the stria terminalis (BNST), 176, 292
bedtimes, inconsistent, 23
behavioral anchors, of restorative sleep, 155–56
behavioral assessment, of breathing pattern, 86, 89–90, 89*t*
Behavioral Sleep Medicine (BSM), focus of, 146
belly breathing, 91, 93, 94, 95, 100
Bergmann, U., 183
Berridge, C., 206
beta activity, wakefulness, active thinking, and, 10
beta blockers, 167
bilateral brain stimulation, 186
bilateral eye movements
  EMDR therapy and, 183
  post-motor vehicle accident case study and, xix
  trauma reprocessing work and, 75, 76, 79, 80
biobehavioral danger response, 104–5
bisoprolol, 167
blood pressure, pre-sleep dipping of, 161
blood volume, LC activation and reduction in, 291–92
Bn. *see* basolateral nucleus (Bn)
BNST. *see* bed nucleus of the stria terminalis (BNST)
body armor, body tension, trauma, and, 116
body distress, sabotaged sleep rhythms and, 123, 124, 148. *see also* somatic distress
The Body Keeps the Score, (van der Kolk, B.), 229
body sensations
  memories around traumatic events and, 75
  sitting with, 163
body tension, resolving root cause of, xxv
Bogdanova, Y., 3
Bonci, A., 265
bonding, raphe nuclei and role of, 233
Borbely, A., 15
brain
  generalized activation of, 288
  brainstem, limbic, and bilateral cortical circuits of, *xxvi*
  restorative sleep and, 9
  systems, neurobiological maturation of, 174–75
  transmission of neural signals in, xi
  see also brainstem
Brain-Body Disconnect, The: A somatic sensory basis for trauma-related disorders (Kearney & Lanius), 230
brain fog, 267, 282, 284
Brain Mechanisms of Insomnia: New Perspectives on Causes and Consequences (Van Someren, E), 202
brainstem, xxv, 80, 95, 174, 284
  disconnecting stimulus and, 265
  hyperaroused, past life-threat moment and, 285
  interoception confronted with threat and, 237
  as master hub of neuromodulation, xi–xiv, xxv
  pathway from neurochemical dissociation, through sleep, to depression, 282, 283

"proto self" and, xii
raphe nuclei in, critical functions of, 233
stabilized, neuromodulatory shift in, 223
three regions of, 207
see also brain
brainstem tegmentum (red nucleus), 176
brain wave activity of traumatized individuals, variance in, 60
breathing
  behavioral assessment of, 86, 89–90, 89*t*
  heart rate and, 103
  retraining, 95
  when in danger, 104–5
  when safe, 103–4
  see also chest breathing; diaphragmatic breathing; whole body breathing; yawning breath
breathing disorders, lethality of sleep-related, 125
breathing patterns, 61
  attunement to, 88–99
  behavioral assessment of, 86, 89–90, 89*t*
  safety and, 102–3
  variance in, during therapeutic session, 102
breathing practice
  introduction to, 94–97
  paradoxical reaction to, 46–47, 48
bright light therapy, 165
Broca's area, 321
broken heart syndrome (takotsubo cardiomyopathy), clinical signature of, 246
Brownlow, J., 5
bruxism, 172
BSM. *see* Behavioral Sleep Medicine (BSM)
Bungner's nuclei, 233

CA. *see* complex apnea (CA)
calming pre-sleep activities, identifying, 162
Campbell, R., 121
Canadian Guidelines for Cardiac Rehabilitation and Disease Prevention, 244
Cappuccio, F., 244
CAPs. *see* cyclical alternating patterns (CAPs)
Clinician-Administered PTSD Scale for DSM-5 (CAPS-5), 127
cardiac rehabilitation (CR), 247, 250
cardiac rehab programs, mental health professionals and, 261
cardiovascular axis of stress, activation of LC-NE system and, 238
cardiovascular conditions, trauma and, 235
cardiovascular disease, as largest cause of mortality, 243
cardiovascular events
  sleep and increased risk of, 262
  treatment of traumatic consequences of, 230
cardiovascular reactivity
  LC-NE and activation of, summary of, 238
  social connectedness and, 243
cardiovascular risk factors, chronic stress and, 243–44

cardiovascular stress symptoms, trauma-informed treatment of, 245–46
cardiovascular system, impact of chronic stress on, 241–42, 242
Carney, C., 63
carotid arteries, stretch receptors in, 111
Carter, M. E., 293
Cartwright, R., 81, 82, 149, 197, 317, 321
case studies
  assessment of current breathing pattern, 90–94
  breathing practice, introduction to, 94–97
  CPAP treatment, patient's transition to adhering to, 141–43
  DBR treatment following a heart attack at home, 249–62
  EMDR treatment of intrusive thoughts, 184–95
  intersubjective cascade, 66–81
  motor vehicle collision: treatments provided after, xv–xxv
  neurochemical dissociation after a heart attack, 268–82
  persistent post-concussive syndrome (PPCS): insomnia returns after successful EMDR treatment, 296–315
  pharmacist robbed at gunpoint: sleep evaluation, 53–56
  relational work with insomnia, 45–53
  trauma treatment of takotsubo heart attack with EMDR, 246–49
  yawning breath, clinical application of, 107–18
Cassidy, C., 206
cataplexy, 26
caudal linear nucleus, 233
caudate nucleus, suppression of cortical excitability and, 202–3
CBT. see cognitive behavioral therapy (CBT)
CBTi. see cognitive behavioral therapy for insomnia (CBTi)
CBTn. see cognitive behavioral therapy for nightmares (CBTn)
CCPs. see clinical choice points (CCPs)
CeA. see central amygdala (CeA)
Center for Epidemiological Studies Depression scale (CES-D), 22
central amygdala (CeA), 176
central amygdala nucleus, interoception confronted with threat and, 237
central nervous system (CNS), Pfaff's five criteria for determining NGC activity is critical for generalized arousal of, 289
central sleep apnea (CSA), 125, 170
cerebellum, 175, 176, 207, 208
CES-D. see Center for Epidemiological Studies Depression scale (CES-D)
change, internal psychic, attunement and, 86–88
chest breathing, 90, 92, 93, 94, 99, 100, 105, 106, 111, 119

childhood parental loss (CPL), 260
Chu, C-S., 126
cingulate cortex, 236
circadian rhythm, basic, honoring, 147
circadian rhythm disorders, 8, 16, 22–23, 123, 124, 148, 170
clinical choice points (CCPs)
  in collaborative assessment, xxviii–xxx
  in TABS model, five-level pyramid of, 38, 38, 39, 57
  using roadmap for, 326
Clinical management of poor adherence to CPAP (Aloia et al.), 138
clinical questionnaires
  purpose of, 43
  TABS sleep repair screening questionnaires, 44t
co-embodiment, of young child with the mother, 230
cognitive arousal
  how brainstem survival responses are cause of, 294–96
  insomnia and, 286–87
  targeting brainstem centers at heart of, 287
cognitive behavioral therapy (CBT), 182
cognitive behavioral therapy for insomnia (CBTi), x, 7, 51, 146–47, 182, 206, 318, 325
cognitive behavioral therapy for nightmares (CBTn), 182, 195
"Cognitive Factors and Processes in Models of Insomnia" (Tang, et al.), 287
cognitive impairment, obstructive sleep apnea and, 141
cognitive processing therapy (CPT), 174, 206
cognitive ruminations, fragmented sleep and, 301
collaborative assessment, five critical clinical choice points in, xxviii–xxx
collaborative intersubjective clinical inquiry
  Part I, 38, 39–40; Part II, 62–64
Colvonen, P., 121
combat veterans
  insomnia and, 18
  nightmares of, 173
  trauma-associated sleep disorder and, 33
complex apnea (CA), frequency of, 125
complex trauma, challenge of, 61
complex trauma patients, frailty of intersubjective relational field and, 39–40
confusional arousals, 16–17, 24–25
connection, raphe nuclei and role of, 233
Consensus Sleep Diary, xxix, 64, 148, 151, *152*
  becoming familiar with, 169
  confidence in using, developing, 169
  introducing use of, 63
  reviewing with patient, 148
  see also sleep diary(ies)
consistent sleep times, 153–54
continuity of sleep, 147, 148

Index 349

Continuous Positive Airway Pressure (CPAP) treatment, 128
　adapting to, 135
　adherence to, 135–37
　anticipating compliance problems with, 124–25
　CAP activity after 30 days of CPAP treatment, 30, *30*
　celebrating patient achievements with, 145
　description of, 134
　initiating, xxx
　irregular or discontinued use of, 31
　Medicare criteria and, 136
　normalized TNF-α levels and, 244
　patient's transition to adhering to, case example, 141–43
　side effects with, 135
Continuous Positive Airway Pressure (CPAP) treatment, steps in intervention process, 137–41
　cognitive challenges, 141
　education and resistance to change, 137–38
　identifying daytime burdens of apnea, 138
　identifying mechanical challenges, 139
　mobilizing supports, 138
　panic attacks and fear of suffocation, 139–40
　relaxation training, 140
　tracking "good days," 141
core sleep, drowsy sleep and, 13–14
Corrigan, F., 206, 207, 210, 216, 306
corticotropic releasing factor (CRF), 229, 240, 293
　acute stress exposure and sources of release of, into LC, 238–39, 263
　LC neurons, major stress, and release of, 291, 292
　oxytocin release and reduction in, 232
cortisol, 14, 17, 131, 132, 133, 171, 229, 234, 283
COVID-19 pandemic, remote work and, 250
CPAP treatment. *see* Continuous Positive Airway Pressure (CPAP) treatment
CPL. *see* childhood parental loss (CPL)
CPT. *see* cognitive processing therapy (CPT)
CR. *see* cardiac rehabilitation (CR)
C-reactive protein (CRP), 234
CRF. *see* corticotropic releasing factor (CRF)
CRF-CNA afferent activation, resident-intruder model studies and, 240
CRF receptors (CRFr2), 229, 234, 263
Crisis Dreaming (Lamberg & Cartwright), 181
critical treatment need(s), identifying, 42
CRP. *see* C-reactive protein (CRP)
CSA. *see* central sleep apnea (CSA)
cyclical alternating patterns (CAPs), 16, 130
　primary insomnia and frequency/timing of CAP subtypes, 19, *19*
　sleep quality and, *12*, 12–13

Damasio, A., xii
danger
　amplified NGC-LC-orexin-thyroid circuit and, 286
　breathing when in, clinical example, 104–5
　evaluating, integrative hub of superior colliculus and, 207–8
　interoceptive signals and, 242
　motor responses to, 176
　NREM sleep disruption and, 17
　sleep impacted by, 23, 35
　see also threats
Daulatzai, M., 28
Davis, J., 171, 182
daytime functioning
　improved, nighttime changes and, 159
　restorative sleep and alertness, 9, 147
　well-being, normal cycling of REM and NREM sleep and, 171
　see also sleep-wake rhythms and patterns
deep brain reorienting (DBR), 195, 199, 200, 264, 266
　agency, patient's response to heart attack, and, 267, 284
　allowing space for tracking pre-affective shock responses (phase 5), 210, 216–20, 252–57, 273–76, 303–6
　attention shift to affective responses (phase 6), 210, 220, 257, 276–77
　clinical case application, for nightmares and insomnia, 211–25
　closure: highlighting role of pre-affective shock: EMDR *vs.* DBR processing, 221–25
　exploring new perspectives that emerge (phase 7), 210, 220–21, 257–59, 280–82
　guiding patient to orienting tension (phase 4), 210, 215–16, 252, 284
　heart attack at home and treatment with, 249–62
　identifying the activating event (phase 1), 210, 212–13, 251, 272, 303
　integrative hub of superior colliculus and, 207–8
　introducing activating event and tracking internal resources (phase 3), 210, 215, 252
　neurochemical dissociation after heart attack case, 268–82
　as a neuroscientifically guided psychotherapy for PTSD, 209
　orienting patient to their present where self (phase 2), 210, 213–14, 251, 273
　reactivation of autobiographical memory and, 324
　reflecting on the therapeutic experience, 277–80
　release of memory fragments through, 315
　reliving the experience *vs.* remembering the experience, 278

deep brain reorienting (DBR) (*continued*)
  sequence of phases in, 210
  summary of session and clinical implications, 225–26, 259–62
  targeted focus of, 227
  targeted resolution of LC hyperactivation and, 205–6
  transitioning from EMDR to, for post concussive syndrome, 300–303
  treatment of cardiovascular events and, 230
  treatment of cardiovascular stress symptoms and, 246
  website, training sessions, 226
  see also eye movement desensitization and reprocessing (EMDR)
deep breathing, 71, 72, 73, 140
deep sleep, 10 *see also* delta sleep
default mode network (DMN), visual processing and, 178
defeat latencies, resident-intruder model of human social stress and, 240
delta activity (slow-wave sleep), deep NREM sleep and, 10
delta waves, 10, 24
dementia, 141
depersonalization, dissociation and, 267, 284
depression, 16, 17, 21–22, 176
  defining sleep signatures of, 21
  pathway from neurochemical depression, through sleep, to, 282–84
  screening for, 22
  sleep apnea and, 26
derealization, dissociation and, 267, 284
de Souza, L., 265
desynchronization, as one of four enemies of sleep, xxv, 123, 124, 160
Developing Mind, The (Siegel, D.), 86
developmental attachment trauma, seven domains of, 61
dialectical behavior therapy (DBT), 206
diaphragmatic breathing, xxiii, 90, 92, 95, 101, 106, 161, 162, 163, 164, 225, 248
  boosting motivation to do, 110–11
  EMDR therapy and, 186–87
  exercises, experiential review of, 107–10
  key messages for therapists, 119
  teaching, 84
  three muscle groups in, 94
  transition to yawning breath from, 111–17
  see also yawning breath
diaphragmatic muscle, 94, 95, 96, 97, 114, 133
digestive conditions, trauma and impact on, 235
Dimesdale, J. E., 137
dipping phenomenon, 161
disembodiment, insecure attachment and, 230, 231, *231*
dissociation, 172, 220
  definition of, 265, 284

derealization and depersonalization and, 267, 284
  key messages for therapists, 284
  see also neurochemical dissociation
dissociative response, becoming a better sleep and trauma therapist, 266–67
dissociative shutdown, xxv
distressing bodily symptoms, pain and numbness as types of, xxv. *see also* somatic distress
distrust of complex trauma patient, managing, 65–66
disturbed sleep, identifying causes of, 155–57
disturbed sleep in trauma, many faces of, 16–34
  alpha-delta sleep, 16, 24
  circadian rhythm disturbances, 16, 22–23
  confusional arousals, 16–17, 24–25
  danger, 17, 23
  depression, 12–22, 16
  insomnia, 16, *19*, 19–21, *20*, 41
  isolated REM behavior disorder, 33, 41
  narcolepsy, 17, 25–26
  nightmares, 16, 17–18, 41
  night terrors, 17, 25, 41
  nonrestorative sleep, 16
  overview, 16–17
  periodic limb movements disorder, 16, 23–24
  restless legs syndrome, 16, 23–24
  restless REM sleep and amygdala adaptation, 31–32
  sleep apnea, 16, 26–31, *27*, *29*, *30*, 41
  sleep paralysis, 16, 32, 41
  sleepwalking, 17, 25, 41
  trauma-associated sleep disorder, 33–34
dizziness, breathing exercises and, 93
dlPAG. *see* dorsolateral PAG (dlPAG)
dlPFC. *see* dorsolateral prefrontal cortex (dlPFC)
DMN. *see* default mode network (DMN)
dopamine, xi, xii, xxv
  depressed patients and, 22
  sleep regulation and, xxxi, 6
dopamine system, activation of kappa opioid receptors and, 268
dorsal motor nucleus of the vagus (DMV)
  LC-NE's activation of cardiovascular reactivity and, 238
  locus coeruleus, cardiovascular signals, and, 291
dorsal raphe nucleus (DRN), xii, 199, 227, 233, 286, 292
  inflammatory processes in traumatized individuals and, 234
  unresponsive caretaker experience and, 234
dorsal striatum, extinguishing of aversive responses and, 239
dorsal visual stream (DVS), 178
dorsolateral PAG (dlPAG), 79, 259, 260, 286, 323
  fight-flight-freeze response and, 208–9
  overwhelming cardiac angina and response of, 267

Index 351

overwhelm response and, 266
reprocessing work and activation of, 70
restoration of emotional responses and, 69
dorsolateral prefrontal cortex (dlPFC), 176
Drake, C., 37
Dream Completion Therapy, 182, 195
dreaming
  downregulation of LC-NE system and, 270
  updating of autobiographical schemas and, 321
dreams
  of decreasing emotional intensity, 318
  key messages for therapists, 195–96
  remembering, 14, 149–50
  rewriting scripts in, 4-step process in, 181–82
DRN. *see* dorsal raphe nucleus (DRN)
drowsy sleep, core sleep and, 13–14
DSM-5
  insomnia disorder (ID) criteria in, 198
  nightmare disorder criteria in, 18, 172–73
  PTSD re-classification in, 80
  somatic symptom disorders in, 228
DVS. *see* dorsal visual stream (DVS)
dyadic developmental psychotherapy treatment, 62
dynorphin (DYN), 209, 269, 273, 282, 283, 284, 286
  heart attacks and release of, 266–67
  memory functions and release of, 270, 272
  orexin neurons and release of, 292
  pain and release of, 266, 296

eCBs. *see* endocannabinoids (eCBs)
electroencephalogram (EEG), 58, 59
electroencephalography (EEG), 9–10, 58, 59
electromyography (EMG), 10
electrooculography (EOG), 10, 58, 59
embodied chronic stress, reversing, 105–6, 119
embodiment, secure attachment and, 230, *231*
EMDR. *see* eye movement desensitization and reprocessing (EMDR)
emotional distress, 148
emotional resonance, hope and, 99
encouraging, intersubjective field and, 60
endocannabinoids (eCBs), 266, 293
endocannabinoid system, 239
endocrine limb, of the stress response, 228, 229, 263
endorphins, 171
endothelial dysfunction, sleep apnea and, 28
enkephalin, 266, 293
EOG. *see* electrooculography (EOG)
episodic memories, 175, 287
  encoding and retrieval of, 323
  semantic memory *vs.*, 322
  sleep-related synaptic plasticity and, 203
Epsom baths, 167
Epworth Sleepiness Scale (ESS), 127, 144, 145
ERRT. *see* exposure, relaxation, and rescripting therapy (ERRT)

ESS. *see* Epworth Sleepiness Scale (ESS)
exercise, essential rest breaks and, 271
exhalation
  breathing when safe and, 104
  diaphragmatic breathing and, 96
  relaxation activated by, 106
  slow and complete, 110–11
  therapeutic breathing and, 97
  yawning breath and, 113–14
explicit memories, 175
exposure, relaxation, and rescripting therapy (ERRT), 182, 195
exposure therapy, 206
eye contact, 60
eye movement desensitization and reprocessing (EMDR), 174, 182, 183–84, 195, 206, 211, 212, 250, 269, 325
  cardiovascular stress symptoms and treatment with, 246
  clinical application: the intersubjective cascade, 66–81
  CPAP treatment and, 138, 140
  eye movements used in, role of, 80
  intrusive thoughts and treatment with, 184–95
  post-motor vehicle accident case study, xix–xxi, *xx*, 296
  takotsubo heart attack and treatment with, 246–49
  targeted focus of, 227
  transitioning to DBR from, for post concussive syndrome, 300–303
  see also deep brain reorienting (DBR)
eye movements
  bilateral, trauma reprocessing work and, 75, 76, 79
  of REM, purpose of, 82
  treatment of intrusive symptoms and, 183
eye-movement storms, depression and, 22

facial expressions, 69, 70
fatigue, sleepiness *vs.*, 24
fear, 266
  of darkness, 20, 21, 44*t*
  of sleep, 18, 19, 20, 20–21, 44*t*
Fear of Sleep Inventory (FoSI), 20
Fear of Sleep Inventory-Short Form (FoSI-SF), 21, 44*t*, 51, 52
feeling felt, 63, 87
fight-flight-freeze response
  breathing when in danger and, 104
  phrenic nerve and, 103
  unresponsive caretaker experience and, 234
fight-or-flight response, 102, 171, 208
  activated sympathetic system and, 88, 93
  fragmented sleep and, 157
  initiation of, 175
  obstructive sleep apnea and, 127
  overwhelm response, activated dlPAG, and, 266

fight-or-flight response (*continued*)
  oxygen desaturation and, 131
  paradoxical reaction and, 98
Fitbits, 168
flashbacks, xxv, 17, 33, 53, 54, 172, 196, 209, 321
  activation of ventral visual system and, 178–80
  alarm reaction of locus coeruleus and, 176
  fragmented sleep and, 302
  life-or-death states and, 268
Flinders, J., 243
Fogel, A., 102, 228
Forster, G., 232
FoSI. *see* Fear of Sleep Inventory (FoSI)
FoSI-SF. *see* Fear of Sleep Inventory-Short Form (FoSI-SF)
Foster, R., 294
fragmented short sleepers, management of, 311–15
fragmented short-sleep insomnia
  casualties of, 294
  clinical features of, 294–96
fragmented short sleep phenotype of insomnia, 286–87
fragmented sleep
  consolidating, 165–68
  sleep diary results, 154
  sympathetic bursts of activity and, 157
freeze state, neuroendocrine response to cardiac angina and, 267. *see also* fight–flight–freeze response
Freud, S., 85, 86
fusiform gyrus, 179

GABA, xxv
Gallese, V., 58
gamma activity, 10
Garmin wearables, 168
Gehrman, P., 3, 5, 37
gender, age at first heart attack and, 250
Germain, A., xii, 3, 5, 18, 37, 121, 324
Gilbert, K., 3
glutamate, xxv, 292
glutamatergic neurons, NREM sleep and optogenetic stimulation of, 294
glutaminergic neurons, motor, cortical, and autonomic responses and, 289
Graeff, F. G., 259, 260
gratitude, review of day and, 164
gratitude journal, 164
grief and loss, 66–78, 266
grounding, EMDR therapy and, 186–87

Halliday, G., 181
Harnett, N., 183
Hartmann, E., 171, 173, 317, 318
Havens, J., 182
health, trauma and impacts on, 235
health psychology, aims of, 245, 264

heart attacks, 230, 315, 319
  dynorphin release and, 266–67
  first, INTERHEART Study on, 243–44
  at home, DBR treatment for, 249–62
  neurochemical dissociation after (case study), 268–82, 284
  prevalence adjusted risk for, in INTERHEART Study, 243
  sleep apnea and, 28
  takotsubo, EMDR treatment of, 246–49
  trauma-informed treatments and, 246
heart rate
  breathing and, 103
  breathing when in danger and, 105
  diaphragmatic breathing and, 111
  dipping of, before sleep, 161
hemispheric encoding/retrieval asymmetry (HERA) model, of episodic memory, 323
hippocampal-amygdala-neocortex network, NREM spindles and "sleep dialogue" in, 295
hippocampus, 80, 81, 129, 130, 149, 175
  dynorphin release and, 267
  explicit memories and myelinization of, 175
  extinguishing of aversive responses and, 239
  integration of limbic responses of, 209
  survival challenge and response by, 207
histamine, xi, xii, xxv
holding the breath, 92, 93
hope, emotional resonance and, 99
hormones, ultradian sleep cycles and, 14
HPA axis, dysphoric state and, 282
Hughes, D., 62
hyperarousal, as one of four enemies of sleep, xxv, 123, 124, 160
hypertension, sleep apnea and, 28
hypnogram, of brain sleep states across night of sleep, 9, 11, *11*
hypocretin-orexin system, narcolepsy and, 25
hypothalamic-pituitary-thyroid pathway, paraventricular nucleus and, 291
hypothalamus, 176, 207
  chronic somatic distress and, 117
  solitary nucleus of, 236
hypoxemia, sleep apnea and, 27
hypoxia, 132, 148
  cardiovascular risk and, 244
  as one of four enemies of sleep, xxv, xxx, 123, 124, 160, 170
  sleep apnea and, 27, 29

IC. *see* inferior colliculi (IC)
ID. *see* insomnia disorder
imagery of your oasis, developing, 164
imagery rehearsal therapy (IRT), 174, 182, 195
immune functioning, sleep and, 150
immunological limb, of the stress response, 175, 228, 229, 263

Index 353

implicit memories, 175, 206, 287, 317
   of accident-related autonomic arousal, resolution of, 311–14
   development of memory circuits, 174
inconsistent sleep times, trauma patients and, 23
inferior colliculi (IC), 289
inferior temporal gyrus (ITG), 176, 178, 179, 195
inflammation
   cardiovascular risk and, 244
   chronic, trauma survivors and, 235
   raphe nuclei and regulation of, 233–35
   sleep and reduction in, 150
   sleep apnea and, 26
   systemic, sleep apnea and, 132
inhalation
   breathing when safe and, 104
   filling of lungs and, 110
innate alarm response, locus coeruleus and initiation of, 175–77, 291
inner confidence, sleep and, 99
Insana, S., 37
insecure attachment
   disembodied experience of self and, 230, 231, *231*
   sleep disorders and, 38
insomnia, xiii, 8, 16, 19–21, 36, 41, 64, 123, 124, 172, 176, 196, 318
   as arousal, Riemann's sleep research and, 201–2
   CBTi as frontline treatment for, 147
   chronic, definition of, 198–99
   chronic, key messages for therapists, 315
   chronic, tense breathing and, 104
   chronic, underlying brain mechanisms in, 200–205
   classic pattern in, 160
   definition of, 19
   fragmented short sleep phenotype of, 286–87
   prevalence of, 197
   primary, frequency and timing of CAP subtypes in, *19*, 19–20
   PTSD as associated sleep disorder with, 19
   relational work with: clinical application, 45–53
   risk for cardiac events and, 244
   screening for, 21
   sleep apnea comorbid with, 140
   studies of, 59
   trauma-induced, 18, *20*, 20–21
   see also deep brain reorienting (DBR); fragmented short-sleep insomnia; imagery rehearsal therapy (IRT)
insomnia disorder (ID), 227
   assessing, in trauma patients, 226
   becoming a better sleep and trauma therapist, 199–200

   definition of, 199, 226–27
   DSM-5 criteria for, 198
   evaluating for, 200
   life experiences leading to, 200
   restless REM sleep at heart of, 199
   studies of, 59
Institute of Medicine, 160
insula, 176, 202, 230, 235
insular cortex, 117, 236
insulin levels, regular meal times and, 165
"in sync" communication, 62, 66
in sync patient/therapist relationship, trauma reprocessing work and, 66–78
intercostal muscles
   diaphragmatic breathing and, 94
   mobilizing exhalation and, 106
INTERHEART Study, on factors related to first heart attacks, 243–44
internal psychic change, active attunement and, 86–88, 101
internal sensations, attending to cascade of, in DBR treatment, 210, 215
International Classification of Sleep Disorders, Third Edition, 125
interoception
   Schulz and Vögele Process Model of, 236, 236–38, 245
   in trauma, 230
interoceptive system, retraining, 245
intersubjective collaborative cascade in trauma treatment, 58–84
   application, 82–83
   becoming a better sleep and trauma therapist, 60–61
   challenge of complex trauma, 61
   clinical application: intersubjective cascade, 66–78
   clinical issues emerging from, summary of, 78–81
   collaborative intersubjective clinical inquiry: Part II, 62–64
   increasing awareness and fostering of, 83
   key messages for therapists, 83–84
   resistant patients, dealing with, 64–66
   sleep as behavior *vs.* as experience, 60–61
   summary of issues, 78–81
   24-hour mind and, 81–82
intersubjective experiences, sharing, 62, 63
intersubjective relational field, 60, 84
   frailty of, complex trauma patients and, 39
   safety and, 79, 80
intersubjective relationship, paying ongoing attention to, 84
intersubjective two-person therapeutic field, defining, 60
intrusive symptoms, eye movements and treatment of, 183
intrusive thoughts, xxv, 47, 196, 318

intrusive thoughts, recurrent, EMDR treatment of, 184–95
  desensitizing and reprocessing trauma, 187
  grounding and diaphragmatic breathing, 186–87
  insight into self-critical thinking, further integration of, 194–95
  Julie's story, 184–89
  origins of pain, 187–88
  pain, depression, and disability, 185
  quieting the negative voice, 188–89
  transformative session: emergence of negative voice, transcript of, 189–94
  trauma treatment, 185–86
iRBD. *see* isolated REM behavior disorder (iRBD)
IRT. *see* imagery rehearsal therapy (IRT)
isolated REM behavior disorder (iRBD), 33, 41
isolation, sleep difficulties and, 46, 47
ITG. *see* inferior temporal gyrus (ITG)
ITG-DMN connectivity, PTSD symptoms and, 180
Ito, H., 265

Janet, P., 229
jaw, tension and pain in, 166–67
Johnson, C., 182

kappa opioid receptors (KOR), 171, 266, 268
Kark, S., 3
K-complex waves, 130
Kearney, B., 230
Kitchur, M., 38, 85
Klein, D. F., 260
Kolko, D., 37
KOR. *see* kappa opioid receptors (KOR)
Krakow, B., 182

Lancel, M., 5
Lanius, R., 60, 230, 234, 235, 283
lateral geniculate nuclei (LGN), 176
lateral habenula (LHb), 22, 282
laterodorsal tegmental nucleus (LDT), 199, 227
laughter, trauma reprocessing work and, 73, 75, 78
LC. *see* locus coeruleus (LC)
LC-NE nucleus, interoception confronted with threat and, 237
LC-NE system. *see* locus coeruleus-norepinephrine (LC-NE) system
LD. *see* lucid dreaming (LD)
LDT. *see* laterodorsal tegmental nucleus (LDT)
left-brain circuits, xxvi, *xxvi*
left hemisphere of brain, 174
Levine, P., 319
Lewis, K. E., 136
Lewy body dementia, isolated REM behavior disorder and, 33
LGN. *see* lateral geniculate nuclei (LGN)

LHb. *see* lateral habenula (LHb)
life-or-death situations
  activated dissociative responses and, 266
  presence of others in, importance of, 273–74
  survival response centers activated by, 286–87
light box, 165
light sleep, 129
limbic system, xxvi, *xxvi*, 174, 175, 207
limb movements, xxx. *see also* periodic limb movements disorder (PLMD); restless legs syndrome
Linden, W., 245
Lindsley, D., 288
locus coeruleus (LC), 175, 176, 199, 203, 208, 215, 216, 227
  amplified survival response and, 291–93
  breathing when in danger and, 104
  cardiovascular and visceral inputs, 291–92
  downregulated tonic activation of, 293
  hyperactivation, deep brain reorienting and, 205–6
  innate alarm system initiated by, 175–77, 291
  norepinephrine and, xii
  orexin pathway and, 292–93
  pain-induced aversive withdrawal responses and, 239
  PTSD and central role of, 205, 210
  REM sleep and critical activity level of, 203, 204
  resident-intruder model studies and, 240, 241
  resolving sleep problems and deactivation of, 325
  restless REM sleep and, 32
  size, 7-Tesla study of, 205
  stress-related symptoms and, 235
  survival challenge and response of, 207
  unresponsive caretaker experience and, 234
locus coeruleus-norepinephrine (LC-NE) system, 199, 200, 318
  cardiovascular reactivity activated by, 238
  dreaming and downregulation of, 270
  LC-NE activity, chronic hyperarousal of, 229, 263
  LC-NE alarm system, restless REM sleep and sustained activation of, 201–2
  LC-NE tonic activation, stabilization of, 239
  tonic activation of, mechanisms behind, 238–39
locus coeruleus-paraventricular feedback loop, 291
long-term memories
  core sleep and, 13
  sleep architecture and, 129–30
loss of control, fear of, 20, 21, 44t, 53
lucid dreaming (LD), 182, 195
Luyster, F. S., 140
Lyons, J., 123

MA. *see* microarousals (MA)
magnesium glycinate, 167

Magoun, H., 288
MAID. *see* Medical Assistance in Dying (MAID)
Mallick, B. N., 202
masks, CPAP, 134, 135, 137, 139, 140
　mask desensitization and, 138
　mask fit, guidance for, 139
　mask habituation and, 138
McKeon, A., 121
meal times, across 10 hours of wake time, 165
medial geniculate nuclei (MGN), 176
medial medullary reticular system, wakefulness activated by, 288–90
medial raphe, 233
medial temporal gyrus, 179
Medical Assistance in Dying (MAID), 66, 67
medically unexplained disorder (MUD), 229
medications, sleep and, 167
meditation, 161, 162, 211
medulla oblongata, 207
melatonin, 11, 167
memory functions, dynorphin release and, 270, 272
memory(ies)
　autobiographical, 175, 203, 285, 286, 287, 322–24, 323
　episodic, 175, 203, 287, 322, 323
　explicit, 175
　implicit, 174, 175, 206, 287, 311–14, 317
　long-term, 13, 129–30
　PTSD, sleep spindles, and consolidation of, 295
　semantic, 203, 322, 323
　short-term, 130
　threat experiences and, 237
memory systems, clinical negotiation of diverse, 321
mental models of security, development of, 87
Merker, B., xii
mesocortical system, dynorphin and dysregulation of, 268
mesolimbic system, dynorphin and dysregulation of, 268
metabolic activity, pre-sleep dip in, 161
MGN. *see* medial geniculate nuclei (MGN)
microarousals (MA), 176
midbrain, 207, 208
Miglis, M., 285
migraine headaches, 94
Miller, K., 5
Miller, M., 244
mixed sleep apnea, 170
MoCA. *see* Montreal Cognitive Assessment (MoCA)
Moldofsky, H., 295
monoamine oxidase-A (MAO-A), reduced, REM sleep deprivation and, 201
Montgomery, P., ix
Montreal Cognitive Assessment (MoCA), 141

mood
　NREM-REM cycling and changes in, 149
　raphe nuclei and regulation of, 233
Morris, L., 205
Moruzzi, G., 288
motor responses, glutaminergic neurons and, 289
motor vehicle collision: treatments provided after (case study), xv–xxv, 296
　advised about concussion, xv–xvi
　conventional treatments and impacts summary, xix, xxiii*t*
　DBR and reactivation of autobiographical memory, 324
　headache intensities for 10-month period after accident, xvi, xvi–xvii
　key symptoms and treatment results summary, xxiii*t*
　noise sensitivity post-accident, xvii–xviii, *xviii*, xxiii*t*
　post concussive symptom relief with trauma sleep therapy, xxiii–xxiv
　smell sensitivity post-accident, xviii, xxiii*t*
　total sleep time before/during EMDR therapy, xx, *xx*, 297–98, 312
　total sleep time first 4 months post-accident, xvii, *xvii*, 296, 297
　trauma sleep therapy as post concussive treatment, xxiv–xxv
　trauma sleep therapy: benefits of, xix–xxi
　see also persistent post-concussive syndrome (PPCS) case
mouth breathing, 139
mPFC
　anticipatory anxiety about panic attacks and, 259
　extinguishing of aversive responses and, 239
MUD. *see* medically unexplained disorder (MUD)
muscle relaxation, xxiii. *see also* progressive muscle relaxation (PMR)
muscle tension, breathing when in danger and, 105
muscular stress, reversing patterns of, 105–6, 119
musculoskeletal pain, sleeplessness and, 295–96
Muse, 168
music, sleep and, 162

NAc. *see* nucleus accumbens (NAc)
Naegeli, C., 206
naps and napping, 155, 158, 167–68, 270
narcolepsy, xiii, xxx, 8, 17, 25–26, 54, 123, 124, 131, 148, 170
nasal pillows, 139
Nash, W., 285
National Child Traumatic Stress Network of the United States, *White Paper on Complex Trauma*, 61
NDI. *see* Nightmare Disorder Inventory (NDI)

NE. *see* norepinephrine (NE)
neck, tension and pain in, 166–67
neck rolls, 167
negative caregiver experiences
    raphe nuclei and, 233–34
    somatic symptoms and, 232–33
negative emotions, sleep and desensitization of, 15
negative voice
    bringing to awareness, EMDR and, 183, 188, 191, 192, 193, 194
    emergence of, transcript of EMDR session, 189–94
    quieting, 188–89
neocortex, 80, 81
nervous system, retraining, 65
neurochemical dissociation, pathway from, through sleep, to depression, 282–84
neurochemical dissociation, 319
    becoming a better sleep and trauma therapist and, 267
    features of, 267, 268, 284, 296
    key messages for therapists, 284
neuroinflammation, sleep apnea and, 28
neuromelanin sensitive MRI (NM-MRI), caudal LC signal study and, 206
neuromodulation
    brainstem as master hub of, xi–xiv, xxv
    definition of, xi
new perspectives, exploring, in DBR treatment, 210, 220–21, 257–59, 280–82
NGC. *see* nucleus gigantocellularis (NGC)
NGC-LC-orexin-thyroid system
    activated, fragmented short sleep phenotype of insomnia and, 286–87, 315
    lack of sleep, social withdrawal pattern, and, 296
    new autobiographical memory and deactivation of, 324
NGC-LC-PAG-VTA-DRN complex, as driver of all PTSD symptoms, 325
Nightmare Disorder Index (Dietch, et al.), 18
Nightmare Disorder Inventory (NDI), 44*t*
nightmares, xiii, 8, 14, 16, 17–18, 26, 33, 41, 53, 54, 55, 64, 123, 124, 159, 172, 199, 227, 315, 321
    activation of ventral visual system and, 178–80
    alarm reaction of locus coeruleus and, 176, 177
    becoming better sleep and trauma therapist and, 174
    description of, 172
    key messages for therapists, 195–96
    pharmacological treatments for, 182
    replicative, 18, 32, 33, 54, 150, 173, 209, 318
    rescripting, 181–82
    resistance to CPAP therapy and, 1236
    restless REM sleep and, 204
    screening for, 18
    specific targeting of, treatments for, 181–83
    spectrum of intensity for, 18
    twofold task management of, 177
    see also deep brain reorienting (DBR); imagery rehearsal therapy (IRT); cognitive behavior therapy for nightmares (CBTn)
night panic, 25
night terrors, xiii, 8, 17, 25, 41, 123, 172, 173, 177, 195, 199, 227, 318
Nissen, C., 197
noise sensitivity, post-accident case study, xvii, *xviii*, xxiii, xxiv
non-rapid eye movement (NREM) sleep, xiii, 58, 81, 149, 172, 203
    danger and, 17
    limb movements during, 23
    night terrors and, 25
    normal state transitions awakenings and, 14–15
    restless sleep and, 203, 205
    shifts from REM sleep to, 81, 82
    silencing of LC-NE brainstem-initiated reactions and, 320
    sleep apnea and, 28
    sleep fragmentation and, 294–95
    sleepwalking and, 25
    stages in, 10, 11, *11*
    three phases of, 129
    see also rapid eye movement (REM) sleep
nonreplicative posttraumatic nightmares, 18
nonrestorative sleep (NRS), xiii, 16, 24, 172, 198, 199, 203, 227, 318
nonverbal responses, trauma reprocessing work and, 68, 70, 77, 78
noradrenaline, 104, 203
norepinephrine (NE), xi, xii, xxv, xxxi, 6, 175, 203, 207, 227, 291. *see also* locus coeruleus–norepinephrine (LC–NE) system
NREM sleep. *see* non-rapid eye movement (NREM) sleep
NRS. *see* nonrestorative sleep (NRS)
NTS. *see* nucleus tractus solitarius (NTS)
N2 sleep, sleep spindles and, 295
nucleus accumbens (NAc), 176
nucleus ambiguus (Amb), 207, 236, 238, 259
nucleus gigantocellularis (NGC), 286, 288, 289, 290, 315
nucleus paragigantocellularis (PGi)
nucleus prepositus hypoglossi (PrH)
nucleus tractus solitarius (NTS), 117, 207, 236, 289, 291
    pain-induced aversive withdrawal responses and, 239
    sleep apnea and, 28

oasis
    of calm, creating, 48–49, 50
    creating, options for activating the braking system, 164

obesity, cardiovascular risk and, 244
obstructive sleep apnea (OSA), 170
　　frequency of, 125
　　screening for, 31
OFC. *see* orbitofrontal cortex (OFC)
Ogden, P., 86
Olanzapine, 182
opioids, regulation of social isolation distress and, 260
optic nerve, 177
orbitofrontal cortex (OFC), 202, 203
orexin-gating switch, sleep-wake response to extreme danger and, 268
orexin-hypocretin system, 131
orexin pathway, locus coeruleus and, 292–93
organ system, waking life and, 15
orienting tension (OT), 208, 227
　　guiding patient to, in DBR treatment, 210, 215–16, 252, 284
　　SC and mobilization of, 175
orphanages, touch deprivation studies in, 232
OSA. *see* obstructive sleep apnea (OSA)
overwhelming experiences, dissociation and intensity of, 265
oxidative stress, sleep apnea and, 28
oxygen, blood saturation levels of, across the night, 27–28, 28
oxygen desaturation, 123, 124, 125, 126, 127, 131, 132, 133
oxytocin
　　attuned presence of a caregiver and, 232
　　breathing when safe and, 104
　　raphe nuclei and, 232
　　REM sleep and, 14
　　snuggling with teddy bear and, 166
　　yawning and, 102

PAG. *see* periaqueductal gray (PAG)
Pagani, M., 80
pain
　　intense, dynorphin release and, 266, 296
　　in jaw, neck, and shoulders, 166–67
　　sleep disruption and, 160
　　uncontrollable, PAG and response to, 267
pain-induced aversive withdrawal responses, 239
Palagini, L., 37
panic attacks, 172, 177, 259, 260, 277, 280
　　CPAP treatment and, 137
　　fear of suffocation with CPAP machine and, 139
　　nocturnal, 127
Panksepp, J., 260
parabrachial nucleus, 117, 236
paradoxical reactions, 98
　　introducing yawning breath and, 111
　　to relaxation, 106
parasomnias, 127
parasympathetic activation, three signals of, 113, 114, 115, 119

parasympathetic braking system
　　boosting, 86, 95, 100
　　sleep and, 111
parasympathetic nervous system (PNS), 103, 104, 112, 119, 156
　　balance between sympathetic nervous system and, 88, 90
　　boosting, sleep and, 65, 83, 95, 101, 161
　　breathing when in danger and, 104
　　deep sleep and, 157
　　mobilizing exhalation and, 106
　　nickname for, 111
　　pre-sleep wind-down and, 118
　　yawning and, 102
paraventricular nucleus (PVN), 291
Parker, J., 123
Parkinson's disease, isolated REM behavior disorder and, 33
Parrino, L., 30
passive behavioral coping response, cardiovascular dysfunction and, 240–41
Patient Health Questionnaire (PHQ9), 22
patients, use of term in text, xxv
pausing and nodding, intersubjective field and, 60
PCL-5. *see* PTSD Checklist for *DSM-5* (PCL-5)
pedunculopontine nucleus (PPN), 199, 227
pedunculopontine structures, acetylcholine and, xii
pedunculopontine tegmental nucleus (PPT), 293
periaqueductal gray (PAG), 175, 176, 199, 200, 215, 216, 227, 289
　　breathing when in danger and, 104
　　central functions of, 267
　　emotional-behavioral response to danger and, 208–9
　　life-or-death experiences and defensive responses of, 266
　　pain-induced aversive withdrawal responses and, 239
　　survival challenge and response of, 207
　　unresponsive caretaker experience and, 234
periodic limb movements disorder (PLMD), 16, 23–24, 54, 130
Perlis, M., 21
persistent post concussive syndrome (PPCS), 288, 314–15
persistent post concussive syndrome case
　　allowing space for patient to track pre-affective shock responses, 303–6
　　email describing experiences after first DBR session, 307
　　identifying the activating event, 303
　　insights from sleep test, 299–300
　　insomnia returns after successful EMDR treatment, 296–315
　　key messages for therapists, 315
　　resolution of autonomic arousal and PTSD and PPCS, 314–15

persistent post concussive syndrome case (continued)
  resolution of implicit memories of accident-related autonomic arousal, 311–14
  total sleep time after DBR therapy: 5 month follow-up, 313–14, *314*
  total sleep time before and during DBR treatment, 312, *313*
  total sleep time between EMDR and DBR treatments, 298, 298–99, 312
  transcript of therapy session later that day, 307–11
  transitioning from EMDR to DBR for post-concussive syndrome, 300–303
Pfaff, D., 288, 289, 290, 291
PFC. *see* prefrontal cortex (PFC)
PGi. *see* nucleus paragigantocellularis (PGi)
pharmacist robbed at gunpoint case, discussion between trainee and supervisor, 53–56
PHQ9. *see* Patient Health Questionnaire (PHQ9)
phrenic nerve, 119
  breathing when safe and, 103
  fight-flight-freeze reaction and, 103
physical distress, as one of four enemies of sleep, xxv, 123, 124, 160, 170
physiotherapy, duration and impact, post-concussion case study, xxiii*t*
Pietrzak, R. H., 235
Pigarev, I. N., 15, 230
Pittsburgh Sleep Quality Index (PSQI), 44*t*
Pittsburgh Sleep Quality Index PSQI-Addendum for PTSD, 5, 44*t*
PLMD. *see* periodic limb movements disorder (PLMD)
PMR. *see* progressive muscle relaxation (PMR)
PNS. *see* parasympathetic nervous system (PNS)
POA. *see* preoptic areas (POA)
polysomnogram, 54
  conveying purpose of, 127–28
  screening for obstructive sleep apnea, 31
polysomnographic (PSG) sleep study, 58–59
polysomnography, 9
pons, 207, 208
positive caregiver experiences
  raphe nuclei and, 233
  somatic symptoms and, 232
posture, therapeutic breathing and, 97–98
PPCS. *see* persistent post concussive syndrome (PPCS)
PPN. *see* pedunculopontine nucleus (PPN)
PPT. *see* pedunculopontine tegmental nucleus (PPT)
Prazosin, 182
pre-affective shock responses, tracking, in DBR treatment, 210, 216–20, 252–57, 273–76, 303–6
prefrontal cortex (PFC), 129, 175, 207, 208
preoptic areas (POA), 291

Pre-Sleep Arousal Scale (PSAS), 51, 52
Pre-Sleep Arousal Scale: Cognitive Experiences (PSAS), 44*t*, 52
Pre-Sleep Arousal Scale: Somatic Experiences (PSAS), 44*t*, 52
pre-sleep rituals, 159
pre-sleep triggers, identifying and removing, 162
pre-sleep wind-down routine, beginning, 118
Preter, M., 260
PrH. *see* nucleus prepositus hypoglossi (PrH)
primary visual cortex, visual signals and, 178
progressive muscle relaxation (PMR), 107, 118, 140, 163, 211, 225
pro-inflammatory cytokines, inflammatory processes in traumatized individuals and, 234–35
pro-inflammatory responses, 229, 234
prosody, 60, 62
"proto self," brainstem and, xii
Pruiksma, K., 182
PSAS. *see* Pre-Sleep Arousal Scale: Cognitive Experiences (PSAS); Pre-Sleep Arousal Scale: Somatic Experiences (PSAS)
PSQI. *see* Pittsburgh Sleep Quality Index (PSQI)
psychoeducation, about role of sleep, 41
psychotherapy, goal of, 285
PTSD, 176
  adherence to CPAP treatment and, 145
  AURORA Study on nightmares and, 178–80
  chronically disturbed REM and, 32
  complex somatic components of, 80
  CPAP and improvement in, 135
  deep brain reorienting approach to, 209–10
  developmental perspective of brain maturation and, 174–75
  disrupted hormone ebbs and flows and, 14
  hyperaroused fear system in, 15–16
  insomnia disorder as transdiagnostic risk factor for, 198, 199, 202
  nightmares, 173
  obstructive sleep apnea and, 126, 127
  PCL-5 and diagnosis of, 51
  protocols, integration of sleep treatment in, xxx–xxxi, 5–6
  resolution of autonomic arousal in, 314–15
  restless REM sleep and, 204
  sleep spindles, memory consolidation, and, 295
  see also disturbed sleep in trauma, many faces of
PTSD Checklist for *DSM-5* (PCL-5), 51, 127, 179
pursed-lip slow exhale, 113, 119
PuttingTraumatoSleep.com, 326
PVN. *see* paraventricular nucleus (PVN)
PVT, wakefulness promoted by, 296

raphe magnus, 233
raphe nuclei, 283

Index

critical functions regulated by, 233
oxytocin and salutary impact on, 232
raphe obscurus, 233
raphe pallidus, 233
raphe pontis, 233
rapid eye movement (REM) sleep, xiii, 14, 81, 133, 159, 203
   activated and fragmented, 20
   characteristics of, 10
   CPAP treatment and, 135
   depression and, 21–22
   discovery of, explosion of sleep research and, 58, 146
   eye movements of, 82
   managing moods and, 149
   normal state transitions awakenings and, 14–15
   restless, amygdala adaptation and, 31–32
   shifts from NREM sleep to, 81, 82
   silencing of LC-NE brainstem-initiated reactions and, 320
   sleep apnea and, 26, 28–29, 29
   sleep architecture and, 129
   sleep fragmentation and, 294–95
   sleep paralysis and, 32
   undisturbed, silenced LC-NE system and, 225
   see also non-rapid eye movement (NREM) sleep; restless REM sleep
rapport, felt sense of, 40
RAS. *see* reticular activating system (RAS)
recovery, stable sleep-wake rhythm and, xiii
Reitav-Thirlwell Trauma Sleep Inquiry for Therapists, xxvii–xxviii*t*, 226
relational work with insomnia, clinical application, 45–53
   corroborating evidence from screening surveys, 51–53
   exploration of sleep and trauma, 50–51
   sleep challenges, discussion of, 45–50
relaxation
   exhalation and, 106
   parasympathetic state of, activating, 88
   surrendering to sleep and, 163
relaxation training, CPAP treatment and, 140
reliving *vs.* remembering the experience, DBR trauma work and, 278
REM instability
   awakenings from, insomnia *vs.* healthy sleepers, 203, 204
   origins of REM sleep hypothesis and, 201–2
REM sleep. *see* rapid eye movement (REM) sleep
REM sleep hypothesis, ramifications of, 202–5
REM sleep without atonia (RWA), 33
Ren, R., 123
repair, definition of, 87–88
replicative nightmares, 18, 32, 33, 54, 150, 173, 209, 318
resident-intruder model of human social stress, 240

resistant patients
   CPAP treatment and, 137–38
   dealing with, 64–66
   empathically exploring sleep problems of, 82
resonance
   definition and function of, 87
   emotional, 99
respiratory sinus arrhythmia (RSA), 103, 119
   breathing when safe and, 104
   mobilizing exhalation and, 106
rest and digest system, 102, 112. *see also* parasympathetic nervous system (PNS)
restless legs syndrome, 8, 16, 23–24, 172
restless REM sleep, 172
   amygdala adaptation and, 31–32
   amygdala frozen in trauma time and, 203
   becoming a better sleep and trauma therapist, 199–200
   failed amygdala adaptation and, 230
   at heart of insomnia disorder, 199
   normal REM sleep with amygdala adaptation *vs.*, 203, 205
   trauma and, 177
   see also insomnia disorder (ID); nightmares
restless REM sleep, targeting, 197–227
   application, 226
   becoming a better sleep and trauma therapist, 199–200
   case illustration of deep brain reorienting, 210–26
   deep brain reorienting and, 206, 209–10
   defining chronic insomnia, 198–99
   key messages for therapists, 226–27
restless REM sleep hypothesis, REM instability: origins of, 201–2
restorative sleep, *11*, 12, 15, 101
   barriers to, understanding, 41
   behavioral anchors of, 155–56
   characteristics of, 16
   educating patient about, 326
   five factors contributing to, 9, 147
   key messages for therapists, 35
   lack of experience with, 57
   optimal, supporting, 7–8
   sleep-inclusive trauma treatment and, 8
   wellness and, 16
reticular activating system (RAS), 10, 237, 288
Richards, A., 295
Richards, D., 136
Riemann, D., 197, 201
right-brain memory circuits, xxvi, *xxvi*
right brain psychotherapy, 62–63
right hemisphere of brain, 174
Rogerian person-centered approach to therapy, 40
rostral ventrolateral medulla (RVLM), 207, 236, 259
RSA. *see* respiratory sinus arrhythmia (RSA)
rumination, xxv, 123, 148, 170, 301

rupture, repair of, 87–88
RVLM. *see* rostral ventrolateral medulla (RVLM)
RWA. *see* REM sleep without atonia (RWA)

SA. *see* sleep apnea (SA)
safe therapeutic environment, awareness and, 48
safety
  breathing and, clinical example of, 103–4
  breathing patterns and, 102–3
  engaging diaphragmatic breath and, 119
  intersubjective field and, 79, 80
  relational space and, 86
  of therapeutic relationship, 258, 261, 279, 284, 319
salience network, 202, 203, 205
  PTSD and central role of, 205
  survival and, 175, 177
  vigilance system *vs.*, 199, 227
salivation, PNS activation and, 113, 114, 115, 118, 119
SA node. *see* sinoatrial (SA) node
SASS and SASSY. *see* Self-Assessment of Sleep Scale (SASS and SASSY)
Satow, H., 246
SC. *see* superior colliculus (SC)
Scarisbrick, P., 295
Schore, A., xxvi, 62, 87, 174
Schulz, A., 228, 236, 245, 246
Schulz and Vögele Process Model of Interoception, 236, 236–38, 245
SCI. *see* Sleep Condition Indicator (SCI)
screening
  for circadian rhythm disorders, 23
  for depression, 22
  for insomnia, 21
  for nightmares, 18
  for obstructive sleep apnea, 31, 124
  options, describing, 56
  questionnaires, 12, 43, 44t, 45
  reflecting on results of, 56–57
  for sleep apnea, 127
secure attachment
  embodied experience of self and, 230, 231
  sleep quality and, 37
Self-Assessment of Sleep Scale (SASS and SASSY), 44t
self-blame and self-criticism, bringing to awareness, EMDR and, 183, 188, 191, 192, 193, 194
self-care, sleep and, 41
self-identity, autobiographical memory and, 175
semantic memories
  encoding and retrieving of, 323
  episodic memories *vs.*, 322
  sleep-related synaptic plasticity and, 203
sense of self, intersubjective experiences and, 62
sensory data, incoming, brainstem centers and integration of, 207

sensory memories, threat experiences and, 237
Seroquel, 182
serotonin, xi, xii, xxv, 229, 260
  oxytocin and, 232
  sleep regulation and, xxxi, 6
  yawning and, 102
setbacks, managing, 159
shallow breathing, chronic insomnia and, 92
shock, 148
short-term memory, 130
Shou, J., 123
shoulders, tension and pain in, 166–67
Shultchen, D., 228
Siegel, D., 38, 58, 85, 86, 87, 99
sighing breath, 92
Singh, A., 202
sinoatrial (SA) node
  breathing when in danger and, 105
  breathing when safe and, 104
  diaphragmatic breathing and, 111
sleep
  alpha-delta, 16, 24
  arousals from, 130
  asking patient about, 56
  befriending, braking activities for, 162
  as behavior *vs.* as experience, 60–61
  brain states during, 10–11
  brief opening dialogue about, 35
  clinical assessment of, in the trauma patient, 42–43, 43t
  consistent times for, sleep diary results, 153–54
  consolidation of autobiographical memory and, 322
  continuity of, 147, 148
  core, 13
  daytime impact of, sleep diary results, 153
  definition of, 40
  drowsy, 13
  duration of, 147, 148
  educating patients about, xxix, 41
  fear of, 18, 19, 20, 20–21, 44t
  five major restorative functions of, 8, 9
  four enemies of, xxv, xxx, 123, 124, 160
  fragmented, consolidating, 165–68
  fragmented, sleep diary results, 154
  health and wellness and, 325
  "homeostatic" drive for, 15
  hypnogram of brain sleep states across night of, 11, *11*
  importance of, 88
  increased risk of cardiovascular event and, 262
  inextricably linked with trauma, 6
  integrating into trauma treatment, 319–20
  medications and, 167
  napping and, 167–68
  nonrestorative, 16, 24, 172
  pathway from neurochemical depression through, to depression, 282–84

poor, compensations for, 155
quality of, sleep diary results, 151, 153
recommended amount of, 160
relationship with your "self" and, 7
as resource for trauma recovery, 8–9
tracking, as descriptive not evaluative, 165–66
tracking, detailed instructions for, 150–51
transition routine into, 161–64
trauma and impact on, 172–73
see also disturbed sleep in trauma, many faces of; non-rapid eye movement (NREM) sleep; nonrestorative sleep (NRS); rapid eye movement (REM) sleep; restorative sleep
sleep aid failures, 64
sleep apnea (SA), xiii, xxx, 8, 16, 26–31, 41, 54, 64, 123, 148, 161, 318
    CAP activity after 30 days of CPAP treatment for, 30, *30*
    daytime burdens of, identifying, 138
    devastating health consequences of, 27–28, 36, 54, 144–45
    impact of, during REM, 28–29, *29*
    meaning of term, 125
    mild, 125
    moderate, 125
    obstructive, screening for, 31
    patients unaware of, 127, 145
    risk for cardiac events and, 244
    screening for, 42, 124, 127
    severe, 125
    as stealth sleep problem, 124
    tracking, 150–51
    undiagnosed, 326
    untreated, consequences of, 126
    untreated, proportion of CAP subtypes in, 27, *27*
sleep apnea, clinical investigation of, 125–35
    arousals from sleep, 130
    breathing problem described, 131–35
    conducting a brief screen for apnea, 127
    conveying increased risks to patients, 126
    conveying purpose of polysomnogram, 127–28
    dealing with resistance to going for a sleep test, 128
    narcolepsy, 131
    periodic leg movements, 130
    review of main findings of sleep test, 128–30
    sleep architecture, 129–30
    sleep efficiency, 129
    spontaneous awakenings, 131
sleep architecture, 129–30
sleep-awake state, orexin pathway, LC, and, 292–93
sleep awareness, including in trauma treatments, 325–26
Sleep Condition Indicator (SCI), 21, 44*t*, 51, 52, 200, 226
sleep cycles, normal, 149–50

sleep deprivation, negative mood and, 46
sleep diary(ies), 12, 23, 56, 84
    adapting to use of, common problems with, 158–59
    behavioral patterns revealed in, 63
    identifying pre-sleep triggers in, 162
    reviewing, to identify areas of difficulty, 169
    see also Consensus Sleep Diary
sleep diary 101, 149–51
    individual nights to overall sleep pattern, shifting focus in, 151
    normal sleep cycles, 149–50
    sleep tracking instructions, detailed, 150–51
sleep diary results, reviewing six key features of, 151, 153–55
    consistent sleep times, 153–54
    daytime impact of sleep, 153
    fragmented sleep, 154
    poor sleep, compensations for, 155
    sleep quality, 151, 153
    total sleep time, 154
sleep difficulties
    exploring, questions for, 43*t*
    four categories of, 123
sleep disorders
    identification of, 59
    spectrum, xiii
sleep disturbances
    active attunement and management of, 99
    cardiovascular risk and, 244
    formulating likely causes of, 148, 169–70
    musculoskeletal pain and, 295–96
    neurobiological roots of, xxxi
    range of, 318
    reframing of, as autonomic dysregulation, 82–83
    resolving, nuances in trauma treatment and, 325
    sequential approach to treating, 6–7
    severe, 282
    targeting, clinical necessity of, xxxi, 6
    treating, integrated approach to, 7
    see also disturbed sleep in trauma, many faces of
sleep efficiency, 129, 134
Sleep Heart Health Study (SHHS), 262
sleep-inclusive trauma treatment, elements in, 8
sleep inertia, 14–15
sleepiness, fatigue vs., 24
sleep intervention plan, developing, xxx
sleep logs, 138
sleep onset REM (SOREM), 131
sleep paralysis, 8, 16, 32, 41, 123, 124, 148, 170
sleep patterns, tracking, 63
sleep positions, choosing, 163
sleep problems
    evolution of, 41
    screening for, xxix

sleep quality
  cyclical alternative patterns and, 12, 12–13
  poor, 198
  secure attachment and, 37
Sleep Repair questionnaires, 44t, 57
sleep research, discovery of REM sleep and, 58, 146
sleep roadblocks to trauma work, identifying and removing, 123–45
  application, 144
  becoming a better sleep and trauma therapist, 124–25
  clinical investigation of sleep apnea, 125–35
  CPAP steps in intervention process, 137–41
  CPAP treatment, adapting to, 135–37
  key messages for therapists, 144–45
  patient's transition to adhering to CPAP treatment: case example, 141–43
sleep spindles, 10, 130, 176, 295
sleep stages, 9–16
  core sleep and drowsy sleep, 13–14
  cyclical alternating patterns, 12, 12–13
  non-rapid eye movement (NREM) sleep, 10
  normal state transitions awakening, 14–15
  objective measurement of, 58–59
  rapid eye movement (REM) sleep, 10–12, 11
  visceral integration and awakening, 15–16
sleep study, obtaining, reasons for, xxix
sleep tests (polysomnograms), 31
  answering questions about, developing confidence about, 144
  conveying purpose of, 127–28
  for fragmented short sleeper, 299–300
  main findings of, reviewing, 128–30
  resistance to, dealing with, 128
  reviewing and identifying key findings in, 144
sleep therapists, trauma therapists as, xxvii–xxx, 57, 326
sleep treatment
  as collaborative process, 56
  relevance of attunement for, 88
  usual pattern of change with, 34
sleep-wake desynchronization, xxv
sleep-wake rhythms and patterns
  autonomic nervous system as driver of, 156
  behavioral observation of, 64
  changing, 55
  curiosity about, developing, 169
  orexin synapses and, 268
  raphe nuclei and regulation of, 233
  synchronizing, 161, 170
  see also zeitgebers, sleep-wake reorganization with
sleepwalking, xiii, 8, 17, 25, 41, 123, 127, 172, 227, 318
sleep window, 156
  definition of, 153
  total sleep time and, 154

slow-wave sleep (SWS), 10, 11, 11, 13, 81, 82, 130, 148, 149
  alpha-delta sleep and, 24
  depression and absence of, 21
  restorative sleep and, 9, 147
smell sensitivity, post-motor vehicle accident case study, xvii, xxiii, xxiv
smiling, intersubjective field and, 60
Smith, J., 294
smooth muscles, 95, 111, 133
SMT. see stress management training (SMT)
SNS. see sympathetic nervous system (SNS)
social connectedness, cardiovascular reactivity and, 243
social defeat stress, repeated, consequences of, 240
social interaction, sleep disturbances and, 296
somatic disorders, definition of, 228
somatic distress
  application, 263
  becoming a better sleep and trauma therapist, 229
  chronic, 117
  key messages for therapists, 263–64
somatic memories, threat experiences and, 237
somatic symptoms
  alarm reactions of LC-NE activation of the brain and, 241
  early attachment experiences and, 230–35
  in psychiatric conditions, research perspective into, 235–38
somatization, description of, 228
somatosensory cortex, 236
somnambulism, 25, 172
SOREM. see sleep onset REM (SOREM)
Spiegelhalder, K., 197
spinothalamic tract, 236
spontaneous awakenings, autonomic dysregulation and, 131
Spoormaker, V., ix
Stepanski, E., 146
Stepnowsky, C., 121, 137
Stern, D., 87
STG. see superior temporal gyrus (STG)
STOP-BANG test, 31, 44t, 45, 54, 127, 144, 145
Strategic Developmental Model (Kitchur), 38
Straus, L., 121
straw breathing, 96, 97
stress, chronic
  as cardiovascular risk factor, 243–44
  cardiovascular system and impact of, 241–42, 242
  evidence of resilience to, from animal studies, 240–41
  as ignored component in treatment, 244–45
  overexpressed eCB response and, 239
  reversing, 105–6, 119
stress cascade, acute traumatic events and, 229

Index 363

stress-induced cardiomyopathy (takotsubo cardiomyopathy), clinical signature of, 246
stress management training (SMT), limits on benefits with, 245
stress response
  endocrine limb of, 228, 229, 263
  immunological limb of, 228, 229, 263
striated muscles, 95, 133
striatum, 267
stroke, sleep apnea and, 28
substance use, sleep disturbances and, 64
suicide, sleep apnea and, 126
sulcus, 176
superior central raphe nucleus, 233
superior colliculus (SC), xii, 175, 176, 199, 227, 289
  breathing when in danger and, 104
  deep layers of, 208
  integrative hub of, 207–8
  intermediate layers of, 208
  interoception confronted with threat and, 237
  survival challenge and response of, 207
  visual processing system and, 177
superior temporal gyrus (STG), 176
survival
  response, locus coeruleus and amplification of, 291–93
  salience system and, 175
  sleep and overarching need for, 17
survival response centers, life-or-death experiences and activation of, 286–87
SWS. *see* slow-wave sleep (SWS)
sympathetic nervous system (SNS), 102, 112, 156
  balance between parasympathetic nervous system and, 88, 90
  breathing when in danger and, 104
  hyperarousal of, 64–65, 123, 124, 148, 160
  insomnia and, 19
  mobilizing exhalation and, 106
  spontaneous awakenings and, 131
  sympathetic overdrive and, xxv
  traumatic danger and nerve fibers of, 176
sympathetic triggers, identifying, 157
synaptic plasticity, restless REM sleep and disruption of, 204
synaptic transmission, definition of, xi

TABS model, xxix, 61, 63, 101, 143
  addressing four elements of, in trauma treatment, 317
  clinical application of relational work with insomnia, 45–53
  embracing, in trauma therapy, 326
  five-level pyramid of clinical choice points in, 38, 38
  productive trauma therapy work and, xii
TABS model, active exploration of sleep concerns, 40–45

clinical assessment of sleep in trauma patient, 42–43, 43*t*
TABS sleep repair survey, 43, 44*t*, 45, 55, 57
TABS sleep repair screening questionnaires, 44*t*, 123
TABS therapy, flexible, modular nature of, 35
TABS treatment priority, deciding on, 57
takotsubo cardiomyopathy, treatment of, with EMDR (case study), 246–49
TALK. *see* Tenderness, Acceptance, Loving Kindness (TALK)
Tamanna, S., 123
Tang, N., 286
TaSD. *see* trauma associated sleep disorder (TaSD)
tearing, PNS activation and, 113, 114, 115, 118, 119
technical difficulties during trauma therapy, 277
tectopulvinar pathway, visual signals and, 178
tectum, 207
teddy bear, snuggling with, 166
tegmentum, 207, 208
Tejeda, H., 265
television viewing, sleep and, 162
temporo-parietal junction (TPJ), 176
Tenderness, Acceptance, Loving Kindness (TALK), self-compassion and, 166
tension, chronic, signals of, 117
testosterone, 14
thalamic pulvinar, 207–8
thalamus, 80, 117, 175
  medium level of sleep and, 129–30
  survival challenge and response by, 207
therapeutic alliance
  conscious, development of, 66
  rupture of, 40, 87
  trauma reprocessing work and, 80
therapeutic alliance, active attunement and, 85–101
  application, 100
  assessment of current breathing pattern, 90–93
  attunement to breathing patterns, 88–90
  becoming a better sleep and trauma therapist, 86
  internal psychic change and, 86–88
  introduction to the breathing practice, 94–97
  key messages for therapists, 100–101
  management of sleep disturbances and, 99
  mechanics of therapeutic breathing, 97–98
  relaying results of assessment, 93–94
  relevance of attunement for sleep treatment, 88
  summary of clinical issues, attunement to breathing, 98–99
therapeutic breathing, 65, 69
  demonstrating, 100
  introducing, to stabilize the autonomic system, 83
  mechanics of, 97–98

therapeutic relationship
  repair of dysregulated autonomic system and, 38
  safety of, 259, 261, 279, 284, 319
therapists, key messages for, xxx–xxxi, 35–36, 57, 83–84, 100–101, 119, 144–45, 169–70, 195–96, 226–27, 263–64, 284, 315
theta activity, lighter NREM sleep and, 10
threats
  interoception when confronted with, 236–37
  salience system and, 175
  see also danger
total sleep time (TST), 148
  first 4 months, post-motor vehicle accident, xvii, *xvii*, 296
  naps and, 167
  in persistent post-concussive syndrome case, 312, *313*, 313–14, *314*
  restorative sleep and, 9, 147
  sleep diary results, 154
touch
  oxytocin release and, 232
  raphe nuclei and role of, 233
TPJ. see temporo-parietal junction (TPJ)
tracking, 87, 99
tracking, tuning in, shifting, repeating protocol, diaphragmatic breathing exercises and, 107, 119
transcranial magnetic stimulation (TMS), 246
transcutaneous vagal nerve stimulation (tVNS), 246
transitions into/out of sleep, clinical examination of, 45–50
trauma
  approaching sleep evaluation for, complex issues in, 53–56
  autobiographical memory system undermined by, 322–23
  autonomic system dysregulation and, 156, 320
  brainstem nuclei dysregulated by, xii
  complex, challenge of, 61
  disruption of self and, 7
  nervous system hijacked by, xiii
  nightmares, restless REM sleep and, 177
  obstructive sleep apnea and, 134
  plasticity of symptom responses to, 6
  response to, longitudinal studies of, 180–81
  sleep and impact of, 6, 172–73
  somatic symptoms and lifelong impact of, 235
  vulnerability to chronic insomnia and, 313
  see also disturbed sleep in trauma, many faces of; intersubjective collaborative cascade in trauma treatment; PTSD; TABS model
trauma-associated sleep disorder (TaSD), xiii, 8, 33–34
trauma-induced insomnia
  chronic, pathways to development of, 20, 20–21
  fear of sleep and, 18
trauma patients
  assessing insomnia disorder in, 226
  clinical assessment of sleep in, 42–43, 43*t*
  management of sleep and, 174
  managing complex sleep challenges of, 148
trauma recovery
  partnership and journey of, 39
  sleep as resource for, 8–9
trauma sleep therapy
  benefits of: recovery journey, xix–xxi
  post concussion symptoms and treatment results, xxii*t*
  as a post concussive treatment, commentary on, xxiv–xxv
  resolution of key post concussive symptoms with, xxiii–xxiv
trauma-stress cascade, somatic symptoms triggered in, 229
trauma therapists as sleep therapists, xxvii–xxx, 57, 326
traumatic events, cascade of responses to, 171–72
trauma treatments
  how to include sleep awareness in, 325–26
  ongoing paradigm shift in, 324–25
  sleep as core target of, xiv
Treating Post-Trauma Nightmares (Davis), 182
trigeminal neuralgia, 184, 185, 189
trust, 39, 85, 99. see also therapeutic alliance
tryptophan hydrolase-2 (tph2), 234
TST. see total sleep time (TST)
tuberomammilary nucleus (TMN), xii, 292
Tulving, E., 322, 323
tVNS. see transcutaneous vagal nerve stimulation (tVNS)
24-hour day-night cycle, active mind and, 81–82, 83
Twenty-Four Hour Mind, The (Cartwright, R.), 81, 321
two hands exercise, xiv–xv

Ullah, M., 123
ultradian rhythm, 11
unobtrusive (stealth) sleep disruptions, danger and, 23
unresponsive caretaker experience, somatic distress and, 234
uvulopalatopharyngoplasty (UPPP), 139

vagal brake, 106
  autonomic nervous system and, 103
  breathing when in danger and, 105
Vagnerova, B., 265
vagus nerve, 111, 119, 207, 236
  breathing when safe and, 104
  dorsal motor nucleus of, 117
  rest and digest response and, 103
Valentino, R. J., 228, 241

Van Bockstaele, E., 228
van der Kolk, B., 229, 321
van Marie, H., 5
van Schagen, A., 5
Van Someren, E., 31, 59, 197, 198, 201, 202, 203, 204, 205, 206, 210, 295, 325
Van Veen, M., 5
ventral striatum, extinguishing of aversive responses and, 239
ventral tegmental area (VTA), xii, 199
ventral visual stream (VVS), 195, 196
  flashbacks and nightmares and, 178–80
  structural covariance network of, 179
  visual processing and, 178
ventrolateral periaqueductal gray (vlPAG), 79, 283, 286, 323
  hypotonic freeze and, 209
  life-or-death experiences and dlPAG shift to, 266, 267
  overwhelming cardiac angina and response of, 267
  overwhelming internal experiences and, 68
  release of opioid shutdown and, 69
ventrolateral prefrontal cortex (vlPFC), 176
vigilance system, salience network *vs.*, 199, 227
visceral integration, signaling of normal morning awakening and, 15–16
Visceral Theory of Sleep, 15
visual emotional memories, consolidation of, 179
visualization, 164
visual processing system, overview of, 177–78
vlPAG. *see* ventrolateral periaqueductal gray (VlPAG)
vlPFC. *see* ventrolateral prefrontal cortex (vlPFC)
vmPFC, extinguishing of aversive responses and, 239
Vögele, C., 228, 236
VTA, 227, 282
VVS. *see* ventral visual stream (VVS)
Vyiazovskiy, V., 294

wakefulness, brainstem and support of, 288–90
wakes after sleep onset (WASO), 154
wake-up time, consistent
  setting, 164
  tracking in sleep diary, 153
Walker, M., ix, 326
WASO. *see* wakes after sleep onset (WASO)
Wassing, R., 31, 203
Watt, D., 260
wearable sleep information, 168
wellness, restorative sleep and, 16
Werner, G., 21
Wernicke's area, 321
where self, present, orienting patient to in DBR treatment, 210, 213–14, 251, 272
White Paper on Complex Trauma, four central goals outlined in, 61

whole body breathing, 117–18, 163
  regular practice with, 107
  teaching to patients, 118, 119
Why We Sleep (Walker), 326
wind-down routine, transition into sleep and, 161–62
women, takotsubo cardiomyopathy and, 246
Wood, S., 240, 241
Wyrofsky, R., 293

Yang, L., 123
yawning, PNS activation and, 102, 113, 114, 115, 118, 119
yawning breath, xxiii, 92, 106
  application, 118
  assigning practice of, 117
  becoming a better sleep and trauma therapist, 106–7
  clinical application of, 107–18
  demonstrating with your patients, 118
  key messages for therapists, 119
  mechanics of, describing, 113–14
  patients' experiences with, reflecting on, 114–16
  personalizing practice of, 116
  post-accident case study, xix
  rationale of, introducing, 112–13
  reviewing results of using, 118
  ten-minute, completing, 118
  transitioning from diaphragmatic breathing to, 111–17
  see also diaphragmatic breathing
Yin Yoga, 161
yoga, 107, 118, 161, 163, 211, 225
Yoga Nidra, 161

Zadra, A., 182
Zayfert, C., 20
zeitgebers, sleep-wake reorganization with, 146–70
  adapting to use of a sleep diary, common problems, 158–59
  application, 169
  becoming a better sleep and trauma therapist, 148
  consolidating fragmentation of sleep, 165–68
  identifying causes of disturbed sleep, 155–57
  issues emerging from sleep diaries, discussion of, 159–61
  key messages for therapists, 169–70
  sleep diary 101, 149–51
  sleep review from sleep diary results, six key features of, 151, 153–55
  summary for therapists, 168
  transition routine into sleep, 161–64
  transition routine out of sleep, 164–65
Zhang, Y., 123
Zung, Hamilton, or HADS depression scales, 22

About the Authors

Dr. Jaan Reitav, a licensed psychologist in Ontario, Canada, has spent his career studying the enigma of sleep, in order to restore its healing functions to patients with sleep disorders, anxiety, depression, pain, and trauma. For 40 years, he has been in independent clinical practice, focusing on the application of psychological interventions to bring about healthy sleep. Across the past 20 years, Dr. Reitav has extended his practice to treating patients with chronic medical problems (cardiac, cancer, diabetes, and stroke) at the Cardiovascular Prevention and Rehabilitation Program, University Health Network, Toronto Rehabilitation Institute. He is professor in the department of clinical diagnosis at the Canadian Memorial Chiropractic College, and, holds certification as an EMDR therapist and a Clinical Complex Trauma Professional. Dr. Reitav has previously authored book chapters to guide clinicians toward better clinical management of sleep problems for both cardiac and pain patients. In the past decade, he has been invited to conduct workshops and clinical presentations on screening and management of sleep disturbances in Canada and internationally.

Dr. Celeste Thirlwell, MD, FRCPC, is a doctor of humanitarian services and a student of consciousness both from the perspectives of Western medicine and ancient wisdom traditions. Her fascination with consciousness and love for humanity led her to her studies in neuroscience, neurosurgery, kundalini yoga, and quantum physics. She has worked as a psychiatrist and sleep medicine specialist focusing on trauma and insomnia in the civilian, first responder, and veteran populations for over 25 years. She completed her psychiatry training at McMaster University and sleep medicine specialist training at the University of Toronto. She has presented nationally and internationally on insomnia, postconcussion syndrome, posttraumatic stress disorder, and moral injury. She continues to search for innovative neuroscience-based strategies to optimize the care of her clients suffering from trauma and insomnia. Dr. Thirlwell incorporates innovative approaches such as yoga, MBSR, EMDR, medical cannabis, electromagnetic field modalities, and neuromodulation in her practice.